Ihsan Al-Issa is professor of psychology at the University of Calgary. A Ph.D. of the Institute of Psychiatry, University of London, and a Fellow of the British Psychological Society, he previously taught and practiced clinical psychology in Britain and the Middle East. His research papers on schizophrenia, behavior therapy, and cross-cultural psychopathology have been published in several international journals. He contributed a chapter to *Experiments in Motivation* (edited by H. J. Eysenck) and his own books include *Cross-Cultural Studies of Behavior* and *Culture and Psychopathology*. He is presently writing an undergraduate textbook entitled *Abnormal Psychology: Theory, Research, and Treatment*.

The Psychopathology of Women

Ihsan Al-Issa

A SPECTRUM BOOK

PRENTICE-HALL, INC.   Englewood Cliffs, N.J. 07632

Library of Congress Cataloging in Publication Data

Al-Issa, Ihsan.
    The psychopathology of women.

    (A Spectrum Book)
    Bibliography: p.
    Includes index.
    1. Women—Mental health. 2. Psychology, Patho-
logical. 3. Sex differences (Psychology) 4. Sexism.
5. Psychiatry—Philosophy. I. Title.
RC451.4.W6A4 1980   616.8'9'07   79-20257
ISBN 0-13-736827-5
ISBN 0-13-736819-4 pbk.

To Moosa and Yoosif

Editorial/production supervision and interior design
by Donald Chanfrau
Manufacturing buyers: Cathie Lenard and Barbara A. Frick

A SPECTRUM BOOK

10 9 8 7 6 5 4 3 2 1

Printed in the United States of America

PRENTICE-HALL INTERNATIONAL, INC., *London*
PRENTICE-HALL OF AUSTRALIA PTY. LIMITED, *Sydney*
PRENTICE-HALL OF CANADA, LTD., *Toronto*
PRENTICE-HALL OF INDIA PRIVATE LIMITED, *New Delhi*
PRENTICE-HALL OF JAPAN, INC., *Tokyo*
PRENTICE-HALL OF SOUTHEAST ASIA PTE. LTD., *Singapore*
WHITEHALL BOOKS LIMITED, *Wellington, New Zealand*

Contents

v

Preface

The background of this book goes back to January 1961 when I started working as a psychologist in a British mental hospital. I shall never forget my first impression of the hospital: the luxury of the medical quarters for the "sane" staff and the stale, unwelcoming stink of the wards for the apathetic, *toothless*, "mad" inmates. The offensive smell of the wards, I was told, was associated with mental illness; at that time I did not question my psychiatric colleagues about the availability of bathing facilities for the patients. Tooth extraction was part of the patients' treatment; it was based on the theory that schizophrenia, a diagnosis given to most residents of the mental hospital, is an infectious disease in which the "schizococcus," a virus which causes schizophrenia, may strike the teeth, the tonsils, the appendix, or the colon, requiring the care of a dentist or a surgeon. Considering schizophrenia and other mental illnesses as infectious diseases has no scientific basis at all. Since my first experience in Britain with the inside workings of a mental hospital I have become more and more aware of many idiosyncratic beliefs and practices of psychiatrists and psychologists. This book aims at familiarizing the reader with many of these beliefs and practices.

The accusation of madness is, of course, not limited to females, and the present volume could have been called *Sex Differences in Psychopathology*. However, I have used the title, *The Psychopathology of Women*, because more women than men are accused of madness and because women are more frequently subjected to psychiatric treatment. As there is no reason to believe that women tend to inherit more "madness" than men do, I have emphasized social factors in order to explain the excessive involvement of women with the psychiatric profession. In particular, I have documented the well-known fact that low social status and lack of power make people—both women and men—more vulnerable to the accusation of madness. The association between being female and being mad may reflect the fact that women have little power to control their destiny and their traditional roles as housewives and homemakers.

Many beliefs of psychiatrists and psychologists emphasize the low status of females and support discrimination against women in our society. The mental health profession has defined female "sanity" and "madness" in terms of a woman's reproductive functions and sexuality: The uterus and hormonal imbalance are considered major causes of her trouble. She is often described as nymphomaniac (over-sexed) or frigid (undersexed), two awful psychiatric labels used to degrade women from the status of sexual object to mental patient. Although a male may be reduced to the status of mental patient, he is usually labeled as a criminal, and sent to prison rather than to a mental hospital. This is just one of many examples given in this book to illustrate discrimination against women by the mental health profession.

Surprisingly, women at the life stage of motherhood—an important role for the survival of society—have become the target of insults and humiliation in psychiatry and psychology. Mothers are not only mad and "out of their minds," but they can cause the schizophrenia, mental retardation, and delinquency of their sons as well as the head-aches of their daughters, and they can drive their husbands to drink and to commit violence and crime. I hope that the research presented in this volume may challenge these misconceptions as well as many others.

Finally, the organization of the book follows the traditional format of textbooks of abnormal psychology and psychiatry: For example, there are chapters on treatment, schizophrenia, depression, hysteria, phobia, hypertension, heart disease, ulcers, asthma, headaches, and so on. I hope that this presentation of the contents will not only familiarize the public with psychiatric theory, research, and treatment, but will also be easy for instructors to teach from, particularly when the book is used as a supplement in courses on abnormal psychology, clinical psychology, counseling, sociology, social work, and women's studies. Most of the material reported in this book has often been neglected by authors of textbooks and general books on psychiatry and abnormal psychology. This is particularly true of the psychological problems specific to females, such as those related to hysterectomy, mastectomy, therapeutic abortion, plastic surgery, and physical attractiveness. I hope that the information presented in this book will help the readers—professionals, students, and the public—to develop insights into the present tragicomic state of the psychiatric profession.

Ihsan Al-Issa

Toward
a Female
Psychopathology

part one

"But I don't want to go among mad people," Alice remarked.

"Oh, you can't help that," said the Cat: "we're all mad here. I'm mad. You're mad."

"How do you know I'm mad?" said Alice.

"You must be," said the Cat, "or you wouldn't have come here."

Alice didn't think that proved it at all: however, she went on: "And how do you know that you're mad?"

"To begin with," said the Cat, "a dog's not mad. You grant that?"

"I suppose so," said Alice.

"Well, then," the Cat went on, "you see a dog growls when it's angry, and wags its tail when it's pleased. Now *I* growl when I'm pleased, and wag my tail when I'm angry. Therefore I'm mad."

Taken from THE ANNOTATED ALICE by Lewis Carroll; introduction and notes by Martin Gardner. Copyright © 1960 by Martin Gardner. Used by permission of Clarkson N. Potter, Inc.

Women
and
Madness

|

Psychiatrists and clinical psychologists are notorious in their readiness to impute madness to others. The list of labels they can use is long enough to enable them to apply one to anybody and everybody. You may be schizophrenic; she is obese or depressive; somebody else is neurotic; and so on. Concepts of madness have been so popularized by textbooks of abnormal psychology and psychiatry, as well as by the media, that they have now become well established in the minds of the public. Many children are now called "crazy" by their parents and teachers. The elderly, housewives, immigrants, and many other persons of low status are similarly categorized. People have become so indoctrinated by psychiatric ideas that they do not hesitate to declare themselves mad.

We are now entrenched in an era of the "madness hunt," a period which is not very dissimilar to the craze of witch hunting during the Middle Ages. Witness, for example, the plethora of textbooks on the abnormal psychology of children and adults. Not unlike textbooks on witchcraft, they serve to affirm the "reality" of mental illness and attempt to justify the existence of the psychiatric establishment. Today, people who report that they hear voices, that they are under the surveillance of the police, or that they assume the personalities of famous individuals (presidents, prime ministers, millionaires, etc.) are hospitalized for mental illness. During the Middle Ages, women who confessed that they had a pact with the devil, could fly on a broom, spread pestilence and illness, or kidnap children and eat them were accused of witchcraft. Nowadays, if you look at an ink blot (the so-called Rorschach Test) and report strange imaginings, then you are mad. In the past, if a spot on your skin was pricked by a pin or a needle and you did not bleed, then you were assumed to be a witch.

And yet people are not randomly selected and accused of madness or witchcraft. Many scientific theories and theological interpretations have been put forward to justify the accusations of madness and witchcraft respectively. The witch was seen as being in league with the devil, while the "crazy" person carries a "disease," has a faulty personality, a deviant childhood, and an abnormal upbringing. The behavior of witches and of the mad is usually explained by suggesting mysterious forces *within* the person and, often, by ignoring the *outside* social context. The concept of "mental illness" is particularly considered as a scientific disease entity, which dissociates it from the religious superstitions of witchcraft. However, when the social contingencies that culminate in labeling someone as a witch or as a mental patient are investigated, a similarity between the two concepts becomes quite apparent. As will be seen, contemporary concepts of mental illness, like witchcraft during the Middle Ages, provide the professional with social labels that serve a social function in today's society.

WITCHCRAFT AND MADNESS

Old civilizations, as well as many non-Western cultures, have attempted to understand nature and man in terms of possession by spirits. The wind, rain, forests, trees, and rivers were thought to be animated by these spirits. People believed that human behavior could also be controlled by the same forces and that spirits could be godly or satanic, with good or evil influences. In Europe during the Middle Ages, it was an accepted theological belief that victims of possession were unwillingly seized by the spirit, and such persons were usually treated by means of exorcism and/or prayer and fasting. There were, however, persons who became witches by voluntarily renouncing

God and making a pact with the devil, thus deserving severe punishment. Indeed, many demoniacs (possessed persons) were encouraged to accuse a witch of causing them to be possessed (being bewitched). Such beliefs and accusations were used during the Middle Ages to confirm the existence of witchcraft and heresy (Spanos, 1978).

Witchcraft was thus established in theological ideology in a way that helped to explain social relations and to control human behavior. A manual, *Malleus Maleficarum* (*The Witches' Hammer*), written in the fifteenth century by two monks, Johann Sprenger and Heinrich Kraemer, established the existence of witches as part of the

Figure 1.1 "The Devil in Love" from *The History of Magic* by Kurt Seligmann. Reprinted by permission of Pantheon Books, Inc.

Figure 1.2 "Test for Witchcraft: Swimming a Witch." From *Witches Apprehended, Examined and Executed* . . . 1613 (Bodleian Library: 4°E 17 Arts). Reprinted by permission of Bodleian Library.

Catholic faith. Furthermore, it indicated that those who denied the existence of witches were heretics. The *Malleus* also outlined methods of detection and management of witches.

The major method of detecting witchcraft was through confession. Once accused, a woman almost always confessed under torture to evil doing. Witchcraft was confirmed by detecting marks, such as a skin lesion, a birthmark, a mole, a scar, or any other spot on the body of the accused. Marks were believed to be branded by the devil

Figure 1.3 "Three Witches Being Hanged" from title page STC 5114, Lambeth Palace Library.

and gave concrete proof of a pact between that person and the devil. Since a body mark could easily be found, the accused was inevitably provided with a concrete evidence of her guilt. A person could also be branded by the devil in such a way as to leave only an invisible mark on the body. Such an invisible mark could be located by pricking: If a pin was pushed into a certain spot and caused neither bleeding nor pain, the person was a witch. Thus, a new profession, witch prickers, was born during the Middle Ages. Finally, a "swimming" test was used to confirm the accusation of witchcraft. It consisted of tying the hands and feet of the accused and throwing her into deep water. If she floated, she was guilty; if she sank, she was innocent. Since many drowned during this test, it is quite possible that the test was a last resort employed by the investigators to rid themselves of the accused without forcing a confession. However, a condemnation of witchcraft was normally followed by burning or hanging.

Witches were thought to have the power to cause pestilence, storms, floods, sexual impotence, and injuries to their enemies. They were also accused of killing their children, and those of others, so that they might eat them or make a salve from the child's insides to rub on chairs, sticks, brooms, or other objects, thereby transforming them into means of aerial transportation; hence the accusation of night flights on wolves, cats, sticks, and so on. The "obscene kiss is another major accusation—kissing the anus of the devil or kissing the anus and genitals of demon-possessed cats" (Rimm & Somervill, 1977). Under torture, women might even confess to having intercourse with an incubus (a male demon).

The Witch: A Mad or an Oppressed Woman?

It is currently believed that most witches were mentally ill persons who were misdiagnosed and mislabeled. Their fantastic confessions are regarded as symptoms of their illness. This view has been documented by authoritative histories of psychiatry (Alexander & Selesnick, 1966; Zilboorg & Henry, 1941) as well as by textbooks of abnormal psychology (for example, Coleman, 1976; Rimm & Somervill, 1977; Ullmann & Krasner, 1975). In commenting on the *Malleus*, Ullmann and Krasner write that the book may be considered "a treatise on witchcraft; the classic fifteenth century abnormal psychology text." Zilboorg (1935), a prominent historian of psychiatry, also concluded that ". . . the *Malleus Maleficarum* might with a little editing serve as an excellent modern textbook of descriptive clinical psychiatry of the fifteenth century, if the word *witch* were substituted by the word *patient*, and the devil eliminated."

Labeling witches as mad women seems to ignore social factors associated with the accusation of witchcraft. Since witches are predominantly females, the accusation of witchcraft (and madness) may be related to attitudes toward and the position of women in society.

The view of the female as inferior, sinful, dangerous, and evil was stressed in works on witchcraft. The *Malleus* claims that "all witchcraft comes from carnal lust, which is in women insatiable." Shirley Weitz (1977) cites Remy, a sixteenth-century author, as saying, "Certainly I remember to have heard of far more cases of women than men: and it is not unreasonable that this scum of humanity should be chiefly drawn from the feminine sex . . . since that sex is more susceptible to evil counsels." Further, the accusation of witch-craft seems to be only part of the tendency of society to ascribe the origin of evil to women:

> The Pandora's box myth comes to mind, as does the idea of original sin in the Garden of Eden. In the latter case, Adam's fall is ascribed to his yield-ing to the temptation to eat the apple offered by Eve. Many other stories tell of temptation emanating from woman and leading to the downfall of man. The legend of the Sirens luring sailors to their death is such an example. Often, especially in a Christian context, the idea of sexual temptation is an integral part of the negative image of woman. The prominent place given to pornographic portrayals of witches' intercourse with devils in Inquisition trials of witches testifies to the existence of heavy sexual repression and the consequent denunciation of those seen as the origin of the forbidden impulse: women. Often there seems to be a one-dimensional view of woman: she is her sexuality, no more, no less. When that sexuality is seen as threatening or evil, so is she (Weitz, 1977).

Mary Douglas (1970) suggests that women were accused of witch-craft because of their powerlessness in society. Poor housewives and mothers, completely destitute of power, were suspects. Barbara Rosen (1969) also described these women as "ill-nourished, over-worked and almost continually pregnant and nursing." For example, "Bessie Dunlop, in Scotland, first met the Devil as she stumbled on an errand, weeping from the pain and weakness of recent childbirth, and in terror that her husband's illness was mortal" (Rosen, 1969). Not only poor mothers and housewives, but also women who under-went a change in their sex roles, so that they became ill-defined and ambiguous in relation to the male (for example, after the child-rearing years or in widowhood and old age), were often accused of being witches (Parrinder, 1958).

In contrast, another group of women who became victims of witchcraft were professionals—midwives, nurses, and healers, for instance—who asserted their power and whose views and behavior challenged the established hierarchical system (again putting them outside mainstreams of society). Their "knowledge of painkillers, abortion, and herbal or faith healing threatened the church's anti-scientific, antisexual, and antifemale doctrines" (Chesler, 1972). It was their help, given to the weak, to peasants, and to other women, that led to the accusations of witchcraft and to severe punishment. Apparently, affiliating themselves with the powerless made them vulnerable to victimization.

Nowadays, many social conditions associated with the accusation of madness, such as being a poor or a rebellious female, seem to be similar to those related to witchcraft. The relationship between sexual status and madness will be amply discussed later in this chapter. It may, however, be noted here that the categorization of women as mad during this century has the same function as accusations of witchcraft had in the Middle Ages (Szasz, 1970; Sarbin & Juhasz, 1978); in both cases, deviation of women from their social roles is attributed either to mental illness or (formerly) to the devil. Szasz (1970) has particularly noted the similarity between the oppression of the witch and the oppression of the person labeled "mentally ill":

> The phenomena called witchcraft and mental illness are actually created through the social interaction of oppressor and oppressed. If the observer sympathizes with the oppressor and wants to exonerate him, while he pities the oppressed but wants to control him, he calls the victim mentally ill. This is why psychiatrists declare that witches were mad. Conversely, if the observer sympathizes with the oppressed and wants to elevate him, while he loathes the oppressor and wants to degrade him, he calls the tormentor mentally ill. This is why psychiatrists declare that the Nazis were mad. I insist that both interpretations are worse than false; by interposing mental illness (or witchcraft, as was the case formerly), they conceal, excuse and explain away the terrifying simple but all-important fact of man's inhumanity to man [woman].

WHICH IS THE MAD SEX?

Madness is not exclusively a female problem. However, women are more often labeled crazy and are more frequently subjected to psychiatric treatment. We have seen that witchcraft in the Middle Ages was attributed to the evilness of women. Nowadays, a daughter, a wife, or a mother is rarely subjected to such accusations. Instead, she is considered crazy, mad, and "out of her mind."

Walter Gove and Jeanette Tudor (1973) examined statistics on sex differences in the rates of mental illness from 1956 to 1970 in public and private hospitals, psychiatric treatment in general hospitals and outpatient clinics, treatment by private psychiatrists, and treatment for emotional problems by general practitioners. They reported that women (age 18 and over) have higher rates than men in all these treatment facilities. The greatest sex difference is found in private practice. Overall, although women receive more treatment for psychosis and neurosis, men receive more treatment for brain syndromes and for the personality disorders (alcoholism and addiction). Further, sex differences in residents of mental hospitals are age-related. Statistics reveal that females are at a disadvantage in their later stages of life because they then tend to remain for a longer time as residents in mental institutions. Mensh (1969) reported that the proportion of women over 60 remaining in mental hospitals two years or more after admission is two or three times greater than for the younger women and about twice greater than for male patients. Howard and Howard (1974) also found that 74 percent of female residents in public hospitals were above the age of 45; this is compared with only 60.6 percent for men. It should be borne in mind that the excessive number of females in mental institutions after middle age may be due to the fact that women live longer than men.

An inspection of seventeen community surveys after World War II by Gove and Tudor (1973) indicated higher rates of mental illness for women than men. However, community surveys taken before World War II, analyzed by Dohrenwend and Dohrenwend (1969), revealed no consistent pattern. Three studies indicated higher rates of mental illness for women; eight showed higher rates for men. These data were confirmed in a later study by the Dohrenwends (1976). They found that the overall rates of mental illness tended to be higher for men in the pre-1950 investigations and higher for women in those published in 1950 or later. One interesting aspect of the Dohrenwends' analysis of community surveys is the finding that the overall rates of mental illness for both males and females increased after 1950.

In Britain, data for admission in psychiatric institutions in 1970 and 1971 is similar to that in the United States (Smart, 1977). The rates of mental illness are higher for women than men. Women are also more frequently hospitalized for psychoses (depression, schizophrenia) and neuroses than men. The same trend is revealed in studies of outpatient clinics and general practice (Kessel & Shepherd, 1962; Logan & Cushion, 1958). As in the United States, there is an excess of hospitalization for alcoholism and drug addiction among men.

In contrast to the United States and United Kingdom findings, there is more mental illness among males than females in many non-Western cultures. This is true in both community studies (Thacore, Gupta, & Suraiya, 1975) and hospital statistics (Ananth, 1976; Bazzoui & Al-Issa, 1966; Rao, 1964). Indeed, Carstairs and Kapur (1976) found that in an Indian village, the number of men with psychotic symptoms is more than three times that of women.

Marital Status, the Rate of Mental Illness, and Hospitalization

Studies reveal that, for women and men, the married tend to have lower rates of mental illness than the unmarried (Bloom, Asher, & White, 1978). However, all studies published after World War II show that married women have higher rates of mental illness than married men. Comparing single women with single men, divorced women with divorced men, and widowed women with widowed men, the majority of studies found that it was the men who had the higher rates (Gove, 1972a).

Overall, the duration of hospitalization is shorter for married than for unmarried persons. Thus, mental hospitals contain a higher proportion of unmarried than married patients. Married women are, however, more likely than married men to remain residents in mental hospitals. It appears that a hospitalized wife tends to be a discarded wife, while the hospitalized husband has a better chance of resuming his marital life. For the single and the divorced or widowed, men are more likely to be hospital residents. This is consistent with the general finding that divorced and widowed men show higher rates of mental illness than do women (Gove, 1972a). There is, of course, the possibility for both men and women that, while in the hospital, they may become divorced or widowed.

EXPLAINING SEX DIFFERENCES

"How am I to get in?" asked Alice again, in a louder tone.

"*Are* you to get in at all?" said the Footman. "That's the first question, you know."

It was, no doubt: only Alice did not like to be told so. "It's really dreadful," she muttered to herself, "the way all the creatures argue. It's enough to drive one crazy!"

Lewis Carroll: ALICE'S ADVENTURES
IN WONDERLAND

Sex differences in the rates of mental illness and the use of physicians and hospitals have been attributed to three factors: (1) "Women *report* more illness than men because it is culturally more acceptable for them to be ill—'the ethic of health is masculine'; (2) the sick role is relatively compatible with women's other role responsibilities, and incompatible with those of men; and (3) women's assigned social roles are more stressful than those of men; consequently, they *have* more illness" (Nathanson, 1975). I now present research attempting to investigate these factors.

Report of Illness

Data from Britain and the United States show that women report more mental and physical symptoms than men (Cooperstock, 1976a; Nathanson, 1975; Wadsworth, Butterfield, and Blaney, 1971). Phillips and Segal (1969) found that even when women and men are matched for physical symptoms, women report significantly more psychological distress than men. Sex differences in the readiness to report physical symptoms appear early in life. In a study of responses to illness among eighth graders, three-quarters of the girls reported not feeling well, but less than three-fifths of the boys had similar inclinations (Mechanic, 1964).

Women may not actually have more symptoms than men, but it is possible that they may report more symptoms because of social factors. Phillips and Segal (1969) suggested that ". . . a person's sexual status affects both the recognition and expression of illness, and his/her help-seeking behavior in response to that illness." Studies of sex stereotypes and mental health discussed later in this chapter would suggest that the expression of malaise and distress by women is more acceptable because these complaints overlap with culturally learned patterns of normal female behavior. Women are expected to report certain personality characteristics that are compatible with sex stereotypes (Broverman, Broverman, Clarkson, Rosenkrantz, & Vogel, 1970). Whereas the expression of symptoms is considered appropriate behavior for women who accept their sex roles, men are expected to "grin and bear it" and to avoid the public display of emotional behavior. Phillips and Segal (1969) argued that "particularly among men illness is looked upon as a feminine characteristic to be shunned. The man who publicly announces that he does not know what it means to be sick thereby improves his masculine status." Men are, therefore, more willing to ignore or conceal their psychological disturbance. Because men evoke more rejection than women when both report the same behavior (Farina, Felner, & Boudreau, 1973; Phillips, 1964), they may *underreport* symptoms in order to avoid rejection. Even among hospitalized patients, men are still unwilling to admit symptoms (Distler, May, & Tuma, 1964).

Physicians may perceive symptoms of female and male patients differently because of sex-role expectations. Physicians take male physical complaints more seriously but assume that those of females are only "in their minds." Jean Lennane and John Lennane (1973) have observed that physical conditions such as dysmenorrhea (painful menstruation), nausea of pregnancy, pain in labor, and infantile behavior disorders are blamed on the mother's emotional problems or her "faulty outlook." Services are also designed to accommodate the female rather than the male patient. For example, services for female psychopathology (e.g., neuroses) are more commonly available than those for men (e.g., alcoholism and drug addiction). In the past, sexually promiscuous women were more likely to be treated than their male counterparts (Mechanic, 1976).

Physicians also use sex-related diagnostic categories in dealing with their clients. Men are more frequently diagnosed as antisocial, alcoholic, and drug addictive, whereas women tend to be labeled as depressive, schizophrenic, and neurotic. Male disturbance is socially visible; people outside the clinic are likely to recognize antisocial behavior without a need for the patient to express himself. However, the female pattern of diagnosis is not as socially visible; others are unable to recognize that the person is, for example, anxious or depressed. In this area of psychological disturbance, unless persons are ready to express themselves and report symptoms, they may easily escape detection, and males may in fact be reluctant to express female patterns of symptoms (Smart, 1977).

Role Obligation and Mental Illness

The sick role is assumed to be compatible with the role obligation of women. It has been suggested that women may have more contact with services because of the relative accessibility and convenience of health service for women; they have more time and incur less loss than men who would lose time from work when attending health clinics. In support of this argument, it is found that the report of sickness is lower among married women than among the single, widowed, or divorced. This is attributed to the more demanding situation of married women, which makes it difficult for them to adopt the sick role (Nathanson, 1975). Similarly, the presence of young children may influence women's report of illness behavior. Brown, Bhrolchain, and Harris (1975) found that women with young children at home tend to have a much lower rate of contact with doctors for psychiatric treatment.

By the same token, Feld (1963) found that among married females with children, working women reported significantly fewer physical symptoms than did housewives. Nathanson (1975) suggests that evidence revealing more first clinic consultation by wives living in flats than in houses may result from the increased social obligations (e.g., interaction with neighbors) of house-dwellers.

Stress and Sex Differences in Mental Illness

Stress refers to any condition that produces a threat or uncertainty about physical survival, identity, and the ability to control one's environment or avoid pain (Lazarus, 1966). It has been suggested that women, because of their biological and social roles, are more predisposed to physical and mental illness. Constance Nathanson (1975) summarized the biological view as follows:

> From this biological perspective, woman is seen as the product and prisoner of her reproductive system. . . . Any imbalance, exhaustion, infection, or other disorders of the reproductive organs could cause pathological reactions in part of the body seemingly remote. The female reproductive system is,

furthermore, particularly vulnerable to disturbance, while that of the male suffers no parallel disability.

In Chapter 6, I shall discuss how, in the past, medicine conceived of hysteria as a disturbance of the womb. Contemporary emphasis, however, is on the social rather than the biological aspects of stress in women's roles. The stress hypothesis has been recently popularized by the work of Gove (1972a, 1976) and Gove and Tudor (1973). They suggested that certain conditions inherent in the female role are conducive to a higher rate of emotional problems in women. For example, married women have only one major social role, that of a housewife, whereas men occupy the roles of workers as well as family heads. Therefore, when women find their marital role unsatisfactory, they are left with no alternative role. Men, can, however, compensate for failure and loss of power in the sphere of work in their role at home. The housewife's work (raising children and housekeeping) is also undemanding and frustrating. Furthermore, her role has low prestige and does not require special skills. Even when a married woman works, her position is less satisfactory than that of a married man. Her job is not only below her educational level but is also considered secondary to her main role as a housewife. Finally, Gove suggests that the role of a housewife is unstructured, which may allow her to brood on her problems, whereas the constant demands on the jobholder force him to be involved with the environment and distract him from his troubles.

In an attempt to explain the increase in the rate of mental illness of women reported after 1950, Gove and Tudor (1973) suggested that the role of women as housewives has become less meaningful and less satisfactory because of changes in the nature of housework in an industrialized society. In the past, because families were large, women spent more of their adult life looking after children. Housework used to be a highly valued activity and required more skills. In the modern nuclear family (consisting only of a couple and their children), child-rearing years are short and domestic skills are replaced by modern conveniences. In contrast to the Gove and Tudor interpretation, the increase in the rates of mental illness for *both sexes* after World War II may be due to a change in the definition of mental illness. Indeed, the definition of mental illness by American psychiatrists has become broader since World War II (Kuriansky, Deming, & Gurland, 1974). A broad concept of mental disorder would enable the psychiatrist to apply the label "mental illness" to a wider variety of life problems.

Apart from the stress hypothesis, unstable men are less likely than unstable women to get married. Sex roles dictate that men adopt a dominant role in courtship; for example, they must play a more aggressive role in making arrangements for dinner, movies, and entertainment in the courtship. Women are expected, however, to play a more passive role. Indeed, it has been shown that the mental health of the man is related to the progress of the courtship, whereas this is not so with the woman (Murstein, 1967). The selection hypothesis may also be used to predict better mental health for the single woman. Since men want to dominate women, they tend to bypass those with "strong independent personalities" (Gove & Tudor, 1973). Thus, the most competent and stable woman would not get married, while the more passive, unstable, and easily dominated woman would.

Many aspects of the female roles described by Gove (1972a) represent some of the realities facing women. However, age, life stage, and social class, which he ignored, are important factors. A young married woman may stay at home to look after young children, which makes many demands on her. In this situation, her work will not be "unstructured," and she will have little time for "brooding" over her problems. An older married woman who does not go out to work may, however, face the situation described by Gove. The excess in the number of female residents of mental institutions above the age of 45 referred to earlier may either indicate a point of life crisis or reflect social attitudes and, in particular, a readiness to discard women at this stage. As we shall see in the following discussion, social class seems to be important in determining female reaction to stress. Furthermore, work outside the home, even given its unsatisfactory nature, may protect women against "mental breakdown."

Life Stress, Life Stage, Social Class, and Illness

Contrary to Gove's suggestion that the life of women is more stressful, Paykel, Prusoff, and Uhlenhuth (1971) found no sex differences in the frequency of stressful life events. The frequency of stressful life events may not be the only crucial factor in "mental breakdown." Indeed, in a community study by Brown and his associates (1975), it was found that working-class women are much more vulnerable to psychiatric disturbance than their middle-class counter-parts *even* when both groups had an equal number of major difficul-ties. The difference between these two groups was in the *kind* of stressful life events. The nature of the difficulties of working-class women seems to be different from those of middle-class women; they tend to be of longer duration and are not directly of their doing. In addition, the difficulties are of the kind about which the women are relatively helpless: a son on probation who says he is unable to get a job, a woman whose landlord wanted to split her rented house into flats, a home due for demolition where three offers of alternative housing had been much too expensive. Many diffi-culties of the middle-class woman seem more amenable to solutions than those of the working-class woman. Class differences in difficul-ties are, however, restricted to women with children at home, and it is at this stage of life that working-class women have the highest rate of disturbance.

The presence of an intimate supportive relationship with a hus-band, a boyfriend, or somebody with whom a woman lives seems to mediate between major difficulties and the onset of illness. Stressful life events tend to cause disturbance only in the absence of intimate relationships. Similarly, lack of such a relationship does not itself bring about disturbance without the presence of a major difficulty. Thus, class differences in intimacy may in part explain rates of dis-turbance in working-class and middle-class women; this is particularly true when the youngest child is less than six. Working-class women in the early stages of rearing their families do not only experience more severe events and major difficulties than the comparable middle-class group, but the quality of their marriages at this stage is, on the whole, poor (Brown et al., 1975).

Other factors that seem to mediate the effect of severe events are (1) loss of one's mother by death or separation before the age of 11; (2) having three or more children aged 14 or less at home; and (3) lack of full- or part-time employment. Having a job seems to be protective even in the presence of the other "risk" factors, such as stressful life events and the absence of an intimate tie with the husband (Brown et al., 1975). As we shall see in the following discussion, work may be related to psychiatric diagnosis because it contributes to the general power of females as well as to their eco-nomic power and decision making. It suffices here to note that the psychological symptoms of women are more affected than those of men by events they could not control; and this would indicate that women's psychological problems are associated with a lack of power to control their lives (Dohrenwend, 1973). Power associated with the social status of women and men should not only affect the degree of control of life events and psychological disturbance but it should also determine their vulnerability to the accusation of madness.

SEX ROLES AND THE ACCUSATION OF MADNESS

One established conclusion from research is that low status is associated with mental illness (Hollingshead & Redlich, 1958). An important question concerns factors involved in a certain social status that make individuals vulnerable to mental illness. The preceding discussion emphasized the relationship between life events, social class, and psychiatric disturbance among women. What follows will discuss the amount of power inherent in social status and its relationship to the accusation of madness.

Ascribed Status vs. Acquired Status

Sarbin (Sarbin, 1969; Sarbin & Juhasz, 1975, 1978) differentiated between ascribed and achieved status in terms of the *degree of choice* prior to entry into any particular status; that is, a high degree of choice is related to achieved status, whereas a low degree or a complete absence of choice is related to ascribed status. At one extreme, ascribed status is granted to persons simply by virtue of their membership in a society; for example, sexual status (male, female), kinship status (mother, father, son) and status related to age (juvenile, adult).[1] At the other extreme, an achieved status is characterized by attainment or option by the persons themselves; for example, physician, student, waiter, football player.

It is the achieved rather than the ascribed status that is associated with legitimate power and prestige. Proper performance of achieved

---

[1]Status refers to a position in a social structure which involves certain *beliefs and expectations* by members of the group. Roles refer to *behavior* carried out by individuals to fulfill their particular status or position.

roles is highly rewarded with public recognition and monetary rewards. In contrast, no positive value is attached to granted roles. Persons are not rewarded for participating in a culture as a male, female, father, mother, adult, and so on; they are only expected to carry out these roles. The nonperformance of achieved and ascribed roles also tends to have different consequences. Failure to enact an achieved role generally does not bring negative evaluation. In the case of occupational and recreational statuses, for example, nonperformance of one's roles (laid off a job, dropped from a team, or dismissed from school) may be construed as a failure or an underachievement or as due to a superior competition or just to a misfortune. It is the nonperformance of the ascribed role that calls for negative evaluation, such as the mother who fails to look after her children. Since ascribed status is the minimal position a person holds in a group, an alternative for the loss of this status is to be degraded to the role of nonperson; that is to say, to the role of a mental patient. Since ascribed roles involve predominantly family relationships, it is not surprising that the accusation of mental illness often comes from a family member (Hollingshead & Redlich, 1958; Linn, 1961; Sarbin & Juhasz, 1978).

In our society, the performance of a man is more heavily weighed in terms of achieved rather than ascribed roles (Marecek, 1978). Conversely, women's behavior is biased toward the performance of ascribed roles. The following discussion would suggest that these roles have some implications for sex differences in mental illness. Because of their achieved roles, men can accumulate more power than women. Women, on the other hand, because they are mainly limited to the familial ascribed roles (e.g., housewife), have few alternative roles and are more liable to the accusation of madness.

Power and the Accusation of Madness

The first stage in the process of accusation of madness is a strained relationship between two persons over role expectations. When the role expectations of A are not being fulfilled by B, A tries to redefine role relation by degrading B. In this situation, the greater the power differences between the two persons, the more likely it is that the less powerful will be degraded and considered crazy, "hopeless, dangerous and inhuman" (Sarbin & Juhasz, 1978). For example, parents tend to accuse their young children of madness, whereas grown-up children label their old parents as "senile." In medieval times and across cultures, the accusation of witchcraft is often preceded by strained relations between two persons of unequal power, and it is the one with the more powerful position who initiates the accusation (Sarbin & Juhasz, 1978). Nowadays, women, because of their weak position in society, are more frequently labeled "crazy":

> The relationship between being female and being mad points up the generally weaker political position of females in our society as well as the fact that they are perceived to be occupying granted rather than achieved statuses. Since the relative involvement of males in achieved roles continues to be much greater than that of females it would follow that a nonconforming female would more likely be perceived against a backdrop of madness while the deviant male would more likely be perceived as antisocial or criminal. It is particularly the strained husband-wife and parent-daughter relation that leads to accusations of madness in our society. Although madness is no longer purely sex-linked as witchcraft or hysteria was, under present arrangements it has remained a condition to which a significant number of females are degraded (or de-personed) by male judges and accusers. When a housewife refuses to care for her children, clean the house, and do the laundry, the explanation sought is usually one that assumes such behavior to be "unnatural." As a result she is likely to be stigmatized as an "unnatural" mother, therefore a non-person and a candidate for a mental hospital. Males are more likely to be caught in nonconforming instrumental acts, such as stealing, acting in a violent manner, or otherwise misbehaving outside the family. Their unwanted behavior is regarded as self-caused, therefore criminal (Sarbin & Juhasz, 1978).

Dair Gillespie (1975) convincingly argued that the weak position of housewives, particularly those with children, is mainly due to their economic dependency and to their inability to make important family decisions. This imbalance of power may determine those who will be agents of hospitalization within the family. Erwin Linn (1961), for example, found that there is a greater likelihood that female patients who had lived with their spouses or parents would be hospitalized by these persons than would male patients in the same living situations. Differences in status within the family seem to qualify tolerance of the patient's behavior. Thus, the spouse or the parent has greater freedom to interfere in the lives of adult women than in those of adult men.

Because of their weak position, even after recognizing a serious problem, wives are usually at a loss at what might be done if their husbands do not accept that there is something wrong with them. Asking for help from friends and personnel in hospitals and clinics, they are often told that there is nothing they can do unless their husbands get in trouble with the police (Clausen & Yarrow, 1955). The police, on the other hand, are unwilling to initiate hospitalization on their own responsibility because they deal with many people who might be "sick," and if they apply lower standards of a psychiatric emergency, they will flood hospitals with as well as involve themselves in extra work. Further, they do not regard commitment as a proper law enforcement task (Bittner, 1967). Outside the family context, men may have strained relations with their employers at work, a situation in which they may have relatively little power, but it is unlikely that they will be sent to a mental hospital (Linn, 1961). They may resolve the conflict by finding another job. When admitted to a hospital, husbands are subjected to shorter treatment and less rehospitalization than wives (Clausen, 1975). Thus, on balance, a wife is more liable to the accusation of madness and to psychiatric treatment than her husband.

The Gas-Light Phenomenon The relationship between the weak position of women and the accusation of madness may be illustrated in the so-called "Gas-Light Phenomenon." "The Gas-Light Phenomenon," the title of a paper by Barton and Whitehead (1969), was based on the play, *Gas-Light,* by Patrick Hamilton. Its theme is a husband's plot to get rid of his wife by driving her into a lunatic asylum. The wife is actually induced to believe that she is going mad, and her consequent distress strengthens the impression that she is mentally ill. The husband accuses her of imagining things. For example, he dims the gas lights; then, he brightens them and tells her there is no difference; he produces odd noises in the house and tells her that there aren't any. He also stresses her poor memory; for example, household articles mysteriously disappear and later turn up among her possessions. He plays upon her morbid fear of going insane and of being hospitalized, as her mother had been: "Then by God, you are mad, and you don't know what you do. You unhappy wretch—you're stark gibbering mad—just like your mother before you."

In questioning whether or not the play bore any relation to real psychiatric treatment, Barton and Whitehead found that the forceful confinement of patients is more widespread than is generally admitted in psychiatric circles. They reported the case of an old lady admitted to a mental hospital following induced fecal incontinence. The old lady was considered a nursing home nuisance, and she was given purgatives regularly. When she started having some "accidents," these were taken as an excuse for removing her to a mental hospital. Other cases of the Gas-Light Phenomenon were also published by Smith and Sinanan (1972):

Mrs. O'N. is 29 and married 10 years. She has six children. Her husband is psychopathic and he uses alcohol abnormally. At the age of 20 he spent six months in prison for assault, and more recently he has been fined for stealing. Mrs. O'N.'s father was admitted to a psychiatric hospital for the first time at the age of 65 from a general hospital where he was being treated for a stroke. With persisting confusion and incontinence a transfer was requested. A younger brother has had three psychiatric admissions with a diagnosis of mental retardation and personality disorder. Mrs. O'N. was admitted to the same psychiatric hospital in October, 1969. During the day, without warning, she became confused, paranoid about neighbours and tearful. Within hours of admission she was semi-comatose, with a temperature of 103.4, a pulse rate of 140 and pretty obvious signs of pneumonia. She was transferred to a general hospital where she recovered uneventfully. Psychiatric assessment there uncovered no illness and particularly schizophrenia was excluded. Her unhappy home circumstances came to light, and she was offered supportive follow-up in the psychiatric out-patient clinic of the general hospital. During her illness her children were placed in care, and shortly after her discharge an attempt was made to treat her husband's alcoholism. He urgently requested in-patient care, and this was arranged. (A year later, in drink, he admitted that he planned the admission crisis to avoid paying 25 rent arrears.) Following his discharge, a new phenomenon appeared during joint interviews by social worker and psychiatrist. He was accusing his wife of madness. During rows that were witnessed he would say: "Tell the doctor about the apparitions you saw." "They (neighbours) all call her mad Mary"; "Tell him about your father and brother in the mental (hospital)—tell him that"; "She's sick, doctor"; "You'll be eating your plum pudding in the mental (hospital)." He threatened to have her certified, and using these rather sadistic tactics he was able to distress her and alarm the treatment team. She insisted in separate interviews that his allegations were false, and at no stage, despite enormous pressure from him, did she show evidence of psychotic illness. She reasoned that her husband wanted the children in care and her in hospital to allow him greater freedom to drink even more.

It was clear that the husband was trying to induce illness in his wife, but she was able to resist his attempts for two years. She was afraid to leave since she was aware that legal separation is difficult to arrange for a poor woman. The case shows the extent to which both society and the professional can tolerate the deviance of men. Furthermore, accusations of madness tend to viciously exploit publicly shared beliefs about mental illness (for example, loss of memory, seeing apparitions, a history of mental illness in the family).

In conclusion, success in inducing mental illness and eventually hospitalizing a marriage partner may, to a great extent, depend on the imbalance of power between the sexes. Indeed, Barton and Whitehead (1969) reported that in one case where the wife of a publican (owner of a public house) shared the work and power of her husband, she was successful in initiating his hospitalization.

SEX STEREOTYPES AND MENTAL HEALTH

"No, that nurse ain't some kinda monster chicken, buddy, what she is is a ball-cutter. I've seen a thousand of 'em, old and young, men and women. Seen 'em all over the country and in the homes—people who try to make you weak so they can get you to toe the line. . . . She may be a mother, but she's big as a damn barn and tough as a knife metal. She fooled me with that kindly little old mother bit for maybe three minutes when I came in this morning, but no longer. . . . Hooowee, I've seen some bitches in my time, but she takes the cake.

". . . She's a bitch and a buzzard and a ball-cutter, and don't kid me, you know what I'm talking about."

Ken Kesey: ONE FLEW OVER THE
CUCKOO'S NEST

The status of women in our society is reflected in sex stereotypes; that is, there exist certain presuppositions about the characteristics and behavior displayed by members of the two sexes. Females are not expected to display aggression or intellectuality or to reveal their sexuality openly; they are expected to be obedient and passive and to cultivate attractiveness and friendliness. Males, on the other hand, are expected to be aggressive, both physically and sexually; they ought to be independent and unemotional (Broverman et al., 1972; Kagan, 1964; Mischel, 1970). Characteristics ascribed to females and males tend to fall into two groups: one representing competence and independence for men and another involving warmth and expressiveness for women. Some of the stereotype characteristics in the competency cluster are as follows (Broverman et al., 1972):

COMPETENCY CLUSTER

Feminine	Masculine
Not at all aggressive	Very aggressive
Not at all independent	Very independent
Very submissive	Very dominant
Very passive	Very active

Here are examples of the stereotypic characteristics in the warmth-expressiveness cluster (Broverman et al., 1972):

WARMTH-EXPRESSIVENESS CLUSTER

Feminine	Masculine
Very tactful	Very blunt
Very quiet	Very loud
Very strong need for security	Very little need for security
Very gentle	Very rough

Broverman and her colleagues (1970) asked seventy-nine practicing clinicians (clinical psychologists, psychiatrists, and social workers) to describe the characteristics of a healthy adult man, a healthy adult woman, and a healthy person of unspecified sex. The findings indicated that female and male clinicians tended to agree closely on the attributes of these three categories; their concept of a healthy, mature man did not differ markedly from their concept of a healthy, mature adult—they were seen as almost the same. In contrast, a healthy mature female was perceived as being significantly different from a healthy adult person. Healthy adult persons and healthy adult men were ascribed characteristics from the competency cluster such as dominant, active, independent, and so on; on the other hand, women were assigned far less of these characteristics. In general, desirable personality characteristics were ascribed more often to a healthy man and to a healthy adult than to a healthy woman.

The results of Broverman and her associates seem to support the hypothesis that a double standard of health exists for women and men; that is, the general standard of health (for an adult person) is applied to men only, while healthy women are seen as significantly less healthy by adult standards. This would suggest that women fit more easily into the "sick" label. Carol Smart (1977), for example, argued that since women are portrayed as "emotional, irrational, unreliable and immature, psychiatrists and doctors, working with the 'natural attitude,' may be more likely to diagnose women as neurotic. Alternatively, because cultural stereotypes of men portray them to be sensible, rational and reliable, a diagnosis of neurosis may be less likely principally because the cause of emotional or irrational behavior in men will be seen as genuine rather than imaginary or trivial. In other words if one is 'rational' (male) the cause of one's complaint must be real, but if one is 'irrational' (female) the cause of the complaint must be unreal (neurotic)." Of course, the study of Broverman and her colleagues (1970) dealt only with the expressed attitudes of clinicians, which may not reflect their behavior in the clinical situation (Stricker, 1977).

Sex stereotypes may influence the clinicians' definition of psychopathology; they may conceive symptoms either as an intensification of or as a breaking away from sex roles (Draguns, 1979). One useful approach to the study of the relationship between psychopathology and sex stereotypes is to find out whether patterns of patients' symptoms reflect the intensification of these stereotypes. A study by Zigler and Phillips (1960) reveals that this is in fact the case. Symptoms in the category of self-deprivation and turning against the self tended to occur more frequently among women (suicidal attempt, suicidal ideas, euphoria, does not eat, self-deprecatory, depressed, mood swings). Similarly, symptoms indicating avoidance of others, such as being perplexed and apathetic, also occur more significantly in women than in men. On the other hand, symptoms in the self-indulgence and turning against others category tended to occur more frequently in men than in women (sexual perversions, drinking, rape, robbery, assault, threatened assault).

Sex stereotypes may affect the definition of mental illness in such a way that breaking away from one's sex role (sex-role reversal) may take on negative valuation and be considered abnormal—for example, aggression, overt sexuality, and intellectuality in women. Abramowitz, Abramowitz, Jackson, and Gomes (1973) have clearly demonstrated that in assessing females and males for the same behavior, clinicians ascribe more psychopatholgy to "liberated" women who challenge accepted values. Kayton and Biller (1972) found that psychiatric diagnosis of men as schizophrenic or neurotic was strongly associated with feminine traits, again suggesting sex-role reversal. A study by Feinblatt and Gold (1976) indicates that sex-role reversal is considered more serious than an intensification of one's own sex role. They found that, in a clinic, a girl who reacted aggressively (the stereotypic reaction of a boy) was perceived as more disturbed than a boy doing the same thing. Conversely, a boy who reacted to a situation by crying (the stereotypic reaction of a girl) was perceived as more disturbed than a girl reacting the same way. Costrich, Feinstein, Kidder, Marecek, and Pascale (1975) also found that university students attribute more serious psychopathology to men who expressed dependency, than to women who expressed the same level of dependency. In contrast, women who expressed aggression were seen as more disturbed than men who did so. These illustrations do not mean that women and men are specially rewarded for showing sex-appropriate but undesirable characteristics; they do, however, indicate that such behavior is tolerated: For example, crying is more tolerated in women, and aggression is more tolerated in men (Stoppard and Kalin, 1978).

Examples of the attribution of pathology to females who reveal sex-role reversal is found in the psychotherapists' descriptions of their "masculine" female clients. Among the most well-known labels in psychiatric literature are the so-called "castrating woman," the "angry woman," and the "intractable woman." The following is a sample of subjective descriptions of these women; most are reported by male therapists.

The castrating woman is frequently acknowledged in Western folklore and in psychiatry. The label "castrating" usually describes a woman who competes with men and rejects the expected submissive feminine role. For a man to threaten another man with castration is considered a sign of authority and the assertion of one's dominance. It is, however, derogatory to call a woman castrating, since this implies a rejection of the dominant-submissive relationship between the two sexes, and she is considered a threat to male authority. Dorothy Tennov (1975) pointed out that the client in psychotherapy is considered castrating when she does not accept the therapist's interpretation of her behavior or does not improve in therapy. Castrating means "anything done by a woman (in this case, the patient) which adversely affects the situation of a man (the therapist)." Diana Russell (1975) traces the origin of the labeling of women as castrating to the sexual situation. Men are threatened by women who take the initiative in sexual relations or who want a lot of sex because this forces them to realize their inadequacy and their inability to perform whenever the opportunity arises. This fact is less apparent if men always take the initiative, but many men feel castrated by women who demand equality in making sexual overtures.

There is also the "angry woman syndrome" described by Rickles (1971). During his thirty-five years of experience in psychotherapy, Rickles became acquainted with female patients who drank excessively and who expressed anger and had uncontrollable tempers. Their spouses are, however, described as showing the opposite (female) characteristics. They are "uniquely passive men who, while disturbed by their wives' behavior, accept it as a cross to bear." These women and their spouses are abnormal because they exhibit a reversal of sex-role behavior; that is, the wives show masculine behavior, while the husbands show feminine behavior. However, if one uses norms applicable to healthy males, the following description of these wives by Rickles may indicate normality rather than abnormality: They are "successful in their careers, dress and comport themselves neatly, and give the appearance of outwardly attractive, well-organized personalities." It appears that their main problem arises from challenging masculine superiority and dominance.

In describing the "intractable woman," John H. Houck (1972) cites Webster's *Seventh New Collegiate Dictionary*. "Intractable" means "not easily governed, managed, or directed; obstinate; not easily manipulated or wrought; not easily relieved or cured; unruly." In the therapy situation, according to Houck, she attempts to be assertive and manipulative. "She is, in nature, anxious, and angry, usually aloof and contemptuous of other women and demanding and suspicious of men." Tennov (1975) suggested that clients of Houck and other psychotherapists are in fact not mentally ill but that they are considered troublesome with respect to fulfilling their "normal" passive feminine roles. She noted that "Houck recognizes some relevance of the woman's external conditions when he recommends that the therapist's concern must often extend to social environmental change, but this turns out to be an attempt, through 'aggressive' therapy, to turn her husband from his 'passivity and diffidence' to a 'posture of strength and resolution—especially towards his wife.' Thus, the environmental changes Houck favors are ones which would further entrap her. Houck is, in essence, asking the husband to keep the 'intractable' woman in line, an approach that is entirely appropriate to patriarchal traditions."

In sum, many psychotherapists tend to associate "masculine" behavior in the female with psychopathology. Psychotherapy with females tends to encourage "feminine" behavior. Ideals of mental health held by psychotherapists for female clients are inconsistent with research indicating that high femininity in both sexes is related to high anxiety, low self-esteem and incompetence (Cosentino & Heilbrun, 1964; Gall, 1969, Gray, 1957; Heilbrun, 1968; Jones, Chernovetz, & Hansson, 1978; Webb, 1963).

The Future of Femininity and Masculinity

Society and its professionals have sanctioned typical male behaviors and considered them the ideals for mental health. Because of this, women are thrown into unresolvable conflict and are damned whatever they do. Whether they show masculine or feminine behavior, they are considered sick. This female conflict—is she to retain her now devalued female role or succumb to the temptation of the privileged male role?—is perhaps more intense in the educated female who has been exposed to an early male-oriented training but is also expected to adopt feminine behavior in adulthood. Barry, Bacon, and Child (1970) summarized the relationship of this conflict to abnormal behavior:

> In our training of children, there may now be less differentiation in sex role than characterizes adult life—so little indeed, as to provide inadequate preparation for adulthood. This state of affairs is likely to be especially true of formal education, which is more subject to conscious influence by an ideology than is informal socialization at home. With child training being more oriented toward the male than the female role in adulthood, many of the adjustment problems of women in our society today may be partly traced to conflicts growing out of inadequate childhood preparation for their adult role. This argument is nicely supported in extreme form by Spiro's (1956) analysis of sex roles in an Israeli kibbutz. The ideology of the founders of the kibbutz included the objective of greatly reducing differences in sex role. But the economy of the kibbutz is a largely nonmechanized one in which the superior average strength of men is badly needed in many jobs. The result is that, despite the ideology and many attempts to implement it, women con-

tinue to be assigned primarily to traditional "women's work," and the in-compatibility between upbringing or ideology and adult role is an important source of conflict for women.

With the de-differentiation of sex roles, however, men are ex-pected to have more adjustment problems than women. Since early school training equally emphasizes achievement and competition for the two sexes, "the new challenge for girls to develop and sustain individual achievement goals does not introduce a radically new motive for most of them." It is the change in the postindustrial era from an emphasis on production and technical skills to an emphasis on "the manipulation of words and ideas, and interacting with people—female socialization—" that might pose adjustment problems to men. For example, one result of the de-differentiation of sex roles is that men are now "expected to contribute their share to the more 'expressive' side of family and social life" (Hoffman, 1977), a behav-ior incompatible with early masculine socialization. During this pe-riod of rapid transition, the well-adjusted woman is not the one who simply steps out of her sex role and adopts "masculine" behavior but the one who can abandon her fear of success (Horner, 1972) and still maintain her capacity for tenderness and empathy in inter-personal relationships.

Sex roles can seriously restrict the range of behavior available to persons as they move from situations calling for masculine-typed behavior (initiative, independence) to feminine-typed behavior (warmth and expressiveness) or vice versa. The alternative is an androgynous individual who is able to incorporate the best of both worlds of masculinity and femininity. As Sandra Bem (1975) noted:

> But it is clear that whatever psychological barriers may turn out to be re-sponsible for the behavioral rigidities of the sex typed and sex reversed subjects . . . there exists a distinct class of people who can appropriately be termed androgynous, whose sex role adaptability enables them to engage in situationally effective behavior without regard for its stereotype as mas-culine or feminine. Accordingly, it may well be—as the women's liberation movement has urged—that the androgynous individual will some day come to define a new and more human standard of psychological health.

In recent years, there has been much interest in the bisexuality of brain organization (Beach, 1977; Diamond, 1977). Although persons have the potential for developing either female or male reproductive organs, it is believed that the brain of both sexes contains mechanisms for both female and male behavior. It is suggested that there are separate systems in the brain for female and for male behavior and that these two systems coexist in all normal females and males. If this view is correct, it would destroy traditional rigid sex roles and sex stereotypes. This would require a new concept of femininity and masculinity, varying in degree within the same individual, and an understanding that the bisexual brain organization potentially permits the individual to be behaviorally or psychologically both feminine and masculine instead of being one or the other.

WHICH IS THE WEAK SEX?

The Female Paradox: High Morbidity
and Low Mortality

Health surveys have consistently confirmed two contradictory observations. On the one hand, women report both mental and physical illness and use physician and hospital services more than men. On the other hand, the death rate for women in the Western world at all ages is substantially below that for men. A British physician described women's biological advantage and their unfavorable morbidity as follows: "It would appear that in some paradoxical way women save themselves from death by becoming ill" (Nathanson, 1976).

In Western countries, the death rate is substantially higher for men than for women. The sex differential has also increased in the twentieth century. In 1900, a woman had a two-year advantage over a man; by 1974, this had risen to 7.7 years (Johnson, 1977). Yet when morbidity is measured by behavioral indices, such as restriction of activity (going to bed, staying at home from work), women report more acute illness than men. Likewise, women also have more contact with physicians and have higher rates of hospitalization, even when obstetric conditions are excluded. Surgical rates for women are also between one and a half to two times the comparable rates for men (Nathanson, 1976). It appears that with the exception of an excess of chronic conditions in men, almost all indicators of morbidity are higher in women. Why, then, do they have a low rate of mortality? Both biological factors and sex-linked behavior are suggested to explain the sex differential in mortality. I shall discuss these two factors separately.

Biological factors   It has been suggested that, on the animal and human levels, males are more susceptible to stress than females (Gadpaille, 1972; Gray, 1971a, 1971b). For example, in training situations, female rats learn faster than male rats to avoid an electric shock. Similarly, in situations where the shock cannot be avoided, female rats defecated less and ambulated more than male rats and hence were considered less emotional (Gray, 1971b). In short, where avoidance is possible, the female rat is superior to her male counterpart. Similarly, where avoidance is impossible, she shows less signs of emotionality and fearfulness. These findings seem to suggest that biological factors which are involved in susceptibility to stress tend to favor the female.

The animal situation seems to have its counterpart on the human level. Many psychophysiological disorders such as ulcers, high blood pressure, and heart attacks are prevalent in men, indicating higher susceptibility to stress. But, as we will see in Chapter 13, these disorders are usually attributed to the occupational situation, which mainly involves men.

Another argument presented to demonstrate the susceptibility of the male to stress is based on the prevalence of sexual dysfunctions in male animals and in men. On the animal level, Gray (1971a) noted that "male dogs, foxes, minks, rats, cats, porcupines and cockerels appear to show a greater reluctance to copulate in a novel environment, in an environment previously associated with pain, and in the presence of other animals higher in the social hierarchy, than do their female counterparts." On the human level, Gadpaille (1972) also observed the general adaptability of the female in her reproductive and sexual functions. He noted that men are weaker physiologically than women. Despite their greater size and muscular strength, they are more vulnerable to disease, and their chances of survival are slimmer. Also, their reproductive function and their sexual development are much more easily upset than those of women. The male's sexual function and sexual behavior is dependent on learning whereas women can still function sexually in total ignorance. The sexual stamina of the male is far inferior to that of the female, and his capacity to perform sexually under adverse psychological conditions is severely circumscribed. Women, on the other hand, can function sexually under many adverse conditions—witness the large number of pregnancies that occur during rape or when the woman is unconscious or suffering severe anxiety. Moreover, there is much greater incidence of homosexuality and all paraphilias in men than in women, and there are sexual deviations peculiar to men, but there are none peculiar to women. Gadpaille concluded that the male is far more vulnerable than the female to psychosexual mislearning and disorder. Yet the generalizations made by Gray and Gadpaille comparing the animal to the human level are premature indeed. As we shall see in Chapters 5, 7, and 13, differences in psychophysiological disorders, fears, and sexual deviations tend to be influenced by the sex status of women and men.

The genetic hypothesis also suggests that high mortality in the male is due to the fact that the female possesses two large X chromosomes, whereas the male possesses one X and a very small Y. Goodman and Gorlin (1970) listed 121 X-linked conditions that females may or do escape or have in a mild form. In contrast, the male tends to have these conditions exclusively or in severe form (for example, color blindness, anemia, thyroid disorders, and clotting disorders). Women are also less susceptible to infections than men and are less likely to die from them. In Chapter 13, I shall discuss the possible relationship between the female sex hormone and heart disease or high blood pressure.

Sex-linked behavior and mortality   Sex-linked behavior is any behavior prescribed by society because of the sexual position of the individual. It has been suggested that behavior related to sex status may drive persons toward or protect them against death. General evidence in support of the effect of social factors and, in particular, sex roles on rates of mortality is indicated by the finding that higher male death rates are not universal. Higher mortality rates among females are more frequently observed in nonindustrialized countries, which shows a reversal of Western trends (Waldron, 1976b).

The importance of sex-linked behavior is very clearly seen in the case of accidents and suicide. It is not only that men drive more but that they tend to drive less safely than women. Male drivers are involved in 30 percent more accidents per mile driven and in 130 percent more fatal accidents per mile driven. Male drivers, more often than female drivers, enter the intersection when the light is yellow or red or fail to signal a turn (Waldron, 1976b). Also, men are exposed to other accidents while at work, and more men than women die from accidental drownings or accidents caused by fire-arms. Suicide, which will be discussed in Chapter 4, is also related to male occupational problems.

Sex-linked behavior can also explain the association between respiratory diseases and smoking or between cirrhosis of the liver and alcohol consumption in man. That men have between five to six times the rates of death from respiratory disease (lung cancer, emphysema) is primarily because they smoke more than women. Apart from cigarette smoking, which contributes to lung cancer, industrial carcinogens, such as working with asbestos, also increase the risk for men. Asbestos is estimated to be responsible for one in twenty lung cancer deaths in the United States (Waldron, 1976b). In Chapter 13, I shall present research suggesting that chronic peptic ulcer and coronary heart disease, which are more prevalent among men, are related to what is considered masculine behavior in Western society.

In contrast to heart disease, respiratory disorders, cancer, and ulcers—the predominant killers of males—chronic conditions such as arthritis and rheumatism, which are more prevalent in women, are less likely to be the cause of death (Nathanson, 1976). Diabetes is the only condition for which higher death rates are reported for women than men, and even here the differential between the sexes, particularly large in the 1920s and 1930s, has significantly decreased in recent years (Hoffman, 1976; Murphy, 1976a). A major con-tributor to diabetes is obesity. Hoffman suggested that since, in recent years, men have become as obese as women, the sex differen-tial has been reduced. Murphy (1976a), however, suggested that a change in sex stereotypes has now affected attitudes toward the diagnosis and treatment of diabetes:

> In the late 1930s, it was well recognized that female diabetics tended to seek treatment later than male ones, and made more difficulties about their treatment. They were more embarrassed than male patients by the need to talk about their urine and have the urine tested, at least to a male doctor, since a "proper lady" at that time did not refer to such "dirty" and sexually-associated matters whereas there were no particular taboos for the males. They showed more sensitivity to the idea of frequent injections with rela-tively blunt needles and ordinary insulin in place of today's extended action insulin compounds than the men did, simply because the men had to main-

tain a facade of being better able to ignore pain. Today this difference in sex stereotypes is much less, and the supervision and treatment of diabetes has become much easier, at least for the patient.

Consistent with the stress hypothesis discussed earlier, Gove (1973) argued that marital status would have a different effect on the rates of mortality for women and men. He reported statistics showing that, in general, mortality rates of the unmarried are higher than those of the married, but the difference between the married and the unmarried is greater for men than for women. Married men derive greater benefits than women from being married, both in the care they receive and in psychological well-being. Both tuberculosis and diabetes require much care (diet, rest, and scheduling major aspects of one's life, such as what to eat, when to eat, and when to take medication). Marriage seems to drastically reduce male mortality in relation to these two illnesses. In addition to tuberculosis and diabetes, statistics reported by Gove (1973) also reveal that marital status protects men against other causes of death, such as (1) mortality involving overt social acts (suicide, homicide, automobile accidents, pedestrian accidents, and other accidents), (2) mortality associated with the use of socially approved "narcotics" (cirrhosis of the liver, which is associated with alcohol use, and lung cancer, which is associated with smoking). The data for these causes of mortality are consistent with the data on mental illness, for they uniformly indicate that the difference between being married and being single (or divorced or widowed) is much greater for men than for women.

Waldron and Johnston (1976) have indicated a recent increase of female mortality from chronic conditions (cancer of the respiratory system, emphysema, heart disease, cirrhosis of the liver) as well as from accidents and suicide. For example, there was a relatively higher rate of increase in lung cancer among women in 1974, which resulted in a declining sex differential in mortality (Johnson, 1977). These reversals of trends in the causes of mortality have been attributed to the "greater participation of women in those occupations previously dominated almost entirely by men. It is predicted that as women come to live and behave in social contexts more similar to those of men, sex differences in stress will decrease, and the health of men and women would grow more similar" (Johnson, 1977). Chapter 13 will discuss recent changes in sex roles and illness.

In conclusion, it appears that the traditional attitudes and behavior of women tend to expose them less to fatal and chronic physical conditions and, in turn, to reduce their rate of mortality. Although such attitudes and behavior work in their favor when they have medical problems, that is not so in the psychiatric area. As we shall see in Chapter 2, psychiatric treatment such as drugs, electroconvulsive therapy, psychosurgery, and psychotherapy have failed to provide solutions to female life problems.

Mortality and Morbidity in Childhood

Sex differences appear so early in life that they may throw some light on the interplay between biological and social factors. There is strong evidence that the male child is more vulnerable to the ravages of birth and childhood than his female counterpart. Similarly, he is more exposed to both physical and psychiatric treatment. All available statistics reveal higher male than female mortality during the first year of life. Similarly, males show an excess of fetal mortality and stillbirth (Gadpaille, 1972; Waldron, 1976b).

Girls show advanced developmental maturity as compared with boys, and this may facilitate early learning and socialization. They show advanced skeletal maturity as measured by the shape and degree of hardening of the bones. Despite the advantage of heavier birth weight, boys tend to do less well in performance during early childhood. They reveal an excess of mental, motor, and neurological abnormalities during the first year of life (Singer, Westphal, & Niswander, 1968). Boys also have higher rates of accidents than girls, and this may, as in adulthood, contribute to the rise in the rate of mortality. As children grow, the rates of accidents increase for boys and decrease for girls (Manheimer & Mellinger, 1967).

In contrast to data reported with adults, there is an excess of psychosis among boys; ratios of boys to girls reported by different investigators range from 1.7:1 to 9.5:1 (Werry, 1972). On the average, three to four times as many boys are labeled psychotic as girls. The high incidence of congenital neurological abnormalities in boys has been suggested to explain a higher rate of mental retardation, learning disabilities, hyperactivity, and poor impulse control. The following discussion will concentrate on mental retardation and behavior disorders in childhood.

Mental retardation First, there are more boys than girls with mental retardation and learning disorders. In spite of a decrease in the tendency to institutionalize women and girls as a form of sterilization, there were still almost 25 percent more males than females in state institutions for the retarded in 1965. Studies of community incidence of mental retardation tend to show an even greater excess of males (Lehrke, 1972). Second, retarded women run a greater risk of having retarded children than do retarded men. Reed and Reed (1965), for example, found twice as many retarded children in families with a retarded mother and a father of "normal" or unknown intelligence as in families with a retarded father and a mother of "normal" or unknown intelligence.

These findings appear to indicate that intellectual abilities are genetically transmitted through the mother to her male child (Lehrke, 1972). However, Nance and Engel (1972) reported that the present excess of retardation among boys may be due to selective factors. During the last two decades, there has been an increase in the differential between the numbers of retarded males and females in public institutions. Contrary to present trends, females prevailed in institutions at the beginning of the twentieth century. These findings seem to indicate that the admission of girls and boys to institutions is influenced by parental attitudes, community pressure, and resources rather than by the actual incidence of retardation. Anne Anastasi (1972) also put forward an environmental interpretation of the finding that there are more retarded children when the mother rather than the father is retarded. She indicated that mothers traditionally play the major role in child-rearing and thus have more influence than fathers on the development of the intellectual abilities of their children.

Behavior disorders I have previously noted that adults become vulnerable to the accusation of madness when there is a strained relationship in the enactment of social roles. Usually, persons who hold less power are those who are victimized and accused of madness. In a strained relationship between a child and an adult, it is almost always the child who is sent for psychological and psychiatric investigation. Children present an extreme example of helplessness and complete dependency on an adult's decision concerning referral to clinics. Childhood problems may therefore reflect the expectations of parents, teachers, and clinicians as well as their tolerance of the child's behavior.

Two patterns of behavior are consistently found in the study of problems of childhood. In one pattern, which is called a *conduct disorder*, the behavior is directed toward the environment—excessive approach behavior, such as destructiveness, fighting, disruptiveness, or temper tantrums. In the other pattern, which is called a *personality disorder*, behavior is directed toward the self (the child)—excessive avoidance, such as fear, anxiety, physical complaints, shyness, crying, and chewing fingernails. The evidence reveals that boys are higher on conduct disorders, whereas girls are higher on personality disorders. Findings in childhood are consistent with those for adults: both show an excess of antisocial behavior among males (Ross, 1974; Werry & Quay, 1971).

Werry and Quay (1971) gave teachers a 55-item checklist of childhood problems that are usually found among clients of child guidance clinics. They found that teachers checked an average of 11.4 problems for each boy and 7.6 problems for each girl. Symptoms that are significantly higher in boys belong to the conduct disorders category, whereas those which prevail in girls belong to the category of personality disorders.

Miller, Hampe, Barrett, and Noble (1971) suggested that the basic problem of children is failure to learn and that there is a differential reaction of girls and boys to this failure. When girls fail, their reaction is more likely to be manifested in social withdrawal, sensitivity, and fear. Boys react to failure by aggression, hyperactivity, and antisocial behavior. "Since children are often referred when they become problems to adults, and since aggression is more likely to become a problem to adults, boys are more likely to be referred to treatment" (Miller et al., 1971).

Studies show that when teachers are used as respondents (Werry & Quay, 1971), there is a higher number of problems in boys than in girls, whereas when parents are the respondents (Miller et al., 1971), the difference between the sexes is eliminated. This would indicate that teachers are less tolerant of the behavior of boys than of girls. The results are also consistent with the finding that school referrals are three times greater for boys than for girls and that many children are not referred to clinics until they enter public school (Rimm & Sommervill, 1977). The presumption of madness by psychiatrists seems to have its equivalence among teachers in their "diagnosis" of male students. In the rating of behavior "symp-toms" among students enrolled in kindergarten, first grade, and second grade, 49 percent of the boys were perceived by teachers as restless and unable to sit still, 48.2 percent were perceived as dis-tractible, and 46.3 percent were perceived as disruptive (Werry & Quay, 1971). The high percentage of boys who are rated by teachers as showing behavior problems has some implications for the defini-tion of abnormality. As Ross (1974) pointed out:

> It makes little sense to speak of behavior problems when nearly half of an unselected population engages in that form of behavior. If one uses the statistical concept of normality, the restless, distractible, and disruptive behavior of the children in this school system would have to be viewed as normal behavior. But the teachers check it off on a problem ("symptom") checklist. Whose problem is it? Could it be that classrooms in elementary school are so structured and teacher behavior so programmed that the "nor-mal," to-be-expected behavior of male children is to emit responses the teacher identifies as restlessness and distractibility? If this is the case, the modification called for is situational-environmental and should not have its focus on changing the behavior of boys so that they "adjust" to what may be an intolerable situation.

In sum, whereas antisocial behavior in men is relatively tolerated or at least is not considered full-blown madness by society, similar behavior may lead to psychiatric treatment in childhood. It seems that adult females and schoolboys are those who are most liable to the accusation of madness in our society.

Women
in Therapy

2

One consequence of interpreting what are essentially human problems in terms of physical illness or psychological disturbance is that the person becomes someone considered in need of treatment. In this view, life problems can be resolved only by the application of the appropriate techniques developed by psychiatrists and psychologists. For example, a woman who has marital problems should not go to an attorney who may suggest a divorce or a legal separation as a solution; rather, she should go to a psychiatrist or a psychologist for treatment. She may be told that she is neurotic or psychotic and that the problem does not lie in her marriage or her husband but in her inability to relate to men or in her immaturity. In short, she is considered sick and in need of medical treatment or psychotherapy (Braginsky & Braginsky, 1974).

Since women are more often subjected to psychiatric treatment than men, the following chapter will deal with the topics of organic and psychological therapeutic techniques, as well as with the ethical question of sex with patients in therapy, from the female perspective.

ORGANIC TREATMENT

Psychotropic Drugs

Psychotropic or psychoactive drugs are defined as those which have, through their action on the brain, an effect on normal and abnormal psychological processes. These drugs are usually identified, according to their action, as major tranquilizers, minor tranquilizers, sedatives, stimulants, and antidepressants. Studies in North America and in European countries indicate that the ratio of females to males in the use of psychotropic drugs is approximately two to one (Cooperstock, 1976a; Gillie, 1975; Manheimer, Mellinger, & Balter, 1968). The majority of women obtain their drugs from physicians, mostly from general practitioners. Physicians are most likely to be the initial suppliers of drugs to women; they contribute to the use of drugs in at least three ways (Prather & Fidell, 1978): (1) multiple prescription, (2) excessive dosages, and (3) repeat prescription. Multiple prescriptions occur when a patient obtains more than one prescription from one or several physicians. A higher proportion of women than men receive multiple prescriptions from physicians (Cooperstock, 1976a).

Repeat prescriptions are those prescriptions that are refilled by the the physicians. Once a woman receives a prescription for a psychotropic drug, she is more likely to receive additional prescriptions (Cooperstock, 1976a). Both initial prescriptions and refills may represent a collusion between physician and patient. The physician may yield to the requests of a patient and, being unable to suggest an alternative, order a refill. In general, the writing of a prescription may serve as a device to terminate a visit, demonstrating to the patient that her visit has ended in a tangible remedy (Prather & Fidell, 1978).

Other sources of psychotropic drugs are stealing prescription pads from the physician's office; borrowing or stealing drugs from friends or family members and, in particular, the mother; or illegally purchasing them from the street (Prather & Fidell, 1978). Sex differences in prescribed drugs noted earlier disappear when the rates of use of over-the-counter drugs are compared. In one study, 36 percent of females and 35 percent of males were using over-the-counter drugs (Abelson, Cohen, Schrayer, & Rapperport, 1973). Among women, those who had taken drugs by prescription from physicians had taken them longer and more regularly than those who had obtained them from other sources (Fidell, 1977).

Why are women prescribed more drugs than men? Historically, according to Ruth Cooperstock (1976b), the medical profession viewed the nineteenth-century American middle- and upper-class women as innately sick, whereas the lower-class woman was depicted as "innately healthy, sturdy and seldom in need of medical care." The innate sickness of the middle- and upper-class women had served the financial interests of doctors by establishing this well-off segment of society as a kind of "client caste" to the medical profession at a time when there was an excess of doctors in urban areas.

Nowadays, there seems to be a collusion between physicians and drug companies. Physicians tend to explain female life problems in psychiatric terms and to prescribe drugs for financial difficulties, loneliness, disobedience of children, and so on (Cooperstock, 1976b). Drug advertisements, on the other hand, tend to reinforce the preju-dice against women by describing them as sicker and weaker than men and by suggesting that drugs will help them adjust to their housewifely role (Seidenberg, 1971). Stimson (1975) found that, in advertisements for antidepressants and tranquilizers, women are portrayed more often than men (a ratio of 15 to 1). The primary message of these advertisements seems to be that women are more likely than men to need these drugs. They depict a harrassed house-wife torn between household chores, child-rearing, and shopping. She may be standing at the sink, crammed between a washing machine and a table cluttered with kitchen objects, with a nagging daughter at her side. Alternatively, they may show a sad-looking woman standing in the supermarket, with shelves of pet food on one side and shelves of toilet rolls on the other. The majority of physicians shown in these ads are, however, portrayed by men (Stockburger & Davis, 1978).

Commercials suggest that married women need and perhaps use drugs more than single women. Studies are, however, inconsistent in this area. For example, a study by Thompson (1973) in New Zealand reveals that married women receive twice as many prescriptions for psychotropic drugs as men and single women. Two North American studies (Fejer & Smart, 1973; Fidell, 1977), however, reveal no rela-tionship between marital status and the use of psychotropic drugs. Employment is not related to drug usage except that housewives report the frequent use of tranquilizers, whereas employed women mention stimulants and sedatives (Prather & Fidell, 1978).

Sex differences in the use of psychotropic drugs are also attributed to the tendency of women to seek professional help and to report symptoms more often than men (Cooperstock, 1976b). Among women who see physicians, those who present more complaints are more likely to receive a prescription for psychotropic drugs (Fidell, 1977). It is, however, found by Dunnell and Cartwright (1972) that women are more likely to take prescribed medication than men even when the two sexes report the same number of symptoms. It is quite possible that it is more acceptable for women than for men to cope with stress by using "pills." Indeed, men tend to mention the use of alcohol rather than "pills" for the purpose of coping (Abelson et al., 1973).

Conclusion   In the study of the use of psychotropic drugs, an important question is whether they are an effective remedy for female problems. The claim of physicians that specific types of drugs are helpful to deal with certain symptoms is not valid. Linda Fidell (1977) found that women who were using major tranquilizers had almost the same symptoms as those given other kinds of psychotropic drugs. The nature of the complaints of these women had nothing to do with what determined receiving the type of drug they were using: Drugs prescribed by the physician appear to be randomly selected.

Studies in Europe and North America reveal a sudden increase in the use of psychotropic drugs when women are approaching middle age (Cooperstock, 1976a; Gillie, 1975; Hemminki, 1974). These years seem to represent stressful periods of their lives. Although drugs may bring temporary relief of anxiety and tension, they may also reduce the possibility of searching for a permanent solution of life problems (Cooperstock, 1976b; Prather & Fidell, 1978; Stimson, 1975). Finally, there has been a recent increase of the rates of both suicide and attempted suicide among women using psychotropic drugs prescribed by physicians (Prather & Fidell, 1978; Weissman, 1974). Thus, drugs may be used to help women to function within the prescribed sex role rather than to take a political action or to seek social solutions to their problems. When drug treatment fails to solve their problems, they may use the same drugs to kill themselves.

Electroconvulsive Therapy (ECT)

Five days later, on arriving for the session, a worried charge nurse said that the patients, while admitting the treatment had done them good, had complained of headache. Lined up outside the treatment ward were the patients with one thing in common—they all had small lesions similar to a second degree burn in the temporal area. A quick examination of the box showed in fact that they had been given ECT straight at 250 volts from the mains. The box was banned and a new one ordered.

J. Easton Jones: "Non-ECT"

In the administration of electroconvulsive therapy (ECT), two electrodes are placed on the patient's temples, where an electric current between 70 and 130 volts is applied briefly (from 0.1 to 0.5 seconds). It is generally agreed that, with the exception of depression, ECT is of little value in the treatment of psychiatric disorders (Maher, 1966; Slater & Roth, 1969). In practice, however, it is applied to a variety of patients. Indeed, Costello, Christensen, Bobey, and Hall (1972) found no relationship between the diagnosis given to the patient and the administration of ECT in a psychiatric unit of a teaching hospital. The researchers concluded that the administration of ECT in that institution was either determined by an unknown factor or that it was randomly assigned to patients. The use of ECT was investigated in another hospital by Jones (1974). He pointed out that "the indications seemed a bit vague, ranging from temporal lobe epilepsy and chronic schizophrenia to depression and poking the medical superintendent in the eye."

Electroconvulsive therapy is administered to females more frequently than to males (Eastwood & Stiasny, 1978). The excessive use of ECT in the treatment of women is apparent in depression as well as in other mental illnesses. It appears that those over 35 of both sexes were given more ECT than those under 35, and more female patients than male patients were over 35; also, the depressed patients were given more ECT than those with other diagnoses, and women were more likely than men to be diagnosed as depressed. These interpretations explain in part the excessive overall use of ECT with women. There is also a belief in psychiatric circles that ECT is more effective in the treatment of women than it is with men (Clinical Psychiatry Committee, 1965).

Evaluation of the therapeutic effects of ECT Although ECT is widely used in the treatment of depression, claims that it reduces suicide or prevents the probability of recurrence of depression appear to be unfounded (Costello & Belton, 1970; Maher, 1966). Two reviews of the literature (Costello & Belton, 1970; Costello, 1976) indicate that studies evaluating the effects of ECT had two methodological faults. First, studies did not use a placebo-ECT group, a situation in which patients go through exactly the same procedure as those in the ECT group except that no electric shock is administered to their heads. Second, they fail to incorporate double-blind conditions; in a double-blind condition, neither the patient herself or himself nor the staff (doctors, nurses) know which group (ECT group vs. placebo-ECT group) she or he is assigned to.

Costello (1976) attempted to satisfy these two methodological requirements. In addition to an ECT group, which is normally administered a shock in the head, a second placebo-ECT group was given a shock to each leg for a period of two minutes. After six treatments, there was no noticeable difference between the effects of a shock administered to the patients' heads and to their legs. As Costello (1976) noted, "On the day of the last treatment the patients' own doctor and two or three ward nurses were asked to judge which kind of treatment had been administered. In only one of the ten patients was there complete agreement. In that case the wrong decision was made. A peripheral shock patient was judged to have had ECT."

Considering the doubtful effects of ECT, it is not surprising that it has come under heavy attacks in recent years. The argument of the anti-ECT group is strengthened by papers such as the one published by Jones (1974), a British general practitioner working in a mental hospital. His paper demonstrates that the use of ECT cannot be relevant to the "improvement" of patients under treatment since in his hospital they were treated for two years with a machine that did not work. More serious objections to ECT arise from its possibly reversible effects on memory and the brain. Roueche (1974), in an article aptly entitled "As Empty as Eve," described a woman in her early fifties who suffered a loss of memory after an ECT treatment for her depression:

> After eight ECTs for the resulting depression, she had no recollection of any part of her hospital stay of nine weeks; on her return home she could not remember what she usually had for breakfast and did not know the meaning of terms such as Blue Cross and Watergate; the contents of books read after her treatment disappeared rapidly from memory; terms associated with her

work as an economist and analyst such as "over-the-counter," "mutual funds" and "odd-lot dealers" had no meaning for her. Because she could not recover her professional past she obtained a disability retirement pension but continued to work without pay as a low level clerk. Four months after her treatment she said she continued to feel "As empty as Eve."

Hemingway, who was treated for depression with ECT, complained how his memory was destroyed and how he was ruined as a writer: "What is the sense of ruining my head and erasing my memory, which is my capital, and putting me out of business?" (Hotchner, 1966).

This anecdotal evidence is not without research support. It has been claimed that ECT has only temporary effects on recent memory. However, Squire (1975) found that post-ECT deficit in memory extends over thirty years, with no apparent differentiation between memory for recent and more remote events. It seems that ECT does affect memory in general but that it incurs greater deficit in the recall of recent than remote events (Squire, Slater, and Chace, 1975).

In conclusion, considering these long-term effects of ECT, it becomes clear that women diagnosed as neurotic or psychotic are well advised to resist this treatment. However, it may be that patients, particularly those who are involuntarily committed to hospital, have neither the will nor the power to reject ECT or any other drastic therapies.

Psychosurgery

Psychosurgery consists of the use of surgical intervention to destroy brain tissue in order to modify behavior and emotions. Although there are several variations of the surgery procedure, it mainly aims at severing the connection between certain areas of the frontal cortex and the rest of the central nervous system (Maher, 1966). The frontal cortex is supposed to be responsible for the feelings of love, empathy, and other emotions as well as for creativity and abstract thinking. Its functions involve almost all of the basic human qualities.

An analysis of all the articles published in the United States between 1970 and 1976 indicates two groups of psychosurgery patients: *first,* the aggressive (violent, assaultive, or hyperactive) patients; and *second,* the anxious, depressive, obsessive, and phobic patients. Sex ratio analysis revealed that 61 percent of the aggressive patients were males, whereas 59 percent of the patients in the other group were females. Overall, there is an excess of females who are given psychosurgery, but this is due to the fact that the second group (anxious, depressive, and so on) has approximately nine times more patients than the aggressive category. These findings do not differ significantly from the sex ratio distribution of these two diagnostic categories in the general population, giving support to the view that because women are more frequently labeled "mentally ill," they are also more likely to be subjected to psychosurgery (Valenstein, 1977).

Effects of psychosurgery   In the evaluation of the postoperative effects of psychosurgery, much attention is given to the elimination of behavior that is disturbing to the hospital staff, to the family, and to society in general. The patient is thus rendered less aggressive and more cooperative or quiet. However, little regard is given to those aspects that are important to the individual, such as intellectual and emotional behavior. Psychosurgery may blunt the patients' intellect, impair their judgment, and reduce their creativity; not only does it make the patients calm, but it also makes them apathetic, irresponsible, and asocial (Chorover, 1974). Effects of the operation are usually subjectively assessed by the psychiatrist or surgeon responsible for the patient's treatment. Mirsky and Orzack (1977), for example, considered the patient as "very much improved" if she said, "The operation saved my life."

The physical complications of surgery include hemorrhages, infections, seizures, weight changes, paralysis, dyskinesias, loss of the sense of smell, bladder or bowel incontinence, and endocrine changes (including irregularities in the menstrual cycle). Behavioral and emotional complications are lethargy (loss of motivation and/or affect), generalized or specific disinhibitions (volubility, lowered personal standards, carelessness, immature behavior, shoplifting, extravagant behavior, irritability, aggression), increase or decrease in sexuality, and inability to work. There seem to be two extremes of reactions to the operation: Patients either become emotionally or intellectually unresponsive (vegetables), or, at the other extreme, they may become impulsive, irresponsible, and amoral (Valenstein, 1977).

A major criticism of psychosurgery is that alternative treatment is often ignored by surgeons. Valenstein (1977) noted that behavior therapy provides a safer and more effective alternative to psychosurgery.

The use of psychosurgery with women and minorities Cases summarized by Roberts (1972) and by Valenstein (1973) seem to indicate that psychosurgery is primarily used with women not to cure their "illness" but to eliminate behavior considered inappropriate for the typical female—that is to say, aggression and overt sexuality. Consider, for example, the case of Julia, who was operated on by Dr. Vernon Mark, one of the proponents of psychosurgery in the United States. Mark and Ervin (1970), in *Violence and the Brain*, reported that psychosurgery had eliminated Julia's violence and assaultive behavior. An examination of the case records before and after surgery has, however, revealed that Julia was "completely destroyed" by the operation. Prior to the operation, Julia was a beautiful 19-year-old honors student whose father, a physician himself, used to be upset by her occasional temper tantrums. After the operation, which was preceded by over sixty electroshock treatments, she lost interest in her environment, including her favorite music (Roberts, 1972). Valenstein (1973) also noted that after two operations Julia was still "a very sick person who was not likely to function in an unprotected environment." There was no change in her epilepsy or her "psychotic" episodes.

In a paper entitled "Psychosurgery: The Final Solution to the Woman Problem," Barbara Roberts (1972) cited the case of a "promiscuous" housewife who ran away from home frequently. After psychosurgery this housewife was apparently cured of her promiscuity and became a model housewife. Roberts noted that it is more acceptable to lobotomize women than men because neurosurgeons consider creativity and sexuality, which the operation totally destroys, as expendable qualities in women.

Middle-aged depressed women are one of the main targets of psychosurgery. Roberts described a case of a woman reported in 1970 by Mark and Ervin. Two operations were claimed to be a great success, even though it was followed by the suicide of the patient. This woman submitted to the operations under pressure from doctors and her mother. She became furious because of the failure of the two operations, but the doctors dismissed her rage as paranoid. When she was allowed out of the hospital to shop, she committed suicide.

Women are more often exposed to psychosurgery because they have more contact with the psychiatric establishment and because their symptoms are more bothersome to others (see, for example, the description of hospitalized schizophrenic women in Chapter 3).

However, men may be victimized by psychosurgery in order to eliminate violence (Chorover, 1974; Mark, 1974). Many transient and situational problems of childhood, such as hyperactivity, are also treated by psychosurgery, resulting in permanent brain damage (Valenstein, 1977). Peter Breggen, an American psychiatrist, after examining reports on cases of psychosurgery, concluded that psychosurgery is "being used to repress the helpless: the poor, the women, the black, the imprisoned, and the institutionalized" (Holden, 1973). Psychosurgery is the most legitimate, the fastest, and the most economical means of social control available to the professional.

Effects of Mastectomy, Hysterectomy, and Therapeutic Abortion

We have just seen that psychosurgery may be used for both females and males. Little attention has, however, been given to the psychological effects of surgical operations that are exclusively female, such as mastectomy, hysterectomy, and therapeutic abortion. Although these surgical procedures may save a woman's life, they may also result in a permanent disfigurement and in psychological disturbance. Since the female breast is a feminine symbol, mastectomy can bring a sense of mutilation or even a loss of feeling feminine (Asken, 1975). Women also show much concern over sexual desirability, interpersonal sexual relations, and dangers to their marriage after the operation. Some common misconceptions among patients with breast cancer are that cancer always recurs and kills, that they will be perceived by others as untouchable, and that they are in some way responsible for the illness (Klein, 1971). Thus, counseling should aim at dispelling these misconceptions and at preparing the patient for postoperative cosmetic reconstruction of the lost breast. During the postoperative period, emotional support is necessary to enable the patient to adapt to the change and to accept her altered body image.

Greer and Morris (1975) demonstrated a relationship between the expression of anger and breast cancer. Among women with cancer, there were a larger number who were either "extreme suppressors" (those who had very rarely, in their adult lives, openly showed anger) or "expressors" (those who had frequently shown temper outbursts). This study suggests that either the extreme expression or suppression of emotions may be associated with breast cancer. However, a replication of this study is needed to estimate the reliability of the finding before final conclusions can be reached about the role of emotions in breast cancer. Indeed, there was a small group of women in the study who had reported a normal expression of anger, and yet they developed malignant tumors.

Hysterectomy, the surgical removal of the uterus, is one of the most common forms of female surgery. Fairnbairn and Acheson (1969) estimated that 19 percent of females by the age of 75 will have had a hysterectomy performed on them. Hysterectomy may be justified purely for sterilization purposes on the grounds that alternative techniques remain inadequate. It may also be recommended on gynecological grounds, such as irregular bleeding and menstrual discomfort. There is a tendency among physicians to suggest hysterectomy because they consider the uterus as a potential future site of pathology indicating infection or hormonal imbalance (Meikle, 1977).

Helen Deutsch (1945) has suggested that the uterus, like the female breast, is of special psychological significance for women since it is closely related to their view of their femininity. Its removal is expected to be followed in at least some women with a feeling of inadequacy and an emotional disturbance. In addition to the common preoperative fears to which patients are prone, many women also experience diffuse nonspecific anxiety following surgery. Depression, neurosis, and psychotic reactions are also reported. Pseudocyesis or false pregnancy is also occasionally noted. Because women may be ambivalent about hysterectomy, it is quite possible that some of them later regret it. In particular, young women still in their child-rearing years show more conflicts and may be more psychologically disturbed after the operation than older ones (Meikle, 1977).

Although some studies reported negative effects of hysterectomy (Lindemann, 1941; Richards, 1974), more recent studies tend to reveal beneficial effects (Meikle, 1977). For example, Meikle, Brody, and Pysh (1977) compared 55 hysterectomy patients, 38 cholecystectomy (gall bladder) patients, and 60 tubal-ligation patients, but they found no support to the view that removal of the uterus leads to greater emotional disturbance than other forms of equivalent surgery. Similarly, no evidence was found to suggest that sterilization by organ removal was psychologically more traumatic than was the case when the uterus remained intact.

Contrary to common beliefs, Huffman (1950) and Patterson and Craig (1963) found no decrease in the erotic response and sexual activities of hysterectomy patients. Meikle (1977) pointed out that operations for gynecological and sterilization reasons tend to be followed by an increase rather than a decrease in sexual satisfaction. As in mastectomy, there is, however, a fear among patients that they might lose their husbands. This fear is mainly based on the mistaken belief in a loss of sexual drive after the operation (Drellich & Bieber, 1958). The husbands' expectations may apparently sometimes take a paranoid form, a belief that after hysterectomy, their wives risk becoming promiscuous (Smibert, 1972).

It is found that, among lower social class groups, the hysterectomized female is considered to be less of a woman (Levinson, 1972; Wolf, 1970). Lower-class women are, therefore, more likely to report adverse psychological reactions from the operation. It is of interest that being poor and having many children are sometimes taken by physicians as sufficient reasons for recommending hysterectomy.

A crucial but relatively neglected area of research is the psychological effect of therapeutic abortion on women who face unwanted pregnancies. The finding that some women become disturbed after abortion argues against granting it. Research suggests that a number of females seem to be psychologically disturbed after therapeutic abortion (Ekblad, 1955; Malmfors, 1958). However, a higher proportion of women who are refused therapeutic abortion also became disturbed (Baird, 1967; Kolstad, 1957; Peck & Marcus, 1966). These studies do not support the view that refusing rather than granting therapeutic abortion is, on balance, better for the mental health of women. Indeed, the beneficial effects of therapeutic abortion have been clearly demonstrated by Brody, Meikle, and Gerritse (1971). They found improvement in many psychiatric symptoms, such as fears, anxiety, and depression, after therapeutic abortion.

In conclusion, conflicting evidence concerning the psychological effects of mastectomy, hysterectomy, and therapeutic abortion suggests that social factors and, in particular, the attitudes of the woman and her associates toward the operation may cause either anxiety, tension, and depression or a feeling of well-being and relief.

WOMEN IN PSYCHOTHERAPY

Women use psychotherapy more than men. Most systems of psychotherapy tend to share certain basic characteristics. Almost all of them use "talking cure," although it is the patient rather than the therapist who does most of the talking. In recent years, there has been a proliferation of the techniques of psychotherapy. Most of them, however, are some sort of variation or extension of psycho-analysis and client-centered therapy. Before discussing the effects of psychotherapy on women, let us first describe the therapy principles used by these two major systems of therapy.

Psychoanalysis

This is by far the most influential system of psychotherapy. It nor-mally requires a large number of sessions—four to five days per week for two to seven years. The basic goal of psychoanalysis is to make the client aware of her unconscious conflicts. The procedure used by the analyst consists of the following:

1. *Free Association and Dreams*   In free association, the client is instructed to say whatever comes into her mind, even though it may be trivial or embarrassing. These associations are important because they symbolize the patient's conflicts. But as the verbalization of the client comes too close to anxiety-provoking material, the association abruptly stops. This phenomenon, which is called resistance, be-comes a focus of attention for the therapist, who attempts to help the patient to break down these resistances. Dreams are also con-sidered symbolic of underlying conflicts. Both associations and dreams have manifest content (what the client verbalizes) as well as latent content (what the manifest content symbolizes). One function of the analyst is to interpret the latent content of associations and dreams to the patient.

2. *Interpretation*   Attempts are made by the analyst to interpret to the clients their associations and dreams. The symbolic connota-tions of the verbalizations or dreams of patients, as interpreted by the analyst, reflect the preoccupation of the psychoanalyst with sex: Elongated objects—a banana, a nose, a pencil—symbolize the penis, whereas closed objects—a box, a room, a mouth—represent the vagina. As a result of the analyst's interpretations, the client can recognize her defensiveness as well as her repressed impulses. She may remember an early painful life event: By "reliving" such an event and linking it with her emotional state—depression, fear, anger—she attains emotional *insight;* this experience is called *cathar-sis.* For example, a woman who told her analyst that she did not like her ugly nose led to her analyst's sexual interpretation (nose = penis),

which in turn conjured from her the memory of a seduction at the age of five. Uncovering past repressed material is essential for cure in psychoanalysis.

3. *Transference*   During analysis, the client develops a strong attachment—a mixture of strong affection, respect, and hostility—to the therapist. These feelings represent those the client has toward major figures in her life, especially her parents. These feelings, which have apparently persisted from childhood and adolescence, are transferred to the analyst—as though he is now her father or another crucial person in her everyday life. Her thoughts and feelings toward these persons now directed toward him.

Psychoanalysts are not expected to reveal countertransference— that is, to show positive or negative feelings toward the client. Since it is mandatory that an analyst should himself undergo analysis, this experience in analysis is believed to make him less susceptible to the temptations of countertransference.

Client-centered Therapy

Client-centered therapy is called "client-centered" because it allows the client to determine the course of therapy, to choose what to talk about, and to make major life decisions without interference on the part of the therapist. Thus the therapist's task is not to ask questions or give answers but rather to restate what the client has been saying in an attempt to clarify the client's feeling. He hears and *reflects* the emotional part of the message. *Reflection* in client-centered therapy is equivalent to interpretation in psychoanalysis. In reflection, the therapist's remark tries to communicate that the client is thoroughly understood. Interpretation, however, goes beyond understanding to an elaboration and explanation by the therapist (London, 1964).

The psychological climate of the therapeutic situation, and particularly the attitudes of the therapist, is given much attention in client-centered therapy. There are three conditions deemed to be necessary for successful treatment. First, *unconditional positive regard:* a respect for the client as a person without passing judgment on the client's beliefs or conduct; second, *empathic understanding:* an attempt to enter into the client's experience and to communicate accurately to her; third, *genuineness:* an effort to relate to the client in an honest and frank manner rather than to hide behind the role of a professional. Ideally, all three conditions seek to establish an active and sharing relationship between equals.

The Effects of Psychotherapy

Women enter psychotherapy because of depression, anxiety, feelings of inferiority, and interpersonal problems. Cultural demands on women as daughters, housewives, and mothers bring dissatisfaction and frustration in their daily living. Psychotherapists, however, tend to attribute pathology to female malaise and psychological problems. Women are mentally sick because they are sexually inhibited or repressed. They may also be fixated in an immature and childish stage of development. Rather than dealing with the source of their frustration and discomfort in the social environment, psychotherapy attempts to manipulate their feelings and attitudes and adapt them to the stress of female living. The apparent disregard of the origin of women's problems by the therapist has resulted in negative rather than positive effects for patients in psychotherapy.

That psychotherapy is harmful to the patient and is a waste of time and money is expressed in a study by Dorothy Tennov (1975). She had tape-recorded interviews with twenty-one women who volunteered to talk about their therapy. One harmful effect of therapy reported by these women was their overdependency on the therapist. Many important life decisions, such as those concerning their marriages or their careers, had been influenced by the therapist, and the decisions they had made were now perceived by these women to be wrong. Concern about the therapy seems to have induced apathy toward their daily routine and to have interfered with their relationships with friends and family members. The financial costs of psychotherapy resulted in social and material deprivation for some of these women. One damaging effect of psychotherapy was that, because of the "continued expectation of help," these women did not seek alternative solutions to their problems. The psychotherapist's concentration was on the motives and irrational fantasies of these women; he did not, in fact, deal with their real life problems.

One disastrous effect of psychotherapy is evident in the finding that rates of suicide among some therapists' clients are exceedingly high. The important question is whether the therapists' behavior is responsible for the high rate of suicide of these patients. Dorothy Tennov believes that some of the behavior of the psychoanalyst and psychotherapist is involved in the patients' suicide. The difficulty of the therapist to relate to his patients and to pay attention to their social environment could be a decisive factor in driving women under psychotherapy to commit suicide (Kahne, 1968). The reactions of psychotherapists to the suicide of their patients are, however, varied. They usually suggest that other persons bear equal or greater responsibility for what happened. The suicide is also considered as an "act of spite" against them. They may react with "anger and a sense of betrayal." After the suicide of his patient, one psychiatrist said, "She fought me all the way, and I guess she finally made her point" (Tennov, 1975).

A survey by the American Psychological Association Task Force (1975) indicated four areas of sex bias and sex-role stereotyping in psychotherapeutic practice. First, therapists foster traditional sex roles by emphasizing the female role as a wife and a mother rather than as a worker outside the home. Second, they use pejorative labels such as seductive, manipulative, and histrionic, as well as encourage traditional passive and nonassertive behavior. Third, therapists also use sexist psychoanalytical concepts, such as penis envy and vaginal orgasm to explain female problems. Fourth, some tend to respond to women as sex objects and seduce their female clients (see "Sex with Patients in Therapy," p. 63).

Dorothy Tennov (1975) has discussed many factors which would suggest that psychotherapy can be more harmful to female than to male clients. Since psychology is male-oriented, the male psychotherapist is unable to appreciate the difficulties experienced by women outside the therapy sessions. His training also puts the woman patient at a disadvantage. The male therapist identifies more, and is more open, with a male patient. For example, some male therapists may consider it wrong to discuss their personal lives and concerns with a female. However, they may feel that it is quite reasonable to share their interests with a male patient (Tennov, 1975). This view is supported by research suggesting that counselors show more empathy with same-sex clients than with clients of the opposite sex (Hill, 1975; Persons, Persons, & Newmark, 1974).

Most females, particularly those who are married, are not paying for their own treatment. The therapist is therefore expected to help the female client to adjust to her husband's convenience. This appears quite reasonable to psychotherapists and psychiatrists, on the principle that "who pays the piper sets the tune."

Considering the harmful effects of psychotherapy discussed earlier, why do women continue to use this service? Since psychotherapy is a male-dominated profession (for every female psychotherapist, there are two males) it is quite possible that the acceptance of psychotherapy by women is closely associated with their general acceptance of the dominance and superiority of the male. Chesler (1972), for example, found that the majority of psychotherapy clients, whether they were males or females, requested a male rather than a female therapist. The reason given by both male and female clients for such a request was that they respected and trusted men more than women.

Should men ever treat women? Phyllis Chesler (1971) noted, in "Patient and Patriarch":

> Male psychologists, psychiatrists, and social workers must realize that as scientists they know nothing about women; their diagnoses, even their sympathy, is damaging and oppressive to women. . . .

She argued that men should not treat women, both because they cannot serve as role models for female clients and because of the imbalance of power between women and men in our society. It has also been suggested that male therapists should not treat women who are extremely dependent and inhibited or who equate femininity with passivity. Such women would benefit more from a female therapist who can model assertiveness within the context of positive female characteristics (Rawlings & Carter, 1977). Similarly, women may seek out a female therapist to help them to clarify their roles as women outside the traditional "man in power—woman subservient" context (Roeske, 1976).

A distinction has been made between traditional therapists and others who are nonsexist or feminist. Men who are nonsexists or feminists are considered qualified to treat women. They may be more appropriate than female therapists who have a sexist approach to therapy (Rawlings & Carter, 1977).

Nonsexist Therapy

Nonsexist therapy is not a new brand of therapy, but it involves certain beliefs and attitudes that can be incorporated into the practice of traditional therapies. In nonsexist therapy, as in traditional therapies, the focus of treatment is on individual change and the modification of personal behavior.

There are at least five characteristics of the nonsexist therapist (Marecek & Kravetz, 1977). *First,* a knowledge of the psychology of women and of sex roles and sex differences in the socialization and life experiences of women and men is essential for a nonsexist thera-pist. *Second,* the therapist should acknowledge the extent of sexism in our society and should be aware of his or her own sexism. *Third,* nonsexist therapists believe in the close relationship between women's personal problems and their social, economic, and political situation. The position of women at home, at work, and in the community must be examined in relation to present sex-role standards and dis-criminatory practices. *Fourth,* the therapist must recognize that there is a relationship between a female's lack of social power and such behaviors as passivity, dependency, submissiveness, and apathy. A nonsexist therapist selects therapeutic techniques that help female clients to be active and independent (for example, assertive training). *Finally,* a nonsexist therapy is committed to viewing each client as an individual, not as a woman or a man. The needs, capacities, and personal goals of the client rather than traditional sex-role require-ments are the basis for understanding the client (Marecek & Kravetz, 1977).

Feminist Therapy

Feminist therapy accepts all the principles of nonsexist therapy. However, these therapists emphasize *sociopolitical* change as basic to *personal* change. The relationship between the goals of treatment and social change is emphasized through a discussion of the ways in which social roles and, particularly, the rights of women influence the client's personal change.

Feminist therapists believe in the principles of self-help and in the equal sharing of resources, power, and responsibility. Therapists who place clients in subordinate roles to an authoritarian therapist reflect women's inferior position in society. Feminist therapists, therefore, deliberately select therapeutic techniques that emphasize their clients' power and responsibilities. The use of contracts is one strategy of equalizing the balance of power between client and therapist. Opening files and case records for clients' inspection and evaluation is another strategy for emphasizing the clients' power. Group therapy, which consists entirely of women, is also used to de-emphasize the power of the therapist (Marecek & Kravetz, 1977). One important contribution of feminist therapy is to provide self-help groups, such as consciousness-raising (C-R) groups, women's counseling centers, abortion referral services, and rape crisis centers. As alternatives to psychotherapy, I will discuss consciousness-raising, assertive training, and systematic desensitization as therapeutic strategies to promote self-help.

Alternatives to Psychotherapy

Consciousness-raising groups   A consciousness-raising group is a type of group therapy without a therapist. Its major aim is to discuss the personal problems of women within the context of their social status. Certain topics are occasionally provided for the group. Examples of such topics include: How I feel about how I look, my relationships with other women, clothes I wear and clothes I prefer, shyness, and how to deal with sexism in my children (Tennov, 1975).

Barbara Kirsh (1974) has described four stages of consciousness-raising therapy. The first stage is "opening-up," where every member of the group is able to express her feelings without criticism. Experiences are shared in a supportive atmosphere. In the second "sharing" stage, problems are discussed not as relating to the individual but to the group as a whole. These problems are also discussed as social or political phenomena affecting all women. It is expected that members of the group will be able to see their problems as relevant to the political and social order and not to their individual inadequacy. A third stage of "analyzing" attempts to relate the subjective feelings of members of the group to the objective analysis of the status of women. Finally, there is a stage of "abstracting," in which attempts are made to find out whether or not social institutions fulfill the needs of women. A major aim of these four stages of therapy is to help women externalize blame and aggression instead of bearing the responsibility of their troubles.

Assertive training: the learning of social skills   Another alternative to psychotherapy that has much increased in popularity in recent years and that deals directly with women's life problems is training in assertive behavior. Many women who are now stepping outside the traditional sex role as housewives and homemakers are being exposed to new situations that require new interpersonal skills. Guilt, fear, and anxiety often prevent women from asserting their rights or expressing their feelings and beliefs in interpersonal situations. The recent emphasis of the women's movement on growth, self-fulfillment, and self-examination has also increased the female awareness of her personal limitations and conflicts (Jakubowski-Spector, 1973).

Lazarus (1973) classified assertive behavior into four groups: (1) the ability to say no, (2) the ability to ask for favors or make requests, (3) the ability to express positive or negative feelings, and (4) the ability to initiate, continue, or terminate a conversation. Apart from verbal cues in assertive behavior ("I do not like my steak"), nonverbal cues, such as eye contact, body posture, gestures, distance from another person, and facial expression, are also important. High assertive subjects are more prompt in their response, speak louder and longer, and show more emotional expression (Eisler, Miller, & Hersen, 1973).

An inability to say no or to refuse requests may include both unwanted requests ("Can you babysit my children this afternoon?") and desirable ones (you are trying to lose weight and someone offers you a delicious piece of cake). Difficulties may also arise in making requests of others. Other problematic situations are disagreeing with others, apologizing to others, admitting ignorance, and terminating unwanted interactions. In addition to situations that require negative assertion, there are situations that involve positive assertion, such as accepting compliments or responding to another person initiating social contact.

Rich and Schroeder (1976) described three conditions in which persons may manifest a deficit in assertion. First, the person may possess assertive responses, but she is unable to identify situations for which these responses are likely to be effective. Second, emotional or cognitive factors (e.g., anxiety or self-deprecation) may interfere with assertive response. Finally, the person may not possess the requisite response. Assertive training aims at overcoming these problems of the client.

Barbara Brockway (1975) dealt with professional women who showed adequate assertive responses; however, these responses tended to evoke a relatively high level of anxiety. These women performed effectively and appeared self-confident inside and outside the training situation, yet they experienced anxiety. Brockway suggested that "perhaps assertive training with professional women should constitute a set of techniques aimed primarily at decreasing anxiety and eliminating conditioned beliefs and attitudes rather than increasing verbal or gestural skills." Two techniques, systematic desensitization and cognitive restructuring, may be used to achieve these aims. Systematic desensitization, which will be described in the following section, can be used to reduce the anxiety of women in specific interpersonal situations requiring assertiveness. Cognitive restructuring is changing one's attitudes, beliefs, and thoughts to make them consistent with the realities of the external environment. It may be used to deal with the client's expectations and perceptions of the interpersonal situation. The negative thoughts of women toward assertive behavior may be partly due to societal stereotypes that regard assertion as desirable for men but not for women. Past experience may have taught them that what is categorized as assertive behavior for men is regarded as aggressive for women (Rich & Schroeder, 1976). In cognitive restructuring, the counselor should, therefore, provide the client with a rationale for her assertive behavior. Apart from acquiring assertive responses, a woman should believe in her right to express her feelings and ideas, and she should believe that assertion is a healthy and a desirable reaction. As Judy Johnson (1975) reported, group assertive training could result in changes in the sex stereotypes and self-concepts of married women.

Systematic desensitization   The behavioral technique called systematic desensitization is useful in dealing with fears and anxieties involving different environmental stimuli, including interpersonal relationships (see the discussion of phobias in Chapter 5). Wolpe (1960) suggested that "if a response incompatible with anxiety can be made to occur in the presence of anxiety-provoking stimuli, it will weaken the bond between these stimuli and the anxiety responses." Muscle relaxation induced by exercise, hypnotic suggestion, or sedatives is considered to be incompatible with anxiety. When a client is relaxed in the office, it becomes possible to counteract the effects of anxiety-provoking stimuli and reduce anxiety.

In the initial interviews with the client, a brief history is taken, and attention focuses on those situations that evoke anxiety. A list, which includes all the possible anxiety-provoking stimulus situations in her or his everyday life, is then constructed. This requires the assistance of the counselor, though the client may help by making a few notes at home. These stimuli are then ranked in stress value, from the least to the most disturbing. (This is called a "stimulus hierarchy.") It is imperative that the counselor ascertains which aspects of the stimulus situation (e.g., size, weight, noise, etc.) are responsible for the client's anxiety, as it is these which need to be emphasized in the counseling sessions. The list of stimuli may consist of from five to twenty items or more.

Following preliminary interviews with the client, a number of sessions are normally devoted to practice in hypnosis procedure (see Chapter 13 for a description of an exercise in muscle relaxation). Whereas in psychotherapy the aim of the treatment is to discover the past traumatic experiences responsible for the patient's fear reactions, a process that may take hundreds of sessions, in systematic desensitization, recovery may be achieved by dealing solely with stimuli existing at present in the patient's everyday life (Kraft & Al-Issa, 1965a). The client, when completely relaxed on a couch or a comfortable chair, is asked to imagine the stimuli listed in the hierarchy. She is asked to indicate if she experiences any anxiety, and the quality of anxiety may be assessed by the nature of her reply ("A lot," "some," "a bit," or "a little"). The stimulus must be repeated until the client feels no anxiety whatsoever. The counselor commences with a "neutral item" that evokes no anxiety at all and then proceeds from the least to the most disturbing item in the stimulus hierarchy. Eventually, the client can visualize formerly noxious stimuli without feeling any anxiety, having been desensitized to these stimuli. When the client has been desensitized to the items in the hierarchy, it will be found that she is no longer anxious in similar situations in her everyday life.

A case reported by Kraft and Al-Issa (1966) may illustrate the use of systematic desensitization to deal with both death phobia and travel phobia:

A woman aged 38. Her case history began at the age of seven, when her mother died. Her father asked her to kiss her mother in the open coffin, but she could not do so, she started crying, and had to be taken away. Following this episode, she developed trembling, which continued for several months, and also a fear of the dark. Eventually these subsided and she had no further symptoms until the age of 26, when she felt faint in the market-place while accompanied by her sister. Following this incident, she developed a fear of fainting and felt that if she fainted she would fail to recover and would die. A year later, she found that she became anxious and panicky when visiting her sister in hospital, and she was severely affected by her sister's death six months later. Following her sister's death, she found that, when reading a newspaper, she could not read anything relating to accidents or death, because this produced sweating, trembling and a feeling that she could not breathe: more recently, she has not been able to read the front page of a newspaper at all. Also, she found that she could not watch any television programme involving medical work in hospital. She developed panic feelings on hearing an ambulance bell and when approaching a cemetery. Since her sister's death, she has found it difficult to walk to work, developing panic feelings on leaving the house, which increase in intensity as she gets farther from home. When travelling with her husband, she develops a fear of fainting and fears that she might consequently die. Because of these feelings, she has been unable to travel on a bus for seven years, following an attack of panic at that time. She last travelled by train ten years ago and by Underground 15 years ago, and now even the thought of travelling by Underground is terrifying to her.

Stimulus hierarchy [stimuli 1–8 for death phobia, 9–18 for travel phobia]

1. Reading the *Daily Mirror*
2. Looking at television
3. Seeing a man of 65 die after illness of varying lengths, e.g. 2 months to 5 seconds
4. Seeing a man die suddenly
5. Seeing a woman die suddenly
6. Seeing an ambulance
7. Seeing a cemetery
8. Seeing a grave
9. Travelling on a bus from one to seven stops
10. Waiting at a bus stop for 1 minute, then increasing by 1 minute intervals to 15 minutes
11. Waiting at a bus stop for 15 minutes and then travelling 7 stops
12. Travelling to Southend with her husband by car, and then returning home after varying intervals of time
13. Travelling to, and visiting, Moorfield's Hospital
14. Being alone at home
15. Being alone in the small bedroom where her brother-in-law died
16. Going to the market alone
17. Going to the cinema alone
18. Travelling on a bus alone from 1 to 12 stops

SEX WITH PATIENTS IN THERAPY

If you had actually screwed me it would have wrecked everything. It would have convinced me that you were only interested in pleasure with my animal body and that you didn't really care about the part that was a person. It would have meant that you were using me like a woman when I really wasn't one and needed a lot of help to grow into one. It would have meant you could only see my body and couldn't see the real me which was still a little girl. The real me would have been up on the ceiling watching you do things with my body. You would have seemed content to let the real me die. When you feed a girl, you make her feel that both her body and her self are wanted. This helps her get joined together. When you screw her she can feel that her body is separate and dead. People can screw dead bodies, but they never feed them.

R.D. Laing: THE DIVIDED SELF

The therapy situation, like all life situations where male-female relationships are involved, may encourage sexual activities. Sex with the secretary, the housekeeper, and the neighborhood housewife is not unheard of. In popular fiction, the doctor is also notorious for peccadilloes with his nurses. These sexual activities may not strike us as strange; however, sex with patients in the professional situation is not just unethical but is an exploitation in the extreme. These activities do not include the use of sex surrogates in the treatment of women with sexual inadequacy (see Chapter 8) but only those where the therapist himself offers to sleep with the patient and claims that it is part of the psychotherapeutic process and is done for her benefit. Psychotherapy may integrate sex as part of its procedure, but there are cases of immature and disturbed therapists who intentionally abuse patients and try to rationalize their behavior.

Who Is the Seductive Therapist?

Van Emde Boas (1966) noted that, in the medical profession, the most frequent "targets" for their patients' sexual desires are gynecologists, closely followed by dentists and family doctors. Psychotherapists are only slightly lower on the list. Kardener, Fuller, and Mensh (1973) surveyed the attitudes of male physicians, including psychiatrists, toward sexual contacts with patients. They found that approximately 5 percent of the sample acknowledged having had sexual intercourse with patients and that 20 percent indicated that there were occasions when such activity might be beneficial.

The seductive therapists are described by Dahlberg (1970) as "neurotic," "depressed," or "sociopathic." They tend to be older than the patient; they are always men; the patients are always young females. They tend to be in a difficult heterosexual situation, to be either separated or divorced. Among the nine seductive therapists studied by Dahlberg, some terminated therapy or payment for their therapy once sexual contact had begun. One therapist suggested sex to his patient under hypnosis. When she refused to pay him for the "treatment," he suggested that he would continue seeing her for sex and would not charge her for it. Some such therapists offered the patients employment, such as secretarial work.

Chesler (1972) found that the termination of these affairs had drastic effects on some of the patients. Some of these women became depressed and attempted suicide. An attempt by one of the therapists to cure the patient's sexual dysfunction was associated with the onset of a headache that lasted for a year after the termination of therapy.

Undoubtedly, the problems of the female patient are exacerbated by the stress involved in her relationship with the therapist. Consider, for instance, a case reported by Dahlberg (1970), where both therapist (age 55) and patient (age 30) were married. The therapist first treated the husband, and then the wife contacted him for problems related to depression and sexual problems. This woman was described as "dependent, helpless and seductive." The therapist offered to cure the patient's sexual problems during a two-week summer vacation with her. Although this offer panicked her, she was willing to have sexual relations with him in the office. The couple tried to take legal action against the therapist, but this was never pursued because of the patient's "paranoid" tendencies, which made the lawyers think that the case could not be won. The patient's panic following the offer of a vacation was calmed down under the influence of sedation. The therapist, however, remained "the enemy" against whom she could organize her "paranoid delusion," and this led to her hospitalization a year later.

Psychoanalysis and Sex with Patients

In 1915, Freud wrote a paper on transference of love in which he pointed out that a patient-therapist love relationship is expected to be induced by the analytic situation. However, he cautioned analysts to control their countertransference tendencies—that is, falling in love with their patients. If the analyst responds to the patient's advances, Freud goes on, "it would be a great triumph for the patient but a complete overthrow for the cure,—the love relationship actually destroys the influence of the analytic treatment."

The well-known female analyst Frieda Fromm-Reichman (1950) also warned that the use of patients, in reality as well as in fantasy, for sexual fulfillments may interfere with therapy. This is particularly so when the analyst is impotent and difficult to arouse. He may harm the patient, because this would demonstrate her inferiority as a sex partner.

Dorothy Tennov (1975) cited an "internationally distinguished former analyst and journal editor as saying that 'two people alone together in a dimly lit room discussing intimate personal details of life—what else can one expect?'" To have successful analysis, some analysts believe that patients should be allowed to act out both verbally and physically. James McCartney (1965) recommended what he called "overt transference," which he defined as "a visible, audible or tangible muscular or glandular reaction to an inner feeling." He required some patients to do more than just talk about their feelings toward the therapist; he felt they needed to caress, fondle, observe, and examine the body of the therapist. In his view, the therapist is also expected to reciprocate these activities and to have intercourse with the patients, especially when the patient cannot find an appropriate person outside the analytic situation. McCartney believes that it is the analyst who should help the patient to act out her sexuality in order to develop from an immature into a fully mature person.

As for male patients, they are sometimes sent to a female analyst to enable them to express overt transference. The behavior of those who remain with a male analyst is well summed up by Wittkower and Robertson (1976):

Erotic transference of male patients to a male analyst is rare apart from homosexuals. However, male patients will often during the course of their analysis, fall in love with women who are connected to the analyst—his wife, his daughter, his secretary, etc. Thus one of our patients compulsively and successfully seduced several female students of his analyst.

The fact that only female cases seduced in psychotherapy are popularized may reflect attitudes toward females and males: Male promiscuity is more tolerated, both inside and outside the therapy situation.

Behavior Therapy and Sex with Patients

In behavior therapy, sex with patients is not considered an integral part of the therapeutic procedure. Though they are expected to positively reinforce their clients, they do not respond to them as sexual objects or encourage them to regard the therapists as anything more than significant therapeutic agents. Lazarus (1974) found that the outcome of behavior therapy is not affected by the therapist's subjective feelings toward the women clients. It was found, however, that in a few instances where women expressed very strong positive feelings for the therapist, this tended to interfere with therapy. The therapist here did not interpret the patients' feelings; rather, he indicated to them that they were capable of the experience of love, an asset that could be useful outside the therapy situation. Lazarus also found that those clients who had shown strong feelings of hate toward the therapist did not remain in therapy.

Sex with Patients in Mental Hospitals

William Schofield, in *Psychotherapy: The Purchase of Friendship*, (1963), described clients of psychotherapy, usually middle-class and upper-class, as having the "YAVIS syndrome"; that is, they are young, attractive, verbal, intelligent, and successful. Residents of mental hospitals may, however, belong to the "HOUND" group (homely, old, unattractive, nonverbal, and dumb). They are the rejects of society. Since they are more helpless and controlled than those in private therapy, they may be more vulnerable to exploitation. Data about sex contact between these patients and hospital staff are, however, hard to come by. In mental hospitals, celibacy rules are rigidly adhered to. It is believed that patients' sexuality, like their minds, has gone astray and been lost. Contraceptives are not usually prescribed to patients.

Sexual deprivation in mental hospitals is reinforced by the complete sexual segregation of patients. It is also widely accepted that tranquilizers seem to affect the sexual potency of male more than female patients. However, anecdotal evidence attests to the generally suppressed sexuality of hospitalized patients. David Cooper (1970) described a young mental patient who, on a visit to London, went to a prostitute; shortly afterwards, his parents urged his transfer to a locked ward in another hospital. In a British mental hospital, a young schizophrenic girl suddenly took off her clothes and forced her way out of the ward. Later, her chasers found her in the bedroom of a male nurse. The male nurse was dismissed and taken to court. The patient ended up in a locked ward (Al-Issa, unpublished observation). The sexual problems of patients in another hospital were so pervasive that Cooper (1970) suggested to the National Health Service in Britain the employment of one or two experienced men or women who would act as "temple" prostitutes to initiate his young patients and who would be paid overtime for these functions. It is apparent that the sexual problems of hospitalized patients are different from those of middle-class private patients in psychotherapy. It is quite possible that the segregation of patients and the absence of legitimate sexual outlets make them more liable to exploitation by the hospital staff.

The Ethical Question

For some years, the American Psychological Association's ethical code had no explicit prohibition on sexual intercourse with patients. In mid-February, 1976, however, the Ethics Committee, in a new revision of the ethic code, adopted the following: "Psychologists make every effort to avoid dual relationships with clients and/or relationships which might impair their professional judgment or increase the risk of client exploitation—sexual intimacies with clients are unethical." The use of surrogates in sex therapy, however, was not considered unethical. The sexual exploitation of female patients only reflects one aspect of the subservient position of women in the therapeutic situation. Unless radical changes in the attitudes toward and the social status of women take place, female sexual exploitation

will remain with us. Sex with female patients is only an extension of
the general stereotype of females as sexual objects:

> The message conveyed by this behavior in a therapeutic setting is that a
> woman's sexual responsiveness is paramount to her emotional adjustment.
> This message from a therapist is particularly debilitating to a woman because
> our culture already defines a woman in terms of sexuality at the expense of
> other aspects of her humanity. The therapist should be countering society's
> definition, not reinforcing it. We believe that how therapists and clients relate
> to each other after the therapy contract is terminated is a private matter
> between two consenting adults and not a professional concern. People should
> be able to do what they want, but they should not be able to call everything
> they do "therapy" (Rawlings & Carter, 1977).

Women, Psychosis, and Neurosis

part two

Doubt is to certainty as neurosis is to psychosis. The neurotic is in doubt and has fears about persons and things; the psychotic has convictions and makes claims about them. In short, the neurotic has problems, the psychotic has solutions.

Thomas Szasz: THE SECOND SIN

Women
and
Schizophrenia

3

If one has an authoritarian system . . . there is no end to the devious uses it will be put to . . . a young woman had been in several mental hospitals, allegedly a schizophrenic. It was clear she had been put there simply because her parents had disapproved of the way she was living as a beatnik, that is, her individual way of trying to find out who she really was. So, like so many others, she is put away, forcibly deprived of all her rights. Of course she kicked and screamed and made a thorough nuisance of herself— again seen as confirmation of illness. I should have thought it was a sign of maybe desperately good health.

R.D. Laing: Interview with Roy Perrot,
THE OBSERVER, 1970

Psychiatrists, as well as laypersons, consider schizophrenia as an extreme state of madness. Schizophrenia may provide one of the best illustrations of deviation from social norms in general and from sex roles in particular. The main symptoms of the schizophrenic woman are hallucinations and delusions.[1] She may hear

---

[1] An *hallucination* refers to reported perceptions (seeing, hearing, smelling, and so on) in the absence of external stimulation. A *delusion* is a personal belief held in the face of evidence usually sufficient to destroy it (I am the Virgin Mary). Psychosis such as schizophrenia is distinguished from neurosis by the presence of hallucinations and delusions.

voices, sometimes flattering and flirtatious, but often insulting and humiliating. Like our dream world, the world of her hallucinations is not a complete bed of roses but can be full of terrifying nightmares. She is also deluded, suspicious, and expectant that all sorts of complex intrigues may undermine her existence. The voices she hears bear witness to the reality of her delusions. These nagging voices keep repeating: "You are a bad woman, you are a bad woman . . . you should kill yourself. . . ."

Consider the case of a 50-year-old woman reported by psychologist Theodore Sarbin (1967). Miss D., she claimed, had romantic

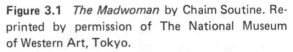

Figure 3.1 *The Madwoman* by Chaim Soutine. Reprinted by permission of The National Museum of Western Art, Tokyo.

conversations at a distance with one Dr. Shields, a man whom she had known only casually some thirty years before her case came to light. Dr. Shields even proposed marriage to her through these "voices." Miss D. had spent all her adult life as a housekeeper for two bachelor brothers. Shortly before her "aberration," the household had moved to a small apartment in a Western city from a semirural area in the eastern United States. After the move, one of the brothers left the home for a job in another city, and the other brother announced to Miss D. that he would be getting married. This would be the first time in her life that Miss D. would be left alone, with no social contacts whatsoever. It was shortly after this, the still-resident brother reported, that Miss D.'s odd behavior became apparent. When questioned about her romantic conversations with Dr. Shields, Miss D. claimed that they were effected by a special electronic device invented by Dr. Shields himself, a man whom she believed to be of an inventive turn of mind and scientific training. The device could transmit and receive like a radio, and it also had x-ray properties so that the operator could see everything Miss D. did at any time and over any distance, even through thick walls. Then one day, the tone of the voices changed. No longer did she hear her affectionate Dr. Shields; now, she heard a strange, threatening, malevolent voice. The device must have fallen into evil hands, into the hands of her country's enemies. So she tried to get help to rescue the machine, first from an attorney and then from the American Legion, the local police, and the F.B.I. Eventually, she was removed from the apartment and placed in a state mental hospital with the psychiatric diagnosis of schizophrenia.

Miss D.'s search for solutions to her existing life problems through vivid imagery (hallucinations) and improbable beliefs (delusions) had brought about hospitalization that could continue for the rest of her life. This chapter will describe the tragic fate of women like Miss D., their ambivalence toward themselves and the world, their loves and hates, and their fears of, or revolts against, parental domination and an oppressive society.

SEX DIFFERENCES IN SCHIZOPHRENIA

It is generally accepted that the overall rate of schizophrenia is the same for females and males in the adult population (Rosenthal, 1970; 1977). There is, however, an interesting age pattern for the hospital admission of schizophrenia for the two sexes. Data published in 1935 by Malzberg (Rosenthal, 1970) and shown in Figure 3.2 reveal that male admission rates accelerate around 12 years of age and peak in the early twenties. This is in accord with the general view that schizophrenia strikes the young. The picture is different for females. The rate climbs more slowly, does not peak until the thirties, and then exceeds that for males in later life. The excess of schizophrenia in the male seems to occur early in life: When cases of early infantile autism are analyzed, for instance, there are about four boys to every girl. In childhood schizophrenia, the ratio of boys to girls is about 1.5:1; in early adolescence, it is about 2:1. Thereafter, the gap narrows, and it closes markedly in the middle to late

Figure 3.2 Number of first admissions for schizophrenia to state mental hospitals in New York, 1929 to 1931, by age and sex. From D. Rosenthal, *Genetic Theory and Abnormal Behavior,* New York: McGraw-Hill Book Co., 1970. (Based on data in B. Malzberg, "A statistical study of age in relation to mental disease," *Mental Hygiene,* 1935, 19.) Reprinted by permission of McGraw-Hill and courtesy of the Mental Health Association, 1800 N. Kent Street, Arlington, Va. 22209.

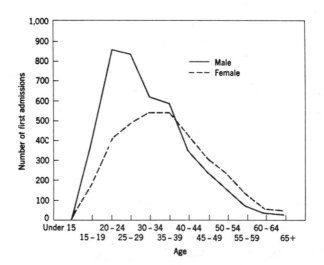

thirties. By the late fifties, about two new female cases are admitted for every male. Altogether, the evidence clearly indicates that schizophrenia manifests itself earlier in the male and later in the female. This picture of admissions to state and county mental hospitals has not changed in more recent years. Data reported by Guttentag, Salasin, Legge, and Bray (1977) for 1972 reveals that, although there has been an excess of schizophrenia in male admissions up to age 35, the trend is reversed in later years.

It appears that when childhood schizophrenia is included in the overall rates of women and men, the latter tend to show an excess of schizophrenia. Rosenthal (1970) suggested that congenital factors that are not genetic in nature could account for the greater vulnerability in the young male. In support of this view, it was observed that among schizophrenic children, there was an excess of organic and neurological cases among boys (Goldfarb, 1970). Another explanation is that "the rates primarily reflect a greater parental anxiety about behavioral disorders in male children, and that males so afflicted are more combative, destructive, and less easy to manage, so that mothers are more prone to bring their boys for professional help than girls" (Rosenthal, 1970).

The age of schizophrenic breakdown in the adult years may coincide with specific stresses related to the sex-roles of women and men. Indeed, when the rates of schizophrenia in different communities are inspected, they reveal inconsistent trends; they show that either women or men can have an excessive rate of schizophrenic breakdown (Dohrenwend & Dohrenwend, 1969), revealing the relative effect of social factors. Murphy (1972) has pointed out that community studies indicate that schizophrenia may strike either men or women in youth, depending on whether or not there are conflicts related to the fulfillment of sex-role expectations. One example reported by Murphy (1972) is taken from a field survey of fourteen rural communities in eastern Canada. He reported that schizophrenia was unusually high among women in the three areas chosen as representing French-Canadian culture. There was an average rate of 13.1 per 1,000 adult women, significantly higher than the rate of 8.8 per 1,000 for men. The excess of schizophrenia among women tends to occur before marriage—around the age of 20—and in later married life—from age 40 to 50.

Murphy indicated that schizophrenic breakdown among French-Canadian females was related to the specific problem of conflicting societal expectations for women, a problem not found in the other communities surveyed. The traditional culture of these areas still saw the ideal woman as one who married early, produced lots of children, worked hard at home, and obeyed her husband. On the other hand, there had been recent educational changes. These had resulted in the women of the communities actually gaining a greater education than the men, who still left school early to help on the farm, and also in their being taught that there were things in life other than the traditional pattern of marriage and family life of their community. So, for those women, there was a sort of generational conflict of values—except with respect to children, the production of which the new school still applauded and advocated. Unless she wanted to leave home, a woman had problems, for she could not overthrow her traditional role in society. Often these women would find a compromise. They would marry local boys, who would be less educated than themselves, and use their education to control their husbands, thus taking over to some extent the traditional male domain of public affairs while they continued to retain the facade of submission to the male. For most of the women, this was a very satisfactory alternative to leaving the community. But there were also women who had little interest in, and little ability for, such leadership in public affairs. How could they survive in such a society? These were the women, Murphy observed, who were particularly prone to schizophrenia, because of the stress involved in playing a role for which they were not properly matched. Murphy also noted that the men of these areas now viewed these educated females with considerable lack of ease because they had the ability to rock the traditional power relationship between the sexes in their society, and this probably heightened their tendency to assign women to the schizophrenic category.

These three French communities were contrasted with another Canadian community of Polish origin where the rate of schizophrenia is reversed, 4.0 per 1,000 for women and 7.9 per 1,000 for men in the adult population. Again, social expectations seem to be involved in precipitating schizophrenia in men. Polish tradition expects young men to leave their homesteads and prove their capabilities before being considered responsible and marriageable adults. The Canadian Pole can do that only by orienting himself to a modern Canadian way of life. These expectations were not directed at girls. Therefore, the rate of schizophrenia among the males of this community was double the rate of females. However, in other, more prosperous, Polish-Canadian communities, the male-female ratio of schizophrenia was equal.

It is to be expected that sex ratios in the incidence of schizophrenia would change across time, especially during periods of change associated with a relative loss in sex role. Murphy (1972) reported that, among the Achinese in Sumatra, such a change has taken place in the present century. At the beginning of this century, a Dutch doctor reported that mental illness among this group was very rare, had a transitory character, and mainly affected women. Twenty years later, and after a long war, a survey of mental illness in the same people indicated a dramatic rise in mental illness that affected men more than women. Two changes seem to have occurred between these two visits to the Achinese: One was that venereal disease had become widespread because of the misuse of Achinese women by the conquering soldiers (this was presumably not stressful enough to these women to cause higher rates of mental breakdown); the other change was the defeat of Achinese warriors, which left them with a very limited role to play, since women were running most of the commercial affairs. It seems that the rate of schizophrenia, which was similar to that of other Malaysian people in Sumatra before this war, had increased about five times because the male suffered a loss in his social role. The actual ratio was 54 male schizophrenic cases against only 9 females, reversing the prewar prevalence of mental illness among the sexes.

Level of education and ethnic origin interact in an interesting way in the incidence of first admissions to mental hospitals for schizophrenia (Murphy, 1977). Among Canadians of British origin, men with low levels of education have a much higher rate than their female counterparts; with high levels of education, sex differences become small and almost diminish. Among Canadians of Dutch origin, a high level of education tends to increase the rate for females but decrease it for males. In Canada, the British section of the population is the dominant group and therefore expects preferential treatment. Even women with low education benefit from this privileged status; because of having English as their mother tongue, they can find employment more easily (as saleswomen, telephone operators, and so on). Males with a low level of education among Canadians of British origin do not, however, benefit from the preferential treatment of their subculture, because Canadian employers prefer unskilled workers from other ethnic groups who are less pretentious and less challenging to their authority. Although the cultural ideal expects the male Canadian of British origin to succeed, his lack of education hinders the fulfillment of such an ideal. Thus, the cultural ideal seems to create more problems for the poorly educated man than for the poorly educated woman but benefits the highly educated of both sexes. The high rate of first admission for schizophrenia among Canadian females of Dutch origin seems to be related to the importance of the family to these women. A Dutch woman finds that her role as a homemaker gives her less power and prestige than in her traditional culture at home. Thus, at all educational levels, a Canadian woman of Dutch origin is going to be less satisfied with her ability to fulfill the cultural ideal. This is more true with the university-educated woman who feels that her education is bringing her very few benefits. In contrast, the life of the male Canadian of Dutch origin does not center around the family, and he seems to find more material satisfaction in Canada than at home; in particular, a high level of education, which brings him more satisfaction, is associated with a low rate of schizophrenia (Murphy, 1977).

In conclusion, data indicate that the age of schizophrenic breakdown in women and men seems to coincide with stresses related to sex-role enactment. In North America, conflicts in youth appear to be factors in the hospitalization of men; the stresses of the middle years are factors in increasing the rate of hospitalization of women. Other factors, such as level of education and ethnic origin, should also be considered in the evaluation of sex differences in schizophrenia.

SEX DIFFERENCES IN SYMPTOMS

For several reasons, it is useful to study sex differences in the symptoms of schizophrenia. First, the content of symptoms may reflect either the tendency to intensify sex stereotypes or the tendency to break away from sex role demands. Second, studying symptoms may give us a lead to the types of behavior that might result in the hospitalization of both women and men. Finally, symptoms may influence the treatment and eventual discharge of the patient from the hospital.

There seem to be at least two possible approaches to the study of sex differences in the symptoms of schizophrenia: One is the study of hallucinations and delusions, which are considered typical of schizophrenia; another is to observe sex differences in the general behavior patterns of patients.

Delusions and Hallucinations

The available evidence seems to suggest that female schizophrenics tend to have more delusions than males (Lucas, Sainsbury & Collins, 1962). The greatest sex differences in delusions occur in the 40 to 50 age group, in which the incidence in the female is twice that in the male (Swanson, Bohmert, & Smith, 1970). A survey of hallucinations in 1934 by Sherman and Sherman, cited by Lucas and his colleagues, indicates that they are more common among women than men. However, a more recent study reveals no sex differences among hospitalized patients (Zigler and Phillips, 1960). Similarly, a community study of a southeastern county in the United States indicates that women report only slightly higher visual and auditory hallucinations than men (11.7% of women and 9.8% of men) (Schwab, 1977).

In a survey of different types of delusions, Lucas and his colleagues (1962) found that women tend to have significantly more sexual delusions, whereas men tend to exceed women in the frequency of delusions of inferiority. An analysis of grandiose delusions indicates that those of men tend to contain significantly more themes related to authority and power, whereas those of women tend to include more themes related to wealth, social status, and skill.

By far the most significant sex differences are revealed in sex delusions; these are more frequent among women than among men and tend to occur more in married than in single women. An analysis of the content of the delusions of both sexes indicates that paranoid sexual ideas, such as the idea of imposed intercourse, were greater in females, particularly those who are single. Delusions of being married, betrothed, pregnant, and of having children also had a higher incidence in females, but again they are more frequent in single than in married women. The only delusions that occurred more often in males than in females were, in the single person, of masturbation and, in the married person, of the spouse's infidelity. "The content appears to reflect the more obvious sexual inhibitions and demands regarding the two sexes in our society—the greater social restrictions on intercourse, for example, in the single females as compared with the single males, the greater pressure on women to conform as regards marriage, and the more explicit condemnation of masturbation in men" (Lucas et al., 1962).

Todd and Dewhurst (1955) used the term "Othello Syndrome" to refer to patients whose central delusional theme is the infidelity of his spouse. This delusion occurs in both sexes but is more frequent and far more dangerous in males. The wives' decreased sexual interest or the husbands' impotence are given as major causal factors. Disparity in the sexual ability of the couple may also be a critical factor—an elderly husband married to a much younger wife.

In contrast to Western patients, Weinstein (1962) noted that sexual ideas are not very frequently expressed in the delusions of native women in the Virgin Islands. When they occur, however, they tend to emphasize violence and attack rather than sexual intercourse itself; for example, they accuse men of assaulting them, or they imagine that a broom standing in the cleaning closet will be thrust into the vagina. Weinstein suggested that the low rate of sexual delusion among native women may be related to social expectations; they are not apt to gain their ends by playing the part of the helpless female or by acting in a seductive fashion. Also, the Virgin Islanders do not structure the environment in terms of sex as do other cultural groups; this does not mean that they are less active sexually in a physical way but that the biological fact of sex does not determine social role to as great an extent.

The content of both delusions and hallucinations may be explained in terms of the attitudes and expectations of the audience (Al-Issa, 1977; 1978). According to this view, a schizophrenic woman tends to report what the professional expects her to say. In a culture where women are reacted to and treated as sex objects, it is not surprising that they report sexual fantasies that are conceived by psychiatrists as delusions and hallucinations. Hallucinations may only be a wish-fulfilling fantasy or an escape from a harsh and unsatisfactory reality. Such hallucinatory experiences of a female are described by Noyes and Kolb (1963):

> One day as she was sitting on the bank of the Potomac River, preoccupied with her problems and dreaming of some means of satisfactory escape from them, she heard the voice of a former lover who had ceased his attentions

as her personality limitations had become more apparent. In this thwarted and distressing state of affairs, she received from the old admirer a message pointing the way to an enchanting fulfillment of her fondest hopes. Although she could not see him, the patient heard the lover direct her to jump into the water, from which he promised to rescue her and row her to Norfolk whence they would sail to Egypt, there to occupy a beautiful castle. So convinced by the vividness of the message that reality was ignored, the woman threw herself into the water where she would have perished except for some chance passers-by. A correct appreciation of her experience would have been too painful and disillusioning, and so she continued to believe in the reality of these autogenous perceptions.

Murphy (1967) suggested that cultural response to delusions can vary with the role or status of the person. Many societies do not tolerate the delusions of widows because they are mistrusted (it is believed that they are a threat to the marital ties of neighbors, acquaintances, and friends). In the French-Canadian villages studied by Murphy, these communities were helpful to their deluded young men rather than to their deluded young women. Young women suspected of delusions were either driven deeper into them, if they were of a somatic nature, or sent into exile, if they were paranoid. Cross culturally, discrimination against deluded women seems to depend on the type of treatment practiced in the societies. Where exorcism of delusions is practiced, there seems to be no discrimination against who will be treated. However, where a sacrifice or other expenses are involved, a family may be willing to pay for the treatment of a son but not for that of a daughter or a wife (Murphy, 1967). The degree of tolerance of some segments of Western society of the delusions or the hallucinations of some of its members may explain in part the finding that half of the "psychotics" in the community are left undiagnosed (Scheff, 1966).

Behavior of Schizophrenic Women and Men

Descriptions of schizophrenia indicate that it embraces a wide range of behavior, much more varied than that of normal persons or patients with other diagnoses. Yet attention seems to have been focused on women and men who show sex-role reversal. Cheek (1964a) found that, on the one hand, as compared with normal men, schizophrenic men tend to be more passive and withdrawn. On the other hand, schizophrenic women were more active and domineering compared to their normal counterparts. Chesler (1972) described schizophrenic women as more openly hostile and violent and more sexually aggressive than male patients. In group therapy, for instance:

> The women walked around more, there was more shouting and screaming. Disrobing and exhibitionism were much more typical of the females. More hostility and assaultiveness were seen among the women and occasionally the therapist or other patients were struck. Sometimes some of them would attempt to embrace the doctor, or would sit on the floor at the foot of the therapist and cling to his feet. This kind of activity was often seen to occur between certain patients, too, but the males in contrast were never seen to exhibit this behavior. The men usually sat in place, the level of noise was markedly less than in the female groups, and they seemed more socially oriented (Weich, 1968).

A stereotype of the schizophrenic woman as hostile, destructive, and promiscuous is well depicted in a case reported by Schulz and Kilgalen (1969). Her behavior was characterized by assaultiveness and combativeness and by frequent running away and self-mutilation. She had, therefore, been locked in restraints to a bed for three months. In her worst moments, during a psychotherapy session, she became very angry and started throwing bottles and smashing glasses. When she occasionally felt better and was less depressed, she usually became nervous, ran away and picked up a man, had sexual relations with him, and finally returned to the hospital after a few days.

The description of schizophrenic women as promiscuous reflects an old psychiatric belief that female overt sexuality is a symptom of mental illness that justifies psychiatric treatment and hospitalization—hence the hospitalization of women with illegitimate children early in this century. Unfortunately, this belief still persists in psychiatric circles. For example, an anonymous (1978) child psychotherapist writes that "premarital and extramarital sex have to be sympathetically accepted in some of our patients because they are part of the illness." A standard textbook of psychiatry also describes a "flare-up" of sexuality as a symptom of schizophrenia:

> Girls throw themselves away on anybody who wants intercourse, with disastrous consequences—one hebephrenic student, daughter of a respectable family, waited behind a hedge on the roadside determined to give herself

to the first passer-by. She had been unable to concentrate on her studies for several months and had spent her days in bed, while drinking and dancing by night in low taverns (Mayer-Gross, Slater, & Roth, 1960).

The rebellious behavior of schizophrenic women may be contrasted with the complete surrender, apathy, and withdrawal of a classical case of a male schizophrenic described by the German psychiatrist, Emil Kraepelin (1968):

The next patient whom I will bring before you today is a merchant, aged twenty-six, who comes into the room under guidance, with closed eyes, hanging head, and shuffling gait, and at the earliest opportunity sinks limply into a chair. On being spoken to, his pale, expressionless features do not show any animation; the patient does not reply to questions or obey orders. If you stick a needle into his forehead or his nose, or touch the cornea, there follows almost a slight blinking or flushing, without any attempt at defense. But during this the patient quite unexpectedly breaks into a slight laugh. If you raise his arm in the air, it falls down as if palsied, and remains in the same position that it took accidentally. After much persuasion the patient at last opens his eyes; he now also gives his hand, advancing it by jerks with stiff angular movements, and remaining in this position. If you bend his head back, he stays in this uncomfortable position, and his leg, which I have raised up, he also stretches stiffly in the air. By degrees one succeeds in calling forth still further signs of automatic obedience. The patient raises his arms if anyone does it in front of him, and imitates pushing and turning movements, whirling his fists with great exactness and rapidity. On the other hand, he does not utter a word, presses his lips together when he ought to show his tongue, cannot be induced to write, and apart from sudden, repeated grins, remains quite mute, but repeats some words shouted out loud to him with closed mouth. He at once obeys the order to go.

The examples given of the behavior of hospitalized females and males may not be universal. Clinical observation of the promiscuous schizophrenic female and the apathetic schizophrenic male may only describe selected cases. Although the proportion of illegitimate births was relatively high among schizophrenic women (19.1 percent among schizophrenics, 7.5 percent among depressives, and 12.7 percent in the general population of London during 1961), Stevens (1970) found that most of these births of schizophrenic women were the result of a serious relationship rather than a casual sexual encounter. Indeed, the high illegitimate fertility of the schizophrenics was not the result of a decrease in social and sexual inhibitions often attributed to psychosis. Similarly, the impression given of schizophrenic women as immoral and undersocialized is not supported by Holzberg (1963). He has shown that they have a harsh "superego" and tend to give a strict moral judgment on social issues. They also display a tendency toward *extreme* moral judgments—that is, being morally very wrong or being morally very right. Schizophrenic women are thus seen by Holzberg as "unique in their tendency to operate under the tyranny of a severe conscience, a tyranny of both 'do not' as well as a tyranny of the 'should'."

In conclusion, cases described in this section may be instructive in raising several questions. It is possible that selective factors may be at work: The overactive aggressive female and the underactive withdrawn male may be hospitalized more readily than those whose behavior is socially acceptable. Also, the behavior of female and male patients may be due to the effects of hospitalization; also, the two sexes may react differently to the adverse effects of institutionalization. Certainly, females showing aggression, hostility, and overt sexuality in a mental hospital would more readily attract the attention of the staff, but we still do not know whether this behavior is the cause or the consequence of hospitalization. Finally, published research on schizophrenia in major psychological and psychiatric journals from 1966 to 1970 (Cash, 1973) and from 1974 to 1976 (Wahl, 1977) tends to show that most researchers used male subjects. One possible reason for sex bias is that female schizophrenics are less willing than male patients to take part in experimental research.

Reversal of Sex Identity in Schizophrenia

Whereas sex role refers to the *behavior* ascribed to women and men, sex identity involves a *belief* in one's femininity or masculinity. Consistent with the clinical description of the "masculine" behavior of the schizophrenic female, it has been suggested that she may differ from normal women at the basic level of sex identity; that is to say, she differs in her belief about belonging to the female sex and in her experience of herself as a female.

Attitudes toward and, particularly, concern about different aspects of the body are thought to be relevant to sex identity. McClelland and Watt (1968) reported that, as compared with normal women, normal males were less concerned about their appearance (such body parts as face, lips, hips, etc.) and more concerned about their strength. Schizophrenic men, however, show the opposite trend; they are, like normal women, more sensitive about how they look than about their strength. Schizophrenic women simply show less concern for all aspects—whether masculine (strength) or feminine (appearance)—of their bodies. Appearance is important for the female, and it is understandable that long-term institutionalization may bring about disturbance in her body image. However, institutionalization cannot explain the reversal found in male patients.

Another approach to the study of sex identity in schizophrenia is derived from looking at patients' drawings of the human figure. Typically, patients are asked to draw a man or a woman to find out whether they can differentiate between the sexes. A woman who draws a picture of a female with male characteristics is assumed to be identifying with the male sex. On the other hand, a male who draws a picture of a male with female characteristics is considered to be identifying with the female sex. Studies using the Draw-a-Man test with schizophrenic patients are inconsistent; in some studies, patients confused the sexes in their drawings, but in others they did not (Burton & Sjoberg, 1964; Kokonis, 1972; Reed, 1957). Patients under stress in a mental hospital often fail to differentiate between the sexes in their drawings because they tend to produce drawings of poor quality. These studies, as well as others, are not clear about whether schizophrenia is the cause or the result of sex-identity reversal.

TREATMENT OF SCHIZOPHRENIC WOMEN

Behavior of hospitalized schizophrenic women that breaks away from sex role expectations would suggest two approaches to treatment in a traditional hospital setting. Treatment would *first* aim at eliminating "masculine" behavior in order to enable the woman to assume the appropriate "feminine" behavior. In the treatment of paranoid women, Modlin (1963), for example, attributed their problems to the lack of male control in their marriage and in the hospital. As part of the treatment, he trained their husbands to be more assertive. He also instructed the staff of the hospital to be firm and authoritarian with the patients. Other aspects of the life situations of these women, particularly those directly related to their symptoms, were, however, completely neglected in the treatment.

Second, since the aggressive and domineering behavior of the female patient brings more disturbance in the hospital ward, it attracts more attention and, of necessity, needs more disciplinary action. Thus, more drastic methods are sometimes used to modify the behavior of schizophrenic women. Ludwig, Marx, Hill, and Browning (1969) attempted to eliminate the aggressive behavior of a thirty-one-year-old schizophrenic woman by shocking her, against her expressed will, with a standard cattle prod. Hospital "treatment" is run for the convenience of the staff rather than for the cure of patients:

> Surgeons prefer to operate on slender patients rather than fat ones, because with fat ones instruments get slippery, and there are extra layers to cut through. Morticians in mental hospitals sometimes favor thin females over fat men, because heavy "stiffs" are difficult to move and male stiffs must be dressed in jackets that are hard to pull over stiffened arms and fingers. . . . Just as personal possessions may interfere with the smooth running of an institutional operation and be removed for this reason, so parts of the body may conflict with efficient management and the conflict may be resolved in favor of efficiency. If the heads of inmates are to be kept clean, and the possessor easily categorized, then a complete head shave is efficacious, despite the damage this does to appearance. On similar grounds, some mental hospitals have found it useful to extract the teeth of "biters," give hysterectomies to promiscuous female patients, and perform lobotomies on chronic fighters (Goffman, 1961).

In order to subdue schizophrenic women, it is to be expected that heavy doses of tranquilizers are prescribed. Kalinowsky (1963) reported some of the effects of such drugs on women. In those on tranquilizers, amenorrhea (nonoccurrence of menstruation), frequently accompanied by swelling of the breasts and by lactation, has been observed. Although tranquilizers decrease the sexual potency of male schizophrenics, Kalinowsky observed that, in some female patients, an increased sexual urge has been noticed. Similarly, evidence indicates that many male patients, after a series of shock treatments, become completely impotent for approximately three weeks (and, after six weeks, slowly regain their former potency); sexual dysfunction, however, is not noticed in the female after this treatment. It is not surprising that the enforced celibacy in mental hospitals bothers women more than men, since women continue their interest in sex while under treatment.

Since one aim of treatment is to help females to adapt to their sex roles, it is not surprising that length of hospitalization is associated with conformity to feminine behavior. McKeever, May, and Tuma (1965) found that, on the first admissions of female schizophrenics, high levels of masculinity on psychological tests indicated a longer stay in hospital. Distler and his associates (1964) also found that schizophrenic women were more likely to be discharged from the hospital if they adopted a feminine pattern of high anxiety and low ego strength than if they revealed the reverse (low anxiety and high ego strength), which is a masculine pattern.

Anecdotal evidence reported earlier indicates that the sexuality of the female is not influenced by institutionalization for schizophrenia. If anything, the expression of overt sexuality may be the cause of her hospitalization. Yet LaTorre (1976) suggested that encouraging sexual activities among patients may help them to regain their sex identity. He cites a study by Nell (1968) in which it was alleged that patients' symptoms improved after such "supportive heterosexual experiences." Apart from ethical questions concerning "forcing" patients to have sex as part of the treatment, sexual promiscuity may have disorganizing effects on married patients (Goffman, 1961).

Schizophrenic Women after Hospital Discharge

How do discharged female patients differ from their "normal" female neighbors? What are the factors that might be involved in the rehospitalization of female ex-patients? Angrist, Lefton, Dinitz, and Pasamanick (1968) attempted to answer these questions. They found that ex-patients did not differ from their female neighbors in severe symptoms, such as hearing voices or seeing visions and lack of control of toilet habits; both groups had low levels of these symptoms. Similarly, the two groups did not differ on symptoms associated with mild problems, such as awkward movements, restlessness, grouchiness, and physical complaints. It is in the area of disruptive and socially unacceptable behavior that the difference between ex-patients and their neighbors often looms large (use of abusive language, excessive swearing, aggressive behavior, idleness, getting drunk often, misbehaving sexually, worrying about health). The ex-patients were also consistently less efficient in carrying out domestic chores, such as preparing morning and evening meals, doing grocery shopping, handling grocery money, dusting, sweeping, doing the usual cleaning, taking care of laundry, and mending. However, former patients who had children living at home were as adequate in child care as their "normal" counterparts. Social participation, such as visiting friends and spending time on hobbies, did not differentiate between the groups (Angrist et al., 1968).

Angrist and her colleagues (1961) found more deviant behavior among ex-patients who were rehospitalized than among those who were not: They had more hallucinations and delusions, such as hearing voices, talking to themselves, seeing people who are not there, feeling that people want to harm them; show more antisocial behavior, including excessive swearing and deviant sexual behavior; and exhibit more disorientation (not knowing what goes on around them) and suicidal or homicidal behavior. Here are some of the incidents reported by husbands and relatives that precipitated the rehospitalization of these female ex-patients:

> She walked around naked with just a straw hat on, staring at the sky.
>
> I thought she should go back to the hospital because of her terrible temper. I worried she might hurt the babies when she was all riled up.
>
> She copied stuff from the Bible and talked of killing others. She was also afraid someone would kill her. (Angrist et al., 1961)

One finding by Angrist and her associates (1961) suggests that refusal to carry out domestic chores may be involved in the rehospitalization of ex-patients. They found that female patients who were rehospitalized performed less well on domestic work: cleaning, cooking, shopping, and looking after the children. Rehospitalized women did not, however, differ from other ex-patients in social interaction or other leisure activities (visiting with friends and relatives, listening to radio and watching T.V., and attending religious services or clubs). It is of interest that there was a small group of ex-patients who were readmitted to hospital, although they were relatively symptom-free and performed their domestic roles as adequately as other ex-patients. It appears that family friction or antisocial behavior, such as alcoholism and sexual deviance, played some part in the readmission of these women to hospital (Angrist et al., 1961).

One important finding by Angrist and her colleagues (1961) is that rehospitalized women tended to be married rather than single.

Since the majority of hospitalized women are married, adaptation to domestic work is necessary in order to reduce the risk of their rehospitalization after discharge. The study by Angrist and her associates strongly suggests that it is the female unwillingness to conform to sex-role demands that leads to rehospitalization.

Marjorie Raskin and William Dyson (1968) studied the adjustment of schizophrenic patients in the community after being discharged from the hospital. It was found that the majority of male patients were dependent on parents or siblings and that one-half were unemployed. The females, on the other hand, were living either on their own or with their husbands, and almost all functioned as homemakers or had outside jobs. These differences are expected, since there are more single male schizophrenics who rely primarily on their families for support. Furthermore, the passivity and inactivity of many male schizophrenics would keep them from getting jobs, whereas females seem to be either socially capable or, at least, active enough to hold a job. Overall, it appears that females adapt more easily to community life than their male counterparts after discharge from hospital.

FAMILY INTERACTION AND SCHIZOPHRENIA

A theory of schizophrenia now rejected by most psychologists is to blame faulty interaction between parents and children for the development of the illness. The family approach to schizophrenia has its roots in psychoanalytical theory. Freud put much stress on sexual seduction by the male and particularly by the father in the development of psychopathology. Later, however, this tendency was reversed as researchers accused the mother for inducing schizophrenia in her children.

In 1948, Frieda Fromm-Reichmann, a well-known female psychoanalyst, was the first to use the awful label, "schizophrenogenic mother," to describe the role of the mother in causing schizophrenia in her children—her coldness and rejection drive these children into schizophrenia. Later, the schizophrenogenic mother has been described by Tietze (1949) as "overanxious, obsessive, domineering, restrictive, perfectionistic, oversolicitous, dependent on approval by others."

Basic to the concept of the schizophrenogenic mother is sex-role reversal in a family with a passive ineffectual father and a dominant aggressive mother. Among the most well-known formulations based on this concept is that of Lidz, Cornelison, Fleck, and Terry (1957). The families of schizophrenics, according to Lidz, show two patterns, one of schism and another of skew. Parents in a family showing schism react in ways similar to those seen in a divorce court: constant antagonism, threats of separation, the derogation of one parent by another. This family pattern is often found in schizophrenic women. In the family showing skew, the serious pathology of one parent dominates the home, and a dependent spouse supports the pathology of a dominant parent. The child becomes the object of a particular intrusiveness by the dominant parent, who is usually the mother, and this behavior is usually supported by a compliant father. This intrusiveness makes the patient a victim to the dominant mother's deviant needs. Schizophrenic men tend to belong to this family pattern.

Research does not give consistent support to family theories of schizophrenia. Contrary to the Lidz theory, other research demonstrated that schismatic parental relations are not more characteristic of schizophrenic females than of schizophrenic males (Becker & Siefkes, 1969). Frances Cheek (1964b) also found no support for the notion of a domineering schizophrenogenic mother. Indeed, in her findings, mothers of both female and male normals were more dominant than the mothers of schizophrenics. Again contrary to expectations, a pattern of an assertive, domineering father and a passive, submissive mother was reported by Sanua (1961) in the families of schizophrenics.

Another theory of the "bad mother" is suggested by Bateson, Jackson, Haley, and Weakland (1956). They postulate a double-bind theory that describes the mother-child relationship and the development of schizophrenia. In their view schizophrenic behavior, such as withdrawal from social interaction, is a reaction to inconsistent communication demanding the performance of mutually exclusive behavior; that is, the schizophrenogenic mother conveys two contradictory messages by means of verbal and nonverbal communication. For example, if a mother begins to feel hostile (or affectionate) toward her child and also feels compelled to withdraw from him, she might say, "Go to bed; you're very tired, and I want you to get your sleep." This overtly loving statement is intended to deny a feeling that is expressed nonverbally through facial cues, but could be verbalized as "Get out of my sight because I am sick of you."

However, in 1966 the psychologist Alan Fontana published a review of such studies of family interaction and claimed that they cannot be accepted as valid because they are based on false assumptions. Three of these assumptions are worth noting here. First, the assumption underlying all such studies seems to be that the way in which family members interact in the experimental situation is the same as the way in which they act normally. This is particularly important because the studies are based on the observation of parents interacting with a schizophrenic *in a hospital*—and this is clearly not a "typical" family situation. It is also assumed that family interaction *now* (i.e., when the patient is schizophrenic) is the same as it was *then* (when the child was becoming a schizophrenic). Finally, it is assumed that family interaction patterns are no different when some members are not present—for in this hospital situation the whole family is usually not present (siblings, especially, are liable to be absent). So, in the opinion of Fontana and many psychologists, the schizophrenogenic mother is no more than a chimera.

Finally, theories of family interaction also ignore the fact that although many families tend to have schizophrenogenic family structures, family members seldom become schizophrenic.

Laing and the Family of Schizophrenic Women

> I was born under a black sun. I wasn't born, I was crushed out. It's not one of those things you get over like that. I wasn't mothered, I was smothered. She wasn't a mother. I'm choosey who I have for a mother. Stop it. Stop it. She's killing me. She's cutting out my tongue. I'm rotten, base. I'm wicked. I'm wasted time. . . .
>
> R.D. Laing: THE DIVIDED SELF

In his study of eleven families of schizophrenic women, R.D. Laing has provided one of the most revealing records of family interaction. Contrary to the stereotype of the schizophrenogenic mother, his interviews indicate that all types of interaction seem to be possible between parents and their schizophrenic daughters. Consider, for example, the Blair family and the King family (Laing & Esterson, 1970). In one family, the daughter is controlled by the father (Mr.

Blair), whereas in the other, she is controlled by the mother (Mrs. King). Mr. Blair had been tyrannizing his teenage daughter Lucie by watching all her movements and by requiring her to account for every minute she spent outside the house, telling her that if she went out alone she would be kidnapped, raped, or murdered. The father snubbed the friends that Lucie brought home and tried to ridicule her. He terrorized her by stories of what would happen if she did not have the "security" of her home. He ridiculed her ideas of being able to follow a career and would say that she was making a fool of herself. When she expressed the desire to be a professional musician, Mr. Blair thought that she was made to be a "gentlewoman."

In this family atmosphere, the "schizophrenic" behavior of Lucie, her flattened affect, and her "delusions" of persecution become understandable. She thought that she was tormented and torn to pieces. She felt people put unpleasant sexual ideas into her head. Mrs. Blair, a helpless victim of her husband, also victimized Lucie. Mrs. Blair's "gossip, nosiness, familiarity, sexual suggestions [and] cheekiness—what in clinical terms would be regarded as a typically paranoid world—" are quite similar to her husband's pattern of interaction with Lucie.

In the King family, however, Mr. King seems unable to rescue his daughter, Hazel, from the grip of her mother. Hazel has no alternative except to yield to the control of her mother, who is herself crippled both sexually and socially. The following description of Mrs. King echoes some of the pejorative stereotypes of the disturbed schizophrenogenic mother:

> Mrs. King is grossly hysterical, giggly, dissociated, frigid, subject to multiple anxieties that she deals with by an extreme entrenchment of herself. For instance, she does not know whether she has had an orgasm or a climax, she is not sure whether or not her husband has "proper" intercourse with her; she is not sure whether or not he uses a contraceptive, or whether he ejaculates inside or outside her. Since her marriage she has hardly ever been outside the house unaccompanied by her own mother or father, apart from visits to the local shops. She has extensive fears of travelling, of meeting people. Her self-consciousness amounts to ideas that people look at her in the street, and that they make ridiculing remarks about her.

Circumstances surrounding the "breakdown" of the daughters of other families described by Laing suggest that these daughters are aware of the restrictiveness of their sex roles. The breakdown seems to coincide with the daughters' attempts to emancipate themselves from the family, to reassert themselves, and to resist the control of parents. Little tolerance, however, is shown toward the daughters' sexuality and toward the expression of emotionality. For example, in the Eden family, as soon as Mrs. Eden heard about the pregnancy of her daughter, she immediately started pumping soap into her uterus, telling her "what a fool she was, what a slut she was, what a terrible mess she was in."

There was also a tendency among some of the eleven families to distort the reports of their daughters and attribute psychiatric symptoms to them. Claire, the Churchs's daughter, was diagnosed as a paranoid schizophrenic with impoverished affect: Everybody, including her parents and the psychiatrists, seemed to agree that she lacked normal affection toward her parents and others. She was described as lacking warmth and as being distant and difficult. Yet the interview with Claire showed just the opposite of what the psychiatrists and her parents were describing as lack of affection. What Claire was concerned about was her parents' lack of *real* affection for her.

In conclusion, the "schizophrenic" daughter, perhaps because of her weak position, tends to become the scapegoat on whom the family's muddled relationships and anxieties appear to be imposed. Although all family members are caught in the closed world of the nuclear family, it is again the mother and not the father who is often blamed by Laing for the sickness of the daughter. But the behavior of the mother may well be a result of interactions with other family members rather than a cause of the daughter's schizophrenia.

SCHIZOPHRENIC MOTHERS

More schizophrenic women than men tend to get married and have children. Schizophrenia "strikes" men early in life, before they have the chance to get married. While he is schizophrenic, the male opportunity for marriage is also significantly more reduced than that of his female counterpart (Bleuler, 1974; Stevens, 1969). Since the probability that schizophrenic females would assume a family role is high, the diagnosis of schizophrenia may interfere with pregnancy and mothering. Schizophrenia may have more adverse effects than other diagnoses because it is most often associated with hospitalization and separation from children.

Pregnancy and Birth Problems

Mednick (1970) found a higher frequency of pregnancy and birth complications in women diagnosed schizophrenics than in women given other kinds of diagnosis or in normals. These complications include anoxia (oxygen deficiency), prematurity, prolonged labor, placental difficulty, umbilical cord complications, illness of the mother during pregnancy, multiple births, and so on. These complications were particularly evident in mothers of children who later developed psychiatric problems.

Obstetrical complications do not, however, seem to be limited to schizophrenia. They are more related to the severity of the disturbance rather than the type of disturbance. Severe disturbance may result in an inadequate concern about physical health and nutrition that may affect the fetus. When compared with other women who are severely disturbed but not schizophrenic (for example, neurotic depressive women), no difference in the degree of delivery complications was found (Sameroff & Zax, 1972).

There is also a relationship between anxiety and tension, on the one hand, and obstetrical complications, on the other. Anxiety may cause biochemical changes that affect the fetus during pregnancy. Anxiety may also influence the delivery process; it tends to prolong labor and to inhibit the help the woman could provide in delivering the baby. Furthermore, anxious women are normally given more medication and tend to have more instrumental deliveries or Caesarean sections in order to speed up their deliveries; apparently, the physician's response to their anxieties seems to increase medical complications (Garmezy, 1974). It appears that both schizophrenic and neurotic-depressive women who tend to have the greatest pregnancy and birth complications also have high levels of anxiety.

The Mothering of Schizophrenic Mothers

One of the first signs of the female "psychotic" breakdown is her inability to care for her children, such as providing meals, setting bed schedules, and other aspects of organizing the household (Garmezy, 1974). One immediate effect of schizophrenia is mother-child separation through the admission of the mother to hospital. Mednick and Schulsinger (1968) found that children of schizophrenic mothers who manifested psychiatric disturbance were those who had been separated at an earlier age from their mothers through hospitalization. There was also a greater likelihood for these children who were separated earlier to be more severely ill and to be hospitalized.

Women who have been hospitalized for mental illness (including 42 percent who were psychotics) do not respond as quickly or as accurately to their infants' cues as do nonhospitalized women (Ganer, Gallant, & Grunebaum, 1976). This study seems to indicate that hospitalization has a negative effect on mothering. In a study by Schachter, Elmer, Ragins, Winkerly, and Lachin (1977), schizophrenic subjects were selected from the clients of a prenatal care clinic: Of nine women, four had had previous hospitalization, two had had outpatient treatment, and the rest had had no previous treatment, but they were diagnosed as schizophrenic for the first time when they contacted the clinic. In contrast to normal mothers, Schachter and his associates found that schizophrenic mothers showed an increased responsiveness and a tendency to demonstrate more positive behavior toward their babies. Further, they were more alert to the feeding demands of their infants. It appears that, although hospitalization may affect the quality of mothering of schizophrenic mothers, the diagnosis of schizophrenia by itself may not impair their mothering.

Sussex, Gassman, and Raffel (1963) studied six 16-year-old adolescents whose mothers were receiving outpatient treatment. The researchers concluded that "the children as a group did not show marked evidence of being adversely affected by the presence of a psychotic mother in the home." Higgins (1966) also found no support for the view that children reared by schizophrenic mothers show less adaptive behavior than children reared apart. Children reared by a schizophrenic mother tend to be asocial in their classroom behavior, more withdrawn in their interpersonal contacts, and less responsive to social rewards administered by the teacher and other adult figures. Children reared apart were more easily upset or irritated by minor accidents and more physiologically aroused under stress. These differences were not regarded as pathological; rather, they only reflected ways of coping with the environment by using approach or avoidance responses. The approach-oriented individual tends to enter into situations and to respond vigorously to stressful encounters. In contrast, the predominantly avoidance-oriented person tends to avoid contacts with environmental challenges and stresses, or, failing this, he or she simply withdraws. This latter type of coping behavior characterized schizophrenic mother-reared children.

Whatever abnormalities are shown by the offspring of schizophrenic women, these may be due to the severity of their disturbance or to social class differences rather than to schizophrenia. As Sameroff and Zax (1978) noted:

> Our results are *not* that offspring of schizophrenic women are a healthy, happy, intelligent, adaptive lot. Our measures have shown that they have high levels of illness, fearfulness, sadness, retardation, and social maladaptiveness. However, this does not make them uniquely different from the offspring of women with other severe or chronic mental disorders, or even children of psychiatrically normal women from the lower socioeconomic strata of our society.

The Role of the Spouse

Support from the father or another adult plays a major role in the adjustment of the children of "schizophrenic" women. The father's presence in the home, his stability, and his attitudes toward mental illness and toward his spouse are crucial to the adjustment of children (Gerty, 1955).

The support a husband gives to his "ill" wife is dependent on his own emotional stability and on his tolerance of disordered behavior. One consistent difference between parents whose children are ill and those whose children are well is the presence of mental illness in both parents (Rutter, 1966). Rutter noted that a relatively low rate of psychiatric illness in the children of schizophrenics may be due to the fact that the schizophrenic's spouse is usually healthy and able to deal with the children. However, this conclusion may not apply to spouses of schizophrenic women, since there is a high frequency of criminal behavior and conviction among their husbands, which would be expected to create problems in the family (Kirkegaard-Sorensen & Mednick, 1975).

Children of male schizophrenics more often spend their entire childhood with both parents than do children of female schizophrenics. Moreover, children of female schizophrenics more often live alone with their fathers than do the children of male schizophrenics with their mothers (Bleuler, 1974). It appears that normal women tolerate, to some extent, the schizophrenic husband and keep him at home (Johnston & Planansky, 1968), but the reverse does not seem to be true.

Joint Hospitalization of Schizophrenic Mothers and Infants

There is a positive relationship between the joint admission of ill mothers and their babies and the child's subsequent adjustment (Garmezy, 1974). Evidence indicates that "with babies 8 weeks to 1 year of age, the schizophrenic mother's presence appeared to have a normalizing effect. Each schizophrenic mother [like a normal mother] differed in her reaction to her child, ranging from great anxiety to constant warmth. The schizophrenic mothers tried to prolong babyhood into the toddler stage, but the clinicians felt that the younger children responded well, and easily formed play relationships with others. In general, these schizophrenic mothers showed little difficulty in caring for their young children while on the ward" (Garmezy, 1974).

In a pioneering British project, Baker, Morison, Game, and Thorpe (1961) admitted schizophrenic mothers and their babies jointly to a mental hospital. Contrary to stereotypes that "psychotics" are dangerous, the researchers noted no hostility to the child. These mothers were able to look after their children throughout their hospital stay. After discharge, these women had shown good mothering and provided their toddlers with much affection. Indeed, their children appeared to be better adjusted than those of many young neurotic mothers. The recovery rate of schizophrenic mothers admitted with their babies was higher than for those admitted without them. Similarly, all jointly admitted mothers were able to maintain responsibility for their babies' care at home, whereas only one-half of the nonjointly admitted mothers were able to function as well.

Other studies support the findings of Baker and his associates. For example, Weiss, Grunebaum, and Schell (1964) reported that jointly admitted mothers looked after their babies adequately. When a mother felt destructive and hostile, she tended to avoid the child. More often than not, the mothers played with their children, and in no instance did they reveal any physical threat to the child. Indeed, another study by Grunebaum and Weiss (1963) found that the children of jointly admitted mothers were well adjusted; only nonjoint admission children fared poorly as compared with children of normal mothers. In contrast, when a baby is born to a woman while she is hospitalized for schizophrenia, the experience of hospitalization seems to affect her interaction with, and positive feeling toward, the infant (Sobel, 1961).

SUMMARY

It is generally agreed that there are no sex differences in the rate of schizophrenia in the general population. However, there is an interesting age pattern for the hospital admission of schizophrenia. There are more schizophrenic persons among young men than young women. At about middle-age or later this tendency is reversed with higher rates among women than men. Community studies reveal that the age of schizophrenic breakdown may vary depending on the extent to which women and men are exposed to conflicts associated with their sex roles. Ethnic background and educational level appear to influence the direction of sex differences.

Hallucinations are equally reported among women and men. However, women report more delusions than men. The excess of sexual delusions among women suggests that these delusions may not be false beliefs but they may reflect true happenings such as sexual assault and abuse.

Cases of schizophrenia revealing sex-role reversal (aggression and overt sexuality in the female, and the passivity and dependency in the male) have attracted the attention of clinicians. It is quite possible that only aggressive and sexual females, and passive and dependent males are hospitalized. And it may be that because the aggressive and sexual behavior of the women is more disruptive in the hospital ward than the withdrawn and passive behavior of the men, they are more severely treated. Their hospital discharge is also related to submission, obedience and other "proper" feminine behavior. Further, female ex-patients who do not function well as homemakers are usually rehospitalized. For both sexes, however, treatment aims at increasing femininity in schizophrenic women and masculinity in schizophrenic men. This is based on the theory that schizophrenia is not only characterized by a reversal in sex role but also by a reversal in sex identity: A schizophrenic woman believes that she is a man and a schizophrenic man believes that he is a woman. Theories relating schizophrenia to the reversal of sex identity receive inconsistent support. However, researchers tend to blame the mothers but not the fathers for the "feminine" behavior of the schizophrenic sons and the "masculine" behavior of their schizophrenic daughters: The seductive, domineering, and over-protective mothers cause the schizophrenia of the children. For example, the British psychiatrist R. D. Laing, who idealized his schizophrenic patients, used abusive labels such as "hysterical" and "frigid" to describe their mothers. Presently, the majority of researchers reject the belief that mothers cause the schizophrenia of their children.

Schizophrenic women tend to have more pregnancy and birth problems than normal women, but they are not different from other patients with the same high levels of anxiety and tension. In general, schizophrenic mothers reveal little difficulties in caring for their babies at home or on the ward when they are jointly admitted with their children. However, hospitalization without the child has a damaging influence on their mothering; it affects their interaction with and their positive feeling toward the baby.

Women
and
Depression

4

Lying awake, calculating the future,
Trying to unweave, unwind, unravel
and piece together the past and the future,
Between midnight and dawn, when the past is all
deception,
The future futureless. . . .

"The Dry Salvages," from T.S. Eliot's FOUR QUARTETS.
Reprinted by permission of Harcourt, Brace,
Jovanovich, Inc.

A dejected mood and a feeling of sadness, hopelessness, and misery are some of the main symptoms of the depressed woman. She experiences no pleasure from activities that used to fill her with joy. Social activities and the expression of love and friendship are no longer meaningful or pleasurable to her. Even those basic activities associated with biological needs, such as food and sex, lose their attraction. All feelings of attachment and love for anyone, including her children, disappear.

Figure 4.1 *Sorrow* by Vincent van Gogh (November, 1882). Transfer lithograph, printed in black, comp: 15 3/8 × 11 3/4″, sheet: 18 1/2 × 14 3/4″. Collection, The Museum of Modern Art, New York. Purchase Fund.

In her low self-esteem, the depressed woman views herself as deficient in characteristics that are important to her feminine identity, such as intelligence, health, beauty, personal attractiveness, and popularity. She may describe herself as inferior and inadequate. She is also pessimistic, and she expects the worst and rejects the possibility of improvement. She criticizes herself for various deficiencies and blames herself for happenings that are in no way connected with her: "I am responsible for the violence and suffering of the world. There is no way in which I can be punished enough for my sins" (Beck, 1967). She complains of tiredness and suffers from insomnia and early waking. Her dominant wish is to avoid, escape, or withdraw from everyone and be left in seclusion. She is now unable to mobilize herself to take her food or her medication. She may wish to kill herself, but she is often too retarded in movement to complete or even to initiate a suicidal attempt.

Depression is divided into psychotic and neurotic depression, sometimes called, respectively, endogenous (coming from within) and exogenous (coming from without) depression. Neurotic and psychotic depression are traditionally differentiated by whether there is a precipitating life event connected with the depression. A person with the neurotic type becomes depressed because of loss, rejection, or some other stressful experience. On the other hand, psychotic depression is assumed to occur in cycles rather than being connected to any discernible life event.

Another basis for differentiating psychotic from neurotic depression is in terms of symptoms. Most psychotic symptoms tend to be related to negative subjective bodily feelings (tired, worn out, powerless), whereas symptoms of neurotic depression are concerned with negative interpersonal events (excessive family or job responsibilities, concern about the welfare of family and friends).

The problem with the division of depression into psychotic and neurotic types is whether the precipitating event can, in fact, be identified. Information is obtained from patients or relatives, and neither source is reliable; past events may be forgotten, distorted or even pass unnoticed. These factors make the diagnosis of psychotic and neurotic depression unreliable. Winokur and Pitts (1964) demonstrated that patients who are diagnosed as neurotic depressives on admission to the hospital are sometimes labeled psychotic depressives on discharge. More recent research has indicated that patients diagnosed as either psychotic or neurotic depressives reported precipitating life events in the nine months before onset, throwing doubts on these two diagnostic types of depression (Brown, Harris, & Copeland, 1977). It may be that the psychotic depression represents a more severe type of the illness. No distinction will be made between psychotic and neurotic depression in this chapter.

SEX DIFFERENCES IN DEPRESSION

There are about two depressive females to one male patient in the United States. Countries other than the United States report a similar excess of depressive females, with the exception of a number of developing countries, such as India, Iraq, New Guinea, and Rhodesia (Ananth, 1976; Weissman & Klerman, 1977). Indeed, the ratio is reversed in India, where there are more depressed males than depressed females (Ananth, 1976).

Sex differences in depression appear to be related to age. Figure 4.2 shows the sex-by-age first admission of cases of depression to state mental hospitals in the United States during 1933 (it is comparable with the sex-by-age first admission curves for schizophrenia reported in Figure 3.2, Chapter 3). The rate of depression is higher for females in the earlier ages, especially from their twenties through their forties. From their fifties on, the rate is somewhat higher for males, but the difference is not as large as that in the earlier periods. With respect to schizophrenia, I noted the opposite trend in Chapter 3: Males have higher admission rates in the earlier ages, while females have higher rates after their middle thirties (Rosenthal, 1970).

In contrast to the pre-World War II picture, recent data indicate that rates of depression are higher for women at every age group, with a shift in the peak of elevated depression to a younger age (Rad-

Figure 4.2 From *Modern Society and Mental Disease,* C. Landis and J.D. Page. Copyright © 1938, 1966 by Holt, Rinehart and Winston, Inc. *Adapted* by permission of Holt, Rinehart and Winston.

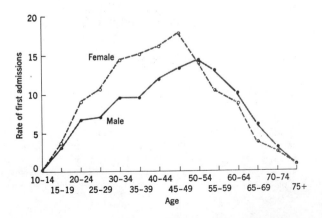

loff, 1975). Other data also reveal a shift in the peak of depression in women from middle age to a younger age group (Brown et al., 1975).

The hospital admissions reported in Figure 4.2 may not be reliable indicators of the incidence of depression, since many factors seem to influence hospitalization. Community studies may give a more reliable picture of the incidence of depression. Using a sample of adults in the southeastern part of the United States, Warheit, Holzer, and Schwab (1973) found that 21 percent of white women were considered severely depressed. This percentage is double that for white men, the same as that for black men, and one-third less than that for black women.[1] Brown and Harris (1978) found that the number of depressive cases among women in North Uist (Scotland) was about half that in Camberwell (London)—5.8 percent and 13.3 percent, respectively. In general, rates of depression in hospitals tend to underestimate much higher rates in the general population. Further, the rates for women vary from one community to the other.

Sex and Depressive Symptoms

Symptoms of depression may be considered as an intensification of what are traditionally considered normal female characteristics, such as dependency, helplessness, hopelessness, passivity, and lack of self-confidence. The association between depression and feminity is supported in a study by Hammen and Peters (1977b). They found that although nondepressed males were rated high on masculinity, depressed males were high on femininity. Whether depressed or not, females were rated high on femininity.

Hammen and Peters (1977a) suggested that, since depressive symptoms are incompatible with what is stereotypically attributed to man, males showing depressive symptoms will be more rejected than females. In this study, normals evaluated a man more negatively than a woman presenting the same depressed symptoms (actually, normal

---

[1]The finding that there is more severe depression among black women than white women is consistent with another study which revealed that in an emergency clinic, behavior which requires hospitalization of female patients is more often perceived as neurotic when the female is white and as schizophrenic (more severe) when the female is nonwhite (Gross, Herbert, Knatterud and Donner, 1969). This may, of course, reflect a general tendency among professionals to give more severe diagnosis (psychosis) to lower class than to a high social class patients (Wilkinson, 1975). Indeed, when factors such as age, sex, social class are controlled, blackness is hardly a significant factor in psychopathology (Warheit et al., 1975).

subjects were presented with the same description but were made to believe that it was a man on one occasion and a woman on the other). The depressed male was not only rejected more than the depressed female, but he was also seen as more impaired. When individuals are asked to consider the ability of depressed persons to function in various roles, depression is perceived to have a more debilitating effect on men than on women. This evidence strongly supports the view that depressed males and females elicit different reactions for exhibiting the same depressed behavior, with males being more devalued and considered more impaired than females. *cuz act feminine*

Since males are rejected for depressed behavior, they may learn to express their psychological stress in alternative ways. For example, it has been suggested that depression and alcoholism are different but equivalent disorders (Weissman & Klerman, 1977). Women admit their depression, whereas men tend to relieve their depression by drinking instead of seeking treatment. The low rate of depression in men, according to this view, is because depressed men may show up in the courts rather than the clinics; that is, a depressed man may get drunk, get into a fight, and end up in court. Of course, for both sexes, alcohol may be used to relieve symptoms of depression; alternatively, alcoholism and its consequent social impairment can lead to depression.

Even when men get depressed, they may express depression differently and may even avoid treatment. Hammen and Padesky (1977) reported that depressed men tend to show an inability to cry, social withdrawal, somatic preoccupation, a sense of failure, weight loss, and sleep disturbance. Women, on the other hand, were characterized more than men by lack of self-confidence and by self-dislike and self-deprecation (in an earlier study by Davis, Lambert, & Ajans [1969] crying was found to be more characteristic of depressed females than of depressed males). Men also reported that they had to be significantly more depressed than women in order to seek help from others or to talk about it with a friend. (This may explain the finding that among depressed male patients, there are more severe than mild cases [Weeke, Bille, Videbach, Dupont, & Juel-Nielsen, 1975].) Men are also more likely than women to reject therapy. Because men's symptoms tend to suppress overt depressive responses, with a greater focus on physical symptoms, their problems may be construed not as depression but as overwork or physical ailment. Thus, depressed men are less likely to be included in statistics on the rates of depression.

SEX HORMONES AND DEPRESSION

Menstruation and Mood

On the approach of a woman in this state, new wine will become sour, seeds which are touched by her become sterile, grass withers away, garden plants are parched up, and the fruit will fall from the tree beneath which she sits.

Pliny (circa 23-79 A.D.): NATURAL HISTORY

If you think you are emancipated, you might consider the idea of tasting your menstrual blood—if it makes you sick, you have a long way to go, baby.

Germaine Greer: THE FEMALE EUNUCH

It has been well established that many women report physical as well as psychological symptoms that appear to be related to menstruation. Among the physical symptoms are headache, fatigue, blurred vision, and intestinal cramps. Dysmenorrhea or menstrual pain may be accompanied with vomiting, nausea, and/or diarrhea. Weight gain, swelling, and feeling bloated are among the most common physical symptoms of the premenstrual week. This temporary weight gain is the result of water retention in the body tissue (Weideger, 1975).

Much attention has been given to emotional changes during the premenstrual and menstrual periods when hormonal levels are very low. Frank (1931) was the first to use the term premenstrual tension to label changes after the twenty-second day of the menstruation cycle. Symptoms of depression, anxiety, and irritability and a feeling of low self-esteem are reported by some women during this time. Katharina Dalton (1961) found that a large proportion of women who commit suicide or engage in criminal acts of violence do so during the four premenstrual and the four menstrual days of the cycle. More than half of children who contacted a clinic with minor colds were brought during the mothers' premenstrual and menstrual periods, a circumstance attributed by Dalton to the mothers' increased anxiety.

Low hormone levels have been traditionally suggested to explain psychological symptoms during the premenstrual and menstrual periods. The physiological explanation resulted in some of the early attempts to cure the symptoms by organic treatment, such as hysterectomy and hormone replacement therapy. However, a careful inspection of the data shows that biological factors cannot entirely explain the appearance of psychiatric symptoms reported by women. One important bit of evidence against a purely organic interpretation of mood changes is that menstrual symptoms are not reported by all women. Indeed, the number of women reporting symptoms varies from one study to another (Weissman & Klerman, 1977). Moos (1969) found that women differ in their patterns of cyclic change. Using the Menstrual Distress Questionnaire, he found that some women experienced mainly dysmenorrhea (pelvic cramps) during menstruation, with no mood disturbance. Other women complained of mood disturbance (irritability, emotional liability) but had no pains or cramps. The severity of the psychiatric symptoms experienced by women is strongly related to their general emotional stability. Coppen and Kessel (1963) found that women who were emotionally unstable reacted more severely to menstruation. Anthropological observations presented by Margaret Mead (1949) also revealed that Samoan women experience only slight pain during menstruation. These findings suggest that factors other than hormonal deficiency are involved in the emotional reactions of women during the menstrual cycle.

Cognitive Factors in Premenstrual Tension

An alternative to the physiological interpretation of menstrual symptoms may be found in the negative attitudes of society toward women and, in particular, toward menstruation. Menstruation has been always considered a taboo in Western society. Young girls are taught to be ashamed of it rather than to celebrate their entry into womanhood at menarche. Since women have traditionally been shunned and considered unclean during this period, this may have been incorporated into their self-image, bringing self-hatred and feelings of worthlessness. Weideger (1975) noted that the menstrual taboo confirms the female negative self-image and represents a source of the shame she feels about her body and her sexuality: Abstinence from sex during menstruation confirms the belief that there is something wrong with the menstruating woman.

Negative attitudes toward menstruation are more common in traditional than in nontraditional women. Karen Paige (1969) found that women who accept the feminine role of a mother also approve of the menstrual taboo. Women who desired motherhood had more menstrual troubles than those willing to pursue careers and child-less marriages. Feminists have suggested that a change in self-image and, in particular, a change in negative attitudes toward menstruation may reduce psychological symptoms in women. Germaine Greer (1970) suggested that women should examine, smell, and taste their menstrual blood as a way of overcoming negative attitudes toward menstruation. The general implication is that any behavior that might enhance the self-image of women will also improve their mental health and emotional stability.

The effects of attitudes and expectations on the mood changes associated with physiological states is consistent with the findings by Schachter and Singer (1962) that an injection of adrenaline (which brings physiological changes, such as tremors, heart palpitations, and face flushing) may bring euphoria or anger, depending on the situation. By the same token, women may feel sick, anxious, and depressed because of their attitude toward menstruation. According to an article in *Time* magazine (1976), instead of saying, "Water retention makes my tear ducts feel full," a woman ascribes negative emotional connotations to those physical states which correspond to her negative opinion of menstruation and says, "I am depressed and about to cry."

Brooks, Ruble, and Clark (1977) found that women who believed that menstruation is debilitating reported significantly higher symptoms for the premenstrual (a day or two before the period) than the intermenstrual phase (7 to 10 days before the period). Women who thought they were premenstrual reported a higher degree of symptoms than women who thought they were intermenstrual, even though the actual cycle phase of the two groups of women was the same (6 to 7 days before the next period was to begin). Self-reports may be an inaccurate representation of the nature and extent of menstrual-related changes and may only reflect expectations about menstruation.

Effect of Other Kinds of Cyclicity

Since there are reports of cycles of emotionality in men, control groups would appear to be essential for the proper interpretation of data on menstruation and psychological symptoms (Parlee, 1973). Estelle Ramey (1972) noted that a study revealed that when male urine was tested for the fluctuating amounts of male sex hormones it contained, a pronounced 30-day rhythm was revealed. Men, however, tend to report less emotional upset during these fluctuations. Anne Seiden (1976) observed that male hormone levels do not only vary with time but also with access to sexual opportunities and, occasionally, with the menstrual cycle of the sexual partner. There is also a lunar cycle for violent crimes, whether committed by women or men (Parlee, 1973). Similarly, studies of females have shown greater mood and behavioral fluctuations with the weekly cycle (work week versus weekends) than with the menstrual cycle, suggesting that factors other than hormonal changes are involved.

In sum, the evidence seems to indicate that the relationship between physiology and behavior is much more complex than the concept of premenstrual tension implies. A causal relationship between menstruation and mood is far from being established.

The Menopause

Apart from physical symptoms, such as hot flashes, sweats, and the estrogen syndrome (vaginal mucosal thinning), the menopause is presumed to increase the risk of depression. The depressive disorder is assumed to be a separate entity labeled involutional melancholia. The patient is supposed to have distinctive symptoms, such as anxiety, agitation, and delusion, during the illness as well as a compulsive personality before the illness.

Although involutional melancholia is supposed to occur immediately after the menopause, the age criterion for its diagnosis is very flexible ranging from 35 years (approaching the menopause) to 60 years (delayed effects of the menopause). Such a flexible age criterion for the diagnosis of involutional melancholia made it difficult to ascertain a direct relationship between hormonal changes and depression. Since depression is not unique to middle-age but can occur during the other stages of life, the American Psychiatric Association decided to drop the outdated and cumbersome label, "involutional melancholia," from its revised system of diagnosis in 1980.

The belief that the menopause increases the rate of depression among women has no support (Hallstrom, 1973; McKinley & Jeffreys, 1974). The average age for menopause has recently risen from the late forties to the early fifties (Cherry, 1976); yet there is now more depression among young women with children than among middle-aged women in their forties or fifties (Brown et al., 1975;

Radloff, 1975). Sales (1978) argues that crisis in middle-age may not be inevitable. By achieving self-understanding and realistic expectations for the future, women may, in fact, find increased satisfaction during the later years. Indeed, research indicates that women whose children have left show more satisfaction and less self-pity than women whose children are still at home (Lowenthal, Thurnher, Chiriboga, and associates, 1975). There are, of course, some women who become disturbed when their children leave home.

The "Empty Nest Syndrome"

The social implications of the menopause may be more important than the hormonal changes. The role of a woman as a wife and a mother may be basic to her self-concept and self-esteem: Loss of self-esteem and feelings of worthlessness and uselessness can be precipitated by the loss of family roles. When a woman devotes considerable time and effort to her home and family, she looks forward to the time when she can derive pleasure from her children after many years of investment. The independence of children and their eventual departure from the home seem to leave a gap that is difficult for the middle-aged mother to fill. She therefore feels useless and apathetic. This reaction is termed the "empty nest syndrome" to emphasize the stress involved in the loss of the maternal role (Deykin, Jacobson, Klerman, & Solomon, 1966). The following verbalization is typical of a depressed middle-aged mother:

> I don't, I don't, I don't feel liked. I don't feel that I'm wanted. I don't feel at all that I'm wanted. I just feel like nothing. I don't feel anybody cares, and nobody's interested, and they don't care whether I do feel good or I don't feel good. I'm pretty useless—I feel like I want somebody to feel for me but nobody does (Bart, 1971).

In her investigation of the empty nest syndrome, Bart (1971) found that middle-aged housewives who were overprotective or who had an overinvolved relationship with their children were more likely to suffer depression in the postparental period than women who did not have such relationships. As compared with working women, housewives tended to have more opportunity to invest themselves completely in their children. Therefore, they were more vulnerable to depression when their roles were suddenly cut down once there were fewer people for whom to shop, cook, and clean. This is consistent with the finding by Radloff (1975) that house-wives were more depressed than working women. Family involve-ment appears to increase the adverse impact of the loss of the ma-ternal role.

Bart noted that a high rate of depression among Jewish women in middle age, when their children leave, is consistent with the empha-sis of the Jewish family on close ties between mother and child. Bart found that Jewish women were twice as likely to be depressed as non-Jewish women. Overall, the data indicate that "women who assume the traditional feminine role—who are housewives, who stay married to their husbands, who are not overtly aggressive and gen-erally follow the traditional female norms are those who respond with depression when the children leave" (Bart, 1971).

Circumstances involving loss (people die, loved ones change, life becomes less pleasant and less meaningful) are universal and should affect both women and men equally. The way the individual handles these circumstances may, however, be crucial, and this, in turn, de-pends on the availability of alternative social roles. For example, Field (1960) described how the depressive role is made temporarily available for women in Ghana and precedes another alternative role sanctioned by the Ashanti religion. Depressed women in large num-bers travel to religious shrines and start accusing themselves of witch-craft. Self-accusation of witchcraft provides them with justification for feelings of failure and worthlessness. The Ashanti woman raises a large family with great care and is an excellent housekeeper and a good businesswoman. When she grows older, however, her husband often takes a younger bride, to whom he gives affection and pos-sessions. This is acceptable in the culture, and there is little the wife can do about it. But she can enact a new depressive role: She can confess that she has been a witch all along; she deserves her present state of being hated and rejected by her husband because of her evil actions. She is then ready to be cured and to step into her next role, that of a discarded wife. Ullmann and Krasner (1969) contrasted the Ghanian women with women in North America, where there are few socially sanctioned roles for persons who find life meaningless. In-stead of having the depressive role as a transitory role that leads to a socially accepted role, the emphasis is put on blaming individuals for their failure, then reinforcing the depressive role as the only alterna-tive for women.

Postpartum Depression

Hormonal changes during the postpartum period tend to be associated with a depressive mood. Brief emotional disturbances—the baby blues—occur with such frequency in the first weeks following delivery that they are regarded as normal. In the nineteenth century, such a depression was called "milk fever" because of its incidence at the beginning of the mother's milk flow. Symptoms of depression, fatigue, irritability, tension, and anxiety are common occurrences after delivery (Pitt, 1968). However, serious psychotic disturbances occur much less frequently, only in about one to two patients per 1,000 deliveries (Kane, 1975). Nevertheless, admissions to mental hospitals tend to increase significantly for women suffering from affective disorders within the first four weeks to three months after childbirth.

In a study of mental illness among married women, Paffenberger and McCabe (1966) found that it peaked in the first months following delivery. Moreover, about half of the women who suffered a postpartum illness had a recurrence in one-third of their subsequent pregnancies. In contrast, the lowest rates of mental illness were found during pregnancy. Another study has also shown an excess of depression during the first three months postpartum (Pugh, Jerath, Schmidt, & Reed 1963). Although hormonal changes may make some women vulnerable to postpartum depression, hormones can not entirely explain depression, since there are cases of women who require psychiatric care after the adoption of an infant (Melges & Hamburg, 1977).

Childbirth is associated with stresses comparable to those experienced during the menopause. Symptoms of postpartum depression indicate the conflicts of these depressed women about their maternal role. They may express excessive concern about the baby's health and welfare, or they may feel guilt about their lack of love or desire to care for the baby. A feeling of inadequacy about taking care of the baby may also be expressed. Delusions may consist of ideas that the baby is dead or deformed. Sometimes, there is a denial of the baby's birth and a belief that the woman is still unmarried or is a virgin. Hallucinatory voices may command the mother to kill her baby. Though infrequent, both suicide and infanticide may occur.

Brown and Harris (1978) found that only pregnancy and childbirth associated with a severe ongoing problem played a part in the development of depression: Some patients were living in quite inadequate housing; others had bad marriages where continued support for the new child was questionable. The authors concluded that "the result clearly suggests that it is the meaning of events that is usually crucial: pregnancy and birth, like other crises, can bring home to a woman the disappointment and hopelessness of her position—her aspirations are made more distant or she becomes even more dependent on an uncertain relationship."

Oral Contraceptives and Depression

The use of oral contraceptives, which contain the female sex hormone, is believed to be associated with increased depression. However, studies do not justify the conclusion that oral contraceptives cause depressive symptoms on a pharmacological basis (Weissman & Slaby, 1973). There is evidence that women with a prior psychiatric history and those with an expectation of negative side effects tend to develop more depressive symptoms while taking oral contraceptives. Mild psychiatric disturbances may develop during the first four weeks of use of contraceptives with high estrogen preparations, but these symptoms gradually disappear.

A large number of women are using oral contraceptives, and so it is inevitable that psychological disturbances may arise during the time these agents are used, but these reactions may be unrelated to the drug (Weissman & Slaby, 1973). Indeed, women on oral contraceptives tend to report both beneficial and adverse psychological effects. Similarly, those using other contraceptive methods (for example, an intrauterine device, or IUD) seem to show the same adverse effects as those on the pill (Moos, 1968).

As yet, research has not sorted out the effects of suggestibility and other psychological reactions to the pill (conflict and guilt over sexual freedom or desire for more children) from the pharmacological effects of oral contraceptives. Therefore, the evidence on the psychological effects of contraceptives is not conclusive.

Effects of Estrogen Replacement Therapy (ERT) and Oral Contraceptives

The belief that female hormones are associated with mood changes has resulted in the use of estrogen in the treatment of depression and premenstrual tension. However, animal experiments in which large doses of estrogen were administered led to the suspicion that estrogen use in humans might result in cancers of the reproductive system. Smith, Prentice, Tompson, and Herrman (1975) found that estrogen replacement therapy brings a significant increase in the incidence of endometrial cancer (the endometrium is the mucuous membrane which lines the uterus). The risk was 4.5 times greater among users than nonusers. In general, women who have suffered from high blood pressure, diabetes, or obesity, or those who have never been pregnant or given birth, have a higher risk of endometrial cancer than other women. Smith and his colleagues, however, found that when this already high-risk group used ERT, their chances of getting endometrial cancer did not increase significantly. Women exposed to the greatest risk of cancer from ERT are those who, on the basis of their medical records, would normally be considered low-risk individuals. In other words, women who have diabetes, who have high blood pressure, who are overweight, or who have never been pregnant are in a high-risk category of endometrical cancer, and this risk does not change appreciably if ERT is used. But for women who are initially of low risk (child-bearing, of average weight, not suffering from diabetes or high blood pressure), ERT increases their risk. A study by Hoover, Guay, Cole, and MacMahon (1976) also suggests that estrogen therapy increases the number of breast cancers. The risk is greater among women who are childless and who have benign breast conditions.

Two more recent studies by Antunes, Stolley, Rosenshein, Davies, Tonascia, Brown, Burnett, Rutledge, Pokempner, and Gracia (1979) and by Jick, Watkins, Hunter, Dinan, Madsen, Rothman, and Walker (1979) have confirmed previous findings of a high risk of endometrial cancer among estrogen users. These researchers also found that this risk rises steeply with both increasing duration of estrogen use and increasing dosage of the hormone. Long-term users have the highest incidence of risk. According to Antunes and colleagues, estrogen users are, on the average, six times more likely than nonusers to develop endometrial cancer, but after five years of continuous use, users run 15 times the risk. Discontinuation of the treatment tends to reduce the risk (Jick et al., 1979). It was concluded that since ERT significantly increases the risk of uterine cancer, it should be prescribed cautiously (short-term treatment using small dosage of hormones) in situations where the benefits outweigh the risks.

The physical side effects of oral contraceptives also seem to provide evidence against the ingestion of artificial hormones. Oral contraceptives, because of the estrogen content, tend to increase the coagulatory action of the blood and, in turn, increase the risk of thromboembolic (clotting) disorders. Studies indicate that the probability of a thrombolic stroke is about nine times greater for women taking the pill. But the probability that an individual female will develop thromboembolic trouble is small. Of every one million women taking the pill, about one hundred will be admitted to the hospital, and about five will die each year from a thrombolic stroke caused by the drug (Williams, 1974). Should the pill fail (only one pill-user in 200 who never skips the pill becomes pregnant each year) and the user become pregnant, the chemicals in the pill can cause birth defects in the fetus. Exposure to hormones during the first month of pregnancy has been linked, particularly in male infants, with defects of the limbs, such as missing fingers, toes, arms, and legs, as well as other defects (Seaman, 1975).

MARRIAGE AND DEPRESSION

Radloff (1975) found that among the married, the divorced, or the separated, women are more depressed than men. Among the single and the widowed, however, men are more depressed than women. In a study of divorced women and men with depression, Briscoe and Smith (1972) found that depressed women were more likely than men to have been depressed during the marriage. On the other hand, depressed men were more likely than women to have become depressed during the marital separation.

Although having a job outside the home tends to reduce depression among housewives, working wives are still more depressed than working husbands (Radloff, 1975). Indeed, both working wives and housewives are more depressed than working married men. The Radloff data reveal that work gives some protection to women against depression.

Depressed female workers and housewives seem to show differential outcomes of treatment. Mostow and Newberry (1975) found that, although there was virtually no significant difference in the severity and type of depression between working women and housewives at the beginning of the therapy, after three months, there were indications that working women were beginning to adjust socially. Housewives, on the other hand, reported impaired performance, disinterest, feelings of inadequacy, and economic difficulties.

A community study by Brown and his associates (1975) found

that working-class women with young children living at home had the highest rates of depression. Even with equivalent levels of stress, working-class women were five times more likely to become depressed than middle-class women (lower social status seems to increase depression for both women and men [Radloff, 1975]). Four factors were found to contribute to this class difference: loss of a mother in childhood, three or more children under age 14 living at home, absence of an intimate and confiding relationship with a husband or a boyfriend, and lack of full- or part-time employment outside of the home. The first three factors were more frequent among working-class women. General levels of satisfaction and intimacy in the relationship with the husband or boyfriend and the amount of emotional support he gave the woman in her role were important factors in preventing depression in the face of life stress. Employment outside the home seems to alleviate boredom, increase self-esteem, improve economic circumstances, and increase social contacts; thus, it can be an antidote against depression. Indeed, Weissman and Paykel (1974) found that patients who work outside the home show less impairment in work during their depression than do housewives. Many depressed women "explicitly sought jobs" to obtain "a new set of relationships and satisfactions" that proved to be therapeutic. Related to the connection between work outside the home and mental illness is the finding by Sharp and Nye (1963). In a study of first admission of mothers, they found that non-employed mothers were given a more severe diagnosis (psychosis rather than neurosis) than employed mothers.

Depression, unlike schizophrenia, does not reduce the probability of a woman getting married (Stevens, 1969). This is consistent with expectations, since men are more likely to marry a submissive and helpless depressed woman than a dominant and aggressive schizophrenic one. Marriage may, however, intensify depressed tendencies in women. Although studies indicate that the married of both sexes have the lowest rate of mental illness (Bloom, Asher, & White, 1978), this is apparently not so among depressed women (Brown & Harris, 1978). As compared with other women, single women had the lowest, whereas the separated, divorced, and widowed had the highest rate of depression. However, the difference in depression between the single and the married was found among working-class rather than among middle-class women; single middle-class women had no advantage over married middle-class women (Brown & Harris, 1978).

It has been suggested that the nature of the work of a housewife is boring and unsatisfying for the educated housewife (Gove, 1972a). Radloff (1975), however, found that, contrary to expectations, the better educated the housewife, the less depressed she tended to be. It was the woman with low education and income who was especially depressed, compared to men. It is quite possible that the educated housewife becomes less depressed because her education makes her feel more hopeful and less entrapped; she may be better equipped to find ways of entertaining herself and of occupying her mind.

Since work gives protection against depression, it is surprising that there has been a recent increase in depression among young females (Weissman & Klerman, 1977). However, depression and, particularly, self-depreciation are found to be associated with the discrepancy between educational achievement and the opportunity for work (Kleiner & Parker, 1963; Rinehart, 1968). Arnold Linsky (1969) found that when few opportunities for jobs compatible with the educational levels of females (and males) are available, the rate of hospitalization for depression is higher. With the increase in the number of educated females, the relationship between job opportunities and depression will become an important area for investigation. In fact, it has already attracted the attention of researchers in depression. Weissman and Klerman (1977) wrote: "Depressions may occur not when things are at their worse, but when there is a possibility of improvement, and a discrepancy between one's rising aspirations and the likelihood of fulfilling these wishes. The women's movement, governmental legislation, and efforts to improve educational and employment opportunities for women have created higher expectations. Social and economic achievement often have not kept pace with the promises, especially in a decreasing job market and where long-standing discriminatory practices perpetuate unequal opportunities."

Depression and Family Life

Depressed women are more impaired in their roles as spouse and mother than outside the home or in their relations with friends and the extended family (Weissman, Paykel, Siegel, & Klerman, 1971). For example, women who are employed outside the home revealed fewer significant differences from comparable nondepressed women. Depression appears to affect family relations more than the occupational role.

As compared with normals, depressed women report more problems in marital intimacy, particularly the ability to communicate with the spouse. Marital relations are "characterized by friction, poor communication, dependency and diminished sexual satisfaction" (Weissman & Paykel, 1974). Such marital problems are often enduring and do not completely disappear with the wife's improvement (Paykel & Weissman, 1973).

Depression appears to impair women's feeling about sex rather than their sexual behavior (Weissman & Paykel, 1974). Although patients reported a marked decrease in their interest in sex, differences between depressed women and normals in the frequency of sexual intercourse were not quite significant. Normals had sexual relations with their spouses about once a week, depressed patients about once every two weeks. However, Weissman and Paykel found significant differences in the quality of the sexual relations. Normal women reported fewer sexual problems, enjoyed sex more, and often initiated intercourse with their husbands. Depressed women, on the other hand, reported sexual dysfunctions and rarely initiated intercourse. A large number of these women associated their illness with past sexual misconduct and conceived of the illness as punishment for their sins.

There is an excess of psychiatric problems and referral to child guidance clinics among children of depressed mothers (Fabian & Donahue, 1956; Post, 1962). These children have a variety of symptoms, including hyperactivity and sibling rivalry. Among 131 cases of parental child murders, 71 percent of the mothers were depressed (Resnich, 1969). Adolescent children of depressed women show deviant behaviors, such as truancy, school dropout, drug abuse, theft, and promiscuity. The depressed mothers of adolescents express "anger, resentment, and intolerance" of their children's independence. They are unable to set limits to the behavior of the children and thus fluctuate between overcontrol and undercontrol, angry outbursts and withdrawal (Weissman & Paykel, 1974). These findings about children of depressed mothers do not clearly indicate whether the depression of the mother results in disturbed behavior or whether it is the other way around. It is quite possible that the mother's depression is precipitated by the behavior of her children. Similarly, lack of communication and absence of intimacy with the husband may, in fact, make women more vulnerable to depression.

We are already familiar with the unfounded belief that mothers may induce schizophrenia in their children (see Chapter 3). In contrast, Brown and his associates (1977) found that the loss of the mother before the age of 11 makes women more vulnerable to depression. However, neither the loss of the mother *after* this age nor the loss of any *other* close relatives, including the father, play any part in increasing the risk of depression in women. Brown suggested that the earlier the mother is lost, the more the child is likely to be unable to learn to master her or his environment. A sense of mastery is probably related to high self-esteem. Low self-esteem and an inability to control and master the environment, according to Brown, are crucial in the reaction of women to stressful life events in adulthood.

EXPLAINING DEPRESSION IN WOMEN

Helpless Dogs, Helpless Women, and Depression

It has been suggested in a previous section that traumatic experience, particularly the loss of the maternal role, tends to promote feelings of hopelessness and helplessness, making women vulnerable to depression. Martin Seligman (1975) has also suggested a more general theory relating traumatic experience to depression and helplessness. He noted a similarity between the behavior of dogs that were placed in an inescapable situation and given electric shocks and the behavior of depressed persons. In his original experiments, dogs were strapped into a hammock and given inescapable electric shocks that were moderately painful in intensity. These shocks were unpredictable because they were not preceded by any warning signal (such as a dimming light), and they occurred randomly in time. Twenty-four hours later, the dogs were given ten trials of signaled escape-avoidance training in a two-way shuttle box: The dogs had to jump over a barrier from one compartment into another in order to escape or avoid the shock. Shocks could occur in either compartment, so there was no place that was always safe, but the response of shuttling or jumping always led to safety. The onset of a signal began each trial, and the signal stayed on until the trial ended. The interval between the start of the signal and the shock was ten seconds. If the dogs jumped the shoulder-high barrier during this interval, the signal was terminated, and the shock was prevented. Failure to jump during the signal-shock interval led to a shock, which continued until the dog jumped the barrier. If the dog failed to jump the barrier within sixty seconds after the signal's onset, the trial was automatically ended. Seligman noticed that those dogs that had received inescapable training behaved helplessly in this situation. They first ran around frantically for about thirty seconds, and then they stopped moving, lay down, and whined quietly. Although they started by struggling a bit, they tended to give up and to accept the shock passively. This shows that when the animal has no control of a traumatic situation, its motivation to respond in the face of later trauma diminishes. Moreover, even if the animal does occasionally respond, and even if response succeeds in reducing the trauma, the animal has trouble learning to perceive or even to "believe" that the response can work any more. Similarly, Seligman (1974) suggested that the depressed patient has learned or believed that she cannot control life situations that relieve suffering or bring gratification.

The motivational deficit in depressive patients and helplessness in dogs is not quite different from the "normal" state of women. For example, housewives, because of a lack of alternatives to an inescapable aversive confinement in the home, may feel helpless. One aspect of this feeling of helplessness is that women are trained not to react by direct manipulation of the environment but by being passive and using their physical beauty and appeal. Beck and Greenberg (1974) suggested that the subjective helplessness of women parallels their objective helplessness and powerlessness in a male-oriented professional and business world. They gave the example of an educated young woman, still nourishing plans of graduate school and a career, but faced in reality with low-status tasks, such as housekeeping, child-rearing, and submissive attention to her husband's needs. Chesler (1972) believes that "depression" is the female style of responding to stress. Helplessness can be considered an intensification of normal female behaviors, such as passivity, dependence, self-depreciation, self-sacrifice, naïveté, fearfulness, and failure.

The Cognitive Approach: Depression is All in Her Mind

A style of thinking characterized by negative expectations is suggested by Beck (Beck, 1976; Beck & Greenberg, 1974) as the basis of depression. The main symptoms of depression are hopelessness and helplessness, which reflect a cognitive triad: a negative view of the self, a negative view of the world, and a negative view of the future. A depressed woman tends to perceive herself as worthless, the world as desolate, and the future as bleak, no matter what she might try to do to improve it.

Beck assumes that it is the distorted thought of persons, rather than their life situations, that is responsible for depression. When the thought represents an inaccurate appraisal of a life event, the emotion will be inappropriate or rather extreme. Beck (1976) gives the following example to illustrate his theory:

> A devoted mother who had always felt strong love for her children started to neglect them and formulated a serious plan to destroy them and then herself.

Beck suggested that in order to understand why this depressed mother would want to end her own life and that of her children, it is important to see the world through her eyes. Her thinking seems to be controlled by faulty ideas about herself and the world. She wrongly believed that she had been a failure as a mother—that she was too incompetent to provide even a minimum care and love to her children. Since it was she who should carry the blame for her presumed failure and inadequacy, she tormented herself with guilt and self-blame.

It is apparent that this theory of depression seeks the cause of depression within the person rather than in the outside environment. It ignores, for example, the life situation of the depressed female, and, in particular, it ignores the possibility that her feelings of incompetence and inadequacy may be compatible with her helpless position rather than being a figment of her imagination.

Behavioral Approach

Lewinson (1974) suggested that a low level of positive reinforcement or reward is implicated in depression. Level of reinforcement, according to this view, is a function of three factors: the number of reinforcers available in the environment, the number of activities and events that are potentially reinforcing for individuals, and the extent to which they possess the skills necessary to elicit reinforcement for themselves from the environment.

The interpretation of depression in terms of a low level of reinforcement would suggest that therapy of depressed women should attempt to increase the range of pleasurable life events as alternatives to family responsibilities. Therapy should also help women to develop skills for obtaining reinforcement from the environment. This may partly be done by increasing their low rate of activity. The evidence discussed earlier, however, suggests that only certain types of activities, particularly those relating to work outside the home, seem beneficial. Thus, encouraging a depressed woman to obtain a job outside the home is "treatment" compatible with research findings. Unfortunately, the major effort of behavior therapists has been to enforce the female to accept her sex role as a housewife and a homemaker. It is claimed that depressed housewives, through reinforcement, can be trained to accept and even to take pleasure in their boring domestic chores. Jackson (1972), for example, reported the treatment of a housewife who was reinforced for carrying out housekeeping activities, such as washing and drying dishes and dusting. Similarly, McLean (1976) assumed that any successful performance can be a powerful antidepressant. These performances may or may not involve pleasant events. This suggestion is certainly contrary to the established evidence that housework, in contrast to a job outside the home, is conducive to depression. Yet McLean went about his therapy by organizing a series of housewifely chores, including cooking and grocery shopping, to treat depressed women.

Apart from the economic independence and personal satisfaction of work outside the home, the evidence is consistent in showing that working women do less housework, while the husbands do more (Bahr, 1974). For instance, there is a "substantial decrease in the number of wives who carry sole responsibility of getting the husband's breakfast, doing the evening dishes, and straightening up the living room when company is coming. Working wives also tend to do less household repairing and do less grocery shopping by themselves" (Blood, 1963). Sharing the house chores may explain, in part, the lower rate of depression among working wives. And yet, McLean (1976) suggests that the dependent behavior of the depressed housewife is maintained by support and help from a husband and children in carrying out house chores; if she verbalizes reluctance to carry out any of her house chores, they will help her. For example, if she said, "I don't know if I feel like making supper tonight," they would say, "That's OK, Mom, we'll cook it tonight." McLean stresses the need for periodic checks to make sure that significant others do not help the housewife and thus reinforce her depressive behavior. But reinforcing the housewife for household chores in "therapy" is contrary to the evidence indicating a relationship between the role of a housewife and mental illness.

Marianne Padfield (1976) found that women, particularly those from lower-class backgrounds, improve regardless of the technique used—she used client-centered therapy and therapy based on reinforcement—when given support to handle the daily business of living. Inadequate life conditions seem to be a major source of stress for these women. They are not well equipped to raise a family and to face other marital problems. Their low income level seemed to be a deterrent to improvement in their depressions. As Padfield noted: "Constant preoccupation about sufficient income to sustain the family was a deterrent to improvement in intensity of depression. It was irrelevant to encourage acitivity if money was unavailable for distractions. It would seem that the major reinforcement of an adequate life-supporting income is a necessary ingredient to improved mental health."

SEX DIFFERENCES IN SUICIDE

The suicide ratio of men to women in the United States is about 3 to 1. Data reported in *Suicide Mortality 1950–1968* (Statistics Canada) reveal that in twenty-five countries men tend to die from suicide more often than women. The lowest rate of suicide for both sexes is in Mexico (men 1.6; women 0.9 per 100,000) and the highest is in Hungary (men 29.6; women 18.0 per 100,000). The rate of suicide among women has greatly increased in the United States in recent years, although that for men has not. Furthermore, women in psychology have a suicide rate about three times that of women in general (Williams, 1974). Similarly, the suicide rate of female physicians in the United States (33.6 per 100,000) is three to five times higher than that expected for women over 25 years old, but the rate does not differ from that of male physicians. However, female physicians commit suicide at a younger age: Almost half of the suicides by women physicians occur before age 40. In contrast, half of the suicides by male physicians occur before age 50. Single women in residency training are the most vulnerable group (Roeske, 1976). It may be that the involvement of females in the professions has contributed to the recent increase in their suicides.

Men tend to have higher rates of suicide than women among the married, single, divorced, and widowed. However, the disparity for males across marital categories is much greater than that for females. For example, for the ages twenty-five to sixty-four, single females in the United States are 47 percent more likely to commit suicide than married females, while single males are 97 percent more likely to commit suicide than married males. Similarly, the disparity for widowed and divorced males compared to married males is much greater than for females in the same categories. For instance, the suicide rate for widowed females is about twice that for married females, whereas the rate for widowed males is over four times that for married males. These findings are consistent with others on mental illness, indicating that marriage is more advantageous to males than to females, whereas being single, divorced, or widowed is more disadvantageous to males than to females (Gove, 1972b).

There are sex differences in the motives underlying suicide. Lester and Lester (1971) found that the majority of men who completed the suicidal act had lost a job or suffered a loss of income within a few years prior to the suicide. Among women, however, the loss of some personal relationship seems to play a role similar to that of a job loss among men. The Lesters felt that these findings make sense, since a man's social status is dependent on his employment and achievement, whereas a woman's standing tends to derive from her relationships with parents, a spouse, or children. That sex differences in suicide become more pronounced in old age, with male rates rising dramatically, may be due to the effect of retirement on men (Calhoun, 1977).

The tendency of male aggression to take more violent forms is reflected in the methods used to carry out suicide. Men use more dangerous methods, and thus fewer survive the suicidal act. This trend is apparent in statistics from both Britain and the United States. Violent methods, such as hanging, firearms, explosives, and cutting and piercing instruments, are more often used by men than by women. Women choose poisoning more often than men (Stengel, 1964). It appears that methods of suicide also depend, in part, on their availability and acceptance in the culture. For example, in Britain, where possession of firearms without a special license is illegal, suicides by shooting are rare; whereas they are common in the United States, since such restrictions either do not exist or are usually ignored. Since the possession and use of firearms is normally less sanctioned for women than for men, it is not surprising that women rarely use firearms to carry out the suicidal act.

Suicide may be committed in association with homicide. West (1966) found that about one-third of the murderers in Britain killed themselves after killing their victims. By the same token, a study of infanticide in Sweden has indicated that a large number of mothers who killed their children subsequently attempted suicide (Harder, 1967). Among depressed patients, those who had attempted suicide expressed more hostility during a psychiatric interview than those who had not (Paykel & Dienelt, 1971; Weissman, Fox, & Klerman, 1973).

SEX DIFFERENCES IN ATTEMPTED SUICIDE

The rates of attempted suicide are higher for women than for men in Europe and the United States. There are, however, some countries, such as Poland and India, that show the reverse tendencies. As in suicide, depression is strongly associated with attempted suicide. Ages 20 to 30, and especially 20 to 24, are the peak risk years. Rates of attempted suicide have now increased to four times what they were twenty or thirty years ago. The vast majority of these unsuccessful attempts are by drug overdose among young women (Paykel, 1976). There are also more attempters among the divorced, separated, and single (predominantly young) than among the married (Weissman, 1974).

Attempts usually take place within the context of a recent serious interpersonal conflict. Typically, this includes marital or family discord, the breakup of an intimate relationship, and the loss of personal resources. Unemployment has been found to be high among male attempters (Weissman, 1974).

The use of *drugs,* and particularly of psychotropic drugs (see Chapter 2), among attempters has substantially increased in the 1960s. Attempters using pills (a female style), as compared with those using more violent methods (a male style), had the least suicidal intent and were using the attempt to obtain help and establish communication. However, they also had the most serious physical effects, and they required medical hospitalization more frequently. Almost all those males using violent methods required involuntary psychiatric hospitalization, reflecting the greater severity of their disturbances (Weissman, 1974).

The *wrist slasher* has usually been described as an attractive, intelligent, unmarried young woman. Recently, however, it was found that wrist cutters are frequently single young men. The age rather than the sex of the wrist cutters seems to be a crucial factor because razor blades are commonly used by young persons of both sexes (Clendenin & Murphy, 1971).

It is believed that men who carry out suicidal acts generally intend to kill themselves, whereas women have something else in mind— namely, to appeal to and influence their environments. As Stengel (1964) pointed out:

> Women seem more inclined to use the suicidal act as an aggressive and defensive weapon and as a manipulator of relationships than men, probably because other means of exerting pressure, such as muscular power, are not at their disposal to the same degree as they are to men. The suicidal attempt is a highly effective though hazardous way of influencing others and its effects are as a rule more lasting than those of the physical violence that men prefer.

Chesler (1972) has also attributed the high rate of attempted suicide to the little power women have to change their environment. She considered the high rate of attempted suicide as one aspect of the "hysterical" reaction of the female—that is, her attempt to manipulate the environment by resorting to emotional and passive reaction. She pointed out that "like female tears, female suicide attempts constitute an act of resignation and helplessness to obtain secondary reward or temporary relief." The Stengel and Chesler interpretations of attempted suicide are consistent with the stereotypic view I documented in Chapter 1, depicting the female as defensive and passive and the male as aggressive and active in the face of stressful life experiences.

SUMMARY

There are approximately two depressive females to one male patient. Although it is traditionally believed that depression peaks at middle-age among females, recent studies indicate a shift in the peak to a younger group in their twenties. Symptoms of depression such as dependency, helplessness, hopelessness, passivity, and lack of self-confidence seem to be more compatible with "normal" female than male characteristics. Therefore, a depressed man is more rejected than a depressed woman; he is also considered more seriously ill. Instead of being depressed, a man may, therefore, react to stress in alternative ways such as drinking and fighting. Even when depressed, men reveal different symptoms from women: Women cry, experience self-dislike and self-depreciation; men, on the other hand, become preoccupied with physical symptoms and report weight loss, sleep disturbance, and a sense of failure.

A depressed woman is typically young, married, working-class, has three or more children under age 14, with no intimate relationship with her mate; she has usually lost her mother in childhood, and she has no job outside the home. Because a job outside the home brings both social and material satisfaction, it serves as the best antidote against female depression. Marriage, particularly among working-class women, tends to intensify depression. It seems to increase their passive, dependent, and helpless behavior. Evidence gives no support to the theory that hormonal changes during the menopause, menstruation, and childbirth are related to depression. Indeed, women who use estrogen replacement therapy should bear in mind that such therapy may not relieve their depression, but it does increase their risk of uterine cancer.

There are more men who commit suicide and more women who attempt it. Male suicide is associated with occupational stress, whereas female suicide is linked with emotional and interpersonal problems. The number of suicides among women has increased in recent years; their involvement in the professions (medicine, psychology) may have contributed to such an increase. Failure of women to complete the suicide act is partly due to the nonviolent methods they use (for instance, drugs rather than guns). It is also believed that men who carry out the suicide act by using lethal methods, intend to kill themselves. Women, on the other hand, use the suicide act to manipulate and influence others: The attempted suicide is an expression of their helplessness, powerlessness, and resignation. To save the life of women who have already carried out an unsuccessful suicide attempt, one must consider the possibility that they were serious about ending their life, because many persons who make a nonfatal suicide attempt tend to make a second successful one.

Women
and
Phobia

5

What I call the destructive anxieties are not the growth of women's minds
and powers, but quite the contrary: the pressures of society and the mass
media to make women conform to the classic and traditional image in
men's eyes. They must be not only the perfect wife, mother and homemaker, but the ever-young, ever-slim, ever-alluring object of their desires.

Marya Mannes: THE ROOTS OF ANXIETY
IN MODERN WOMAN

The phobic woman offers one of the best examples of how women
react to stress by the intensification of what are considered normal feminine characteristics, such as dependency, helplessness,
avoidance, and withdrawal from significant social and other daily
activities. Marks (1969) defined phobia as a special form of fear,
originating from the Greek word *phobos* and meaning flight, panic-
fear, or terror, that (1) is out of proportion to the demands of the
situation, (2) cannot be explained or reasoned away, (3) is beyond
voluntary control, and (4) leads to avoidance of the feared situation
(a phobia may also lead to immobilizing the person). There are two
groups of phobias. One group is associated with external stimuli
and falls into four subgroups: (1) agoraphobia, (2) social phobias,
(3) animal phobias, and (4) miscellaneous specific phobias (high

Figure 5.1 *The Shriek* by Edvard Munch (1896). Lithograph, printed in black, sheet: 20 5/8 × 15 13/16″. Collection, The Museum of Modern Art, New York. Matthew T. Mellon Fund.

places, darkness, germs, heat, storms, poison, etc.). The second group of phobias is related to stimuli that are internal to the patient and thus cannot be avoided (obsessive phobias).

FEARS OF CHILDREN AND ADULTS

A person can hardly go through childhood without some fears of real or imaginary situations. Kagan (1971) reported that females express more fears than males in infancy. They become upset by novel stimuli at an earlier age than males. A female infant under six months old is more likely than her male counterpart to cry in a strange laboratory or in an unusual situation. When a mother and infant were first situated behind a wire barrier and the mother was then signalled to put the infant on the opposite side, many one-year-old girls "froze" and began to cry. They preferred to remain close to the mother. Boys, on the other hand, were more likely to start some activity or attend to some event in the surroundings. Tennes and Lampl (1964) also found that female infants exhibit more intense fear than boys in response to strangers. Other studies, however, found no sex differences in fear of strangers, except that girls tended to display the fear at an earlier age than boys (Lewis & Brooks, 1974; Robson, Pederson, & Moss, 1969).

Kagan (1977) explained the relatively low level of fearfulness in infancy among boys by their tendency to initiate action in situations of uncertainty. Even though such action may be task-irrelevant, the activity may protect them against fear. Girls' earlier display of fear, motor inhibition, and the tendency to stay close to the mother may be due to the fact that the female is biologically precocious in relation to the male, and this may result in advanced psychological functioning. Girls therefore show earlier cognitive development and awareness of their surroundings. Their fear reaction is only an attempt to assimilate unfamiliar events or to resolve the uncertainty they generate. As Kagan (1977) noted, "The infant female may pay for her early physical precocity with more frequent bouts of fear during the first year."

A potentially fear-arousing situation that preschool children have to face is the initial settling into a group. Girls seem to cope better with this new situation; boys were found more likely to cry than girls (Blurton-Jones & Leach, 1972). Whereas boys were fearful and inhibited, girls walked more, talked more, and laughed more during the first day at nursery school (McGrew,1972). Boys settled in less well and expressed more distress than girls during the first week at a play group (Smith, 1974). Smith suggested that studies finding more fear among boys raise the question that children arriving at play groups may be a selected sample and that mothers may be more protective of girls and thus may be sending only less fearful girls to a play group.

Jean MacFarlane (1954) reported that fears tend to decrease with age for both sexes. The average percentage of fears from early childhood up to age 13 was 33.7 for boys and 25.4 for girls. Thus, girls seemed to have an advantage over boys during childhood. At age 13, however, girls had approximately five times more fears than boys. Although girls tend to have less fears than boys in play groups in childhood, most studies reveal that school phobia—refusal to go to school—is more prevalent among girls (Conger, 1977; Kessler, 1966). The peak age for school phobia in the United States and England is about 11 or 12.

Self-reports of fear in adolescence and adulthood show that females rank consistently higher than males. A study of young persons (average ages: males = 19.5 years; females = 18.7 years) indicates that, with the exception of fear of noise, which is about equal in both sexes, females exceed males in fears related to tissue damage (the prospect of surgical operation, dead animals, dead people); social-interpersonal (feeling rejected, looking foolish), animal (dogs), classical (enclosed places), and miscellaneous fears (strange places, failure, making mistakes) (Grossberg & Wilson, 1965). The prevalence of fears among women is revealed for normal persons, hospitalized patients, and patients in psychotherapy (Hersen, 1973). These sex differences emerge regardless of the kind of self-report questionnaires used.

It has been suggested that, because of social expectations, males are less likely to admit fears than females (Hersen, 1973). This explanation receives little support. For example, responses of women and men on fear schedules are not differentially affected by social desirability or by the tendency to endorse socially acceptable items (Farley & Mealiea, 1971; Geer, 1965). Most studies also do not show either a greater tendency among boys and men to lie and be defensive or a tendency among girls and women to be more candid in reporting anxiety (this evidence argues against the suggestion discussed in Chapter 1 indicating that sex differences in mental illness are due to the readiness of women to report symptoms) (Block, 1976). Nevertheless, men reveal a discrepancy between the report of fear and approaching a fear object. Whereas high-fear females showed agreement between verbal and motor responses and did not approach a small German shepherd, high-fear males, on the other hand, approached the dog (Geer, 1965). This raises the possibility that high-fear males are affected by social expectations in a real-life situation but not during a verbal report situation.

To summarize, girls are more fearful than boys in infancy, but this tendency is reversed at age 4. Studies of nursery school children and play groups indicate that boys show more fears. On the average, girls seem to have less fears throughout childhood and up to early adolescence, at which time they surpass boys. In adolescence and adulthood, studies consistently indicate a prevalence of fears among females.

TYPES OF PHOBIA

Agoraphobia

The Greek word *agora* referred to a public, open marketplace that was a social, mercantile, and political center of the city. Among the main symptoms of agoraphobia are fear of going out into the open; fears of closed places, such as elevators, theaters and churches; fears of travel by ship, train, and airplane; fears of tunnels and bridges; and fears of having hair cut or hair done and of leaving the home or of remaining alone at home (Marks, 1969, 1977).

Agoraphobia is the most prevalent kind of phobia, accounting for half of all phobic patients. On the average, 84 percent of these cases are females, of whom 89 percent are married. Among these married agoraphobics, 20 percent work and 20 percent remain at home willingly. The remaining majority of agoraphobic women are housewives who want to work but are not allowed to do so. It is this last group that has the most severe phobia. It appears that the more pressue is put on the reluctant housewife to remain at home, the more she becomes fearful of public places (Fodor, 1974).

Agoraphobia usually begins between ages 13 and 35. It may have a sudden or gradual onset, and it may last for many years or only a few days or months (Marks, 1977). On the average, agoraphobia usually develops five years after marriage in women with dependent personalities, a time when they feel more trapped in marriage, particularly when they have young children to care for (Fodor, 1974). These findings bear similarities to those discussed in Chapter 4 documenting the increase of depression among married women with young children (Brown et al., 1975).

Social Phobias

Fear and anxiety relating to social and interpersonal situations begin in adolescence when the child starts breaking off family ties. Social phobias reflect the involvement of girls and boys in social activities, such as giving a talk in public or meeting people at parties. Unlike most phobias that occur more in women than men, social phobias are equally distributed among the sexes (Marks, 1977). Fodor (1974) observed that social phobias in females tend to coincide with the stage when they are struggling to overcome family and social pressure to keep them dependent and within the feminine role. She gives the example of a woman who developed severe speech anxiety in college around the time when she was trying to assert herself by informing her parents that she no longer wanted to become a nun like her older sister.

The prospect of recovery from social phobia is quite good (Marks, 1969). Unlike agoraphobic patients, these patients appear to be relatively independent; for instance, they work or live away from home. They have not fully accepted their female dependency and nonassertiveness; social anxiety is only a symptom of their struggle to break away from feminine behavior and low status.

Although both the agoraphobic and the social anxiety patient show fear of crowds, agoraphobic fears center on being crushed, enclosed, or suffocated by a crowd rather than focusing on fears of being seen or watched by people in a crowd. It is the patient's belief that he or she is being observed that precipitates social phobia. Marks (1969) described these patients as being afraid of eating and drinking in front of others for fear their hands might shake as they hold their fork or cup or for fear they might have a lump in the throat and be unable to swallow while being watched. The victims of social anxiety may also avoid seeing people in public (in buses or in the street).

Animal Phobia and Other Specific Phobias

Although rare in adults, animal phobias tend to appear predominantly in women. In a series of twenty-three patients with animal phobia, Marks (1969) found only one man. The predominance of women seems to be even greater than in agoraphobia. Rutter and Graham (1970) observed that although animal phobias are found initially in both boys and girls, they become rare in boys as early as age 10 or 11. Other specific phobias tend to be equally distributed among the sexes. In these phobias, fear tends to be aroused by a specific stimulus or locus: heights, thunder, traffic, closed places, and the like.

Obsessive Phobias

Obsessive phobias are quite uncommon in clinical practice. Taking into consideration a large number of studies reporting sex differences in obsessions, Beech (1974) concluded that no sex is more predisposed to obsessions than the other.

Obsessions are an excessive preoccupation with unwanted thoughts, despite active resistance against their intrusion. A mother may be unable to rid herself of the idea of strangling her baby in its sleep (Marks, 1977). Obsessive thoughts are usually associated with compulsive rituals—repetitive actions some persons feel compelled to carry out against their wishes. The mother who is obsessed by the thought of killing her baby may compulsively check the house to ensure that she has removed all knives and other sharp instruments. Fears of contamination may lead to excessive washing.

Phobic patients with irrational fears reduce them by avoiding the fearful situation or object (crowds, animals). Obsessionals have fears about their own feelings, and therefore they carry these fears around with them, so to speak. Those who claim to fear dirt feel compelled to think of and look for dirt by checking the cleanest possible situations instead of avoiding them. A woman obsessed with the idea of possible injury from glass splinters would be more afraid of fragments she suspected but could not find at home than of the glass splinters she actually found and removed with her bare hands.

Obsessive phobias of harming people (fears of killing, stabbing, strangling) may lead to the avoidance of weapons. A housewife may have to hide sharp knives in her kitchen far out of reach in order to remove temptation. Mothers may need to have constant company for fear they will strangle their babies if left alone. It is, however, rare for these patients to carry out these activities. How obsessions affect the patient's life and those of the people around her is illustrated in the case of Rose (Mellet, 1974).

Rose, a 32-year-old housewife, was suffering from chronic obsessions. After the birth of her third child, she became obsessed by thoughts that safety pins might be lost in the baby's vagina; she might drop a duster into the lavatory pan and then use it, smearing furniture; she might touch the genitals of strangers; she might say "VD" in ordinary conversation or push a child in a baby carriage in front of traffic. In the morning, her anxiety was sometimes so high that she would drag at the coat of her husband, begging him to stay home when he was about to go to work, or she would call

Figure 5.2 Lady Macbeth ("Out, damned spot, out, I say!"), trying to wash out the blood, is a classic case of obsessive phobia. The Picture Collection, The Branch Libraries, The New York Public Library.

him later to come home from work. She considered these morbid thoughts as outside her control and not as part of her normal personality. They also made her extremely depressed.

Rose remembered an incident that occurred several years preceding her present illness. While she was working in an office, she had thought of passing urine and had then wondered whether the content of the lavatory pan was in the teapot on the office desk. In the hospital, she had been frightened lest she would lift her skirt and forget herself. One early symptom that might be related to her present illness was her memory of being worried about school lavatories. She remembered that she used to stay there for a long time. Also, at the age of 14, she had had a bladder infection. While she was talking to the psychologist about this infection, she feared that she would say "VD." She associated VD with lavatories. As a typist at the age of 15, she feared that she would type "VD" in the middle of a letter. This forced her to leave her job.

In the hospital, Rose was given desensitization sessions combined with group therapy, antidepressive drugs, electroconvulsive therapy (ECT), and modified narcosis (giving a sedative drug dosage where the timing is such that the patient is arousable for meals), but the treatment brought little improvement. Rose continued drug therapy for many years after her discharge.

Obsessions related to prohibited actions and temptations (torture, rape, and incest) are extremely anxiety-provoking. The patient may, however, engage in ritualistic activities (compulsions) in order to avoid the intrusion of these thoughts. The following case of a school-mistress demonstrates how rituals are used to avoid sexual thoughts:

A 47-year-old school mistress of superior intelligence, married with one daughter and with a history of 36 years of duration of compulsive thoughts and rituals. Recalls that at the age of 10, after hearing a passage from the Bible—"to blaspheme against the Holy Ghost is unforgivable"—became preoccupied with this thought. Shortly afterwards, words like "damn," "blast," "bloody" came to her mind despite all her attempts to resist them. The "blasphemous thoughts" elicited guilt and anxiety which she found could be alleviated by repeating any activity on hand a certain number of times. By the age of 13, these intrusive thoughts became of a direct sexual nature, centred on the sexual words and the idea of having sexual intercourse with the Holy Ghost. The associated anxiety continued to be allayed by performing repetitive acts, e.g., dressing and undressing, writing and rewriting, walking up and down staircases, retracing her steps.

At age 29, attended a psychiatrist for 9 months with little improvement. At 31, deteriorated and was admitted for 3 months; had ECT and drugs and left unimproved. Soon after developed a compulsive urge to kill her husband and daughter and was leucotomized at the age of 32. Two years later embarked on psychoanalysis and continued with it for 11 years. At the end of the analysis was much worse. Now not only the intruding sex words and thoughts about the Holy Ghost evoked ritualistic behavior, but also any activity with sexual meaning, e.g., shutting drawers, putting in plugs, cleaning a pipe, wiping tall receptacles, putting on stockings, eating oblong objects, doing things four times (association with four letter Anglo-Saxon words), stepping on patterns in the shape of sex organs, entering underground trains, etc. Whenever possible avoided these activities, e.g., stopped eating bananas and sausages, and her life became a "misery." For instance, it took her hours to dress or to travel short distances. Attributes this change to the psycho-analysis since in it she learned about the extent of sexual symbolization. After 2 years of supportive psychotherapy and drugs with another psychiatrist, was referred to the National Hospital to be considered for another leucotomy. This was decided against and was referred to this Department for behavior therapy in March, 1964 (Meyer, 1966).

Hypochondriasis and Illness Phobia

All of us are subject to some physical sensations, such as slight pains and aches, occasional headaches, and stomach disturbances. However, these sensations do not attract our attention, and they may pass unnoticed. To the hypochondriac patient, on the other hand, these sensations become magnified into symptoms of physical illness. The concept of hypochondriasis involves three elements: bodily preoccupation, disease phobia, and the conviction of the presence of disease. A hypochondriac patient may have one or a combination of two or even three of these elements. The most frequent complaint of hypochondriac patients involves the head and the neck, with the abdomen and chest being the second sites most involved.

The types of illness or symptoms used by hypochondriac patients seem to reflect their past experience with the illness and their previous health history. The illness may have been experienced by a parent with whom the patient identifies. Hypochondriasis in the family during childhood could make one more perceptive of bodily sensations, which might then be interpreted as signs of disease (Marks, 1977).

Hypochondriasis may also reflect worries about diseases that are fashionable in the culture. For example, Marks noted how campaigns to educate the public about tuberculosis caused many hypochondriac patients to adopt a fear of that disease. Now it is unfashionable to fear tuberculosis, whereas cancer and heart disease are much commoner worries and are more frequently seen in hypochondriac patients.

The mode of onset and the course of hypochondriasis differs in important respects between the sexes. A high proportion of male cases occur in middle age. There is commonly a history of marked but not disabling health consciousness and athleticism; these male patients have devoted many years' effort to the cultivation of bodily prowess. The symptoms are frequently focused on the heart, but they may be concerned with abdominal or genital discomfort, muscular pain and weakness, or strange feelings in the head or in the spine, for which erroneous or bizarre explanations are advanced. These anxiety symptoms are somatic in nature and, when they first occur, have an adequate physiological causation. But by the frequency of their recurrence, they promote a sense of uneasy awareness of bodily functions and an anticipation that things might go wrong (Slater & Roth, 1969).

In the female, hypochondriasis tends to have emotional justification. It may start with an actual illness that is perpetuated because of the advantages attained, such as sympathy and affection, by remaining unwell. The symptoms represent an illness with which the patient has already been made familiar. Alternatively, symptoms may be picked up by imitation, from association with other patients. Many of these female patients have been subjected to a succession of abdominal, gynecological, and orthopedic operations before referral for psychiatric advice (Slater & Roth, 1969).

In short, hypochondriasis in men reflects worries about physical well-being; in women, it is used to affect relations with others and to get sympathy and attention. He is worried about his physical strength; she uses her physical complaints to obtain more strength and more control over the environment.

Hypochondriac symptoms may take an extreme and even delusional form in depressed middle-aged women. Complaints of constipation, for example, may become exaggerated into the delusion that the bowels are entirely blocked—a belief that cannot be changed despite the daily passage of a stool. Constipation and lack of appetite may be followed by the belief that the food is rotting in the stomach (Slater & Roth, 1969). Depressed patients with hypochondriac complaints tend to be twice as likely as depressed patients without these complaints to have had a history of illness before adulthood (Kreitman, Sainsbury, Pearce, & Costain, 1965).

EXPLAINING PHOBIAS

According to psychoanalysts, a phobia symbolizes a conflict associated with repressed sexual and aggressive instincts. When the phobic is faced with a stimulus that symbolizes a conflict (that is, it represents the sexual and aggressive instincts being repressed), it arouses her or his anxiety and tension. By itself, the stimulus should normally elicit little fear; it is a fear stimulus for the phobic only because of what it symbolizes. Besides repression, displacement—a defense mechanism in which the person transfers attitudes and emotions from one object to another—is involved in phobia. For example, a girl who hates and fears her mother may displace such emotions to irrelevant objects such as cows. A cow becomes a symbol of mother; the conscious fear of a cow is equal to the unconscious fear of the mother. Similarly, a fear of open places may symbolize the unconscious fear of women of the opportunity for sexual adventures.

Behaviorists do not consider fears and phobias as symbolic of underlying conflicts but as the result of an association between a stimulus and an aversive experience. The classic example is Watson's well-known experiment with little Albert, an 11-month-old boy who was fond of animals. Watson developed a phobia for white rats in this boy by standing behind him and making a loud noise by banging an iron bar with a hammer whenever Albert reached for the beloved animal. Albert developed a phobia of white rats as a result of the association between the loud fear-producing noise and the animal. Similarly, Albert's fear generalized from the white rat to other objects with similar characteristics—white and furry (Watson & Rayner, 1920).

How a heat phobia has developed in a young woman through a traumatic experience is illustrated by Kraft and Al-Issa (1965a):

A 24-year-old female patient was suffering from heat-phobia dating back to the age of five. When she was five years old, she witnessed a fire in which the charred bodies of two children were carried out of a burning house. She was terrified by the whole event, but appeared to show remarkably little emotional reaction towards it, and subsequently forgot about it. The patient developed phobic symptoms in relation to heat almost immediately after the traumatic incident. She showed great reluctance to put her hands into warm water and washed herself in relatively cold water (about 72 degrees

Fahrenheit) which she, however, regarded as fairly warm. As a child, she was terrified of striking a match and only succeeded in doing so for the first time at the age of fourteen. She also experienced considerable difficulties in relation to drinking and eating hot foods. Later, she found that she could not touch an electric hotplate either "on" or "off," and could not use a hot iron. At the age of ten, she first realized that she avoided looking at the burns on the left side of her aunt's face, because this gave rise to anxiety. There were several other occasions when looking at burns produced a great deal of anxiety. The patient had received psychiatric treatment at various hospitals, but shock therapy and various drug combinations did not relieve the patient of the present symptoms. [The patient's treatment consisted of desensitization, which was described in Chapter 2.]

Although most psychologists reject the psychoanalytical approach to phobia, the question is whether the behavioral principles are satisfactory in explaining all phobias. In the case of heat phobia reported by Kraft and Al-Issa (1965a), it is clear that a traumatic event related to heat was discernible in the patient's life history. However, it is often difficult to detect any such event at the start of phobias (Marks, 1977). This is particularly true in the case of agoraphobia: the shops, streets, elevators, and trains have not been associated with any aversive experiences in the lives of agoraphobic women. Consider, for example, the following case, reported by Marks (1977): A woman who has agoraphobia complains that each time she waits for a bus she has "a wave of panic, breaks into a cold sweat, and wants little else than to rush back home." Just thinking about the bus stop arouses her panic. No traumatic experience associated with the bus stop was apparent. This woman has not once been attacked while waiting for the bus. Obviously, relating her phobia to a specific life event is not helpful.

Another finding incompatible with using the behavioral approach to explain phobias is that there are cases in which fears become attached to stimuli that are not directly involved in the traumatic experience. Marks (1977) gives the following example: "A four-year-old girl was playing in the park. Thinking that she saw a snake, she ran to her parents' car and jumped inside, slamming the door behind her. Unfortunately, the girl's hand was caught by the closing car door, the results of which were severe pain and several visits to the doctor. Before this she may have been afraid of snakes, but not phobic. After this experience a phobia developed, not of cars or car doors, but of snakes. The snake phobia persisted into adulthood, at which time she sought treatment from me."

Marks (1977) suggests that this case can be explained by the concept of "response preparedness," a tendency of some situations rather than others to arouse fear, regardless of prior exposure. Marks believes that these fears may be innate and that they appear to be related to special dangers that were important during the evolution of the human species. (For example, fears of snakes and heights belong to this group; writhing and jerky movements seem to frighten both monkeys and humans.)

Yet it is quite difficult to use the response preparedness models to explain the fears of agoraphobic women of going out into the street, shopping, having a hairdo, or just remaining alone at home. Phobias are more prevalent among females, and there is no reason to believe that they are more predisposed to phobias than males. Indeed, animal work reveals that males are more fearful than females (Gray, 1971b). The reversal on the human level, with more fears among females, would suggest the influence of social factors on sex differences in fearfulness.

Social Approach

Rather than explaining phobia as related to specific stimulus situations, it may be understood as a response pattern that is triggered in situations sanctioned by the culture. The phobic response pattern is characterized by avoidance, dependency and lack of assertiveness (Andrews, 1966); it can arise from early interpersonal and, in particular, familial learning situations in which avoidance and dependency are experienced as adaptive for a child. This response pattern may continue in adulthood.

In phobia, according to this view, the precipitating events only trigger a previously learned avoidant-dependent pattern. As Lazarus (1964) pointed out, "The precipitating event in Miss A's life was the minor car accident which apparently reinforced previous parental admonitions [warnings of various dangers] and led to a more complete pattern of dependency and withdrawal in terms of past learning."

It is therefore not surprising that the behavior of the phobic patient is not always related to the potential danger in the situation. Seidenberg (1972) reported a case of a married woman who complained of fear of losing her mind, fear of going out in the street and of going into stores, and fear that she might harm her three-year-old daughter: activities related to her role as a housewife. Yet she was able to work part-time as a door-to-door canvasser for a research corporation. Her relatives were alarmed by this dangerous venture because this work brought her into "inner city" districts. In contrast to her fear in supermarkets and beauty salons, she suffered no fear in this "outside" work. Her phobia is only relevant to functions associated with her sex role: "Her 'breakdown' occurred at the point when she painfully realized that without some change or correction, her future life would be a continuum of a past which was characterized by submission to authority, absence of choice, and a general exclusion and isolation from the significant stimuli of life. This woman's symptoms allowed her to separate herself from the fate of the young women with whom she grew up and who now surrounded her in the suburbs. . . . She withdrew from the role of shopper and hair-dryer captive" (Seidenberg, 1972).

How fears and phobias are related to female status is well demonstrated in "fears of success." Horner (1972) suggested that anxiety may be the price a woman has to pay for her success. Women become anxious about achieving success as a result of negative consequences, such as social rejection or the feeling of being unfeminine. Since many young women are now stepping out of their traditional domestic roles to compete with men for training and advancement in the job market, it is expected that fear of success will be intensified. Moulton (1977), for example, described professional women in therapy whose anxiety started with their promotion to executive jobs, at which time they became subject to disapproval by male coworkers. Moulton also described middle-aged women with "re-entry anxiety." These women were taking courses in continuing education or were resuming employment in order to enable them to occupy themselves or to be financially independent. In re-entering college or the job market after fifteen or twenty years as homemakers, they had to face fears about achieving independence or overcoming strongly held beliefs of intellectual inadequacy. In recent years, both career choice and career development have, indeed, become a major source of conflicts and anxiety for females (Nadelson, Notman, & Bennett, 1978).

The recent approach to phobia as a culturally learned behavior pattern would suggest that therapy should aim at changing the patient's strategies of avoidance and dependency. To counteract avoidance tendencies in an agoraphobic woman, she has to learn a whole new way of looking at threatening situations, a way that usually characterizes man in our society. Terhune (1949) described such a manly attitude: "The thrill of being afraid and daring to do in spite of the fear is one of man's greatest and most continuously rewarding experiences." Similarly, agoraphobic women can be helped not by being desensitized to the street and shops but by helping them to be assertive, self-sufficient, and independent. A typical example is a woman who was treated by Goldstein (1970) simply by being told that her anxiety was related to her nonassertiveness with her husband and her in-laws. The patient explained how her agoraphobia disappeared: "I told my husband to get out of the house—I didn't want to have anything more to do with him and I told his parents off and I feel fine."

Finally, it is quite possible that what is considered phobias among women may not be irrational fears but appropriate reactions to real dangers. In examining the fears of black women (which are significantly higher than those of white women), Warheit, Holzer, and Arey (1975) found that these fears are an accurate description of real-life situations in which these women live: Blacks are more often subjected to bodily harm and homicide than whites. It is therefore realistic of them to fear strangers, and to be frightened of the possibility of injury. The fears of women in agoraphobia (fears of going out or of being alone) may be related to the high risk of being sexually assaulted and abused by men (see Chapter 11). It appears that the whole life situation of the female should be considered in explaining excessive fears and anxieties.

Marriage and Phobia

The relationship between phobia and interpersonal relations is well illustrated by women who develop their phobias after marriage. Symonds (1971) described women who had been active, independent, and self-sufficient before marriage, but whose marital lives seemed to have the opposite effect on them. Their active social and occupational life outside the home was replaced by fears of traveling, crowds, and social gatherings. Symonds gave the case of Mrs. M., a professional woman who complained of fear of traveling or of being alone. She developed her symptoms just a year after marriage. The background of Mrs. M.'s phobia was characterized by her submission to the irrational demands of her husband. For example, he had a fear of germs, and he had insisted that they wear masks until the baby was eighteen months old. He would not allow anyone to baby-sit for the child, so they were forced to take him everywhere. He did not trust restaurants, and he would never eat out or allow the child to eat out.

Although the marriage situation may precipitate agoraphobia, many housewives acquire their fears before marriage. However, agoraphobia may be so compatible with the housewife role that it is hardly noticed by the parties concerned. Eric Berne (1967) noted that fears of public places are not expressed simply because a woman yields to her restrictive role as a housewife and remains confined to the home but that they are part of playing the house-wife game with friends or a spouse. Berne argued that agoraphobia may only be an expression of the "If it weren't for you" game often played by couples. He gives the case of Mrs. White, who con-tinuously complained to the psychiatrist as well as to her friends that her husband was restricting her social activities. According to Mrs. White, Mr. White was so restrictive that she was not even allowed to learn to dance, something she had always loved to do. Through the successful assertive training of this woman in therapy, the husband became less sure of himself and more compliant to her wishes. Mrs. White was now able to engage in different social activities. She joined dancing classes, but only to find out that she was scared of dance floors. Similar social activities met with the same fate, bringing out her morbid fears and anxieties. Mar-riage seems to have enabled her to complain that she could do all sorts of things if it weren't for him. Berne suggested that the husband was, in fact, performing a very real service for his wife by forbidding her to do something she was deeply afraid of and by preventing her from even becoming aware of her fears. Briefly, the case of Mrs. White demonstrates how the marital situation reinforces a phobia acquired earlier by the housewife.

In the treatment of female agoraphobia, improvement may not be welcomed by the husband (Hafner, 1977). Many husbands seem to adapt to the phobias of their wives, and recovery can have an adverse effect on them. Hafner noted that, in the group he studied, improve-ments in the wives' phobic conditions resulted in increased self-dissatisfaction and hostility on the part of the husbands. In the follow-up of these cases, he noted:

One husband attempted suicide about four months after the treatment. He said that he did so because since his wife's recovery he had felt useless and inadequate: she was no longer almost totally dependent on him in the way she had been while agoraphobic. Two husbands became depressed when the focus of dissatisfaction within their marriage shifted back from the wives' agoraphobia to their own sexual difficulties, which they were unable or unwilling to discuss. In four husbands (including the one who attempted suicide) their wives' recovery re-awakened abnormal jealousy which had lain dormant as long as the wives had been unable to go out alone; this led to unpleasant arguments and markedly increased marital disharmony, which the wives attempted to reduce by partially resuming their agoraphobic behaviour (Hafner, 1977).

Wives may also adapt to the phobias of their husbands; the recovery of the husband may be troublesome for the wife. In a follow-up of a male case of traffic phobia treated by Kraft and Al-Issa (1965b), it was noted that although the patient remained symptom-free, his wife contacted them complaining of anxiety and phobic symptoms. She found that she could not tolerate his new level of adjustment and wished that he might have another accident. In fact, she became so desperate that she thought very seriously of separation. Kraft and Al-Issa noted that, although the wife's complaints could well be related to other factors, it was surprising that the appearance of her symptoms should coincide so closely with the successful treatment of her husband. There was also a striking similarity between the symptoms of both wife and husband—her fear of traveling alone seemed to closely parallel his fear of riding a bicycle in traffic. As treatment was relatively short, and since it induced rapid changes in the husband's behavior, it had brought about important repercussions on the patient's social environment. It is quite possible that the wife had adjusted to her husband's phobic symptoms by being sympathetic and protective toward him, but cure of the husband might well have brought about a breakdown in her adjustment. This case, as well as others where one member of the family is phobic, indicates that phobia is not only limited to a circumscribed stimulus but that it also involves the whole interpersonal relationship with other members of the family.

SUMMARY

Similar to depression discussed in Chapter 4, phobia may illustrate how women react to stress by the intensification of what are considered "normal" feminine characteristics such as dependency, helplessness, avoidance, and withdrawal from significant social and other daily activities. During childhood, there are no sex differences in fears and anxieties. However, during adolescence and adulthood, females surpass males in almost all kinds of fears. Agoraphobia, which accounts for half of phobic patients, is most common among married women. Many of its symptoms are related to the housewife's activities: Fear of shopping, fear of going to the hairdresser, and fear of staying alone at home. Animal phobia, which is equally common among girls and boys in childhood, is found almost exclusively among females in adolescence and adulthood.

Obsessive ideas and compulsive actions seem to occur equally among women and men. Again the female symptoms seem to be related to her role as a mother and a homemaker: Thoughts of harming and killing her baby may lead to hiding sharp knives to avoid such temptation; obsession with dirt usually results in continuous rituals of cleaning and dusting. Female obsessive fears of illness (hypochondriasis) seem to have emotional justification; they may start with a sickness that is perpetuated because of sympathetic and affectionate advantages enjoyed by the woman. In males, however, fears of illness reflect worries about physical health during middle-age (the heart, the stomach, the head, the genitals, and so on).

Psychoanalytical theory considers phobias to be symbolic of unconscious sexual and aggressive conflicts. Behavioral theory, however, traces the origin of phobias to traumatic experiences associated with the object of phobia. Unfortunately, the unconscious conflicts suggested by psychoanalytical theory are not open to direct observation and, thus, their existence cannot be investigated and confirmed. Behavioral theory may, however, explain some phobias (fear of the dog that bit you), and yet it may not explain female fears. For example, women usually develop agoraphobia after marriage without any traumatic experiences associated with streets, shops, elevators, or traffic. It is quite possible that the agoraphobic response, which is characterized by avoidance, dependency, and lack of assertiveness, is compatible with the housewife role: She is not expected to have an active public life. (We noted in Chapter 2 that professionally successful women who reject a phobic pattern of behavior are labeled "castrating" by men.) Many of the fears reported by women may not be irrational reactions, but appropriate responses to real danger. I note in Chapter 11 that the proba-bility of a female being sexually assaulted and abused is very high. It is, therefore, not surprising that they would report fear of strang-ers and fear of injury.

Women
and
Hysteria

6

The majority of the ancients and almost all followers of the other sects have made use of ill-smelling odors (such as burnt hair, extinguished lamp wicks, charred deer's horn, burnt wool, burnt flock, skins, stems, and rags, castoreum with which they anoint the nose and ears, pitch, cedar resin, bitumen, squashed bed bugs, and all substances which are supposed to have an oppressive smell) in the opinion that the uterus flees from evil smells. Wherefore they have also fumigated with fragrant substances from below, and have approved of suppositories of spikenard [and] storax, so that the uterus fleeing the first-mentioned odors, but pursuing the last-mentioned, might move from the upper to the lower parts.

Soranus of Epherus: GYNECOLOGY, circa 130 A.D.

The prototype of the "hysterical" woman is the farmer's wife. One day, she wakes up but finds out that she cannot walk or talk. There is now not a single thing she can do. She is no longer milking the cows, feeding the animals, or doing the cooking and washing. An exploited worker, she is now on strike. She has decided, presumably unconsciously, to use body language to express herself to her tyrant husband. For many years, she has been doing things for him or with him, but it is now all over. The slave driver has forced her into illness.

Conversion hysteria is diagnosed where there is a body dysfunction without a known organic illness. It is assumed that the emotional problem is converted into physical symptoms. These symptoms range from ordinary pains and aches to paralysis, convulsions (seizures), or even blindness and deafness. Although the dramatic reaction of the farmer's wife used to be familiar to psychiatrists and physicians in the past, it is now rarely heard of. In addition to the hysterical paralysis of the farmer's wife, other forms of hysterical behavior seem to be disappearing in this century:

> . . . Behavior that includes "kicking about" and "waving the arms and legs" is met with distaste and lack of sympathy and is tolerated at best only among shrieking mobs of teen-aged girls in response to their current idols. . . . Unacceptable today would be the fainting ladies of the Victorian period, partly because they would altogether fail to evoke any sympathetic response in their social environment and partly because the skill of fainting gracefully has almost disappeared. With the increasing awareness of conversion reactions and the popularization of psychiatric literature, "the old-fashioned" somatic expressions of hysteria have become suspect among the more sophisticated classes, and hence most physicians observe that obvious conversion symptoms are now rarely encountered and, if at all, only among the uneducated of the lower social strata (Veith, 1965).

Hysterical reaction in its milder forms is, however, still with us. Instead of extreme behavior, such as convulsions, blindness, or paralysis, hysteria may be expressed as vague pains or discomforts in some parts of the body. They may not be totally incapacitating, but they do interfere with the person's ability to follow normal activities.

"Hysteric," like the labels "neurotic" or "schizophrenic," has pejorative connotations in psychiatry and in public use. The so-called hysterical woman may be described as emotionally immature, excitable, shallow, and, often, demanding and seductive in interpersonal relationship (Coleman, 1964). Psychiatrists also use the awful label "histrionic" to describe female clients. This is a subcategory of hysteria, listed in the official *American Psychiatric Association's Diagnostic and Statistical Manual* as "Hysterical personality, histrionic style." Her personality typifies stereotypes of the seductive female. Histrionics are described as "vain, egocentric individuals, displaying labile and excitable but shallow affectivity. Their attention-seeking and histrionic behavior may encompass lying and pseudologia phantastica [weaving fantastic stories]. They are conscious of sex and appear provocative" (Brody & Sata, 1967). Taylor (1966) described the histrionic woman as temperamental and ostentatious. Although she is extroverted and charming socially, her behavior is tainted with artificiality and insecurity. She is flirtatious and sexually attractive, but she is often unable to react with sexual emotions. She tends to attract many victims, but these men "have to content themselves with a promise of sexual intimacy that never materializes, or, if it does, is a cold and heartless affair" (Taylor, 1966). Taylor also described a "hysterical spite reaction" directed against those with whom histrionic women were once in love, such as employers, doctors, or psychotherapists. This reaction would consist of emotional scenes, paramnesia (distortion or falsification of memory), and pathological lying.

INCIDENCE OF HYSTERIA

In one study carried out in a general hospital, there were four women to one man among a group of patients discharged with a diagnosis of hysteria (Lewis & Berman, 1965). Psychiatrists who work in general hospitals consistently report more hysterical symptoms than their colleagues with a more limited specialist experience in the same institutions (Mayou, 1975).

It is difficult to know the exact rates of hysteria. It is quite possible that many persons with hysteria end up in the general practitioner's clinic and the surgeon's operating room rather than in the psychiatric clinic. For example, Pauline Bart (1968) compared women who entered a neurology service but who were discharged with psychiatric diagnoses with women entering a psychiatric service of the same hospital. She found that 52 percent of the psychiatric patients on the neurology service had had a hysterectomy, as compared with only 21 percent on the psychiatric service. This study shows that, although the neurological patients were expressing psychological distress through physical symptoms, they were treated by the use of surgical procedures. It is also noted by Pflanz (1976) that there is a high rate of appendectomy for girls just after menarche. Again, general abdominal complaints by young women often lead physicians to the diagnosis of appendicitis and to appendectomy (Pflanz, 1976). Moreover, what are considered hysterical symptoms may only reflect the fact that women in general tend to report physical symptoms more than men (Brodman, Erdman, Lorge, & Wolff, 1953; Phillips & Segal, 1969).

Throughout history, hysteria has been considered a female disease, but in both World Wars, large numbers of male hysterics were reported among servicemen. Whenever a predominance of male hysterics is found, they are usually considered as compensation cases (different forms of so-called compensation neuroses, such as blindness and other disabilities, are adopted by men to collect insurance or pensions), hypochondriasis or malingering[1] (Buss, 1966; Chodoff & Lyons, 1958).

Anne Seiden (1976) has observed similar sexism among physicians and psychiatrists where ill-defined body complaints are more likely to be called "hysteria" in women, whereas comparable symptoms in men are more likely to be called "hypochondriasis" (referring literally to chest pain). She noted that this bias is reflected in physical examinations, during which male physical complaints are taken more seriously. The average adult patient visiting any physician's office with almost any complaint is likely to have the heart and lungs examined (thus detecting evidence of the prime killers of middle-aged men), while the average woman, unless she comes with specific complaints related to these organs, is much less likely to receive thorough breast and pelvic examinations (which might detect cancer, the prime killer of middle-aged women).

Pauline Bart (1968) noted that it is poor and ignorant women who are more likely than their better off sisters to be diagnosed as hysterical. Bart studied women between ages 40 and 59 who were admitted to the neurological service and who emerged with a psychiatric diagnosis, usually of hysteria. These women tended to come from poor, rural areas where they do not have available a "psychiatric vocabulary of discomfort." They experienced themselves as physically ill as a way of expressing psychological distress. A similar group

---

[1]Physicians seem to consider both hysterics and malingerers as "liars" who report physical symptoms with no organic basis. However, the "hysteric," who is usually a female, does not know that she is lying; she is, therefore, described as both irrational and insane. The male malingerer, on the other hand, is assumed to know that he is lying; his behavior is, therefore, considered both rational and sane.

of women who contacted the psychiatric service and expressed their distress in psychiatric rather than physical terms were urban residents of higher social status.

VARIETIES OF HYSTERICAL REACTION

One immediate result of the hysterical reaction of the farmer's wife is to enable her to avoid the drudgery on the farm and at home. A hysterical reaction may also serve as an avoidance response in other situations. For example, avoidance of sexual intercourse is thought to be the cause of vaginal anesthesia, a hysterical symptom that might be involved in orgasmic dysfunction. This anesthesia is usually present with some sexual partners but not with others (this has its parallel in men who suffer from phallic anesthesia with some partners but not with others or only during intercourse but not when masturbating). Notice how disabilities in hysteria are not consistent in all situations but are only selectively shown by the patient.

An extreme avoidance reaction is the development of a trance in a dangerous and fear-arousing situation. Women suspected of witchcraft in the Middle Ages went into a trance in order to avoid torture and humiliation, and some even developed insensitivity to pain (analgesia) or touch (anesthesia). Female singers may develop aphonia, a partial paralysis of the muscles of the vocal cords. They remain in a state of "my voice is gone" while they are on stage. Why does a singer who is making a living out of singing have a desire to lose her voice and, in fact, develop hysterical aphonia? Clearly, female singers who develop aphonia are ambivalent about their occupation, and the symptoms may serve as an escape from the singing situation, which is apparently aversive and anxiety-arousing (Taylor, 1966).

Hysterical symptoms are sometimes designed not to avoid a situation but to fulfill a strong desire, such as having a child, which can bring about hysterical symptoms mimicking pregnancy: amenorrhoea and an enlargement of the abdomen and breasts, as in pregnant women. Doctors may be deceived, particularly when the simulation of pregnancy extends to normal labor. These women may narrowly escape Caesarean operations.

We must emphasize again that not only women but any person may use an hysterical reaction to deal with stress. Take, for example, the case of a 40-year-old man described by Brady and Lind (1961): It was the wife who was now the strong force in the family, and the man had to depend on her for making important decisions. He was also exposed to constant harrassment from both his wife and his mother-in-law. One day, as he was with the family shopping for Christmas, he suddenly became blind—that is to say, hysterically blind. Thus, the use of illness behavior in hysteria provides both sexes with an escape from unpleasant and distasteful situations. It may also enable them to fulfill some of their hopes and dreams; in the next section, I discuss how selective forgetting can help to avoid unpleasant life experiences and to achieve a wish-fulfilling fantasy.

Dissociative Reactions

Hysteria may sometimes manifest itself by blocking off certain life experiences from memory or conscious recognition. People may forget their names, their ages, and their places of residence. They may not be able to recognize relatives and friends. They may sometimes wander away from home but, after a period of time ranging from weeks to many years, suddenly recover and start wondering how they got into their present situation. These persons cannot remember what happened during this period of amnesia (loss of memory). When amnesia is involved in an hysterical reaction, it is labeled dissociative reaction.

We sometimes try to forget unpleasant experiences, but the hysteric tends to repress the whole stressful situation, including certain aspects of personality. The person uses "forgetting" as an avoidance response or as an escape from a situation that is no longer tolerable. Masserman (1961) described such a situation in the case of Mrs. Bernice L. This housewife substituted an intensely desirable way of life, personified by Rose P., who used to be an intimate friend, for her unhappy present life:

> Bernice L., a forty-two-year-old housewife, was brought to the Clinics by her family, who stated that the patient had disappeared from her home four years previously, and had recently been identified and returned from R., a small town over a thousand miles away. On rejoining her parents, husband and children she had at first appeared highly perturbed, anxious, and indecisive. Soon, however, she had begun to insist that she really had never seen them before, that her name was not Bernice L.—but Rose P.— and that it was all a case of mistaken identity; further, she threatened that if she were not returned to her home in R. immediately, she would sue the hospital for con-

spiracy and illegal detainment. Under treatment, however, the patient slowly formed an adequate working rapport with the psychiatrist, consented to various ancillary anamnestic procedures such as amytal interviews and hypnosis, and eventually dissipated her amnesias sufficiently to furnish the following history:

The patient was raised by fanatically religious parents, who despite their evangelical church work and moralistic pretenses, accused each other of infidelity so frequently that the patient often questioned her own legitimacy. However, instead of divorcing each other, the parents had merely vented their mutual hostility upon the patient in a tyrannically prohibitive upbringing. In the troubled loneliness of her early years the patient became deeply attached to her older sister, and together they found some security and comfort; unfortunately, this sister died when the patient was seventeen and left her depressed and unconsolable for over a year. After this, at her parents' edict, the patient entered the University of A. and studied assiduously to prepare herself for missionary work. However, during her second semester at the University, she was assigned to room with an attractive, warm-hearted and gifted girl, Rose P., who gradually guided the patient to new interests, introduced her to various friendships, and encouraged her to develop her neglected talent as a pianist. The patient became as devoted to her companion as she had formerly been to her sister, and was for a time relatively happy. In her Junior year, however, Rose P. became engaged to a young dentist, and the couple would frequently take the patient with them on trips when a chaperone was necessary. Unfortunately, the patient, too, fell 'madly in love' with her friend's fiancé, and spent days of doubt and remorse over her incompatible loves and jealousies. The young man, however, paid little attention to his fiancé's shy, awkward and emotionally intense friend, married Rose P. and took her to live with him in Canada. The patient reacted with a severe depression, the cause of which she refused to explain to her family, but at their insistence, she returned to the University, took her degree, and entered a final preparatory school for foreign missionaries.

On completion of her work she entered into a loveless marriage with a man designated by her parents and spent six unhappy years in missionary outposts in Burma and China. The couple, with their two children, then returned to the United States and settled in the parsonage of a small midwest town. Her life as a minister's wife, however, gradually became less and less bearable as her husband became increasingly preoccupied with the affairs of his church, and as many prohibitions of the village (e.g., against movies, recreations, liberal opinions and even against secular music) began to stifle her with greater weight from year to year. During this time the patient became increasingly prone to quiet, hazy reminiscences about the only relatively happy period she had known—her first two years in college with her friend

Rose P.—and these years, in her daydreaming gradually came to represent all possible contentment. Finally, when the patient was thirty-seven, the culmination of her disappointments came with the sickness and death of her younger and favorite child. The next day the patient disappeared from home without explanation or trace, and her whereabouts, despite frantic search, remained unknown to her family for the next four years.

Under treatment in the Clinics, the patient recollected that, after a dimly remembered journey by a devious route, she finally reached A., the college town of her youth. However, she had lost all conscious knowledge of her true identity and previous life, except that she thought her name was Rose P. Under this name she had begun to earn a living playing and teaching the piano, and was so rapidly successful that within two years she was the assistant director of a conservatory of music. Intuitively, she chose friends who would not be curious about her past, which to her remained a mysterious blank, and thereby eventually established a new social identity which soon removed the need for introspection and rumination. Thus the patient lived for years as though she were another person until the almost inevitable happened. She was finally identified by a girlfriend acquaintance who had known both her and the true Rose P. in their college years. The patient at first sincerely and vigorously denied this identification, resisted her removal to Chicago, where her husband was now assigned, and failed to recognize either him or her family until her treatment in the Clinics penetrated her amnesia. Fortunately, her husband proved unexpectedly understanding and cooperative, and the patient eventually readjusted to a fuller and more acceptable life under happily changed circumstances (Masserman, 1961).

A dramatic version of memory loss is reported in the rare cases of multiple personality. Typically, the person has two or more personalities that alternate—within minutes or years. These personalities may reflect an exaggerated version of conflicts and ambivalence in the normal personality of the individual. It is not unusual that, when the normal personality is conformist, the other personality takes the other extreme of nonconformity. One well-known case of multiple personality is that of Eve White and has been reported by Thigpen and Cleckley (1957). Eve White, a 25-year-old woman, complained of severe and blinding headaches, often followed by blackouts. Her history showed serious marital problems, which were followed by divorce from her husband. Added to the stress of marriage were financial problems that forced Eve to live with grandparents, away from where she worked. In therapy, she gave the impression of a sad, retiring, conventional, and passive person, trying to deal with personally frustrating situations. In one session, however, she was seized by a sudden pain, and she put her hands to her head. Thigpen and Cleckley reported the transformation in her personality as follows:

> After a tense moment of silence her hands dropped. There was a quick, reckless smile and, in a bright voice that sparkled, she said, "Hi there Doc!" . . . There was in the newcomer a childishly daredevil air, an erotically mischievous glance, a face marvelously free from the habitual signs of care, seriousness, and underlying distress, so long familiar in her predecessor. This new and apparently carefree girl spoke casually of Eve White and her problems, always using she or her in every reference, always respecting the strict bound of a separate identity. When asked her own name, she immediately replied, "Oh, I'm Eve Black" (Thigpen & Cleckley, 1957).

At the end of the therapy and after the recall of an early traumatic experience in which her mother had forced her to kiss her dead grandmother, a new personality emerged. This personality was an integration and a compromise between the two separate personalities of Eve White and Eve Black. She called herself Evelyn, which was originally Eve's full name. Later, Evelyn remarried and was able to establish a stable family life.

Both Bernice L. and Evelyn were suffering from intolerable life situations. Both of them had a strong desire for an alternative lifestyle. Bernice L. rejected the role of a housewife and traveled to her old college town to impersonate Rose P. and to start a new life. Evelyn, on the other hand, was able to take short respites from a serious, guilt-ridden, introverted personality through another sensuous, care-free extroverted personality.

FACTORS IN HYSTERIA

Hysteria and Female Sexuality

The word "hysteria" itself implies that it is a female rather than a male disturbance. The label is derived from the Greek word "hystera," meaning womb. In the past, the womb was considered the source of sexual desires in women, and it was thought that sexual frustration might cause its movement. It was believed that the sexually frustrated uterus, while wandering all over the body, blocks breathing passages and causes distress. Therefore, hysterical young girls were usually advised to get married. If this failed, they were encouraged to produce children.

Although the sexuality theory of hysteria had been rejected as early as the second century by Galen, the belief in a relationship between sexual frustration and psychiatric symptoms in general and hysteria in particular survived for a long time. Taylor (1966), for instance, observed that sexual intercourse has often been recommended not only for hysteria but also for the treatment of other illnesses (see p. 63, "Sex with Patients in Therapy").

The relationship between sexual difficulties and, particularly, traumatic seduction and hysteria was also stressed by Freud in his publication, in 1896, of a paper entitled "The Aetiology of Hysteria." He based his conclusions on eighteen fully analyzed cases, all of whom had been seduced. Freud considered the crucial age of seduction to be three or four. Seduction at a later age, at eight or ten, might not lead to hysteria. He divided his cases into three groups, according to the source of sexual excitement. First, the child may be assaulted and abused by a stranger against the child's will. By far the largest number of cases formed a second group where an attendant (a maid, a nurse), a parent, or a relative initiated the child into sexual intercourse and maintained this relationship for some time. Sexual relations between children of both sexes, mostly between brothers and sisters, form the third group. Hence, the psychiatric label "conversion hysteria," as first used by Freud, indicated that the individual had converted her sexual conflicts into physical symptoms.

Psychological and Social Factors

Although all hysterical persons have the common characteristic of physical symptoms that bear superficial similarity to organic disease but have no underlying physical basis, the cause is not exclusively sexual. Let us think again about the farmer's wife. Initially, she found herself in a stressful and unpleasant situation. Her desire to avoid this situation was thwarted by a lack of alternatives to being a housewife. Illness presented one available solution to her problem. As her stress continued, physical symptoms started to appear. At this stage, she became less aware of the relationship between her symptoms and her life problems. Her original wish to be sick gradually became more difficult to identify. Through autosuggestion, her desire to be ill led to a conviction that she was truly ill. (The appearance of physical symptoms, particularly the dramatic ones, must, however, require an exceptional power of autosuggestion.) The conviction that one is ill is called hypochondriasis. The aches and pains of the hypochondriac person are subjective; there are no objective physical symptoms. In hysteria, however, the subjective conviction of the patient is supported by objective symptoms.

Many of the women described by Freud and other psychoanalysts as similar to the farmer's wife have conflicts related to their feminine roles. When a woman finds herself trapped, illness may be the only escape from or avoidance of stress. A classical example is the case of Anna O., who was treated by Breuer and Freud (1955). Anna O., at the age of 21, had to nurse her ill father. The physical and emotional energy she invested in him affected her health, and she had to give up her nursing duties. She developed a squint, a severe disturbance of her vision, and a paralysis of the muscles at the front of the neck. Freud explained her symptoms as symbolic of a sexual conflict related to incestuous cravings for her father. However, Thomas Szasz (1974) has given an alternative interpretation to these hysterical symptoms:

> Anna O. thus started to play the hysterical game from a position of distasteful submission: she functioned as an oppressed, unpaid, sick-nurse, who was coerced to be helpful by the very helplessness of a sick person and by her particular relationship to him. The women in Anna O's position were—as are their counterparts today, who feel similarly entrapped by their small children—insufficiently aware of what they valued in life and of how their own ideas of what they valued affected their conduct. For example, young middle-class women in Freud's day considered it their duty to take care of their sick fathers. . . . Today, married women are generally expected to take care of their own children; they feel that they are not supposed to delegate this task to others.

Szasz goes on to emphasize that the basic conflict of Anna O. was between a wish to be a good daughter who should take care of her father and a wish to be an independent person who wanted a family of her own.

Illness behavior and bodily dysfunction are not desired by most people because they are against survival in the world at large. However, the reaction of others to sick persons may sometimes perpetuate this behavior. When life is made easy for the invalid, it is not surprising that people continue to behave so when they are no longer ill. This may begin as a simple malingering, but it may become hysterical "illness." In hysteria, the person is not looking for medical treatment but is, perhaps, asking for affection or attention from others. The farmer's wife, for example, may be telling her husband that she cannot go on functioning in the house and on the farm unless she gets some help. One might ask why she does not use words instead of body language to communicate with her husband. Szasz (1974) provides an answer:

> The point is that when some persons in some situations cannot make themselves heard by means of ordinary language—for example, speech or writing—they may try to make themselves heard by means of protolanguage, for example, weeping or "symptoms." Others in other situations may try to overcome this obstacle in exactly the opposite way, that is, by shifting from ordinary language spoken in a normal tone of voice to ordinary language spoken in a shout or in a threatening tone. Obviously, the weak tend to use the former strategy, and the strong the latter. When a child cannot get his mother to listen, or a wife her husband, each might try tears; but when a mother cannot get her child to listen, or a husband his wife, each is likely to shout.

Hysterical behavior seems to be closely associated with a lack of legitimate power to achieve one's goals. Persons who adopt illness behavior have few alternatives for success in changing their environment. Thus it is not only women but also other low-status individuals (children, the uneducated, lower-class persons, and the oppressed) who may resort to hysterical reactions (Bart, 1968; Szasz, 1974; Lewis, 1976).

Hysterical Reactions: Non-Western Style

That hysterical reactions are more prevalent among females in both Western and non-Western cultures would suggest common sociocultural factors related to the development of these disturbances. As in the West, hysterical behavior among non-Western females appears to be related to their sexual status in society.

One hysterical disturbance that frequently afflicts Eskimo females in the arctics is *piblokto* (Parker, 1962). In *piblokto,* a woman starts screaming, sobbing, making wild gesticulations, and running out on the ice naked—the attack usually ends in weeping. Parker suggested that this reaction is related to the low status of Eskimo females. He noted that *piblokto* is particularly common among women who are abused or rebuffed by their husbands. As compared with her Western sister, the Eskimo female is not in a very enviable position. According to Parker, her role carries with it more disabilities and less prestige than that of a man: She has little or nothing to say about whom she marries and, during marriage, her sexual potential is considered as the property right of her husband (it is not unusual for Eskimo husbands to exchange wives for certain periods or to permit another man to have sexual access to their wives without their consent).

Another reaction, which is mainly prevalent among lower-class Malaysian females in Southwest Asia, is *latah* (Murphy, 1976). It is characterized by a high level of suggestibility, an irresistible impulse to imitate the actions and words of others, and a strong startle or fear reaction—the *latah* jumps violently, freezes, utters a cry, and, very commonly, shouts obscene exclamations. Clearly, this reaction is related to ambivalence with respect to submissive behavior (Aberle, 1952). In *latah,* the female is almost completely resigning herself to the guidance and suggestions of others (Murphy, 1976). Her extreme passivity and hypersuggestibility may be considered as an intensification of what is considered a "proper" female behavior in the West (see Chapter 1).

Finally, "epidemic" hysteria is reported, mostly among young girls, in both Western and non-Western cultures (Sirois, 1974; Teoh & Tan, 1976). Teoh and Tan described such an outbreak of hysteria among Malaysian adolescent girls in a boarding school. Among the behaviors shown by these girls are hyperventilation—rapid, deep breathing—screaming, and complaining that they are seeing ghosts and devils. Such behaviors are not unlike those of hysterical persons in the West; Teoh and Tan depicted the Malaysian girls as rather immature, seductive, sentimental, and superficial.

SUMMARY

Hysterical persons are not ill persons. They are only adopting illness behavior in order to communicate with their social environment. In dealing with these persons, two questions must be asked. First, what are the learning conditions that bring about the simulation of symptoms of physical illness? I emphasized the reward value of illness. All societies make life comfortable for the ill person. Alternative be-havior may also be punished. Thus, individuals who are punished excessively for talking may stop talking altogether and use physical symptoms to express themselves. Second, what is the meaning of a physical symptom to a particular person? Is it used to escape, to avoid, or just to have more control of a situation? Women, and par-ticularly housewives, have few alternative roles. Being trapped into a limited role would explain the flight into compensatory, wish-fulfilling, and amnesic roles or into the sick role. Hysterical reac-tion may be temporarily eliminated by hypnosis and suggestion, but, as a response style, it is expected to be repeatedly used unless the am-bivalence and conflicts involved in the life of the female are resolved.

Sex
and the Woman

part three

Life plays a dirty trick on women. . . . The men think you're gorgeous when you're too young to know anything about life. How well I remember how hard it was to take any interest in my husband when I had been changing diapers all day. Now I have much more time and interest for sex, but my husband is the one who's beat. He does tax returns to make extra money on the side—I know he feels like rolling over and going to sleep at the end of the day.

Susan Jacoby: "WHAT DO I DO FOR THE NEXT 20 YEARS?"

The
Sexual
Woman

7

Sexuality has always been relatively controlled in all societies. Female sexuality is, however, more subject to this control than male sexuality. Many myths have characterized the understanding of the sexual response of women by psychologists and other professionals. Consider, for example, the psychoanalytical belief that female sexuality is passive, a belief entirely based on reports of inhibited patients from middle-class pre-war Viennese society. In contrast to the psychoanalytical view, our present knowledge is based on Masters and Johnson's meticulous observations of the different stages of female sexual response.

THE FEMALE SEXUAL RESPONSE

In a microscopic exploration aided by physiological measures, Masters and Johnson (1966) noted that the first stage in female sexual response is the *excitement phase*. Its first sign is lubrication (the moistening of the vagina with a lubricating fluid) within 10 to 30 seconds after the onset of sexual stimulation. The *clitoris*, which is located just above the entrance to the vagina, increases in size (like

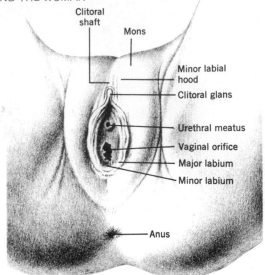

Figure 7.1 Female genitalia. From Nason and Dehaan, *The Biological World,* New York: John Wiley & Sons, Inc., 1973.

Figure 7.2 Male genitalia. From Nason and Dehaan, *The Biological World,* New York: John Wiley & Sons, Inc., 1973.

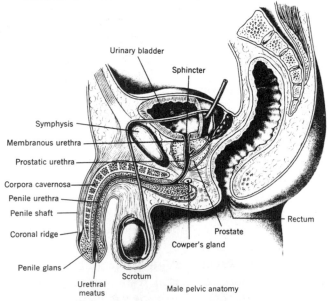

the male penis, the clitoris has a shaft with a bulb, the glans, at the tip). The breasts begin to swell, and the nipples become erect. As erotic tension increases during the excitement phase, the inner lips (minor labia) begin to swell, and the outer lips (major labia) at the entrance of the vagina open slightly to facilitate intercourse. The vagina also expands to as much as three times the diameter it has when it is sexually unstimulated. Breathing becomes heavier, and muscular tension, pulse rate, and blood pressure increase. Masters and Johnson observed that two-thirds of women exhibit sex flush during this phase. Sex flush is a measles-like rash that first appears on the upper part of the abdomen and then spreads out over the breasts.

In the second or *plateau phase,* the reactions noted in the excitement phase are enhanced and intensified. One important change, however, is the appearance of what Masters and Johnson called the "orgasmic platform." It is the swelling of the outer third of the vagina, reducing its diameter by as much as 50 percent. The dilation of the vaginal passway is due to vasocongestion—that is, an excessive flow of blood into the thick network of veins of the vagina. The clitoris also rises from its normal position overhanging the pubic bone and retracts farther from the vaginal entrance. There is also a noticeable increase in the rate of breathing.

The third phase of the female sexual response is *orgasm.* Whereas ejaculation presents a concrete sign of male orgasm, the major observable feature of female orgasm is a series of rhythmic contractions of the muscles of the outer third of the vagina and the swollen tissues surrounding it. Physiological reactions, such as pulse rate, blood pressure, and breathing rate, reach a peak. Many muscles of the body (arms, legs) contract in a state of spasm. The sex flush also becomes most pronounced.

Finally, the *resolution phase* comes in the aftermath of orgasm. Orgasm releases blood from the engorged blood vessels as well as reduces muscular tension throughout the body. As the swelling around the nipples subsides, they appear as if they were undergoing further erection. The increased prominence of the nipples and the rapid disappearance of the sex flush are considered reliable signs that the woman has undergone orgasm. Perspiration may cover her entire body, or it may appear only on the soles of her feet and the palms of her hands. It may take as long as half an hour before the body returns to its sexually unstimulated state. However, if a woman reaches the plateau phase but does not experience orgasm, the resolution phase may take as long as an hour. All other physiological functions, such as pulse rate, blood pressure, and breathing rate, gradually return to normal.

Female Orgasm

One important finding by Masters and Johnson is that although men tend to have a refractory period (a period where they cannot become sexually aroused or have another erection), women do not have such a period. Sexual stimulation immediately after orgasm may bring about a second orgasm. It is indeed possible that a series of a half a dozen or even a dozen orgasms may take place without reaching the resolution phase. This multiorgasmic response seems to be an exclusively female phenomenon. Contrary to common beliefs that men possess a stronger sex drive, "they are not nearly so capable as women of multiple orgasms. Only about 6 percent to 8 percent of men are able to have more than one orgasm during each sexual experience, and when the capacity for multiple orgasm exists, it is usually found only in very young men. . . . Those men who have a second orgasm shortly after the first relate that the pleasure of the first is superior to that of the second, in direct contrast to women's subjective reports" (McCary, 1967). The female's superior capacity for multiple orgasm also goes against the popular belief that it is "natural" for women to be monogamous and for men to be polygamous (Schofield, 1976).

The intensity of orgasm varies, however, from one woman to another. Judith Bardwick (1971) described three types of orgasmic response in the female. Pattern A (minimal or minor orgasm), which is common for young and relatively inexperienced women, is the achievement of a plateau state of arousal that seldom reaches the orgasmic level. Resolution occurs slowly, and the woman enjoys the experience without frustration. This is sex with affection but no physical gratification. In Pattern B (moderate orgasm), the woman "stays at the plateau level and with some stimulation can have recurrent orgasms." Experimentation with sex maximizes her feeling, sensation, and physical pleasure. There is more of a response to physical sensations than in Pattern A. Pattern C represents an orgasm closest to that of the male. "The woman reaches a high plateau state, swiftly achieves a maximal orgasm, and experiences a swift and total resolution. Similar to the male, she will take 15 to 20 minutes at least to recover from this resolution phase." This pattern is the least-reported level among women.

The mystery of female orgasm has always fascinated men. A question that has often been asked is whether or not women experience sexual pleasure in the same way that men do. Tiresias, a Theban soothsayer, is reported to have been walking on Mount Cylene when he came upon two snakes copulating. He killed the female and for this reason was changed into a woman. He was satisfied with this change, because, as he noted, a woman enjoys intercourse ten times more than a man. He was punished again by being changed back into a man. In a recent study, Vance and Wagner (1976) asked females and males to write short descriptions of what an orgasm felt like. These descriptions were then shown to three groups of judges—obstetrician-gynecologists, clinical psychologists, and medical students. They were asked to mark each description male or female, depending on whether they thought it was written by a woman or a man. These judges were unable to distinguish the sex of a person from the person's description of her or his orgasm. This study indicates that orgasm may not be experienced differently by females and males. It is, however, doubtful whether subjects in this study were able to translate the emotional and sensual experience of orgasm into accurate verbal description. Shere Hite (1976) recorded the description of orgasmic experience by females. The following are some examples:

"I'm high—I breathe fast—also lightheaded, in dream world, sounds are distant, time suspended."

"Like an awakening and the beginning of life."

"Fantastic, almost unbearably ecstatic."

"Happiness, energy, thrills, ecstasy, lying in whipped cream."

"On the edge of an earthquake."

"Warm, tingly, heady. Specific parts of the body come into focus as they are touched, and I feel loved, wanted and worthwhile."

Clitoral vs. Vaginal Orgasm

According to Freudian thinking, clitoral stimulation is a game played only by little girls. Mature women have a different game to play. They are expected to transfer their sexual response from the

clitoris to the vagina. Clitoral orgasm has been described by psychoanalytical authors as an expression of immaturity, neuroticism, masculinity (based on the analogy between the penis and the clitoris), and sexual abnormality (Robinson, 1959).

It is now well established that all female orgasms are physiologically the same (Kaplan, 1974). They are triggered by clitoral stimulation and expressed by vaginal contractions. Indeed, orgasm is generally more easy to achieve through direct clitoral stimulation than through coitus. Hite (1976) found that only 30 percent of her female subjects could have orgasm regularly from intercourse without direct manual clitoral stimulation. However, all women had orgasm from clitoral stimulation during manual stimulation with a partner or during masturbation.

There is an anatomical difference between the female sexual and reproductive functions that is not present in the male (Koedt, 1970; Rotkin, 1972). The male's sexual and reproductive behavior is the same; both sexual satisfaction and reproduction can be fulfilled by the same act and through the same organ, the penis. Females, however, have separate organs to fulfill the two functions of sexual satisfaction and reproduction. The clitoris is the sexual organ, whereas the vagina has reproductive functions, such as menstruation, receiving the penis, holding semen, and as a birth passage. Anne Koedt (1970) noted that the emphasis on vaginal orgasm attempts to define women sexually according to what pleases men. Sexual penetration is preferred by men because the vagina provides the best physical stimulation for the penis: It supplies the necessary friction and lubrication. In accord with this view, we shall see in Chapter 8 that, because of ignorance of the functions of the vagina and the clitoris, many women who do not get enough clitoral stimulation during intercourse and thus do not achieve orgasm are considered sexually inadequate.

Cross-cultural studies reveal that, in most societies for which there are data, men tend to take the initiative and, without extended foreplay, to proceed toward a climax without much regard for synchrony with the woman's orgasm. Many reports indicate that coitus is primarily completed for the man's pleasures, with little attention given to the woman's response. Her orgasm is secondary to his. For example, a survey of several African ethnic groups in Guinea indicates that women overwhelmingly reported passivity during coitus and inability to achieve orgasm (Davenport, 1977). Clitoral stimula-

tion, which is needed in order for the female to achieve sexual arousal and sexual satisfaction, seems to be disregarded.

ATTITUDES AND SEXUAL BEHAVIOR

There are wide variations among peoples of the world in the restrictions placed on sexual behavior. Societies range from those that restrict sex to the marital situation to those that encourage sexual experimentation and sexual exploration during early childhood (Ford & Beach, 1952). A world view of attitudes toward sexual behavior is reported by Murdock (1949). He analyzed cross-cultural data on 118 societies to find out the regulation of sexual behavior before and after marriage. With the exception of a Chinese group and a group of New England whites, the preliterate peoples of the world constituted the sample (North American Indian tribes, Africa, Oceania, Eurasia, and South America). Among these societies, only three seem to have a general taboo against all sexual intercourse outside marriage; these are the American whites, and the Ashanti and Timne societies of West Africa.

It appears that a distinct difference between restrictive and permissive societies is that the former tend to emphasize the productive function of sexual activity within the context of marriage. In contrast, permissive societies tend to associate sex with many social phenomena, such as marriage, kinship, social status, reproduction, and ceremonies (Murdock, 1949).

Societies that encourage premarital intercourse are organized so that all children born outside of marriage do not suffer social disabilities or stigma. The social legitimacy of infants is not determined by the circumstances of birth, and children are given full status as adults when they reach the equivalent of an age of majority. Only a few societies deny full social status to children born outside marriage, and these are societies that try to keep all intercourse confined to legitimate spouses. There are also physiological factors that seem to be conducive to very few pregnancies in societies that allow premarital sexual experimentation. There is a period in every individual's life when she is capable of engaging in sexual intercourse with a low probability of conception. Although it varies from one person to another, it usually occurs during adolescence and is therefore called adolescent sterility (Davenport, 1977).

In restrictive societies, including North America, a double standard is usually practiced in dealing with females and males: The sexuality of females is more repressed, and their sexual experience is more limited than that of males. In most societies that practice segregation and chaperonage to control the sexual behavior of adolescents, boys are less carefully watched than girls. For example, among the Kiwai Papuans of New Guinea, girls are closely chaperoned by their parents and are usually kept in ignorance of lovemaking for some time. The boy, however, is not similarly restricted, and he usually takes the initiative in an attempt to get around the rules. Similarly, in most restrictive societies, the disgrace and punishment for any sexual misbehavior is directed toward the girl rather than toward the boy. The Hopis, for example, place all the blame for illegitimate pregnancy squarely on the girl who is involved, whereas her male lover is not regarded as being at fault at all (Ford & Beach, 1952).

In American society, sexual behavior has been predominantly controlled by traditional standards that stipulate either abstinence until marriage or a personal acceptance of premarital intercourse only when the partners are in love or engaged. The standards for men held by both sexes tend to be more permissive in regard to sexual intercourse prior to marriage or in the absence of a love relationship. Both women and men agree that it is important to them that women be virgins at marriage; both would be less willing to encourage their sister than their brother to have intercourse with someone the sibling loved; both would lose more respect for a girl who engaged in sex without love than for a boy who did so; and both have higher standards of sexual morality for females than for males (Kaats & Davis, 1970). These double standards, which are upheld for women and men, are reflected in sexual conduct; women enjoy less sexual freedom than men. Kinsey, Pomeroy, Martin, and Gebhard (1948; 1953) reported that 48 percent of women had had premarital intercourse and that 26 percent admitted having had extramarital intercourse. For men, however, 85 percent had had premarital intercourse, and about 50 percent had had intercourse with other women since they married.

Studies in the 1960s reveal that at that time there was less acceptance of the traditional American standards of sexual behavior among both sexes, and yet male-female differences still remained. For example, men were still much more likely than women to have their first experience of sexual intercourse with someone they did

not love and to have a greater number of sexual partners. There had been changes in sexual behavior in the sixties since the Kinsey study, but such behavior was still carried out within the confines of "permissiveness with affection" (Reiss, 1967).

There have been, however, dramatic changes in the sexual behavior of young females in the seventies. Hunt (1974) observed that one-third of the females (single and married combined) in the Kinsey data had had premarital intercourse by age 25. His data revealed that by age 25 nearly half of his married sample and nearly three-quarters of his single sample had done so. Thus, the incidence of premarital sexual relations for young women has doubled from the late 1940s to the early 1970s. Yet again, this increase in sexual freedom occurred within the confines of traditional standards that stipulate a personal acceptance of premarital intercourse only when partners are in love or engaged.

How far have adolescents moved toward sensuous sex without affection? Among adolescents with sexual intercourse experience, Sorensen (1973) observed two main subgroups; the serial monogamists (those nonvirgins who have a sexual relationship with *one* person they love) and the sexual adventurers (those nonvirgins who freely *move from one sex partner to another* with no feeling of obligation to be faithful to any partner). His data revealed that 15 percent of boys and 28 percent of girls were serial monogamists. There were, however, 24 percent of boys but only 6 percent of girls who were sexual adventurers. Although these data show that adolescent girls are now more sexually liberated than their mothers, they are still consistently more conservative than boys in attitudes, values, and behavior. It appears that the promiscuous female (sexual adventurer) who is the product of the sexual revolution in the 1970s represents only a small minority of the female population.

The Threat of Female Sexuality

According to Sherfey (1970), the female's unsatiated capacity for orgasm is not suitable for sedentary or monogamous cultures. Primitive women's sexual drive was too strong and aggressively erotic to withstand the disciplined requirements of settled family life, where paternity is important. Before the existence of family life, the pre-civilized woman had apparently enjoyed full sexual freedom and was often totally incapable of controlling her sexual drive. Sherfey

predicted that the present increase in the sexual freedom of women, through their relative economic independence and their use of contraceptives, would destroy family life and might necessitate a countermeasure of repression. She gives the increasing rate of divorce as a symptom of the decline in family life.

Sherfey's basic assumption may, however, be inaccurate. It is doubtful that a society has ever existed without sexual rules; societies differ in their degree of permissiveness, rather than in the absence of regulations for sexual behavior (Davenport, 1977). Even non-Western societies with extreme permissiveness in premarital and extramarital sexuality have been able to maintain family life, showing that female sexual freedom is not incompatible with the existence of the family.

Whereas Sherfey suggested that the free expression of female sexuality might lead to the destruction of family life, other psychiatrists feel that recent sexual permissiveness has increased the rate of sexual dysfunctions in men (Ginsberg, Frosch, & Shapiro, 1972; Moulton, 1977). In a paper entitled "The New Impotence," Ginsberg and his colleagues argued that when the repression of women had been lifted in the seventies, bringing increased sexual freedom, it resulted in an increase of impotence among younger men. In fact, cases presented by Ginsberg do not show that women were the cause of the sexual problems of his male clients; rather, these men had chronic problems related to sex: They were anxious, inexperienced, and sexually inhibited men. The women, on the other hand, were quite normal: One wife complained that she was unsatisfied with sexual practices limited to foreplay; her husband never attempted intercourse because he thought that it was dirty.

Ruth Moulton (1977) suggested that the "New Feminism" is having adverse effects on both husbands and wives. Besides impotence and premature ejaculation, some husbands respond to the general independence and sexual freedom of their wives by sexual withdrawal and sexual indifference. They refuse to attempt intercourse with the wives for months or years—a strategy that, in the past, was more used by women. The wives then feel unloved and may turn to lovers. Some of the reactions of the husbands are overeating or becoming domineering and possessive.

Ginsberg and Moulton report only isolated and perhaps exaggerated clinical cases. Nevertheless, changes in sexual standards and sexual behavior may require new adjustments for both women and

men. Women may sometimes overreact to their newly discovered sexual needs. However, most men have not been able to change their behavior, standards, and expectations to enable them to enjoy the emerging female sexuality. They tend to become anxious when they lose their dominant position in the sexual situation; for example, Mirra Komarovsky (1976) found that male college students feel they are threatened by the female sexual initiative.

The adverse reaction of men to women who want to give free expression to their sexuality is very much related to sex-role stereotypes where the female is expected to be submissive in the sexual situation. However, according to one researcher:

> The gradual breakdown of sex-role stereotypes should make for an increasingly greater role flexibility that would facilitate interchangeability between passive and active roles in initiating relationships as well as in playing out specific roles. As masculinity and femininity become meaningless concepts, men and women should feel free to pursue and be pursued; to choose and be chosen; to alternate between active and passive sexual roles (Safilios-Rothschild, 1977).

SELF-STIMULATION

Exploration and self-stimulation of the sex organs are some of the early sexual activities of females and males. The Kinsey findings, however, show that males are more likely than females to stimulate their sexual organs. Studies in the late sixties reveal that rates of masturbation for college women differ only slightly from those found by Kinsey in his 1940s samples, thus giving little support for the notion of a substantial change in masturbatory behavior among college women (Kaats & Davis, 1972). Although evidence in the early 1970s (Hunt, 1974) indicates a dramatic change in self-stimulation among women, the gap between the sexes still remains.

Since sex differences in self-stimulation have been found in different cultures (Ford & Beach, 1952), this question became a subject for many interpretations. Some scholars, notably Ford and Beach (1952) and Bardwick (1971), suggested that the shape and location of the male genitals make them more accessible to stimulation than those of the female. It is easier for the male to induce in himself genital sensations closely resembling those obtained from sexual

intercourse. The female has to employ a penis substitute in order to be able to obtain a comparable effect. This argument is not convincing for several reasons. First, females rarely use a penis substitute for self-stimulation. Second, the present interpretation considers only vaginal stimulation and ignores the importance of clitoral stimulation in masturbation. Finally, the belief that self-stimulation rarely leads to sexual satisfaction (for example, because of the inaccessibility of the female organs) is not accurate. Hite (1976) indicated that of the 82 percent of women who said they masturbated, 95 percent could achieve orgasm easily (in just a few minutes) and regularly whenever they wanted. Masters and Johnson (1966) also found that, contrary to general belief, women are more likely to obtain multiple (and more intense) orgasm with self-stimulation than with intravaginal intercourse. The superiority of self-stimulation may be due to the fact that few men can maintain an erection long enough to produce multiple orgasms in their partners. In masturbation, a woman may continue to experience orgasm until physical exhaustion terminates the session. The average female will usually be satisfied with three to five manually induced orgasms. With mechanical stimulation, such as an electric vibrator, in which long sessions are less tiring, a woman may experience between twenty and fifty orgasms (Brecher & Brecher, 1966; Dodson, 1974).

Sexual Attitudes and Self-Stimulation

Since women are capable of responding to and even of achieving stronger orgasm in self-stimulation than in coitus (Masters & Johnson, 1966), sex differences in the actual practice of this behavior may reflect the repression of female sexuality. In the Hite study, most women said they enjoyed masturbation physically but not psychologically. "Psychologically, they felt lonely, guilty, unwanted, selfish, silly, and generally bad. . . . Almost all women have been brought up not to masturbate." The repression of female sexuality is well illustrated by medical procedures practiced in the past to correct female masturbation. Donald Hastings (1966) listed "amputation or cautery of the clitoris, restraining devices such as straitjackets to make the genitals inaccessible to the hands, miniature chastity belts, sewing the vaginal lips together to put the clitoris out of reach, and even castration by surgical removal of the ovaries." Hastings goes on to point out that there seem to be no references

in the medical literature to the surgical removal of the testicles or the amputation of the penis to stop masturbation. He speculated that if women instead of men had composed the medical profession of the time, these drastic measures would have been applied to boys to stop them from masturbation.

One recent indication of the changing attitudes toward masturbation in professional circles is its use for the rehearsal of sexual responses in the treatment of female sexual dysfunction. Therapists use masturbation as an initial step in the development of heterosexual response (Lo Piccolo & Lobitz, 1972; Masters & Johnson, 1966; 1970; Pomeroy, 1966; see also Chapter 8).

Sex Differences in Sexual Stimulation

One explanation of sex differences in masturbation is that women and men differ in the conditions under which sexual arousal is likely to occur. It is assumed that men are more easily aroused by a larger number of external stimuli, such as films, literature, and erotic art (Kinsey et al., 1948; 1953; Mann, 1971; Schmidt, Sigusch, & Schafer, 1973). Thus, men become sexually aroused without the actual presence of, or physical contact with, a potential partner. For women, however, this contact is necessary before they are sexually aroused. Men are also more often sexually aroused by the sight of the sex organs, and they much more frequently initiate a sexual relationship after some genital exposure or genital manipulation (Davenport, 1977).

Recent evidence, however, revealed that there is only a small difference between the sexes in response to erotic stimuli (*The Report of the Commission on Obscenity and Pornography*, 1970; Schmidt et al., 1973; Zuckerman, 1971). Hunt (1974) also reported that, within one generation, the number of men aroused by erotic material doubled, whereas the number of women increased four times. Moreover, the findings by the Commission on Obscenity and Pornography (1970) indicated that some females (e.g., younger, more liberal, and more sexually experienced) report greater sexual excitement in response to erotic material than some male subjects (e.g., older, more conservative, more inhibited, and less experienced). It appears that differences between the sexes may not be in the physiological-sexual response to erotic stimuli but in the report of these experiences and that women tend to deny sexual excitement

unless there are extended erotic cues to make their arousal legitimate (Heiman, 1975). It is therefore not surprising that there is a low relationship between sexual arousal (vaginal blood volume changes) and the female subjective report of arousal (Heiman, 1977).

Clinical Evidence on Erotic Stimuli

That man may obtain sexual excitement in the absence of genital stimulation by or contact with a woman is illustrated in clinical reports indicating that voyeurism, exhibitionism, and fetishism tend to be almost exclusively male phenomena. Voyeurism refers to the act of looking at some form of nudity instead of engaging in normal sexual intercourse as a source of sexual satisfaction. Although it is difficult to find female cases of voyeurism in clinical reports, interviews with women concerning their fantasies and sexual behavior (Friday, 1973; 1975) reveal that women do not only respond to sexually explicit visual stimuli (pictures, filming, and live men and women) but that some of them also indulge in voyeuristic activities. For example, one of the less overt but common voyeuristic activities of women is called "crotch watching," which is observing men's trousers in order to obtain sexual excitement, a behavior similar to "breast watching" by men. As the following case reveals, other more overt forms of voyeuristic activities do occur:

> A forty-year-old single woman complained that a middle-aged man who lived in the opposite house was creating a public nuisance by exposing his erect penis while lying on his bed. The man admitted his exposure but denied that he was creating a public nuisance, because the woman had to stand on a piece of furniture in order to see him. Furthermore, she had been observing him for many years and because she had never complained, he had thought that he was doing her a favor. In the course of the legal investigation, it was learned that the woman not only stood on a piece of furniture but also used binoculars. The man was acquitted. However, the mystery remained as to why the woman, after so many years, complained about the man's behavior (Hirschfeld, 1948).

It is possible, as the above case demonstrates, that voyeuristic behavior of women is under-reported because of a compliant male partner who tolerates her behavior. Voyeurism in the male also tends to take a more aggressive form and thus come to the attention of the police. How society sometimes overlooks and even allows

certain behavior in the female but not in the male is well illustrated in exhibitionism, which is also reported by clinicians in men only.[1] Calhoun (1977) noted that "should a woman choose to undress regularly in front of a window, male observers are unlikely to be disgusted or to report the incident to the police. Furthermore, modern dress codes give women ample opportunity for mild exhibitionism, an advantage not shared by men." Fetishism is another type of sexual behavior found only in males, and yet clinicians report that it may occur among females in association with other activities, such as kleptomania (stealing unneeded goods from stores).[2] Stoller (1977) observed that occasionally women discover that laying hands on certain objects (usually cloth) with an intent to steal results in sudden orgasm.

Although voyeurism is rarely reported in women, it nevertheless consists of an area of male deviance in which women are used as sexual objects either through payment (as in the case of the prostitute) or through coercion (as in the case of the wife, daughter, son, or other relatives). Consider, for example, scoptophilia, a form of voyeurism that refers to an excessive interest in looking at the genitals or at the sex act as a sexual stimulus. Scoptophilia may be expressed in the form of troilism (or triolism), where a sexual partner is shared with another person while one looks on, after which the onlooker may or may not share the sexual partner. Hirschfeld (1948) reported the case of a husband who forced his wife to commit adultery so that he might observe her in the act. He would invite a foreign business connection over for dinner. He would then hide in another room and watch while his attractively dressed wife met the guest and informed him that her husband had been called away on urgent business. She would wine and dine the guest and then "seduce" him. She would have sexual intercourse with the guest on the divan in order to give the husband a clear view of the affair. She would then quickly dismiss the guest in order to allow her husband to rush forth from his hiding place to carry out "the sexual act with his wife with passionate ardor." When the wife threatened to divorce

[1]Exhibitionism refers to a condition in which sexual excitement is produced by exhibiting the genitals to others, usually strangers. This is followed by masturbation.

[2]Fetishism involves sexual excitement by means of an inanimate object (leather boots) or a body part (the hair or the foot), not as a substitute for the person, with the implication that the original owner of the fetish would be preferred if she or he were present, but because the object is preferred to its owner.

the husband because of these demands, he threatened to accuse her of adultery on the basis of the acts to which she objected. Another case described by Hammer (1968) is one of incestuous troilism in which the father would call his preadolescent son and daughter into the bedroom, make them strip, and direct them to perform sexually. This was done under the rationalization that he would save the daughter from outside temptations and that it was better to get sexual experience at home where she was safe from infection and evil influence.

In conclusion, women do not only practice and enjoy self-stimulation but are also capable of developing a wide range of sexual interests and behavior. However, social inhibitions and controls may modify and interfere with female sexuality. Many sex differences may only reflect these social controls and the different learning experiences of women and men.

SEXUAL BEHAVIOR DURING PREGNANCY, POSTPARTUM, AND MENSTRUATION

Pregnancy is both psychologically and physically stressful to the female. It is therefore expected to affect her sexual behavior. The scant attention given to this area of research may, however, be due to the reluctance of the professional to associate motherhood with sexuality. As Butler and Wagner (1975) noted, "The medical world has accurately reflected the societal view which has considerable trouble in accepting sexuality and pregnancy at the same time in the same person. Whether the impending motherhood of the pregnant woman raises unconscious resistances in the physician (usually male) by mixing the unmixables, lover and mother, is one speculation."

Masters and Johnson (1966) found that during the first three months of pregnancy, women who had had previous pregnancies reported very little change in sexual interest, with the exception of a small number who reported either an increase or a decrease. Most of the women having their first baby reported a reduction in erotic interest and responsiveness. During the second trimester of pregnancy, Masters and Johnson found a general elevation in sexuality on the behavioral level as well as in fantasy and dreams. The last trimester witnessed the greatest drop in sexual interest and activity.

A study by Solberg, Butler, and Wagner (1973) found a consistent decrease in the sexual interest and activity of the majority of 260 women during pregnancy. Not only had the frequency of intercourse decreased as pregnancy progressed, but there had also been a decrease in the frequency of orgasmic experience and orgasmic intensity. Only a small number reported an increase in orgasmic intensity during all stages of pregnancy. The report by Masters and Johnson (1966) of an increase in sexual interest and activity during the second trimester is not consistent with this finding. "It has been suggested that the volunteer quality of the Masters and Johnson population may have biased their population toward individuals with a particular interest in sexuality" (Butler & Wagner, 1975).

Data on sexual activity during the last trimester may have been affected by the warning of physicians to pregnant women not to engage in sexual intercourse until after the baby was born. In the Masters and Johnson (1966) study, some doctors had instructed the women studied not to engage in intercourse during the entire last trimester, whereas others had forbidden coitus only during the last month. Some of these women reported that, regardless of medical advice, they themselves gradually lost interest in sex during the last trimester; others reported that their husbands had lost interest in them.

One reason for discontinuing coitus is the fear of harm to the fetus. It is, however, widely accepted that, with the exception of women who carry a risk of abortion, there is no reason that women should abstain from sex during the first six months of pregnancy. For the habitual aborter, in sexual intercourse and even more so in masturbation to orgasm, intense contractions of the uterus may carry a risk of abortion.

Similarly, fear of infection during the last three months of pregnancy does not have much ground. In some women, particularly those who are pregnant with a first baby, a little "spotting" or bleeding may occur during intercourse. These are cases where coition should be given up. Such cases, though very rare, need medical attention (Brecher & Brecher, 1966).

Butler and Wagner (1975) gave a cautionary note about the danger of sexual intercourse during pregnancy. A rather infrequently practiced method of cunnilingus consists of the male forcing air into the vagina. Some women report high excitement and even orgasm with

this technique. There is a risk of death in using this technique with pregnant women. Death may result from blowing air into the vagina, from whence it enters into the veins and arteries, preventing blood circulation (medically called air embolism) (Butler & Wagner, 1975).

As expected, coital positions may have to be modified during pregnancy. Butler and Wagner (1975) reported a drastic decrease in the male-superior position, which was used by couples approximately 80 percent of the time before pregnancy. The side-by-side position became the most frequent in the last trimester. The rear entry position, which had been rarely practiced before pregnancy, became much more popular.

In the Masters and Johnson (1966) study, after the babies were born (postpartum), strong sexual interests returned to some women within two weeks, but others remained uninterested for three months after childbirth. Mothers who were breast-feeding up to the third month reported a more immediate return to a higher level of sexuality than the others. They were also more interested in resuming sexual activity with their husbands after childbirth. These mothers also reported sexual stimulation during breast-feeding: They often reached a plateau level of sexual arousal. Some women who breast-fed expressed guilt feelings concerning their sexual arousal during nursing. Others even stopped breast-feeding because of guilt feelings.

Some women experience regular fluctuations of sexual desire not only in pregnancy but also during the menstrual cycle. Benedek and Rubenstein (1942) found that with the gradual increase of estrogen during the first half of the menstrual cycle, women become active, extroverted, and heterosexual. The desire for copulation is usually accompanied by a feeling of well-being and alertness. During the second half of the cycle, active sexual tendencies are modified by a receptive and passive predisposition. Maximal sexual desire most commonly occurs either a day or so before or after the period of menstrual flow.

Udry and Morris (1968) investigated the frequency of sexual behavior during the menstrual cycle. There is a gradual increase in the rate of intercourse and orgasm until there is a peak round the time of ovulation. In the latter half of the cycle, there is a decline, with a brief increase just before menstruation. The finding that women are more sexually responsive during midcycle and just before menstruation should be used in sexual counseling.

SEX AND THE AGING WOMAN

Whereas men reach the peak of sexual responsiveness and potency around the age of 17 or 18, declining gradually thereafter, women reach their peak in their late thirties and early forties. Their rate of decline is, however, slower than that of men. During the peak period, particularly after the birth of several children, women respond rapidly and intensely: Vaginal lubrication occurs instantly, and multiple orgasms are frequently reported. The increase in sexual responsiveness may not be due to biological factors but to the female loss of inhibition and to a greater security in her relationship with an accepting partner (Kaplan, 1974).

There is a wide variation among women in sexual functioning during the *menopausal* years. Some women report a decrease in sexual desire, whereas others indicate a noticeable increase in sexual appetite during the menopause. Similar variation is found in the reports of *postmenopausal* women. The findings from sixty-one menopausal women studied by Masters and Johnson (1966) show that the intensity, rapidity, and duration of the response to sexual stimulation were reduced with advancing age through all stages of the sexual cycle: There was less lubrication; the sex flush became more restricted; there was a delay in the reaction of the clitoris to direct stimulation and a reduction in the duration of orgasm. Isadore Rubin (1966) has also pointed out that because of lowered hormone production in the female with advancing age, for example after menopause, the thinning of the vaginal walls and reduced lubrication may make intercourse quite uncomfortable and even painful for *some* women. Some may find penetration and the friction of inter-course painful or complain of a burning sensation on urination.

To counteract the thinness of the lining of the vagina, estrogen replacement therapy may be recommended. In some cases, local application of a simple lubricant between the lips of the vulva will relieve the discomfort entirely. Estrogen cream applied locally to the vulva and vagina may thicken the tissue and eliminate the discomfort.

Postmenopausal changes do not seem to apply to all women, however. Rubin (1966) gives the example of three women past the age of sixty who were still capable of vaginal expansion and lubri-cation, although there was an observable senile thinning of the vaginal walls and a shrinking of the major labia. Rubin attributes

the sexual response of these women to the fact that they had maintained intercourse regularly once or twice a week for their entire adult lives. These three women were contrasted with other women who had intercourse infrequently (once a month or less) or who did not masturbate with regularity. Five or ten years after menopause, these women had difficulty in accommodating the penis whenever they had the rare opportunity for intercourse. Although there is evidence indicating a close relationship between activity levels in the earlier years and those in the later years, it may not indicate causality. It may simply show that those with the strongest sex drive were also more sexually active, both in the early and in the later years. If this were true, it would demolish an old myth that one can use oneself up sexually and that it is necessary to save oneself for the later years (Rubin, 1966).

In contrast to men, whose capacity for multiple orgasm declines with aging, women remain capable of multiple orgasm throughout life. Older men often show a longer time of sustained erection than they had in youth, though ejaculation may be less frequent or even absent (Busse, 1973).

Sexual activity of women during the later years depends to a certain degree on the capacities and desires of their husbands. First, husbands are, on the average, three or four years older than their wives. Second, with age, the response of the husband tends to drop more than that of his wife. Thus, you have the interesting situation where younger women report that they do not want intercourse as often as their husbands, whereas older women express the desire to have intercourse more often than their husbands. Thus, in order to maintain the sexual activity of her husband:

> From middle age onward, a wife had better take steps to jolt her husband out of his rut, to use her imagination and experience to bring surprise into their sexual activity. . . . Even though she has been content enough to let the sexual relationship rock agreeably along in a uniform pattern for years, it is never too late—or too soon—to open new doors to adventure and romance (Davis, 1956).

After their fifties, women do not have to cope only with a marked decline in the sexual desire of men; in addition, there is a decrease, because of death, in the number of men. Even after 65, a woman

may seek out sex partners and certainly can respond to sexual opportunities. That availability of sex partners affects the female's sexual activities is revealed by the finding that although 25 percent of 70-year-old women still masturbate, many women cease having intercourse during their fifties and sixties (Kaplan, 1974).

Women
and
Sexual Dysfunctions

8

This does not mean failure to enjoy sex when one is dead with fatigue, when children are hammering on the door, in the middle of Union Square, or generally, with the wrong man, at the wrong time, all of the time every time, or with the wrong vibrations. Males of the vending machine type (put a quarter in and an orgasm comes out) should take note of this. Nor does it mean failure to get a mind-blowing orgasm on every single occasion. If it does mean these things, every woman is frigid. Nor does it really apply to non-response if the man is clumsy, hurried and phallus-struck. We assume you know all this. Real frigidity is when a woman who loves her man and isn't consciously scared of any part of sex still fails to enjoy it when they've both taken trouble to see that she should.

Alex Comfort: THE JOY OF SEX

When the norms forbade all extramarital sex relations, a girl or woman could easily refuse male requests. When the norms are permissive, she has nothing to hide behind. If she does not wish to engage in sex relations—and most teenage girls probably do not—she is left in an exploitable position. If in the past she had to say no to safeguard her self-respect, she must now say yes for the same reason—to avoid the dreaded epithet *frigid*.

Jessie Bernard: "THE FOURTH REVOLUTION"

Sexual dysfunction is defined as "the inability of the individual to function adequately in terms of sexual arousal, orgasm or specifically coital situations" (Williams, 1974). Since the term "frigidity," as traditionally used by clinicians, is an overinclusive label that involves a variety of sexual problems and implies pathology, it has now been replaced by the term sexual dysfunctions (Sotile & Kilmann, 1977). The following are the types of sexual dysfunctions that are commonly reported by clinicians (Kaplan, 1974; Masters & Johnson, 1970).

1. *General Sexual Dysfunctions* A female with general sexual dysfunction usually describes herself as devoid of sexual feelings. She is also unable to respond to sexual stimulation; for example, physiological responses, such as vasocongestion and lubrication, hardly ever develop in the sexual situation. Williams (1974) noted that some of these women may consider coitus as "a tedious ordeal" or a "frightening experience." Others may, however, enjoy physical contact with a partner, even though sexual arousal does not take place.

There are two types of general sexual dysfunctions. If a woman has never been sexually aroused with a partner, it is called *primary* sexual dysfunction. If, however, she had been responsive in the past with someone but has difficulty with her present partner, it is called *secondary* sexual dysfunction.

2. *Orgasmic Dysfunction* Orgasmic dysfunction refers to the inability to achieve the orgasmic phase of the sexual response. It is *primary* if the woman has never achieved orgasm at all. It is *secondary* if she had been orgasmic in the past but cannot achieve it now.

Orgasmic dysfunction may depend on the circumstances (Williams, 1974). It is *situational* if a woman can experience orgasm in one situation but not in others; it is *absolute* if the woman cannot achieve orgasm in coitus or with any other kind of stimulation. Williams (1974) noted that women with orgasmic dysfunction may have a strong sexual drive and can be easily aroused and develop vasocongestion and lubrication but cannot reach orgasm. Some women seem to have a very high threshold for triggering off the neural mechanism involved in orgasm. That is, they require prolonged, continuous stimulation of the clitoral area before they are "ready." Such women will clearly be nonorgasmic in a penile vaginal intercourse situation of a few minutes' duration. Thus, orgasmic

dysfunction may only reflect the fact that conditions conducive to orgasm vary from one person to another.

3. *Vaginismus* Vaginismus is an involuntary closing of muscles at the entrance to the vagina, making penetration and intercourse impossible. This relatively rare condition may develop independently of orgasmic dysfunction. However, repeated failure in attempts to have coitus may have devastating effects on the general sexual adjustment of the partners and make the sexual situation anxiety-provoking for the female.

4. *Dyspareunia* A rare sexual dysfunction is dyspareunia or painful coitus. More than any other sexual dysfunction, dyspareunia can have organic causes, such as infection, structural pathology, and the decrease in lubrication that accompanies aging.

FACTORS IN SEXUAL DYSFUNCTION

Both constitutional and psychological theories have been postulated to explain female sexual inadequacy. Constitutional theories are based simply on the observation that there are individual differences in sex drive, arousal, and orgasmic capacity.

Although constitutional factors may contribute to some cases of sexual dysfunction, psychological factors are involved in most cases. Psychoanalytical theory has been widely used to explain sexual dysfunction. It is considered by psychoanalysts as an hysterical condition, based on psychic conflicts and manifested in sexual anesthesia. Vaginal anesthesia is only one variation of hysteria. The cause of vaginal anesthesia is, therefore, not dissimilar to that of stocking anesthesia (loss of the sense of touch in the skin areas covered by stockings) or other types of anesthesia. Psychoanalysts also believe that sexual dysfunction, as part of an hysterical reaction, has its roots in the parental relationship and, particularly, in an incestuous attachment to the father. The psychoanalyst Wilfred Abse (1974) pointed out that incestuous fixations in childhood and sexual frustrations in adolescence affect the adult sexual life of both females (sexual dysfunction) and males (impotence). But incestuous desires toward parents that involve a conflict between the forbidden and the tempting affect women more than men. This is so because of the sharp contrast between woman as mother (the forbidden) and woman as "harlot" (the sexual) projected in the attitudes of men.

A woman is expected to have an image of the sacred mother but to behave like a harlot with her man; she is required to be simultaneously the Mother of God and the temptress of men.

Stekel (1963) indicated that, although incestuous wishes are shared by all children, the neurotic woman who has not gotten rid of such wishes shows that she is still a child. He presented a case to demonstrate the interaction between childish "neurotic" behavior and sexual dysfunction. Sexual difficulties were precipitated by a traumatic experience when the husband prevented a patient from continuing a childhood fantasy to relieve her guilt about early sexual behavior. This married 40-year-old woman had the habit of playing like a small child while her husband was away. She would lock the door and sit on the floor with her old dolls. One day, the husband returned home unexpectedly, discovered her childish hobby, and destroyed all her playthings. She immediately fainted and consequently became seriously ill for a month. On recovering from her fever, she became depressed and developed sexual problems. She also began to steal dolls from department stores. When her newly accumulated collection was discovered by her husband, she seemed to have no recollection of the thefts. Her early history showed that she had been petted by her brother at the age of 11. She also used to sleep with an aunt who used to pet and stroke her body, calling her "my dolly." At 13, she became the mistress of her piano teacher, though full intercourse did not take place until she was 15, when she was seduced by a physician. She had other affairs before marriage, but she was faithful to her husband. Stekel considered these dolls as symbolic of her sexual adventures; her doll play enabled her to maintain a precarious marital adjustment. The dolls represented separate love affairs. (They were, in fact, given names similar to those of her lovers.)

Brown (1966) gave three interrelated factors as causes of sexual dysfunction: (1) envy of the male, either in the form of penis envy or masculine protest or both; (2) masculine identification, and (3) rejection of femininity. Although a disturbance in the feminine role seems to underlie the theoretical orientation of psychoanalysis as expressed by Brown, sexual dysfunction has been treated as a disease in psychiatry and psychoanalysis. In the following, I shall emphasize a sociopsychological approach to sexual dysfunction.

A basic assumption of the sociopsychological approach to sexual dysfunction is that fear, anxiety, and guilt are inhibitory factors in

female sexual response. Inhibitory anxiety is connected either with the sexual act or with anxiety-provoking stimuli associated with sexuality. The female may have undergone specific individual or social conditioning against sexuality in general and against heterosexuality in particular. This attitude may develop through a traumatic personal experience at a certain period of her life. I will describe a case in the section on "The Treatment of Sexual Dysfunction" where a man had traumatized a woman by exhibiting himself to her. Rape is, of course, one of the most traumatic experiences conducive to sexual dysfunction (see Chapter 11), but any early aversive experience with men may condition the female against heterosexual relations. Fears of pregnancy or venereal disease may also become inhibitory factors. Females may also be deliberately trained, by their parents and others, to be sexually unresponsive. Helene Deutsch (1945) has expressed the view that "in many women, bourgeois morality or their mothers' malicious frigidity has created the idea that coitus is a sacrifice they must make to the dirty needs of men, and they must dutifully let it happen to them." Bardwick (1971) described sexual dysfunction as an unconscious fear of prostitution. This fear was explained by Chesler (1972) as a result of the separation between love and sex and the socializing of women to fear love and to condemn sex. How the fear of sex is transmitted from mother to child is effectively described by Cameron (1949):

> A typical situation is one in which the wife, from the onset of marriage, has been unable to gain sexual satisfaction, usually because of anxieties concerning sex instilled during her own childhood. . . . The wife then raises the age-old cry that the husband does not care for her for her own sake, but simply wants to use her as a means of sexual satisfaction, and then, by illogical but very human extension declares: "All men are brutes: every one of them wants only to make use of women." The marriage becomes a battleground, with the mother turning to the girls as her allies, and at the same time indoctrinating them with this fear of sex, and therefore, of men: "I never want you to go through what I have had to endure." In this way, sex fear, with accompanying hostility, frigidity, and other neurotic mechanisms, may be perpetuated down through several generations.

Masters and Johnson (1970) have found that religious orthodoxy, involving negative attitudes toward and anxiety connected with sex, is associated with a repressive family environment. Among 193 women who had never achieved orgasm, 41 were described as the products of rigidly channelized religious control (18 were Catholic,

16 were Jewish, and 7 were from a fundamentalistic background). The case of Mrs. A., reported by Masters and Johnson, illustrates the relationship between sexual and social value systems and future sexual adjustment:

> The young woman described a cold, formal controlled family environment in which there was complete demand for dress as well as toilet privacy. Not only were the elder brother and sisters socially isolated, but the sisters also were given separate rooms and encouraged to protect individual privacy. She never remembers having seen her mother, father, brother, or sister in an undressed state. The subject of sex was never mentioned, and all literature, including newspapers, available to the family group was evaluated by her father for possibly suggestive or controversial material. There was a restricted list of radio programs to which the children could listen.
>
> The only time her mother ever discussed a sexual matter was the day of her wedding. Mrs. A. was carefully instructed to remember that she was committed to serve her husband. It would be her duty as a wife to allow her husband "privileges." The privileges were never spelled out. She also was assured that she would be hurt by her husband, but that "it" would go away in time. Finally and most important, she was told that "good women" never expressed interest in the "thing." Her reward for serving her husband would be, hopefully, in having children.
>
> She remembers her wedding night as a long struggle devoted to divergent purposes. Her husband frantically sought to find the proper place to insert his penis, while she fought an equally determined battle with nightclothes to provide as completely modest covering as possible for the awful experience. The pain her mother had forecast developed as her husband valiantly strove for intromission.
>
> When seen in therapy, Mrs. A. had no concept of what the word masturbation meant. Her husband's sexual release before marriage had been confined to occasional nocturnal emissions, but he did learn to masturbate after marriage and accomplished ejaculatory release approximately once a week without his wife's knowledge. There was no history of extramarital exposure.
>
> As would be expected, at physical examination Mrs. A. demonstrated a severe degree of vaginismus in addition to the intact hymen. . . . When vaginismus was described and then directly demonstrated to both husband and wife, it was the first time Mr. A. had ever seen his wife unclothed and also the first time she had submitted to a medical examination.

Up to this point, I have emphasized conditioning and social repression as factors hindering both sexual arousal and sexual satisfaction in women. More recently, Sherfey (1972) and Mednick and

Weissman (1975) have explained sexual dysfunction in terms of an existential conflict. This conflict first arises out of the hypersexuality of the female; that is, each orgasm tends to increase pelvic constriction and hence increase the readiness of the female for further orgasms. Since most male sexual partners cannot meet the woman's level of repeated readiness for orgasms, her sexual dysfunction is seen as a "self-protective outcome of an approach-avoidance conflict"; she wants the pleasure of orgasm, but she becomes unresponsive sexually in order to avoid chronic pelvic congestion. It must be noted that the Sherfey theory is based on the simple observation that men achieve orgasm before women and that they may refuse to continue stimulating their women or that they may have difficulty maintaining a sufficient erection to bring them to orgasm. There is generally considerable disparity in orgasmic times between men and women. A man usually achieves orgasm within four minutes of intromission, whereas a woman needs from ten to twenty minutes of sexual intercourse before she obtains orgasm (McCary, 1967). (With oral-genital stimulation or during masturbation, a woman usually reaches orgasm in less than 4 minutes.) This discrepancy between the orgasmic responses of the two sexes during intercourse makes women more vulnerable to sexual dissatisfaction than men.

It has been suggested that the sexual response of the female is susceptible to psychological influences. Any psychological intrusion can reduce her level of excitation. She is, for example, more arousable when she stops thinking about her sexual participation, about what she is supposed to do, feel, or think. She is more sexually aroused when she feels most and thinks least (Bardwick, 1971; Masters & Johnson, 1970). Another related factor is the belief that female sexuality is tied to the quality of the relationship and her feelings about it (Williams, 1974). It is assumed that women are bothered more by the negative qualities of the relationship, particularly recent events, such as arguments, hurt feelings, or the manner of approach. Women seem to be culturally conditioned to be sensitive in the sexual situation.

Other Factors in Sexual Dysfunction

Hostility and aggression toward the male may cause sexual dysfunction. Oswald Schwarz (1949), in *The Psychology of Love*, pointed out that some women with sexual dysfunctions are of the "fighting"

type, unable to release themselves in sexual pleasure. They do not tolerate the idea of having sex with a man because it symbolizes dependency. Other factors related to female sexual problems are the inadequacies of husbands. Brown (1966) described these husbands as "essentially 'marital morons' . . . so clumsy, crude, or inept that they are incapable of providing the normal stimulation necessary for their wives to experience sexual satisfaction." Brown cited the Dickinson and Beam (1932) results, where the inadequacy of husbands contributed to the sexual dysfunction of 15 out of 100 women. These women described the inhibitions of their husbands as follows: "He will not touch my vulva"; "He thinks it wrong to make clitoris friction"; "He thinks coitus is carnal"; "He fears pregnancy"; "He thinks no decent woman asks for it"; "He will never dress or undress before me."

There is a great variation among females in their choice of lovers (Williams, 1974). Thus, a wife may be thought sexually inadequate because she is unable to reach orgasm with her present boyfriend or husband, yet she may respond freely and completely with another man. Take, for instance, the case, reported by Gratenberg (1950) of a female patient who married an old man, had children, but never experienced orgasm with him. During therapy sessions, the woman was obsessed by the question of her inability to have orgasm with her husband. Grafenberg described the conclusion of the therapy as follows:

> Bored by the repeated discussions with her, I finally asked her if she had tried sex relations with another male partner. No, was the answer, and reflectively she left my office. The next day, in the middle of the night, I was awakened by a telephone and a familiar voice, who did not give her name asked: "Doctor, are you there? You are right," and hung up the receiver with a bang. I never had to answer any further sexual questions from her.

Sexual dysfunction may also become a habitual lifestyle or a game played to bolster the shaky interpersonal relationship of a couple. Since both partners are reinforced by this game, sexual problems tend to be perpetuated. Eric Berne's (1967) intriguing transactional analysis of sexual dysfunction is an example. This begins with the husband making advances to the wife and being repulsed. After further attempts, the wife declares that he does not really love her for herself—all he really wants is sex. For a time he is checked, but

then he tries again and meets the same resistance. Weeks, perhaps months, pass, and now the wife has become informal, even forgetful. She'll walk through the bedroom half-dressed or ask her husband to bring her a towel when she's in the bath. At parties, she may even become flirtatious with other men. Eventually, the husband reacts and tries once again, but again he is repulsed. Now arguments break out: The usual topics are the wife's recent behavior, other couples and their lives, or their own financial situation. The arguments end with the slamming of doors and the two of them retiring to separate rooms. Now the husband has had enough. He decides that they will find a way of living together without sex. The wife again becomes "forgetful," but now the husband is unmoved by her provocation and makes no advances when she forgets her towel or walks around with little on. She becomes even more "forgetful" and eventually goes up to him and kisses him. At first, he remembers his resolve, but as the kisses become more passionate, he believes that he's succeeded at last, especially when his initial advances are not repulsed. He becomes bolder, but just at the critical moment, the wife withdraws and cries out that this little episode has proved it—all he really wanted was sex! Again there is uproar and quarrelling and retirement to separate rooms with much slamming of doors. It is this "uproar," the last following the repulse, that provides the perverse satisfaction to both partners from this game. The best way to stop the game, or not to get involved in it in the first place, is to decline the uproar— not to react to the wife's reaction. Then she is left in a state of dissatisfaction, and this may become so strong that she will eventually become more compliant. For her, the quarrel, the uproar, is a kind of substitute for the sex act itself. Such sexual games among couples seem to have their origin early in life. Berne cites the story of a little girl described by Dickens in *Great Expectations*. She comes out in her starched dress and asks a little boy to make her a mud pie. Then she sneers at his dirty hands and clothing and tells him how clean she is.

Recent evidence indicates that the incidence of female sexual dysfunction has decreased in the 1970s (Moulton, 1977). Moulton noted that her clients who sought therapy in the 1950s suffered from fear of sex. During the 1970s, however, women in treatment have shown freer sexual attitudes. Many of them were divorced, had rejected marriage, and were looking for a better sex partner (in contrast to some of the women in the 1950s who were in desperate need

to find a husband). Whereas women in the 1950s had rarely engaged in extramarital sex, many of the women treated twenty years later had had one or several extramarital affairs. Most women clients in the early group were unable to achieve orgasm by any method, but this was true of only a small number in the later group. Overall, sex did not play as important a role in the marital conflicts of women in the 1970s as it did in the 1950s.

THE TREATMENT OF SEXUAL DYSFUNCTION

An initial stage in the treatment of sexual dysfunctions is to try to obtain information about the female's physical potential for orgasm. Hastings (1966) suggested the following questions:

1. Has the woman ever achieved orgasm? Under what circumstances?
2. Can she achieve orgasm by means of masturbation?
3. Under what circumstances does she experience sexual arousal?
4. Has she achieved orgasm with a sexual partner other than her husband?
5. Does she notice sexual arousal in dreams or fantasy during the day? Upon reading erotic literature? On seeing suggestive movies?
6. Do arousal and orgasm occur under any other circumstances?
7. What are her usual responses during arousal and genital union?

If the therapist finds that the female experiences sexual arousal or orgasm in any situation at all, this is reassuring of her sexual potential. The therapist will then proceed in using any of the techniques described in this section. Psychoanalytical theory considers sexual dysfunction as the manifestation of maladjustment and immaturity (neuroticism), and treatment thus requires long-term probing into the past of the patient. As in other types of neurotic symptoms, the analyst has to work through the early unconscious sexual conflicts of the patient. Psychoanalysis is time-consuming, and since it takes many years before improvement is in sight, it may then be too late to salvage a sexual relationship. Even psychoanalysts themselves have expressed disappointment over the lack of success of analytic therapy in many cases (Brown, 1966).

The main assumption underlying the behavioral approach to sexual dysfunctions (and impotence) is that anxiety and fear are the

main inhibitory factors preventing normal sexual responses. When the patient is completely relaxed by hypnosis or other methods, she may be desensitized to the stimuli that arouse her anxiety in sexual situations. Lazarus (1963) used behavior therapy with sixteen married women with sexual dysfunctions. These cases illustrate the diversity of etiological factors. They ranged from faulty attitudes acquired in childhood, resulting in conditioned avoidance of sexual activities, to a feeling of hostility and resentment toward men in general and toward husbands in particular. The mildest case reported by Lazarus was of a woman who could have intercourse in the normal position but whose husband's sexual satisfaction depended on varying the sexual positions. She thought that her husband behaved like an animal and needed treatment. Her aversion to postural variation had arisen from her childhood experience on the farm where she had occasionally been forced to witness animals copulating. In using systematic desensitization (see Chapter 2), she was asked to imagine large animals copulating nearby; that is, the nearer the animals, or the larger the animals, the more anxious she felt. As soon as her anxiety about the sexual activities of animals was reduced in the therapy situation, her sexual inhibitions in the bedroom underwent a change. In another case, the problem was related to distractability and a hypersensitivity to auditory stimuli. During sexual intercourse, the patient would be excessively upset by the sound of a distant motor vehicle or an imagined footstep. While hypnotically relaxed, she was asked to imagine increasingly disturbing sounds: For example, she was asked to imagine that while having intercourse in a hotel room, she could hear people walking and talking in the corridor. Lazarus found that in cases where clear-cut areas of inhibition are involved, behavior therapy produced significant improvement. In other cases where the sexual dysfunction was complicated by other disturbances, behavior therapy was not very effective. Among the failures in the Lazarus cases was a woman whose therapy was complicated by homosexual proclivities. Although she regularly achieved clitoral orgasm during masturbation, heterosexual stimulation was described by her as "locally anesthetising."

A case reported by Kraft and Al-Issa (1967) shows how an early traumatic experience can initiate fears of sex and sexual dysfunction. A twenty-five-year-old female complained of difficulties in making a satisfactory adjustment toward members of the opposite sex. She

herself attributed this to an incident at the age of ten when a man exposed himself to her while she was traveling in a no-corridor train. She felt that she had lost all physical interest in men from that time onward.

She found intercourse, as well as all physical contact, with her husband quite revolting. Eventually, she attempted suicide and was admitted to a hospital. At this stage, she claimed that she hated all sex. When talking to a man, she would not think of him as a potential sexual object. She could not bear his putting his arm around her, nor could she consider sexual relations with him. When alone with a man, she feared that he would assault her sexually, but she did not feel threatened when surrounded by a group of people. She had received psychiatric treatment, including electroshock and various drug combinations, at various hospitals, but none of these treatments had been effective. At one hospital, it was felt that her condition was due to a latent homosexuality, but there was no substantial evidence to support this assumption.

Her treatment was based on the method of systematic desensitization. During the first three interviews, a list of anxiety-provoking situations was compiled. The items were arranged in ascending stress value from situations that were relatively easy—for example, talking to a man in a crowd situation—to the most difficult situations, those involving sexual intercourse with a man. In between, there were situations involving men smiling at her, dancing with her, kissing her, and so on, comprising twenty-six items in all.

The patient, completely relaxed by means of hypnosis, was asked to imagine the items in the stimulus hierarchy, commencing with the least disturbing and proceeding to the most anxiety-provoking situation. There were eighty-four desensitizing sessions in all, each lasting an hour and a half. Toward the end of the treatment program, she reported that she could now cope with sexual intercourse without any difficulty whatsoever.

Behavior therapy is also applied to the treatment of dyspareunia (painful intercourse) and vaginismus. This disorder is characterized by a spasm of the muscles surrounding the vagina and its entrance. The muscles become so tight that even the lubricated tip of a finger cannot be introduced into the vagina. That the cause of the disorder is emotional tension and anxiety rather than physical defect is shown by the finding that under general anesthesia, bougies (i.e., lubricated

cylinders) can pass with ease. Haslam (1965) noted that spasm of the muscles could thus be removed by reducing the anxiety of the patient: A patient could be desensitized by training her to insert bougies of different sizes in her vagina. Haslam reported the following case:

Mrs. Th. was twenty-three, and had been married for two years. The marriage had never been consummated. She gave a history of having been examined P.V. by a general practitioner when young, and having been very scared by this. She was afraid to touch or insert anything into the vagina (e.g., a tampon). The marriage was continuing on the basis of mutual masturbation, which both parties enjoyed. The husband had had previous sexual intercourse with another girl, but was reluctant to attempt to force his wife in any way. If intercourse was attempted she became very tense and pushed him away.

Their trouble had started on the honeymoon, when the husband had failed to penetrate, due to his inability to maintain an erection following a surfeit of champagne. After this, neither party had been confident and intercourse had never taken place. . . . [When] deconditioning was commenced . . . the patient was rather unco-operative and one had to proceed very slowly. Gradually her confidence increased. She tolerated the number four bougie [bougies were numbered according to size] for a short period, but was tense, arched her back and complained histrionically of pain when it was introduced. However, when the bougie had been introduced and left for a few minutes she was gradually able to relax and in this way confidence was increased. Progress was slow, however, and it was not until the tenth session that she was able to tolerate the passage of a number eight bougie and retain it in place herself. Up till this time she had refused to contemplate passing the bougie herself at all, and had had two (unadvised) traumatic failed attempts at intercourse at home which had shaken her confidence and delayed improvement. It was decided, therefore, to resort to the number four bougie for the purpose of getting the patient to pass it herself, and two sessions were spent in encouraging this procedure. At the fourteenth session she succeeded in passing the number six bougie herself and departed very pleased with her accomplishment. She returned for the next session saying that intercourse had been partially successful and that her husband was at last beginning to believe in the possibility of some improvement. One more session of deconditioning was held, and following this intercourse was successful and enjoyable.

In other cases, manual vaginal dilation, where the therapist digitally dilates the client's vagina, was used in the treatment of vaginismus (Dawkins & Taylor, 1961; Elgosin, 1951).

Masters and Johnson's Treatment Technique

In their treatment of sexual dysfunction, Masters and Johnson (1970) start with the assumption that both partners should be involved in the treatment of sexual dysfunctions. Similarly, the use of a team of male and female cotherapists is thought necessary. They start therapy by taking an extensive sexual history from each partner in order to determine the couple's conceptions of sex and their value system. After initial abstinence from any type of sexual interaction during the first days of therapy, couples are encouraged to explore each other's bodies and sensate areas but without feeling the urge for sexual performance. The couple have daily meetings with the therapists to discuss their problems and to learn sexual techniques for use in the privacy of the bedroom. An important stage in their therapeutic procedure is training in "sensate focus" (see Figure 8.1). In the privacy of their bedroom, the partners should be in the nude, and no physical weariness, stress, or tension should be present. The co-

Figure 8.1 Nondemand position for sensate-focused lovemaking. From Abse et al. *Marital and Sexual Counseling in Medical Practice,* Hagerstown, Md.: Medical Department, Harper & Row, Publishers, Inc. Reprinted by permission of Harper & Row, Pub., and Lois M.R. Louden.

therapists arbitrarily assign one partner to initiate interaction and ask her or him to introduce physical touch to the spouse. By fondling and massaging certain areas of the body, the other partner not only obtains sensate pleasure but also discovers with the other partner her or his individual levels of sensate focus. If neither partner has any idea of her or his physical preference, a trial-and-error approach is followed. The trial-and-error method may be preferable in all cases, since it may culminate in discoveries of new sensate pleasures. At this stage, neither partner is allowed to approach or touch the genital area of the other, nor should the wife's breasts be handled. Neither specific sexual stimulation nor specific physical sexual expression is allowed. That is, the pressure of sexual performance from either partner with the aim of sexual release (orgasm, ejaculation) is discouraged. The aim is to make the partner think and feel sensuously without the pressure of sexual performance. There are no demands for personal reassurance or for the need to rush to return the favor. The only commitment is to exchange giving pleasure with the other partner. Overall, the partners learn that sex involves not only physical expression but also a sensory awareness of the pleasures of touch, vision, smell, and sound. Physical sex comes later in the therapy, when the two partners feel comfortable and relaxed.

Masters and Johnson (1970) reported the results of studies of two types of sexual maladjustment in 342 women. One group, who had primary orgasmic dysfunction (i.e., those who have never achieved orgasm throughout the whole life span), had a success rate of 83.4 percent. A second group, who had secondary or situational orgasmic dysfunction (failure to achieve orgasm after having had at least one orgasm), had a success rate of 78.2 percent.

It is of interest that, for the single male clients who had no satisfactory sexual partner to bring to therapy, Masters and Johnson (1970) provided specially trained female partner surrogates. For the single female client, however, no male partner surrogates were provided. Masters and Johnson used the term *replacement partner* to describe those partners brought by a single woman to the therapy situation. In the Masters and Johnson studies, unmarried women were denied therapy without a replacement partner. Partners brought by women did not usually have the expert knowledge of the surrogates used for men. Masters and Johnson argued that this double standard for women and men was justified because of "women's

need for a relatively meaningful relationship," a condition that is difficult to reach in a brief, two-week period. A man, on the other hand, can consider "a partner surrogate as he would a prescription for other physical incapabilities." The Masters and Johnson practice may, of course, reflect societal double standards that can also be seen in the laws that protect the client of prostitutes and accept his promiscuity but punish her for soliciting.

The Use of Self-Stimulation and Erotic Stimuli

A combination of the use of erotic stimuli and training in self-stimulation is used by Lo Piccolo and his associates (Lo Piccolo & Lobitz, 1972; Lobitz & Lo Piccolo, 1972). Their sex therapy is the most economical, since it is carried out by the person in the form of "homework" assignments. In general, the client is instructed that, during masturbation, she is to focus on any erotic stimulus that is currently arousing, whether it is literature, pictures, or just fantasy. The stimuli may range from heterosexual erotic materials to homosexual fantasies. Once aroused, the client masturbates to orgasm. However, just prior to orgasm, she is asked to switch her focus to fantasies of sexual activity with her partner. On subsequent occasions, the client is instructed to switch to fantasies of the partner at earlier points in time, until fantasies of the partner become sexually arousing and the artificial stimuli previously used are no longer necessary. For clients who have difficulty in fantasizing their partners, the therapists supply a Polaroid camera and instruct them to photograph their partners in sexual activity. Then, the clients use these photographs in lieu of fantasy.

In cases of women who have never experienced orgasm from any source of physical stimulation, fantasy and erotic materials alone do not enhance the arousal level enough to produce orgasm. In such cases, the therapists used a nine-step masturbation program that has proven highly successful in producing the client's first orgasm. The nine steps follow a graduated approach model to desensitize the client to masturbation.

Step 1 The client is given the assignment to increase her self-awareness by examining her nude body and appreciating its beauty. She may use a hand mirror to examine her genitals and to identify the various areas with the aid of diagrams provided by the therapist.

Step 2   The client is instructed to explore the genitals tactually as well as visually. To avoid performance anxiety, she is not given any expectation that she will become aroused at this point.

Step 3   Tactual and visual exploration is focused on locating sensitive areas that produce feelings of pleasure when stimulated.

Step 4   The client is told to concentrate on manual stimulation of identified pleasurable areas. At this point, the female discusses with the therapist techniques of masturbation, including the use of a lubricant.

Step 5   If orgasm does not occur during Step 4, the client is told to increase the intensity and duration of masturbation. She is told to masturbate until "something happens" or until she becomes tired or sore.

Step 6   If orgasm is not reached during Step 5, the client is instructed to purchase a vibrator of the type sold in pharmacies for facial or body massage. In the most difficult case seen by the therapist, three weeks of daily 45-minute vibrator sessions were required to produce orgasm.

Step 7   Once the client has achieved orgasm through masturbation, the husband is introduced to observe her. This is designed to desensitize the female to displaying arousal and orgasm in the husband's presence. This will also serve as an excellent learning experience for him.

Step 8   The husband is instructed to manipulate his wife in the manner she has demonstrated in Step 7.

Step 9   Once orgasm has occurred in Step 8, the couple is instructed to engage in intercourse, with the husband stimulating the wife's genitals either manually or with a vibrator. Heterosexual erotic pictures or literature are used throughout the nine-step masturbation program.

Kaplan (1974) combined psychotherapy with sex therapies used by Masters and Johnson and Lo Piccolo and his associates. Individual psychotherapy was designed to deal with the psychological problems interfering with sexual responsiveness. Betty Dodson (1974) has used self-stimulation and mutual masturbation extensively as a type of group therapy to enhance the sexual response of her clients. Erotic imagery is used in self-stimulation in order to counter early conditioning denying sexual thoughts and sexual desire.

Other Specific Techniques

Helena Wright (1959), a British gynecologist, suggested that, without adequate rhythmic friction, no sexual satisfaction was possible for either women or men. Man learns his preferred rhythm in the course of masturbation or premarital experience. The wife must find her preferred rhythm of friction and teach it to her husband. To achieve this, the husband places his hand over the wife's clitoral region, keeping it relaxed and flexible. The wife can then put her hand over his and move his fingers in any way she likes. Those wives who learn that the clitoral region gives pleasure when suitably stimulated find it easy to transfer to sexual intercourse.

"Muscle therapy" is also used in the treatment of sexual dysfunction. Kegel (1952), a gynecologist, found that patients with urinary stress incontinence could be helped, without surgery, by an exercise for strengthening the pelvic vaginal muscles (the pubococcygeus muscles that surround and are attached to the walls of the vagina). Awareness and control of these muscles seem to increase by daily exercise. After this exercise, some of the women noticed that both sexual arousal and sexual satisfaction had increased. Hall (1952) also proposed that vaginismus can be treated by having a woman practice contracting and relaxing her vaginal muscles, which will enable her to have voluntary control of these muscles.

Only a small percentage of female sexual dysfunctions is due to physical disease. In rare cases, inhibition of the sexual response can result from physical factors; for example, pelvic endometriosis (inflammation of the mucous membrane which lines the uterus) might cause pain during intercourse. Hormonal dysfunctions may also be involved. Medical advice must be sought when physical abnormalities are thought to be involved.

Is Orgasm Necessary for Happiness?

Many authorities, including Kinsey and his associates (1953), have emphasized the view that orgasm should not be used as the sole criterion for satisfaction in sexual relations. A distinction is made between sexual satisfaction obtained from sexual arousal and that obtained from the social aspects of sexual relationship. Wives may obtain sexual satisfaction from giving pleasure to their husbands.

Mace (1958) described wives who never experienced orgasm and who were not bothered by this lack unless reminded that there was something wrong with them. He pointed out that these women were not cold and unresponsive physically but were affectionate and capable of giving and receiving tender love. Although they did not reach orgasm, they enjoyed sex relations with their husbands. "In their quiet way they respond to the warmth and intimacy and closeness of the sexual embrace."

Bardwick (1971) asked a group of married or engaged female students why they made love. A very small number of them reported that it was for pleasure. The majority of both married and unmarried subjects responded that it made them feel close. Frequently, there were responses such as: "It is an experience of our love"; "It makes him happy"; "He wants it"; or "It is expected." It appears that orgasm, defined in terms of physical pleasure and direct bodily sensations, is not experienced by a large number of females. Hite (1976) found no consistent relationship between *not* having orgasm during intercourse and not liking it. Eighty-seven percent of women, whether orgasmic or not during intercourse, most frequently gave affection and closeness as their basic reason for liking intercourse. It appears that the "joy of sex" is a subjective experience, which may or may not be related to orgasm.

In contrast, the psychoanalytical view of female orgasm is not only that it is necessary for sexual fulfillment but that it is also an antidote against neurotic and psychosomatic disturbances. In his book, *The Function of the Orgasm,* Reich (1942) has indicated that there is a positive relationship between undischarged sexual energy and different behavioral disturbances. Hamilton (1929) also suggested a relationship between orgasmic dysfunction and being neurotic:

Unless the sex act ends in a fully releasing, fully terminative climax, in at least 20 percent of copulations, there is likely to be trouble ahead. The least serious consequence is a chronic sense of tense, restless unsatisfaction. It is, I think, one of the most suggestive findings of my research that, of the 46 women who are inadequate as to orgasm capacity, 20 had been diagnosed at one time or another in their lives as more or less seriously psychoneurotic . . . while only one of the 54 women who could have orgasm with reasonable frequency had ever been regarded as psychoneurotic.

The relationship between sexual adjustment and marital happiness is affected in part by the expectations of the couple. Conservative couples have different expectations of marriage than couples with liberated attitudes. What is viewed as a satisfactory sex life by an inhibited couple may be frustrating to a liberated couple. This may explain the early findings by Terman, Buttenwieser, Ferguson, Johnson, and Wilson (1938) showing a small relationship between the regularity of female orgasm and satisfaction with marital sex. Perhaps women did not expect or feel entitled to sexual satisfaction in the past generations. With sexual liberation, however, modern women consider orgasm not only extremely important but also a basic right in the marital relationship. One would now expect a strong relationship between orgasm regularity or sexual satisfaction and marital happiness. In the early 1960s, Clark and Wallin (1965) found that two-thirds of married women who had orgasm all or most of the time indicated that they enjoyed marital intercourse very much, as compared with one-sixth of those who rarely or never had orgasm. More recently, Hunt (1974) found even stronger associations between the sexual side of marriage and marital satisfaction. The majority of married women and men for whom marital sex was pleasurable in the past year rated their marriage as being very close. Among women and men who reported that their marital sex was lacking in pleasure, "virtually none rated their marriages as being very close, and only a few as being fairly close."

Quite apart from the cultural conditioning and social expectations that may make orgasm important in marital satisfaction, physiological factors may play a crucial part (Hunt, 1974; Masters & Johnson, 1966). Orgasm relieves the discomfort and irritation caused by pelvic congestion during sexual arousal.

Throughout this chapter, I have emphasized orgasmic dysfunction. Abse (1974), however, gives the example of a woman who required only the sight of a married man with whom she was infatuated to trigger an orgasm. When he entered a room in which she was socially engaged with other people, the sight of him walking in her direction was enough to release an orgastic experience, usually interpreted by others as a swoon. Polatin and Douglas (1953) reported a case of a 25-year-old schizophrenic woman who had spontaneous orgasm without masturbation or sexual fantasy. It may not be that orgasm is spontaneous but that this female was not aware of the

erotic stimuli associated with sexual arousal. "Spontaneous" orgasm may, however, be as problematic as orgasmic dysfunction.

SUMMARY

Sexual dysfunction may refer to a woman unable to respond to sexual stimulation or to achieve orgasm; but it may also mean that a woman finds intercourse painful, or experiences muscular spasm at the entrance of the vagina, making penetration and intercourse quite impossible. Attempts by psychoanalysts to explain sexual dysfunction in terms of unconscious sexual desire toward the father have not been helpful to the female. An alternative sociopsychological approach to sexual dysfunction suggests that fear, anxiety, and guilt are inhibitory factors of the female sexual response. Fear and anxiety may develop as a result of a traumatic experience associated with sex, such as sexual assault or rape. Also, in a repressive family environment, negative attitudes toward sex may develop and interfere with the sexual response. Many cases of sexual dysfunction may, however, be the result of a lack of adequate sexual stimulation: Because the man achieves orgasm before the woman, he refuses to continue stimulating her until she achieves orgasm. Men may also be clumsy or inept in the sexual situation. Sex therapy, therefore, involves training couples in the use of adequate techniques as well as reducing their guilt and anxiety toward sex. Understanding the female and male normal sexual response (described in Chapter 7) is basic to a satisfactory sexual relationship.

Women
and Homosexuality

9

Perhaps the only women in the culture who do not despise themselves because they are women, are the active lesbians—at least those who do not imitate men—the many lesbians who look and act intensely feminine. They have wholly identified with the beauty ideal, so much so that they despise men because men are not women and because men really don't admire women, not the way they wish to be totally admired.

Una Stannard: "THE MASK OF BEAUTY"

The word "homosexual" has often been associated with the male. This may reflect a linguistic confusion between the Greek word "homo" meaning "same" and the Latin word "homo" meaning "man." The homosexual woman is usually called a lesbian, a label derived from the island of Lesbos on which the poetess Sappho lived with a group of women (c.620–c.565 B.C.). Although tradition has it that Sappho was happily married and had a daughter, her overwhelming passion for women was as deep as any love of a woman for a man.

Labels are originally used to describe specific behavior in a specific situation. Later, however, these labels are used to include the whole person. As early as 1948, Kinsey warned us against categorizing per-

sons as heterosexual or homosexual; rather, he said, we should speak of individuals as having had certain amounts of heterosexual or homosexual experience. Kinsey went on to say that the term "homosexual" should not be used as a substantive that stands for persons or as an adjective that describes persons. He recommended that it should be used to describe the nature of the overt sexual reactions or the sexual stimuli to which persons respond. A similar view was expressed by Alan P. Bell (1975):

> There is no such thing as homosexuality. By this I mean that the homosexual experience is so diverse, the variety of its psychological, social and sexual correlates so enormous, its originating factors so numerous, that to use the word "homosexuality" or "homosexual" as if it meant more than simply the nature of a person's sexual object choice is misleading and imprecise. When a male or female patient announces his or her homosexuality to the physician, the doctor must conclude nothing more than that the patient becomes erotically aroused by persons of the same sex. As we consider the diversity of homosexual experience, we shall see the crucial mistake in inferring anything more. To put it another way, there are as many different kinds of homosexuals as heterosexuals, and thus it is impossible to predict the nature of any patient's personality, social adjustment, or sexual functioning on the basis of his or her sexual orientation.

Any kind of woman, then, can be a lesbian. She may be single or married with children. Like everybody else, she may be rich, poor, stupid, or intelligent. The only difference is her sexual preference. The label "lesbian" describes only one aspect of her behavior. However, a lesbian is not accepted by society but is regarded as abnormal and sick. In 1973, the American Psychiatric Association voted to exclude homosexuality from its list of mental illnesses. Nevertheless, the label still retains its negative connotations. Throughout the years, strong emotional reactions toward homosexuality and an intolerance of homosexual persons have created many misconceptions about it. This chapter will aim at examining both research and societal beliefs about the homosexual woman.

INCIDENCE OF LESBIANISM

Little attention had been paid to the incidence of lesbianism before the Kinsey Report (1953). Thirteen percent of the Kinsey females had had some homosexual experiences, compared to 37

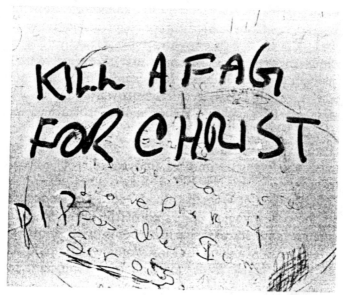

Figure 9.1 Anti-homosexual graffiti in a public bathroom.

percent of the male sample. However, some studies reveal a significantly higher rate of female homosexuality (Caprio, 1954).

It is difficult to estimate the true incidence of homosexuality among women: Because of negative attitudes and the social ostracism of homosexuals, many of them remain "in the closet," keeping their homosexual activities secret. There must be many hidden lesbians among married women and other females. As the following case shows, "coming out" involves many adverse consequences:

> For Elaine Noble, 31, the first avowed lesbian to be elected to state office [to the Massachusetts legislature in 1974], coming out . . . cost her job as an advertising executive, her female lover, who was afraid to be seen with her, "and at least for a time, a certain portion of my sanity." There were obscene phone calls, dirty words written on her car, slashed tires. People looked on her as "a freak, a tattooed lady." "I wonder, if we knew the cost," she says, "would we still have done it" (*Time*, 1975).

The relativity of the concept of homosexuality also makes it difficult to separate the homosexual from the heterosexual. As Sydney Abbot and Barbara Love (1972) put it:

> At what moment does a woman step outside the boundary of acceptable relations with women? When she feels emotion for another woman? If she becomes bisexual? Only if she sleeps for a time exclusively with one woman?

Although one needs to have a single sexual experience with another woman in order to be labeled a homosexual or a lesbian, some psychiatrists, particularly those who are psychoanalytically oriented, are notorious in their indiscriminate use of the concept of latent homosexuality or "unconscious lesbianism." The latent homosexual does not need to show overt sexuality toward the same sex to be given this label. Two cases of unconscious lesbianism reported by Dr. Eustace Chesser (1971) may illustrate the point. In both cases, there was no evidence of any emotional attachment to women. In fact, one of the women admitted that the idea of sexual contact with a woman horrified her. "She didn't want sex of any kind, whether with a man or woman." Evidence for the unconscious lesbianism of the other woman consisted of the fact that she broke off an engagement and started sharing rooms with another woman. According to Chesser, a good-looking woman who could have many boyfriends but who still finds sex with men repugnant must be a lesbian. The women he described, however, were so timid and sexually repressed that they could hardly be sexually aroused by either men or women. It seems that, according to Chesser and other psychoanalysts, the concept of unconscious lesbianism may be applied to any woman. However, rather than being unconscious lesbians, some women tend to hide their homosexual tendencies consciously in order to survive in a predominantly heterosexual world.

Female homosexuality has attracted little attention, and this may have brought about an underestimation of its incidence. Psychologists and psychiatrists have, for the most part, investigated only male homosexuality. On the societal level, female homosexuality arouses less ethical and legal concern than male homosexuality. For example, although male homosexuality has been made a crime, female homosexuality is not considered an offense in most European countries. Chesser (1971) pointed out that, historically, lesbianism did not excite the same horror as male homosexuality because of the prevalent ignorance of the nature of the sexual act:

> It was believed that semen contributed the whole of the embryo. The womb was merely a receptacle in which the embryo was nourished. Since male homosexuality, like masturbation, resulted in loss of semen it seemed more heinous than the frictional pleasure of the female.

Bailey (1955) interpreted legislation against male homosexuality as reflecting male-female status: "The lesbian's practices . . . do not

imply any lowering of her personal or sexual status, and can be ignored by a society which is still, in some respects, fundamentally androcentric. To 'corrupt' a younger girl by initiating her into the pleasures of tribadism is thought trivial compared with the 'corruption' of a youth by 'making a woman of him,' or inciting him to inflict such a degradation upon a fellow man.''

Differential attitudes toward male and female homosexuality may reflect the nature of the female participation in the sexual act and the concern of society for the procreational function of sex. That is, whereas exclusively homosexual females may be ready or could even be forced to have sexual intercourse and be impregnated, exclusively homosexual males can hardly be aroused by the female, making intercourse and procreation impossible.

SEX ROLE AND LESBIANISM

One popular belief about the homosexual woman is that she is aggressive, competitive, and masculine in physical appearance and dress. She is a woman who wants to be a man, smoke a cigar, and play football (the stereotype of the homosexual male is the "limp-wristed faggot" who may work as an interior decorator, a hairdresser, or a ballet dancer). It is therefore not surprising that the homosexual woman has been described as a seductive and aggressive female who combines active homosexuality and transvestism (cross-dressing). A stereotype of the lesbian is illustrated by Rubenstein (1964) in the case of N. N. was a young girl of average feminine appearance, but from the age of 10 onward, she had shown a strong desire to behave in a masculine manner, cutting her hair short and wearing masculine clothing. This tendency was encouraged by an older girlfriend of a domineering personality to whom she was very attached and was ready to submit. She also showed a preference for boys' games throughout her childhood. From puberty on, she had had love affairs with girls about her own age with whom she insisted on taking the active role. She liked her partners to be feminine, and she enjoyed stimulating them by manual masturbation. She always developed very tender feelings for her friends and felt depressed when they eventually left her for boyfriends.

The presumed relationship between homosexuality and sex-role reversal may be seen in the psychiatric classification of homosexuals into passive and active types. The passive homosexual takes the

female role in sexual contact, whereas the active homosexual takes the masculine role. Although homosexuality has traditionally been considered an abnormal behavior by psychiatrists, the passive homosexual male and the active homosexual female are considered more abnormal than the active homosexual male and the passive homosexual female. The homosexual is considered more abnormal when she or he shows sex-role reversal by taking the role of the opposite sex in the sexual relationship. Recent research has shown that there is no clear-cut classification of active and passive homosexuals. Homosexual couples alternate between these two roles (Saghir & Robins, 1969; Saghir, Robins, & Walbran, 1969).

Abse (1974) noted that the roles played by a homosexual female couple may take various forms. They may sometimes reflect the mother-daughter relationship, and sexual intercourse itself may emphasize all those facets of lovemaking concerned with tenderness, including gentle caresses and endearments. At other times, there is a greater emphasis on playing a male role by the dominant partner (the butch), whereas the more passive partner (the femme or fem) responds as "his" wife. Also, tribadism (opposition and friction of the female genitals) occurs as one woman lies on top of the other in order to stimulate coitus. Some lesbians may freely exchange roles, for the "male" player may be left unsatisfied unless there is role reversal. The butch may maintain the illusion of masculinity by the manner of dress, a short haircut, an absence of makeup, or the assumption of the male's economic role. The butch may also initiate heterosexual intercourse by wearing a dildo (artificial penis), sometimes one with a vibrating, electrically powered rubber tip. Except for the butch, lesbians are undistinguishable from other females in physique, dress, or mannerisms.

Martin and Lyon (1972) suggested that the butch-femme idea came about because it is an advantage to be a man. Some lesbians who are convinced that they are more masculine than feminine tend to equate masculinity with aggression, power, and superiority and femininity with passivity, inferiority, and softness. In this thinking, they are following social stereotypes by equating femininity with inferiority. Other lesbians may learn early that if you are sexually attracted to a woman, you should play the masculine role—that is, get yourself a wife. They find that "heterosexual marriage is the only available and accepted model for women setting up housekeeping." Another reason for going through the "butch" stage is

simply for identification. "If you look like any other woman on the street, how in the world are you going to find other Lesbians, or, more to the point, how are they going to find you? So stereotyping yourself may serve a plus function at the beginning of one's gay career." Finally, an interesting butch-femme pattern is when the couple try to act out the entire male-female dichotomy in their partnership. The femmes insist that their butches wear only male clothing and that they appear and act as nearly like the stereotyped male as possible. Most of these femmes have been divorced more than once. It appears that they have been so badly treated by men that they cannot bear the idea of remarrying. Thus, the butch-femme relations adopted by some lesbians appear to reflect various motivational and situational factors rather than intrinsic sex-role tendencies. Basically, a lesbian does not want a "man." As Abbott and Love (1971) put it, a lesbian "discovers that a woman who wants a woman usually wants a woman."

The association between active homosexuality on the one hand and the aggression and the superiority of the male on the other is also found in other cultures. Ford and Beach (1952) reported that cultures in which violence and mastery are regarded as attributes of the male are also constantly aware of active homosexuality as an expression of virility. The Iatmul of New Guinea offer such an example: They have at least eleven words for sodomy, and these are frequent terms of abuse. In this society, passive homosexuality is regarded as the fate of captives in war. In describing homosexuality in the traditional Arab Middle East, Al-Issa and Al-Issa (1970) pointed out that, at a certain age, young boys must leave the world of women and children (that is, female and young members of the family at home) and join the exclusive society of men. Their strong need to belong to the male world is exploited by older adult males in order to induce them to homosexual practices. As the culture looks down on this passive sexual role (that is, the feminine role), these young boys soon assert their virility, and, in their turn, they start playing the roles of active homosexuals.

In contrast, Ford and Beach (1952) describe a form of institutionalized male homosexuality where taking the female passive role is not degrading but brings considerable prestige and power in the community. In some societies, the man who assumes the feminine role is regarded by other members of the community as a powerful shaman. Among the Siberian Chukchee, such an individual puts on

women's clothing, assumes feminine mannerisms, and may become the "wife" of another man. The couple copulate anally, the shaman always playing the feminine role. In addition to the shaman "wife," the husband usually has another wife with whom he indulges in heterosexual coitus. The shaman may, in turn, support a feminine mistress.

Lesbians are similar to transsexual women in their sexual orientation: Both are sexually attracted to females. However, the transsexual woman, although a physically normal woman, believes that she is a man. A lesbian may adopt masculine behavior, but she does not consider herself a man. Furthermore, a transsexual woman loathes her breasts, genitals, and other feminine characteristics because they interfere with her male self-concept. She may go as far as undergoing an operation for sex change.

In conclusion, sexual relationships between lesbians are quite similar to those between a woman and a man. They are often mutual, but they can sometimes be one-sided. Generally, there are no strict husband or wife roles in homosexual relations, although a minority might occasionally assume a predominantly insertor or insertee role during the sexual act.

HOMOSEXUAL VS. HETEROSEXUAL WOMEN

Sexual Behavior

Homosexual arousal of homosexual women is reported at an earlier age than the heterosexual arousal of heterosexual women (Saghir & Robins, 1973). In the Saghir and Robins study, about one-half of the homosexual women denied ever having had a romantic attachment to a boy or a man. However, the majority of those homosexual women with a history of heterosexual attachment developed their feelings during the adolescent years. In contrast, heterosexual women developed sexual feelings during the preadolescent as well as during the adolescent years. Findings reveal that homosexual orientation tends to occur early in the lives of homosexual women.

Riess (1974) reported that, although the sexual activity of homosexual women is less frequent than that of a heterosexual group, they tend to have orgasm more frequently and more easily. However, masturbation plays a greater part in the life of the homosexual than

in that of the heterosexual woman. Also, factors other than sex tend to be important to homosexual women; although they find sex satisfactory and enjoyable, the meaning of the female-female relationship seems to depend less on sex than love, warmth, contact, and a sense of oneness.

Parental Relationships

The parental background of homosexual women has attracted the attention of research workers. Most studies have their starting point with the finding by Bieber, Dain, Dince, Drellich, Grand, Gundlach, Kremer, Rifkin, Wilbur, and Bieber (1962) that the family of the male homosexual shows a pattern of a seductive, controlling mother and a withdrawn, hostile, rejecting father. Researchers expected the opposite behavior in the parents of lesbians. The data, however, tended to be inconsistent. Kaya, Berl, Clare, Eleston, Gershwin, Gershwin, Kogan, Torda, and Wilbin (1967), for example, found that female homosexuals have intimate and controlling fathers, though their mothers did not differ in behavior from a heterosexual group. Likewise, Gundlach and Riess (1968) did not find a difference between the parents of the two groups. Saghir and Robins (1973) observed a significant tendency of homosexual women to describe their mothers as dominant (53 percent), in contrast to the mothers of heterosexual women (23 percent). They tended also to describe a poor relationship with the mother and a closer and more mutual relationship with the father (Saghir & Robins, 1973). From these studies, it may be concluded that there is no unique pattern that distinguishes the families of homosexual from those of heterosexual women.

A study by Siegelman (1972) revealed that the parental background of lesbians is more disturbed than that of heterosexuals. However, when the family background of a group of homosexuals scoring low on neuroticism (emotional instability) was compared with a sample of heterosexuals with similar scores, there was no significant difference between the groups. Indeed, it appears that it is not sexual orientation but the degree of emotional stability that is the deciding factor in daughter-parent relationships. In a more recent work, Siegelman (1974) also found that the tendency of homosexuals to report more rejecting, less loving, or more demanding parents tended to be related to their level of emotional stability

rather than to homosexuality. However, homosexuals in general reported less closeness to their parents and less family security. These women felt more distant, insecure, misunderstood, and unhappy with their parents than heterosexual women.

One important factor that might affect the relationship between a lesbian and her parents is the negative attitude of these parents toward homosexuality. Ruth Simpson (1976) reported that when a number of heterosexual women were asked how they would feel, and what they would do, should they learn that their daughters were lesbians, their responses were negative: "I would take her to a psychiatrist immediately and have her cured"; "I would rather she would get pregnant—at least that would be normal"; "I would see to it that she was married as soon as possible"; "If her father ever found out he'd kill me." Simpson (1976) wrote: "The family closet, the only temporarily safe place for the young homosexual, cannot help alienating the child from the parent. As the young lesbian reaches her teens, she sometimes feels obliged to have sexual relations with a boy. Often, in such cases, she is motivated partly by the hope that her parents won't suspect her true sexuality. This adds further to the sense of alienation and resentment that inevitably builds up between child and parent."

Psychological Disturbance

Studies usually show no significant difference in abnormalities between homosexual women and heterosexual women. Saghir and Robins (1969; 1973) found that homosexual women are no more neurotic or psychotic than their heterosexual counterparts. The occurrence of depression and neurotic disorders is quite similar among the two groups. The majority of homosexual women attributed their depression to specific events mainly related to their homosexuality, often to the break-up of a love relationship with another woman (Saghir & Robins, 1973). Saghir and Robins noted that the only significant difference between homosexual women and heterosexual women is in the prevalence of excessive and problem drinking in the former group.

Louis Diamant (1977) has demonstrated that, in a group of young lesbians and heterosexual women matched for age, education, and occupation, there is no difference in the emotional stability (neurotic behavior) of the groups. However, the lesbians were more

outgoing and sociable (extroverted), and more politically liberal than heterosexual women. Diamant suggested that what is labeled "neurotic" by practitioners may only be a stress reaction of some lesbians to their unfavorable minority status. There are, in fact, some studies showing homosexual women to be lower than heterosexual women on objective psychological measures of mental illness, such as hypochondriasis, hysteria, depression, paranoia, and schizophrenia (Ohlson & Wilson, 1974). An earlier study by Hopkins (1969) also revealed that homosexual women had more positive personality characteristics: They were more independent, more resilient, more dominant, and more self-sufficient than heterosexual women.

LESBIANS VS. MALE HOMOSEXUALS

Lesbians begin their homosexual activities later in life than homosexual men. Only a small proportion, about 24 percent, of homosexual women became involved sexually prior to the age of 15, as compared with three-fourths of homosexual men, who became sexually active before that age (Saghir & Robins, 1973).

Lesbians tend to form more stable and long-term relationships than homosexual men. The one-night stand or casual contacts and frequent changes of partners seem to characterize male homosexuality. Although in general, men are more promiscuous (engage with more sex partners) than women, homosexual men seem to be much more promiscuous than heterosexual men (Kinsey et al., 1953; Saghir & Robins, 1973). Cruising of public places, such as parks, beaches, movie houses, streets, and bars, is a male rather than a female activity. In order to find sex partners, homosexual women usually start a relationship and continue it over a period of time before any sexual contact occurs. The potential partner is most often found in a socially acceptable setting, such as in the school or college where they are enrolled, or at parties, social gatherings, homosexual bars, or in the context of athletic activity and work. Their "cruising" is not significantly different from that of heterosexual women.

The male homosexual's constant search for a partner may bring him into conflict with the law. It is, for instance, not unusual for homosexual men to respond to graffiti at a public lavatory for a casual sexual encounter. Eustace Chesser (1971) described the case

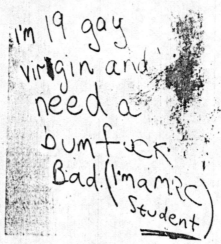

Figure 9.2 Bathroom graffiti.

of a schoolmaster who responded to an invitation for a rendezvous. A man was waiting on a seat in the park. He was neatly dressed and good-looking. "I approached him and he smiled. When I sat down and smiled back, his expression changed." He said, "I am a police officer and I am going to charge you with importuning." The schoolmaster appeared in court and was fined. The magistrate told him that he should be ashamed of himself and that he was not fit to be in charge of boys. He lost his job, and it was impossible for him to continue in the teaching profession or even to live in the same town.

The casual sexual encounters of the homosexual male would indicate his interest in the physical rather than the emotional aspect of the relationship. Homosexual men, in fact, tend to be more

Figure 9.3 Bathroom graffiti.

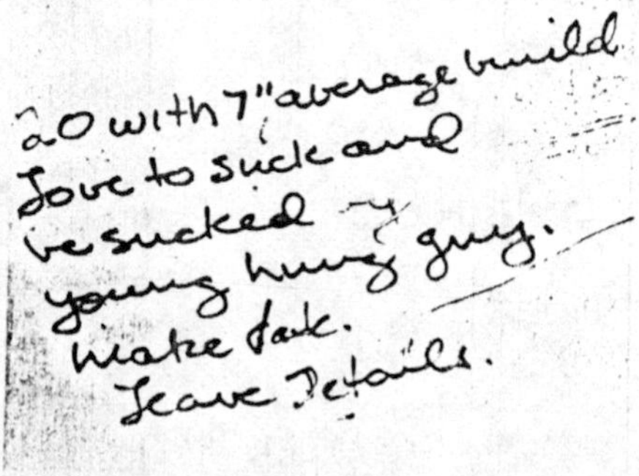

sexually stimulated by the physical characteristics of the partner than do homosexual women (Bell, 1975). Homosexual women, however, invest more emotionality in their relationships and expect more out of them than homosexual men; they, therefore, react more intensely to the break-up.

A significant number of both homosexual women (20 percent) and men (18 percent) tend to get married. But, as expected, there is also a high rate of divorce among married homosexual persons. In their heterosexual experiences, homosexual men tend to experience fears of sexual impotence, whereas homosexual women experience fears of harm or physical injury to their genitals in relation to intercourse. However, neither homosexual women nor homosexual men are disgusted by the sight of the genitals of the opposite sex (Saghir & Robins, 1973).

HOMOSEXUAL TECHNIQUES

Sex with a woman includes: touching, kissing, smiling, looking serious, embracing, talking, digital intercourse, caressing, looking, cunnilingus, undressing, remembering later, making sounds, sometimes gently biting, sometimes crying, and breathing and sighing together.

Liz, my roommate, and I have oftentimes made love when one of us has emotional problems—the love of friends. In this case, Liz had a bad experience and I made love to her. I first kissed her forehead, then her lips, and then very gently massaged her breasts. Gently kissing and rubbing them, sucking her nipples. While doing this, she usually either squeezes my breasts or rubs my shoulders. I then caress her vagina and perform cunnilingus on her. I then take the position of the man and let her kiss and hug me. This is when the emotion comes out. If she wants to, she then makes love to me (Hite, 1976).

Manual-genital stimulation is the most prevalent sexual practice among homosexual women (Saghir & Robins, 1973). All homosexual women practice it at one time or another in order to achieve orgasm. Similarly, cunnilingus, which involves oral-genital activity, seems to be universal among homosexual women.

Another practice is full-body contact, which involves body to body friction or pressure (tribadism). Saghir and Robins found this practice infrequently used by about one-third of homosexual women. Object-genital insertion is employed by over one-fourth of homosex-

ual women. In three-fourths of those who used objects on themselves or with others, the object used was a penis-shaped structure made of hard rubber. A much smaller number in a group studied by Hunt (1974) employed an artificial penis on another woman (2 percent). Compared with homosexual women, none of the heterosexual women studied by Saghir and Robins reported the use of inanimate objects for vaginal self-insertion or as a practice in their relationship with men.

THE HOMOSEXUAL WOMAN, SOCIETY, AND THE PSYCHIATRIC PROFESSION

Apart from her sexual orientation, the homosexual woman hardly differs from other women. She is no more psychotic, neurotic, or emotionally disturbed (Hooker, 1957; Riess, 1974; Saghir & Robins, 1969). Because of social attitudes, however, the lesbian is discriminated against as a woman and as a homosexual. Gene Damon (1970) observed that discrimination against women is even noticed in homophile organizations. Those "organizations open to both male and female homosexuals practice the same sort of sexual denigration of women as does the heterosexual society at large. When they *are* members, no matter how loyal, they seldom hold office, and if they do it is, yes, secretary or treasurer. . . . When you examine . . . the bond that should bind these people, the male and female homosexuals, it is simply intolerable to find the social prejudices reinforced here." Sydney Abbot and Barbara Love (1971) also noted that:

Lesbians are doubly outcast, both as women and as homosexuals. Lesbians, like all women, are not encouraged to be independent or to educate themselves; as women they are always treated as inferior. On the other hand, they are denied the benefits of the sexist system: financial security, recognition in the home, maternal power. They suffer the oppression of all women but are not eligible for any of the rewards. Whereas heterosexual women are moving from a position in society that is privileged—wife and mother—to a freer position, lesbians are a minority fighting for the right to exist. The lesbian suffers the oppression of all women—only more so. Women get lower pay than men on the job, while lesbians are fired when their sexual preference is discovered. (Lesbians have not yet reached the level of tokenism.) A woman in college is fighting for grades equal to men's, but a lesbian is coping with

fears and anxieties about being expelled. A divorced woman has a nearly un-challenged right to her children, but a lesbian's children are forcibly taken from her. Men are satisfied if a woman remains silent, but a lesbian triggers anger and hostility. A gigantic law suit should be instituted against schools, industry, and the psychiatric profession for severe psychic damage done to homosexuals, as well as to women.

Homosexual women are slightly more involved with psychotherapists than heterosexual women. A majority of homosexual women go for therapy during a period of depression or to alleviate their guilt feelings; there was only a minority who went into therapy with the aim of a change in sexual orientation (a majority of heterosexual women also went into therapy to deal with depression [Saghir & Robins, 1973]).

Traditionally, psychotherapists aim at changing the sexual orientation of homosexual persons. Psychoanalytically oriented psychotherapy has generally failed to accomplish this aim. More drastic therapeutic techniques have been used on homosexual men, in particular on those who are institutionalized. Valenstein (1973), for example, reported that psychosurgery had been used in the treatment of homosexual criminals. By far the most frequently used method for changing sexual orientation is aversive therapy—that is, associating homosexual arousal with aversive stimuli such as an electric shock (Feldman & MacCulloch, 1965; 1971). This method has almost always been associated with the treatment of homosexual males. Since only male homosexuality used to be illegal, a large number of criminal homosexual men were available for treatment in institutions. The absence of aversive treatment with females may be the result of their unavailability in institutions, since female homosexuality has not been considered a crime.

Indeed, reports concerning the treatment of homosexual women are very rare. One exception is a study by Blitch and Haynes (1972) in which they emphasize the use of systematic desensitization, role-playing (playing certain roles in the therapy situation to overcome the client's social deficiencies, such as increasing her ability to accept compliments, to disagree with friends, and to assert her feelings), and the use of masturbation fantasies. Ullmann and Krasner (1975) also discussed the treatment of homosexual women. They suggested that the first step for dealing with a homosexual female is to aim at the "development of good interpersonal relationships, with both women and men. As such, we are likely to focus on stick-

ing up for one's legitimate rights, being able to express one's feelings and having them respected. After a good relationship has been established with a male, the treatment is similar to that for orgasmic dysfunction."

It may not be possible to tackle the problems of homosexual women by changing their sexual orientation, but it may be possible to do so by dealing with social discrimination against women and other minority groups. The basic problems of these women are economic and social rather than sexual in nature:

> By her very nature the lesbian is cast in the role of breadwinner and will be a member of society's working force most of her life, since there is no male in her life to support her. Because of traditionally low pay for "women's work" the lesbian is very much concerned with equal job opportunities for women and with "equal pay for equal work" laws. Because of her anticipated longevity in the working force she is vitally concerned with equal opportunity for education and professional careers for women. Because she is taxed as a single person at the highest available rate regardless of her commitments she is also concerned with the tax deductions for head of household espoused by many women's rights groups. Because she may be a working mother she has a definite stake in proposals for child centers. Because of societal pressures against her lesbian commitment she may find herself involved with men and therefore might very well have need of birth control information and/or abortion (Martin & Lyon, 1972).

Some radical homosexual women, in fact, consider lesbianism as a political stance rather than a sexual preference. For these women, heterosexuality represents one aspect of a limited and restricted female role. They can no longer have sex with men who consider them solely as sex objects rather than as persons. Indeed, the meaning of women's liberation for these "nouveau" lesbians is making a "conscious choice of opening themselves up to making *love* to women rather than having *sex* with men" (Rule, 1975).

What, then, is the role of the professional in dealing with the female homosexual? It is important that the professional helps the woman to come to grips with the urgent problems that bring her to the clinic. These problems may include depression, anxiety, or alcoholism. Or they may be related to her relationship with her partner (guilt feelings, reactions to a broken relationship, and so on). As far as sexual orientation is concerned, the professional should help the female adjust to her homosexual role (for example, by

using behavioral techniques, such as desensitization, to reduce her anxiety and tension) rather than taking a negative stand and trying to eliminate homosexual behavior by drastic techniques (shock therapy).

In 1974, Gerald Davison, in his presidential address to the Association for the Advancement of Behavior Therapy, strongly supported the view that persons engaging in homosexual behavior should not be treated for sexual orientation change. He noted that "the very existence of sexual reorientation programs might very well impede social change towards a lessening of cultural prejudice and of legal oppression." Davison believes that, because society and the professional view homosexuality as a pathological condition, homosexual persons are pressured against their will into seeking treatment. He suggested that "as behavior therapists and clinicians, we might perhaps pay more attention to the quality of human relationships, to the way people deal with each other, rather than to the particular gender of the adult partners" (Davison, 1974).

Traditionally, homosexual persons are treated as sick persons. The major issue facing the professional, as well as society at large, is whether to accept homosexuality and other "deviations," such as schizophrenia and depression, as an aspect of a natural and varied human potential or to consider them as illnesses to be cured or contagious diseases to be shunned and isolated. The labels "homosexual," "schizophrenic," and "depressive" arouse the fears of "normals" because they awaken those elements of human behavior that are repressed through severe socialization. "Normals" fear the homosexual person because she or he reminds them of their own repressed bisexuality. Schizophrenics are feared because they openly manifest the "normal's" repressed irrationality. The depressive person also arouses anxiety because she or he expresses the repressed emotionality of the "normal." However, it is only by accepting bisexuality, irrationality, and emotionality as parts of themselves that "normals" may be able to live in peace with these minorities.

Women,
Alcoholism,
Drug Abuse,
and Criminality

part four

If hed fucker maybe she could get the money out of his pocket. But he just talked. The hell with it. She hit him over the head with the bottle. She emptied his pockets . . . Give me my wallet you goddam whore. She spit in his face and told him ta go fuck himself. . . Tralala screamed in his face that he was a no good mothafuckin sonofabitch and then started kicking him. . . Ya lousy fuckin hero. Go peddle a couple of medals if yaneed money so fuckin bad.

. . . and more came 40 maybe 50 and they screwed her and went back on line and had a beer and yelled and laughed. . . and she laughed and she drank more and more and soon she passedout and they slapped her a few times and she mumbled and turned her head but they couldnt revive her so they continued to fuck her as she lay unconscious on the seat in the lot and soon they tired of the dead piece. . . tore her clothes to small scraps put out a few cigarettes on her nipples pissed on her jerkedoff on her jammed a broomstick up her snatch then bored they left her lying amongst the broken bottles rusty cans and rubble of the lot. . .

Hubert Selby, Jr.: LAST EXIT TO BROOKLYN

Women, Alcoholism, and Drug Abuse

10

MacDuff: What things does drink especially provoke?
Porter: Lechery, sir, it provokes, and unprovokes; it provokes the desire,
but takes away the performance.

MACBETH, II, iii

Drug use is a universal phenomenon. Human beings seem to be highly motivated to ingest certain substances, such as tea, coffee, alcohol, marijuana, and other drugs, in order to achieve mood changes and to reach an altered state of consciousness. Drug use and abuse is, however, traditionally considered a male behavior. This chapter deals with the relationship between sexual status on the one hand and alcoholism and drug abuse on the other.

SEX DIFFERENCES IN ALCOHOLISM AND DRINKING

Alcoholic women form between one-sixth and one-fifth of alcoholics in the United States (Jellinek, 1960; Lisansky, 1957). This ratio, however, varies from one treatment setting to the other. For example, figures from private clinics indicate no sex differences in alcoholism (Schuckit & Morrissey, 1976).

Sex differences in the rates of alcoholism must be related to the extent to which women and men are normally allowed to use alcohol. In North America, studies with students as well as with other adults in the 1950s and 1960s clearly show that drinking is strongly associated with male rather than with female roles (Forslund & Gustafson, 1970). The report of alcohol use was significantly lower among females (Slater, 1952; Straus & Bacon, 1953). However, studies carried out in the late 1960s show that the gap between the sexes has decreased considerably as a result of an increase in the rate of drinking for women. For example, surveys of teenage alcohol use between 1968 and 1971 reveal that the difference between boys and girls in the use of alcohol was decreasing at most grade levels each successive year (Wechsler & McFadden, 1976). Similar trends were found in a national survey of drinking practices conducted in the United States in late 1964 and early 1965, using a random sample of persons age 21 and older (Cahalan, Cislan, & Crossley, 1969). It was shown that there had been an increase in drinking for both sexes during the last twenty-five years: The percentage of American men who drink rose from 75 to 77 percent, and the percentage for American women rose from 56 to 60 percent. The increase in the percentage of women who drink was, however, twice as large as that for men. As each percentage point represents approximately one million people, the increase in the drinking of females was indeed substantial. Nevertheless, heavy drinking was reported by only 5 percent of women, but by 21 percent of men (a heavy drinker is one who drinks nearly every day, with five or more drinks at a time at least occasionally, or one who drinks at least weekly, usually with five or more drinks on most occasions).

In the early 1970s, the rate of drinking among the sexes seems to have equalized. In a survey carried out in 1974, Henry Wechsler and Mary McFadden (1976) reported that there was no overall difference in the frequent use of alcohol between the sexes among students (grades 9–12) from several high schools in two Massachusetts communities (Town A and Town B). Similarly, there were no sex differences in the number of students in Town A who had been intoxicated on beer, wine, or distilled spirits during the year. (Intoxication is defined in terms of self-reports of getting drunk on beer, wine, or hard liquor.) In Town B, however, significantly more girls than boys reported intoxication on wine and distilled spirits, whereas a larger, but not significant proportion of boys said they had become intoxicated on beer during the year. Although the gap between the sexes in the frequency of drinking in high school has diminished, in a study of groups of men and women in thirteen universities, Ruth Engs (1978) found almost five times as many males (20.1 percent) as females (4.3 percent) who were heavy drinkers.

There have also been some recent changes among women and men in the consequences of drinking related to driving (Argeriou & Paulino, 1976; Whitehead & Ferrence, 1976). Traditionally, women drink less and drive less than men, and their arrests for drunken driving are relatively low (Rimmer, Petto, Reich, & Winokur, 1971). However, figures for the period between 1972 and 1975 show that rates of collision and drunken driving were increasing among females and, in particular, among young women under the age of 21 (Argeriou & Paulino, 1976; Whitehead & Ferrence, 1976).

Diminishing sex differences in the consumption of alcohol or in drunken driving among young persons should predict similar changes in the rates of alcoholism in the general population. The rates may also reflect changes in the traditional social attitudes toward the drinking of women and men, which are discussed in the next section.

ATTITUDES TOWARD FEMALE DRINKING

Traditional North American attitudes toward drinking and drunkenness reflect double standards: Both females and males think that it is worse for women to drink. Straus (1970) has, in fact, found that women were somehow more indoctrinated in the prevalent stereotypes than men. Although both sexes were more intolerant of drunkenness in women, women were more tolerant of male drunkenness than males themselves.

Gomberg (1974) noted two aspects of the double standard toward drinking. One reflects the division of labor among the sexes, and the other relates to the loss of emotional inhibitions and sexual restraints through alcohol. Alcohol is assumed to affect women's sensitivity to the needs of others and to her roles as wife, mother, daughter, sister, housekeeper, and nursemaid. The temporary incapacity caused by alcohol is considered a threat to the family, particularly in sensitive areas, such as child care. Indeed, Child, Barry, and Bacon (1965) found that, cross culturally, societies with large sex differences in child-rearing tend to have large sex differences in alcohol consumption; that is to say, the more women have exclusive responsibility for child care and homemaking, the less they are allowed to drink. The study of Child and his associates also shows double standards in the use of alcohol for the disinhibition of emotions. For example, they found sex differences in societies in which drinking is expected to elicit aggression, a behavior almost universally considered masculine rather than feminine. It appears that the more a society emphasizes female versus male stereotypes (looking after children versus tilling the field), the less women are encouraged to consume alcohol.

Straus (1970) reported that both women and men felt that drinking results in sexual excitement or that it accompanies and facilitates petting, necking, and sexual intercourse. However, the association between sexual promiscuity and alcohol is more stressed in the female. This may, of course, be simply due to the fact that although men become impotent by large amounts of alcohol, women are able to take part in sexual activity or at least be sexually available while under the influence of alcohol. Since alcohol is expected to disinhibit emotional responses (aggression, sex), drinking may be used by women and men as an excuse for taking part in sexual activities. The evidence does not, however, support the view that alcoholic women or women who become drunk are more likely to engage in sexual activity. If anything, the evidence suggests a decrease of sexual interest in alcoholic women (Kinsey, 1968; Levine, 1955); they tend to find sexual relationships frightening, uncomfortable, and painful (Blane, 1968). It is quite possible that sex may be used by the lower-class alcoholic woman to obtain alcohol. Similarly, sexual promiscuity may also be related to the locale of drinking and to drinking partners (Lisansky, 1957).

The double standard for the two sexes is shown in the attitudes of college students toward the disinhibition of sexual and aggressive responses caused by alcohol (Straus, 1970). In response to a question about "going too far" in drinking, men felt that male drinkers would be considered as "going too far" in terms of their *aggressive,* violent, and antisocial acts—for example, abusing others, swearing, fighting, getting out of hand, and reckless driving. These male subjects saw "going too far" in females in terms of *sexual misbehavior*—for example, flirting, petting, and sexual promiscuity. The women in the sample explained "going too far" in terms of sexual activity for both sexes; although they predominantly felt that males were *sexually ag-*

gressive when drinking—such as trying to force one to neck with them—they thought that females were *sexually seductive*—that they indulged in "arousing sexual behavior," "making passes" at men. Thus the sex stereotypes discussed in Chapter 1 seem to be reflected in beliefs about the effects of alcohol on women and men.

EFFECTS OF ALCOHOL ON WOMEN AND MEN

There are both physical and behavioral effects of alcohol. Because of their excessive drinking, men are expected to have more physical complications than women; for example, men report more blackouts and cirrhosis of the liver. This section will deal primarily with the behavioral effects of alcohol.

Drunkenness is usually differentiated from intoxication. Drunkenness refers to inappropriate behavior as a result of drinking, whereas intoxication is the level of alcohol in the blood. Morgan Jones and Marilyn Jones (1976) reported that, when body weight is controlled, women become more intoxicated than men following a given dose of alcohol. A possible explanation is that the total body weight of men is composed of more water than that of women. Since alcohol is distributed throughout the body in proportion to the water content of body tissues, alcohol tends to be more diluted in the body of the male than in the female (the male body has more muscles, which contain more water). Jones and Jones also reported that, during the premenstrual period when hormones are low, there is also a higher level of intoxication for a given dose than during other periods of the cycle. They suggested that estrogen levels may affect the degree of intoxication by alcohol.

Apart from the physical effects of alcohol, the behavioral effects of alcohol—will she or he withdraw, be friendly, or be aggressive?—seem to be influenced by learning and past experience. Barry (1976) noted that cross-cultural variation in reaction to alcohol indicates that it usually releases whichever behavior is accepted in the culture; it may be assertiveness and aggression, or it may be sociability and friendliness. Since our society encourages men and women to express different behaviors, alcohol may also affect them differently.

Since drinking and alcoholism are traditionally more prevalent among men than among women, theory and research have attempted to understand them in relation to male rather than to female behavior. One approach to explain the effects of alcohol is that drinking satisfies the dependency needs of the alcoholic male. His craving for maternal care is satisfied by heavy drinking, which produces a state similar to infantile dependency. It is assumed that the female is given more opportunities by society to be dependent and that she is therefore less motivated to seek alcohol (Beckman, 1976).

A theory that seems somehow opposite to the dependency hypothesis is postulated by McClelland, Davis, Kalin, and Wanner (1972) in *The Drinking Man*. The need for power is viewed as the underlying factor in heavy drinking and alcoholism. Alcohol is expected to enhance masculine characteristics, such as aggression, assertiveness, and self-reliance, and to decrease feminine characteristics, such as dependency. The relationship between male heavy drinking and aggression suggested by McClelland is found in experimental research as well as in almost all non-Western societies (Horton, 1943; Taylor & Gammon, 1975).

Although studies investigating the factors underlying heavy drinking used male subjects, it is assumed that women who are heavy drinkers or alcoholics are having problems related to their feminine identity; drinking is a sign of a rejection of femininity and an adoption of the masculine role (the need for power). It is argued that "women are under less pressure to drink heavily, particularly during adolescence, than are men. If they do drink heavily, they are to some extent assuming a masculine role. While young men may think that drinking is a way of showing their adulthood, women may feel it is a way of showing that they can do anything men can do" (Beckman, 1975).

Schuckit and Morrissey (1976) hypothesized that, if alcoholic women engage in "masculine" behavior more often than nonalcoholic women, they are also more likely to hold a job and to show a higher rate of college attendance than women in the general population. Studies tended to support this hypothesis, suggesting a relationship between "masculine" sex-role behavior adopted by women and the probability of developing alcoholism. These findings may, however, be the result of a sample bias; that is to say, the groups studied might have included a large number of employed and highly educated women, a group who tends to seek treatment for their drinking problems more often than alcoholic housewives. There is, of course, the possibility that both employment and college education bring the female into a predominantly male environment and give her more opportunity to learn heavy drinking, which is typical of the male (Keil, 1978).

In contrast to their male counterparts, women may not become aggressive after drinking. Wilsnack (1976) noted that, when females were asked to list adjectives to describe how they felt after taking two drinks, they mentioned "warm," "considerate," "expressive," "pretty," "feminine," and so on. In accord with this finding, Wilsnack hypothesized that women drink to increase their feelings of femininity and womanliness. In support of this hypothesis, she found that alcohol decreases the female concern with power and assertiveness and increases a woman's positive feelings and her sense of contentment. She also found that the feminine attitudes, interests, and values (cooking, raising children) of alcoholic women did not differ from those of nonalcoholics; in fact, they tended to value the maternal role more highly than the other group. Again, the view that alcoholic women are "masculine" is not supported.

Wilsnack (1976) suggested that alcoholic women may have sex-role conflicts between what they consciously accept as the traditional feminine role and their unconscious masculine identification; although they reveal feminine behavior, they unconsciously doubt their adequacy as women. Beckman (1978) found no indication of sex-role conflicts among the majority of alcoholic women. She also found that nonalcoholic women in treatment for psychiatric problems did not differ from alcoholic women on masculinity-femininity measures. It was concluded that, whatever problems alcoholic women have in the area of sex-role identification, these problems are not unique to alcoholic women but are shared by other women with emotional problems.

Effects of Alcohol During Pregnancy

It has been recognized since ancient times that drinking may affect the fetus. A statement attributed to Aristotle says, "Foolish and drunken hairbrained women most often bring forth children like unto themselves, morose and languid" (Streissguth, 1976). Unfortunately, serious research in this area has been conducted only during the past decade.

In 1942, Haggard and Jellinek, in their book, *Alcohol Explored*, reported high rates of miscarriage and childbirth mortality in the children of alcoholic women, and yet they attributed these events to poor nutrition and family stresses rather than to alcohol. Likewise, a high incidence of mental retardation, epilepsy, and behavioral disorders were thought to be the result of the "poor stock" of alcoholic families.

The first researcher who established a link between abnormalities in childhood and alcoholism was the American pediatrician, Christy Ulleland (Ulleland, 1972; Ulleland, Wennberg, Igo, & Smith, 1970). In her study of infants who failed to thrive, she observed one environmental factor common to all of them: They all had alcoholic mothers. It is assumed that growth deficiency and developmental delay in these children were the result of the poor care given by alcoholic mothers. Later, however, this was found to be untrue, because these children continued to fail to thrive, even after they were given proper care. Therefore, Ulleland attributed their growth deficiency to the prenatal influences of alcohol rather than to the kind of care they received after birth. Further research on children of chronic alcoholic mothers led to the discovery of the so-called "Fetal Alcohol Syndrome" (Jones, Smith, Ulleland, & Streissguth, 1973). Children with this syndrome were characterized by prenatal growth deficiency (short birth length and low birth weight), retarded physical growth after birth, physical deformities, mental retardation, and delayed motor development.

The amounts of alcohol actually consumed during pregnancy by mothers of children with the fetal alcohol syndrome is varied and does not implicate any specific kind of alcohol drink (Streissguth, 1976). For example, one mother drank two quarts of red wine daily; another mother drank one quart of red wine plus undetermined amounts of hard liquor daily, and so on. It is, however, important to note that there are alcoholic mothers whose children do *not* have the fetal alcohol syndrome. Thus, the amount of alcohol that may cause this syndrome is still undetermined.

PATTERNS OF DRINKING AND ALCOHOLISM IN WOMEN

Alcoholic women are significantly older than men when they first drink, as well as when they first drink to get drunk (Bromet & Moos, 1976). Ullman (1970) found that more men than women became intoxicated to some degree during the first drinking experience.

Women were more likely than men to have had their first drink at home with their parents. Conditions under which the first drink is taken may predict future patterns of drinking behavior. The setting in which girls had their first drink under family supervision and control may bear some relationship to the general finding that fewer women report problem drinking. Drinking with the family may also make them more vulnerable to the influence of parental patterns of drinking.

Lisansky (1957) found that a significantly greater proportion of alcoholic women drink alone, presumably at home. One frequently reported pattern is going to bed at night with a bottle or sipping at home during the day. They mention wine as their favorite beverage. Although wine is considered a more ladylike beverage than beer or hard liquor, it may also be conducive to "plateau drinking" among women. Plateau drinking is when alcoholics frequently imbibe small amounts during the course of a day. Some recent studies give support to the tendency of women to indulge in continuous drinking (Rimmer et al., 1971; 1972; Schuckit, Rimmer, Reich, & Winokur, 1971). Others have, however, suggested that women are more likely to be periodic or bout drinkers than men (Madden & Jones, 1972; Wanberg & Horn, 1973). It is suggested that wine is associated with continuous drinking, whereas spirits are associated with periodic drinking (Jellinek, 1960). Since women now become drunk as frequently as men on both wine and spirits (Wechsler & McFadden, 1976), sex differences in the patterns of drinking may be diminishing. Situational factors may also influence patterns of drinking. Suburban living may encourage continuous drinking, which would not necessarily interfere with homemaking. Periodic drinking seems to be more compatible with work outside the home.

The tendency of alcoholic women to drink alone and at home may affect the consequences of alcoholism, such as arrests or hospitalization, which are significantly more frequent among men than among women attending outpatient clinics (Bromet & Moos, 1976; Lisansky, 1957). Alcoholic women tend to keep out of public view and out of difficulties in the community. These so-called "hidden drinkers" or "secret drinkers" are not a public nuisance but remain in the seclusion and security of their homes.

Another finding related to female patterns of alcoholism is the tendency of alcoholic women to use drugs (tranquilizers, sedatives) more than alcoholic men (Curlee, 1970); this difference has not, however, been found in Britain (Rathod & Thomson, 1971). The greater usage of drugs by female than by male alcoholics appears to parallel the same tendency in the general population. Cahalan and his associates (1969) also found a strong relationship between drinking and cigarette smoking, but this was more evident in women: Eighty-one percent of heavy-drinking women smoked cigarettes, compared to only 19 percent of nondrinking women.

Many descriptions of alcoholic women seem to characterize the middle-class housewife. Lisansky (1957) has, however, compared this outpatient group with lower-class State Farm women (prisoners). The State Farm women tended to be excessive drinkers at an earlier age than did the outpatient group. They were also younger, even though they had been alcoholics just as long as the outpatients. Alcoholism or, at least, problem drinking tended to appear in the families of 92 percent of the State Farm women but occurred in a much smaller proportion in the relatives of the others. The State Farm group also had more psychiatric symptoms. Similarly, bout drinking has been found to be more prevalent among lower-class alcoholic women than among other groups (Mayer, Myerson, Needham, & Fox, 1966).

The pattern of lone drinking is not universal for alcoholic women. The State Farm women tended to drink publicly in bars and taverns. They were also more frequently hospitalized or arrested than the outpatient group. Sexual promiscuity was frequently reported in association with their drinking; it was reported in the records of about half of the State Farm women, as compared with only 11 percent of the outpatients (Lisansky, 1957). Myerson (1959) reported that the higher rates of promiscuity of lower-class prisoners are coupled with evidence of involvement in prostitution. Homosexuality is also more evident in lower-class alcoholic women, with rates as high as 20 percent (Schuckit & Morrissey, 1976). Data, however, reveal higher rates of sexual dysfunctions among higher-class women (Schuckit, 1972a; 1972b).

MOTIVATIONS FOR DRINKING

Life situations and the immediate problems of women may play a major role in precipitating drinking. Indeed, women mention specific past experiences, such as a parent's death, a divorce, an unhappy love affair, or an abortion, as the reasons for their drinking. Men, however, attribute their excessive drinking to individual reasons, such as feeling bored, tense, irritable, and shy (Lisansky, 1957; Ullman, 1970). A more recent study by Mulford (1977) shows that alcoholic women reported more major crises than men during the year before admission for treatment; they reported a major illness, an accident in the family, a major financial setback, and divorce or separation.

Winokur and Clayton (1968) suggested that alcoholism in women is a part of, and perhaps secondary to, another psychiatric condition rather than a separate entity. This suggestion was based on the finding that there was a high incidence of depressive symptoms, suicidal thoughts, and delusions among alcoholic women. It is concluded that women use alcohol to reduce depression and other symptoms. In support of this view, Winokur and Clayton pointed out that the late onset (middle-age) of problem drinking and alcoholism in women tends to coincide with the onset of depression. However, both depression and alcohol abuse may be the result of social problems during middle age.

In contrast to female alcoholism, which is associated with depression, male alcoholism tends to be associated with a previous diagnosis of sociopathy (Schuckit & Morrissey, 1976; Schuckit, Pitts, Reich, King, & Winokur, 1969). Men tend to combine alcoholism with antisocial behavior more often than women. In such cases, alcohol abuse is assumed to be a symptom of an underlying antisocial lifestyle. Sociopathic alcoholism is characterized by an early age of onset of drinking problems, by more marital problems, and by a younger age of admission to a hospital. In contrast, depressive alcoholics, who are predominantly female, have the opposite characteristics: They have a later age of onset, fewer years of alcoholism prior to hospitalization, fewer physical symptoms related to alcoholism, and higher rates of suicide attempts. Schuckit and Morrissey (1976) noted that differences between male and female alcoholics may reflect these differences between sociopathic alcoholics, who are predominantly male, and depressive alcoholics, who are predominantly female. Winokur, Rimmer, and Reich (1971) found that when only primary alcoholics (neither sociopathic nor depressive) are compared, differences between the sexes tend to be drastically reduced.

Menstrual tension has also been considered to explain alcoholism in women (Beckman, 1975). Belfer, Shader, Carroll, and Hormatz (1971) found that 67 percent of menstruating women related the onset of their drinking episodes to premenstrual tension. Podolsky (1963) also related premenstrual tension and depression to alcoholism in women. However, other studies did not find any direct relationship between premenstrual tension and alcoholism (Driscoll & Barr, 1972; Lisansky, 1957). Instead, Lisansky emphasized the overall emotional adjustment of women and, particularly, the degree of their acceptance of physiological changes during menstruation.

There is some relationship between the incidence of gynecological-obstetrical problems, such as infertility, miscarriages, and hysterectomy, on the one hand and alcoholism and heavy drinking on the other (Kinsey, 1966; 1968; Wilsnack, 1973; 1976). Studies are, however, inconsistent about which comes first—drinking or reproductive problems. Some of these studies (Kinsey, 1966; 1968; Curlee, 1970) seem to indicate that women were problem drinkers before their gynecological-obstetrical problems occurred. Others reported by Wilsnack (Wilsnack, 1973; 1976; Pattison, 1975) reveal that most alcoholic women had their reproductive problems several years before they embarked on excessive drinking. Thus, whether or not heavy drinking is caused by gynecological problems is not clear. It may be that, as a result of these problems, a woman may develop a sense of inadequacy about and a lack of preparation for fulfilling her adult role and that, consequently, she may indulge in heavy drinking (Kinsey, 1968; Wood & Duffy, 1966).

In conclusion, the motivation for and the function of drinking may have implications for the development and treatment of alcoholism; for example, drinking to reduce anxiety and tension is more conducive to addiction than drinking as a result of specific external and environmental factors. It is more difficult to deal with inner tension and anxiety, which typically motivate males, than with the family problems that motivate female drinking.

MARITAL STATUS AND ALCOHOLISM

Client: He used to . . . drink . . . (long pause)
Therapist: . . . and . . .
Client: . . . the bum beat me . . .
Therapist: . . . and . . .
Client: . . . he really didn't care about the family . . .
Therapist: . . . and you wish you had him back.
The client immediately began sobbing.

Sheldon Cashdan: INTERACTIONAL PSYCHOTHERAPY:
STAGES AND STRATEGIES IN BEHAVIORAL CHANGE

In alcoholics of both sexes, the rate of those who are married is much lower and the rate of those who are divorced or separated is much higher than in the general population. Proportionately, there are also more single alcoholic men (23 percent) than single alcoholic women (16 percent) (Mulford, 1977). Married alcoholic women report excessive alcoholism and problem drinking in their husbands. Lisansky (1957) pointed out that the likelihood of a woman marrying an alcoholic is approximately 1 in 10, whereas that of a man marrying an alcoholic is about 1 in 50. Bromet and Moos (1976) found that 15 percent of alcoholic men and 52 percent of alcoholic women reported that their spouses were heavy drinkers. These studies have, however, used predominantly lower-class subjects (Schuckit & Morrissey, 1976). Studies of alcoholic women from higher classes show as few as 6 percent having alcoholic husbands (Wood & Duffy, 1966).

Marital status varies with the social class of alcoholic women (Schuckit & Morrissey, 1976). A great number of lower-class alcoholic women are single, separated, or divorced. Prisoners are predominantly unmarried; only 20 to 30 percent live with their husbands. In contrast, more than half of the patients from higher socioeconomic groups were living with their husbands before entering treatment. The number of both legitimate and illegitimate children is higher in the lower-class alcoholic women, a finding that may reflect social class differences with or without alcoholism.

Data suggest that women often become problem drinkers in association with husbands who themselves have alcoholic problems, but this phenomenon rarely works in the other direction (Lisansky, 1957; Rosenbaum, 1958; Wanberg & Knapp, 1970). Surprisingly, women's magazines do not portray the husband as a contributing factor to female alcoholism. On the contrary, he is depicted as supportive to his alcoholic wife and as helping her to recover from alcoholism. His alcoholism is, however, attributed to his nagging wife (Chalfant, 1973).

Gomberg (1974) pointed out that nonalcoholic husbands of problem drinking women may react in a variety of ways: "protectively, unforgivingly, with denial, with anger, and so on." Although marital problems may drive the alcoholic woman to seek help with her drinking, there is generally little information about the response of the husband to her drinking. Since alcoholism is more prevalent among men than among women, the study of the adjustment of the nonalcoholic wife to her alcoholic husband has attracted much at-

Figure 10.1 A Greek woman helping a sick man in a drinking party. Reprinted by permission of the Martin von Wagner Museum der Universität Würzburg.

tention. I shall, therefore, deal in the remaining part of this section with the problems of wives of alcoholics.

The Wives of Alcoholics

It has been frequently observed that the wives of alcoholics are more disturbed than the wives of nonalcoholics (Edwards, Harvey, & Whitehead, 1973; Orford, 1975). Two explanations for their disturbance have been given. On the one hand, it is believed that their choice of alcoholic partners is a manifestation of pathology previous to marriage; they marry an alcoholic to fulfill perverse personal needs. On the other hand, these wives are considered the victims of a stressful situation brought about by the alcoholism of their husbands.

Researchers who emphasize the pathology and personality disturbance of the nonalcoholic spouses of alcoholics suggest the following:

The deviance, or potential deviance, of the alcoholic spouse is often a conscious or unconscious attraction, that the non-alcoholic spouse often has an "investment" in the alcoholic's continued drinking, and that should the latter's deviance cease the non-alcoholic spouse may attempt to engineer his return to deviance or may herself break down. Prominent among these ideas is that of non-accidental mate choice along complementary lines. In particular, the theme of the attraction of opposites along the dominance-submissiveness axis is repeatedly to be found in the literature. The strong-assertive woman attracted to the weak-submissive man is a recurring story (Orford, 1975).

To be the wife of an alcoholic is as awful and pejorative as to be labeled a schizophrenogenic mother (see Chapter 3). Lewis (1937) described the wife of the alcoholic as an aggressive woman who marries a man with a dependent personality and who creates situations that enable her to punish him. More amusing is the categorization of these wives into four types by Whalen (1953). There is the "Suffering Susan," who, to punish herself, chooses an abusive and irresponsible husband who will make her life miserable. The "Controlling Catherine" uses marriage to dominate or to express her resentment toward men, and so she chooses a weak, inept husband. The "Wavering Winnifred" fluctuates between support and condemnation of the husband's alcoholism, but, in order to be loved, she seeks a weak husband who needs her desperately. And, finally, the "Punitive Polly" is the one who needs an emasculated husband to control and punish.

In support of the view that the wife has a vested interest in the alcoholism of her husband, it is claimed that the wives of alcoholics fought their husbands' attempts to get help, undermining the treatment so as to keep the husbands ineffectual (Boggs, 1944); the recovery of the husbands was followed by wives' physical symptoms, anxiety, phobias, depression, and even psychiatric hospitalization (Kalashian, 1959; Macdonald, 1956).

The weight of the evidence is in support of the stress hypothesis; that is to say, the behavior of the alcoholic's wife is a reaction to stressful situations created by the presence of an alcoholic in the family (Orford, 1975). Many studies suggest that the husband's drinking affects the wife's adjustment. Wives of alcoholics tend to have fewer pathological disturbances during their husbands' periods of abstinence (Haberman, 1965). Although the wives of alcoholics manifest more psychophysiological symptoms than those of non-alcoholics, these symptoms diminish drastically when the husbands become abstinent or when the wives leave their alcoholic husbands (Bailey, Haberman, & Alksne, 1962). These findings lend no support to the suggestion that the wives of alcoholics show mental breakdown when their husbands become abstinent. Also, the view that attraction of opposites is involved in the marriage of alcoholics is questionable (Orford, 1975). Similarity between husband and wife was found to be a determining factor in marriage (Berscheid & Walster, 1969).

The behavior of the wives of alcoholics cannot be seen in isolation; it is the result of interaction with their husbands. These wives appear to respond to the intensity and frequency of the alcoholic episodes of their husbands. Their coping behavior tends to change in response to different situations and, in particular, during the husband's stages of drinking (social drinking, excessive drinking, alcoholism, abstinence) (James & Goldman, 1971; Edwards et al., 1973).

Game analysis of alcoholism by Eric Berne (1967) suggests that the wife of an alcoholic may take different roles in dealing with a difficult situation: "at midnight the Patsy, undressing him, making him coffee and letting him beat up on her; in the morning the Persecutor, beating him for the evil of his ways; and in the evening the Rescuer, pleading with him to change them."

In conclusion, the evidence (Edwards et al., 1973; Orford, 1975) shows that the wife of an alcoholic is neither an aggressive woman who marries an alcoholic so that she may dominate him, nor does she become disturbed when her husband becomes abstinent. On the contrary, research indicates that she tends to improve when her husband stops drinking. These wives have basically normal personalities. Their reaction is similar to that of other women under stress.

TREATMENT OF ALCOHOLIC WOMEN

The treatment of alcoholism tends to be oriented toward the male rather than toward the female. Sex differences in the development and reaction to alcohol would predict that treatment settings designed for men may not be suitable for women (Schuckit & Morrissey, 1976).

In general, alcoholic females, like their male counterparts, are not seen for treatment until the drinking problems have gone on for some years. Lindbeck (1972) emphasized the role of professionals in identifying "concealed" alcoholism in women. Women seek help for physical, emotional, or family problems more often than men. They may not know that they have drinking problems. Indeed, only a small number of them may go to the physician specifically for this purpose (Johnson, 1965). Chafetz, Blane, Abram, Golner, Lacy, McCourt, Clark, and Meyers (1962) reported that physicians are able to identify less than half of alcoholics in a group of patients. Moreover, physicians are more likely to miss those who are employed, maritally stable, and not involved with the police. It appears that the middle-class alcoholic woman is more difficult to detect than her lower-class counterpart. Detection of heavy drinking and the consumption of other drugs during pregnancy is, of course, of vital importance for the health of the fetus.

Alcoholic women are not only considered more abnormal than other women, but it is thought that they are more difficult to treat (Gomberg, 1974). Studies of prognosis (outcome of treatment) are inconsistent, showing worse, no different, or better prognosis for women than for men (Beckman, 1976). Many factors seem to affect the outcome of treatment of alcoholic women. Alcoholism in the client's father, the degree of alcohol-related illness (for example, cirrhosis), and the use of drugs other than alcohol indicate poor outcomes. Those who are younger, those who began heavy drinking at a later age, and those who were alcoholics for fewer years present better prospects. Secondary alcoholism with depression, which is prevalent in women, shows a favorable outcome. Likewise, successful treatment seems to be associated with hospital admission as a result of an attempt or threat of suicide. In contrast, sociopathic alcoholism, which is more prevalent in the male, seems to have a poor outcome (Schuckit & Morrissey, 1976). Thus, many factors are involved in the response of women and men to treatment.

That women drink in response to specific situations may make it easier to deal with their alcoholism; this is in contrast to the male, who uses alcohol to reduce his anxiety and tension. It may well be that women prefer individual therapy and that men prefer group therapy because of differences among the sexes in the patterns of alcoholism and in the problems underlying drinking (Gomberg, 1974). Bromet and Moos (1976) summed up the implication of sex differences for treatment as follows:

> The greater prevalence of heavy drinking among relatives of alcoholic women and of solitary drinking suggests that environmental stimuli may facilitate their drinking behavior. One important goal of therapy might be to change the social climate in the home in ways that are conducive to a more abstinent lifestyle. On the other hand, among men [and lower-class or working women] the social contingencies outside the home might be more relevant.

Wilsnack (1976) suggested that the treatment of female alcoholics should deal with the social pressure put on them to conform to traditional feminine values. For the female who is undergoing rapid change in her sex role, the women's movement and consciousness raising may help her to overcome conflicts relating to traditional sex roles and hence reduce her reliance on heavy drinking.

DRUG ABUSE

> But no doctor can tell you anything your own bones don't know. And I can let the doctors in on something. I knew I'd really licked it one morning when I couldn't stand television any more. When I was high and wanted to stay that way, I could watch TV by the hour and love it. Who can tell what detours are ahead? Another trial? Sure. Another jail? Maybe. But if you've beat the habit again and kicked TV, no jail on earth can worry you too much.

> Billy Holiday: THE LADY SINGS THE BLUES

In the discussion of psychotropic drugs in Chapter 2, I was concerned with the legal medical use of drugs. I shall deal here with the illegal nonmedical aspects of drugs. Since drug abuse is primarily considered a male problem, females have been neglected in both research and treatment (Prather & Fidell, 1978; Suffet & Brotman, 1976). There is, however, enough data on female drug abuse, particularly on marijuana in youth and on heroin addiction in adulthood, to suggest that sex roles influence drug use and abuse by women and men.

Sex Differences in Drug Abuse

In general, surveys of the illegal nonmedical use of drugs (marijuana, psychedelics, heroin, etc.) report higher rates in men than in women (Suffet & Brotman, 1976). However, the age of the persons investigated, as well as the date of the study, seems to determine differential rates of drug use among women and men (Prather & Fidell, 1978). If the population studied consists of adults, men are more likely than women to be users of marijuana and other drugs. In the survey conducted for the National Commission on Marijuana and Drug Abuse (*Drug Use in America,* 1973), statistics clearly reveal that, although the number of males is more than double that of females among adults who use marijuana, it is only slightly higher among male than female youth. Studies undertaken *before* the 1970s are more likely than those carried out *after* 1970 to report that more men than women use drugs (Johnson, Donnely, Scheble, Winer, & Weitman, 1971; Wechsler & McFadden, 1976).

Initiation and Patterns of Drug Use

Studies reveal that most females learn the use of drugs from males (Suffet & Brotman, 1976). Among male and female users, it is usually the experienced male who introduces the drug to an inexperienced female (Freeland & Campbell, 1973).

Women tend to start marijuana use at a later age than men. They also make less heavy and less frequent use of the drug (Prather & Fidell, 1978). Although both male and female users usually obtain their marijuana from men, women report being *given* their marijuana, whereas men *purchase* their drug (Bowker, 1975; Prather & Fidell, 1978). It is also reported that the majority of male users have, at some time, sold marijuana, whereas the majority of women have never done so (Goode, 1970).

The use of marijuana seems to be associated with the use of psychotropic drugs (Prather & Fidell, 1978). Among those who obtain these drugs through nonmedical sources, three-fourths of the men and one-half of the women also use marijuana. However, those who obtain psychotropic drugs through medical sources are no more likely to use marijuana than nonusers of psychotropic drugs.

Female narcotic addicts are usually introduced to the drug by a male (Prather & Fidell, 1978). O'Donnell (1969) studied male and female addicts who use narcotics, barbiturates, and alcohol to find out the effects of marriage partners on each other. Results revealed that marriage to an addicted male is related to the later addiction of his wife but that marriage to an addicted female does not result in the addiction of the husband. A study by Howard and Borges (1970) of how drugs (heroin, barbiturates, etc.) are injected found that 68 percent of males, but only 29 percent of females, had "hit" themselves. Since many female addicts are dependent on males for their drugs, it is quite possible that males tend to administer these drugs to the female addict.

Female addicts start the use of narcotics about the same time as their male counterparts, with the majority falling between the ages of 16 and 25 (Ellinwood, Smith, & Vaillant, 1966). Black female addicts reported marijuana as the first illegal drug they used, whereas white females used psychotropic drugs first (Chambers, Hinesley, & Moldestad, 1970). Female addicts report using other drugs in addition to heroin, whereas men tend to use heroin only (Prather & Fidell, 1978).

Karen File (1976) observed that female addicts take five roles in order to meet their needs for narcotics: They may be sellers, bag followers, hustlers, workers, and dependents. She found that the most frequent role is that of a hustler, who engages in various illegal activities, such as shoplifting and prostitution, in addition to drug distribution in order to support her habit. About one-fifth of female addicts work at least part-time, and slightly fewer are housewives (dependents). Eight percent are currently sellers, and these women are almost always involved in a dealing partnership with a male. A small group of female addicts are bag followers, who work with a dealer to support their habits. Bag followers are described as "attractive, usually white, and young. . . . They will carry heroin on their persons since the police are reluctant to search females on the street."

In their "street roles," females and males are divided according to sex, at least in so far as status and risk are involved in these roles. Bag followers are exclusively females, a role in which young and beautiful women are exploited by male dealers. Males tend to be sellers, in contrast to females, who usually assume dependent roles. Although both sexes are largely involved in hustling, females usually engage in shoplifting and prostitution, whereas males rob, con, burgle, or pimp. For the female addict, these roles are not stable. A bag follower may be dropped by her "old man," and she may then resort to other sources, such as dealing or hustling. Similarly, a dependent female may lose her secure position and may be forced to walk the street (File, 1976).

WHY DO WOMEN AND MEN USE DRUGS?

There has been much concern among adults at the rapidly increasing rate of drug use among the young generation in the 1960s and early 1970s. It is felt that the use of drugs among young people represents not only a personal experience but also an alternative lifestyle that challenges basic middle-class values. A typical picture of the drug user is the hippie who has rejected middle-class values, such as competition, aggression, delayed gratification, and material success, as life goals. The alarming picture of the drug scene has started research into the factors contributing to drug use.

Parents and Drug Use

Adults may serve as a model to adolescents who become involved in the drug culture. Thus, drug use by adolescents may only be an aspect of adult indulgence in drugs. As Conger (1977) put it, "The adult who smokes cigarettes, has two martinis at lunch, takes amphetamines to restore energy, tranquilizers to relax, and barbiturates to sleep—even though he or she may be doing it to cope in a high-pressure, competitive society—is just as surely a product of a drug culture as the youthful drug user seeking a new high."

Evidence in the United States (Kandel, 1974) and Canada (Smart & Fejer, 1972) reveals that the use of illegal drugs (marijuana, LSD) by young persons is strongly related to the use of drugs by their parents. For example, the use of psychotropic drugs by the mother increases the probability of marijuana use by the daughter. Furthermore, the father's as well as the mother's use of alcohol tends to increase the probability of marijuana use by their children (both daughters and sons).

Psychological and Social Factors

Drugs may be chosen according to the desired effects (Rogers, 1977). For example, girls may use amphetamines to control weight, to study for examinations, or to get high and to achieve a euphoric state. However, there are sex differences in the factors underlying the use of drugs.

Narcotics   Brown, Gauvey, Meyers, and Stark (1971), in a study of heroin addicts in Washington, D.C., compared the reasons for first heroin use given by thirty-five adult females and ninety-eight adult males. Although curiosity and the influence of friends were the reasons cited most often by addicts of both sexes, 20 percent of the women, but only 7 percent of the men, gave "relief of personal disturbance" as their reason for trying heroin. Other studies suggest that because of low self-esteem, women take narcotics to enhance their self-image and to gain acceptance by a peer group (Prather & Fidell, 1978). As in the case of alcoholic women, it has been suggested that the use of heroin helps women to deny their femininity and, in particular, their desire for passivity and dependence (Ball & Chambers, 1970).

In a review of studies of female heroin addicts, Suffet and Brotman (1976) concluded that, although the behavior of these women appears to be deviant, they tend to hold traditional female values. Miller, Sensenig, Shocker, and Campbell (1973) also found that ". . .sex role stereotypes of values emerge among addicts who are popularly thought to reject so many common cultural values. . . . Males place emphasis upon values related to achievement and competence, and females place more emphasis on values related to interpersonal and intrapersonal sensitivities."

These conventional values of heroin addicts may be contrasted to the prevalence of shoplifting and prostitution among women addicts (Chambers et al., 1970; Prather & Fidell, 1978; Suffet & Brotman, 1976). Suffet and Brotman noted that this discrepancy may be explained in terms of the social and economic position of female addicts. Many of these women are isolated socially and have no social or economic support. They are unmarried, poor, and predominantly unemployed (78 percent are unmarried; 50 percent have children; only 32 percent live with a spouse or other relative; 66 percent have not completed high school; and 86 percent are unemployed). Thus, their economic need may drive them to illegal activities. Since female opium addicts tend to belong to a lower social class, it is quite possible that, as Gilbert Geis (1970) noted, the use of the drug may represent "a response to an unappetizing, frustrating, and unrewarding way of life."

Marijuana Whereas narcotics seem to be predominantly used by lower-class persons, marijuana is a popular drug among middle-class youth. Marijuana, to the young, is like alcohol to the adult. However, marijuana induces passivity and awareness of the self; it appeals to the middle-class youth who wants "to escape, not to become deeply enmeshed in a ruthless schedule, insistent demands, pressures, and expectations" (Geis, 1970). For the male middle-class adolescent user of drugs, marijuana (and LSD) reduces the "intolerable demands of masculine role performance." Marijuana may be desired by adolescents because it reduces aggression, in contrast to alcohol, which tends to increase aggression (Taylor, Vardaris, Rawitch, Gammon, Cranston, & Lubetkin, 1976).

It has been suggested that marijuana use may be a symptom of a new trend among the young in American society, of moving toward a condition in which strength and aggression are no longer fashionable (Geis, 1970). This suggestion is of particular interest, since it seems to indicate the opposite motives underlying alcohol use by men (for example, see McClelland et al. [1972], on p. 232, for a discussion of drinking, aggression, and the need for power.) Indeed, Geis (1970) has put forward a hypothesis to explain marijuana use by men that bears some similarity to the hypothesis put forward by Sharon Wilsnack (1976) to explain alcohol use by women in terms of a desire to feel feminine. Geis wrote:

> It is this thoroughgoing trend toward legitimization of feminine roles for men that lies behind the use of drugs and the adoption of hair styles and other characteristics by middle class male adolescents. I think that today's middle class youths are unable to fill the socially articulated masculine roles, particularly as the drive to push them into such roles becomes more desperate.

There are no systematic studies that relate marijuana use among females to specific feminine behavior. However, female users tend to have the same values as male users: They are less religious, more liberal, and more unorthodox in their lifestyles than nonusers (Prather & Fidell, 1978). Both male and female users select nontraditional careers and major in the liberal arts. "For men, nontraditional careers include studying the arts or social sciences as opposed to engineering or business. For women the nontraditional career means a shift away from homemaking and motherhood and from traditional majors such as home economics or elementary education, and a movement towards the liberal arts" (Prather & Fidell, 1978).

Women who use marijuana tend to be different from nonusers in their sexual behavior; they tend to date more, and they report being more sexually active than nonusers. The more a woman's relationship with men is equalitarian, the more likely it is that she will use marijuana (Goode, 1970; Prather & Fidell, 1978). Indeed, among student populations, sex differences in the use of marijuana are eliminated when only those who subscribe to a freer and unconventional lifestyle are investigated. For example, a survey by Suchman (1968) among West Coast university students found that 5 percent of the women and 14 percent of men smoked marijuana at least once a week. However, when lifestyle factors were taken into account, differences in the rates of smoking marijuana narrowed: Among students who approved of premarital sexual intercourse, 33 percent of the women and 34 percent of the men smoked marijuana.

In conclusion, it appears that marijuana use, unlike alcohol, which intensifies sex-role behavior, tends to reduce aggressive behavior in the male. Research is needed to ascertain the specific effects of marijuana on women and men in a controlled laboratory setting.

Treatment of Drug Abuse

Female addicts experience specific problems that are not dealt with in a male-oriented program (Prather & Fidell, 1978). Very little attention has been given to their need for birth control counseling or contraceptives in these programs. Similarly, provisions for child care are lacking in residential addiction treatment centers. As Prather and Fidell (1978) noted, "The addict mother then faces a dilemma of relinquishing the custody of her child or seeking child care from relatives or friends. Since both social agencies and her family frequently regard the woman with a drug history as an inadequate mother, the woman encounters difficulty regaining custody of her children once she has completed the treatment program."

Treatment of female addicts reflects discrimination against women in the occupational sphere. Job training, career counseling, and job placement are rather neglected for women. Women generally receive training in traditionally female jobs, such as domestic or laundry work. The treatment staff tends to be predominantly males (Levy & Doyle, 1974) who are not only insensitive to the requirement of the female addict but who also tend to exploit her sexually (Prather and Fidell, 1978). Prather and Fidell (1978) concluded, "Because of the numerous problems that women encounter in treatment centers, it is probably not surprising that fewer women enter treatment than men, that women have a lower retention rate than men, and that women experience a lower success rate than men."

One uniquely female problem is related to pregnancy and to the children of addicted mothers. In a study reported by Suffet and Brotman (1976), statistics reveal a dramatic increase in the number of pregnant addicts; in 1960, one in every 164 deliveries involved an addicted mother, whereas in 1972, the rate was one in 27 (a six-fold increase). Moreover, two-thirds of these women had addicted babies. These results underline the crucial problems relevant to pregnant addicts and their children.

The pregnant addict Addiction may not only affect the female, but it also has adverse influences on her child. It is therefore necessary that the pregnant addict receives counseling and that her child be given special care. Unfortunately, little research has been done on these women and their children (Mondanaro, 1977).

The pregnancies of addicted women are usually unplanned. Because heroin and methadone interfere with the normal menstrual cycle, most addicted women are used to missing their periods. (Methadone hydrochloride is a synthetic narcotic related to heroin and is regarded as equally addictive physiologically, but it is substituted for heroin as a preliminary step to complete withdrawal, causing the patient less distress.) Family planning and early detection of pregnancy should be available to all women of child-bearing age, because addicted women are frequently unable to detect their pregnancies until the fourth or even the sixth month. Because many female addicts tend to have pelvic inflammatory diseases (infection in the Fallopian tubes), the insertion of an intrauterine device (IUD) is highly dangerous. Therefore, other birth controls, such as the pill, the diaphragm, tubal ligation, and vasectomy, should be weighed carefully and judged on an individual basis (Mondanaro, 1977).

Pregnant addicts usually show strong dependence on their men, but they tend to get little assistance at home (Mondanaro, 1977). There is a high rate of battering among these women. Their spouses or partners are often involved in drugs; they are usually unemployed and secure money by stealing, passing bad checks, selling drugs, and pimping.

Heroin babies tend to be full-term but relatively small. Women who conceived, maintained, and delivered on methadone have larger babies than women who conceived on heroin and were then placed on methadone later in their pregnancies. It has been suggested that the positive effect seen in the birth weights of methadone babies is probably due to the prenatal care given to the mothers and to the attention that they pay to nutrition during their pregnancies. Thus, if women using heroin received all the prenatal care and the social services offered to women in methadone programs, they too would have larger and healthier babies.

Since addicted babies, particularly those addicted to methadone, may not experience visible symptoms of withdrawal until five days after birth, they are usually hospitalized for a period of five to six days. Without treatment, the baby may die of convulsions or dehydration (Mondanaro, 1977). The larger the addicting dose of any narcotic drug used by the mother, the more severe the withdrawal symptoms. Likewise, symptoms increase in severity with multiple addiction (methadone and heroin, methadone and barbiturates). Withdrawal symptoms are irritability, a high-pitched cry, increased muscle tone, inability to coordinate sucking and swallowing, inconsolability, and vomiting. In mild cases of withdrawal, swaddling tends to relieve symptoms. When the irritability of the baby increases, various tranquilizers may be given. Addicted babies do not respond positively to rocking or handling. Mothering does not seem to have a calming effect on them.

In summary, studies suggest that a follow-up of the addicted baby and counseling of the mother to enable her to handle her baby are essential for the well-being of both mother and child.

SUMMARY

In most cultures, drinking is considered a male rather than a female behavior. The more a society emphasizes the functions of the female as a mother and a homemaker, the less she is allowed to drink. It is assumed that drinking interferes with her family functions, such as child-rearing. It is also believed that drinking is not "proper" for the female because it increases her aggression and sexual promiscuity. However, with the ongoing breakdown of sex roles and sex stereotypes, the gap between the sexes in drinking habits is gradually narrowing and diminishing. This is particularly true among high school and college students in North America. Alcohol tends to have different effects on women and men: It intensifies feminine characteristics in women and masculine characteristics in men. It makes her warmer, more considerate, and more expressive, but it makes him more aggressive and enhances his feeling of power.

The typical female heavy drinker is the one who has her first drink with the family. Her drinking pattern is more influenced by family members (parents, husband) than the male's. She is described as a "secret drinker" who sips wine at home during the day and goes to bed at night with a bottle. Her drinking is often associated with depression; male drinking is often related to antisocial behavior. She drinks because of specific family and interpersonal crises, including health problems. He drinks to reduce his irritation, boredom, and anxiety. The non-alcoholic wives of alcoholic men tend to be psychologically disturbed, but this seems to result from living with an alcoholic husband.

Although the illegal, nonmedical use of drugs is considered a male rather than a female habit, sex differences are found more often in studies of the sixties than of the seventies, and more often among adults than among young persons. Females tend to be introduced to drugs by males. In general, parental use of drugs is associated with drug use by the children. Female heroin addicts tend to hold conventional feminine values. However, because they are poor, they usually support their habits by stealing or prostituting. Whereas heroin users tend to be lower-class, marijuana users often belong to the middle-class and reject middle-class values. In contrast to alcohol, marijuana decreases rather than increases aggression in men.

Treatment of both alcoholism and drug addiction is designed for the male rather than the female. Many problems specific to females such as pregnancy and child care are usually neglected in existing treatment programs.

Criminal Women
and
Delinquent Girls

II

What are little girls made of?
Sugar and spice and everything nice.
What are little boys made of?
Snakes and snails and puppy-dog tails.

Children's rhyme

Females are traditionally conceived of as law-abiding citizens. Gibbens and Ahrenfeldt (1966) reported that, in most Western countries, there are about ten men convicted for every adult woman and about six boys for every girl among juveniles. Females are not only less likely to engage in criminal behavior than their male counterparts, but they also get involved in different kinds of offenses, most of which are not considered serious. More women than men are tried for offenses related to cruelty to children, shoplifting, brothel keeping, and prostitution, whereas more men are tried for violence, drunkenness, theft from unattended vehicles, burglary, housebreaking and shopbreaking, embezzlement, bigamy, and incest (Walker, 1965).

In juvenile delinquency, a distinction is usually made between criminal offenses, such as assault or theft, and status or juvenile offenses, which include a wide spectrum of behavior that is illegal by virtue of the person's age. Such status offenses, considered normal for adults but delinquent for minors, may include gambling, consuming alcoholic beverages, running away, wandering in the streets at night, sleeping in alleys, and disobedience of parents. Boys tend to get more involved in criminal behavior, such as joyriding, burglary, auto theft, and, more recently, in the illegal use of drugs, particularly marijuana. Girls are more often reported for running away from home, incorrigibility (uncontrollable by their parents), and promiscuity.

Female crimes have been regarded as victimless and as constituting little threat to the social order; they usually involve trivial offenses causing little injury or monetary damage to others. However, there has been much concern in recent years about the involvement of women in crimes of violence that are traditionally committed by men. It has been suggested that there is a shift in female criminality from victimless crimes (running away, promiscuity, shoplifting) to homicide, armed robbery, and gang activities (Adler, 1975). This chapter will discuss the relationship between sexual status and criminal behavior. First, theories to explain sex differences in the rates of crime are discussed. Second, crimes committed predominantly by females, such as prostitution, shoplifting, and running away, or by males, such as homicide and robbery are described. Finally, problems related to crimes against women and young girls are presented.

THEORIES OF CRIMINALITY IN WOMEN

Biological and Personality Theories

Most theories of female criminality attempt to link crime to an inherited biology or to an unfortunate personality (Smart, 1977; Widom, 1978). About the end of the nineteenth century, Lombroso and Ferrero (1895) suggested that women inherit physical characteristics that predispose them to carry out specific crimes. For example, prostitutes are unusually attractive; likewise, murderesses and violent women are endowed with unusual physical strength.

More recently, Cowie, Cowie, and Slater (1968), in *Delinquency in Girls,* described the criminal female as having "impaired physical health . . . [and as being] oversized, lumpish, uncouth and graceless, with raised incidence of minor physical defects." It is clear that these authors have overlooked social factors that might have affected the physical appearance of the institutionalized girls they studied. Because of their lower-class background, they had poor diets, inadequate medical care, and fewer opportunities to satisfy middle-class standards of appearance for teenage girls (Smart, 1977).

Criminality in women is also explained in terms of chromosomal abnormalities (chromosomes are the carriers of the genes, the units of heredity). It was suggested that whereas normal women carry two chromosomes (XX), criminal women have an extra chromosome (XXX). Studies revealed that one percent of criminal women have an extra chromosome (Telfer, Richardson and Chock, 1968; Widom, 1978). Although these chromosomal abnormalities occur ten times more often among criminal women than among women in the general population, the rate is too statistically insignificant to account for most criminal behavior.

Pollack (1950), in *The Criminality of Women,* saw the low rate of criminality in women as an artificial indication of their deceitfulness and ability to disguise their crimes. According to his view, women are actually more criminal than men, but, because of their deceitfulness and evil, they can mask their criminality. For example, in the privacy of the home, women are more able to disguise their crimes. Mothers may engage in child neglect or child molestation without being detected. Because they are in control of the kitchen, they can kill discretely by poisoning their victims. Outside the home, women manipulate men to commit crime but remain immune from arrest. What is the evidence for the deceitfulness of women and the honesty of men? Pollak found support for his view in the biology of the sexual response of women and men:

> Not enough attention has been paid to the physiological fact that man must achieve an erection in order to perform the sex act and will not be able to hide his failure. His lack of positive emotion in the sexual sphere must become overt to the partner and pretense of sexual response is impossible for him, if it is lacking. Woman's body, however, permits such pretense to a certain degree and lack of orgasm does not prevent her ability to participate in the sex act (Pollak, 1950).

In Chapter 1, I discussed a similar view—held in the Middle Ages— which justified accusations of witchcraft by citing the "evilness" and "sexuality" of women.

Personality theory suggests that criminals of both sexes are high on traits such as neuroticism (emotional instability), extroversion (impulsivity), and psychoticism (being solitary, not caring for people, being troublesome, inhumane, cruel, aggressive, and so on) (Eysenck, 1964; Eysenck & Eysenck, 1973). Female prisoners, in particular, show an extremely high level of psychoticism, indicating that they are more disturbed than male prisoners (Eysenck & Eysenck, 1973). Farley and Farley (1972) suggested that the behavior of delinquent girls may be an expression of a sensation-seeking need, a desire for variation in stimulus experience. The Farleys found that delinquent girls who are high on such a need on psychological tests tended to make more escape attempts and were more frequently punished for disobedience and fighting than other delinquent girls.

Both biological and personality theories conceive of the individual as being predisposed to breaking the law because of inherent characteristics. Later in this chapter, I discuss how situational factors are crucial in determining the rates of different types of criminal behavior among women and men.

Socialization, Conformity, and Criminal Behavior

Differences in the rate of crime among the sexes are explained by the tendency of women to be more ethical and to adhere more often to the moral codes of society (Walker, 1965; Gibbens & Ahrenfeldt, 1966). Three questions are relevant to the present interpretation of criminal behavior. First, are there sex differences in the development of moral reasoning? Second, are the ethical values of women more internalized and their moral judgments more severe than those of men? Third, does the evidence gleaned from the criminal behavior of women support the view that women are more conformist than men?

According to Laurence Kohlberg (1975), a psychologist at Harvard, there are three stages of development in moral reasoning: the preconventional, the conventional, and the postconventional stages. In the preconventional stage, the child's behavior is self-centered; concepts of right and wrong are based on what one can do without being caught or on what leads to self-gratification. At this stage, the child is relatively unaware of external rules or standards. During late childhood, the child passes a conventional stage, which is identified by the concepts of "good girl" and "good boy." Persons do not behave according to what is right or wrong, but they are more likely to conform in order to obtain rewards. At this stage, there are certain elements of fairness, reciprocity, and equal sharing, but they are always seen in physical and pragmatic terms. Reciprocity, for example, is not based on justice but is a question of "you scratch my back and I'll scratch yours." The final stage of moral development is the postconventional or the ethical stage, which involves more abstract reasoning. The individual adheres to personal principles, which may result in a clash with conventional standards of society. Although some studies suggest that girls are overrepresented at the "good girl" level, the overall evidence reveals that boys and girls are quite similar in their moral development (Maccoby & Jacklin, 1974).

However, female values seem to be more highly internalized and humanistic than those of males (Conger, 1977). In a study of fifth- and seventh-graders by Hoffman (1975), it was found that moral transgressions are more likely to produce guilt in females and fear of detection and punishment in males. Females also show more consideration of others than their male counterparts. Hoffman (Hoffman, 1970; Hoffman & Saltztein, 1967) suggested that these differences between the sexes are the result of different child-rearing practices for boys and girls; the use of less power assertion with and the expression of more affection toward girls are more conducive to the internalization of values and to the development of a humanistic orientation. There is also increasing pressure on males to achieve and to succeed, goals that may often be in conflict with concerns about the welfare of others (Hoffman, 1975).

Explaining crime in terms of socialization puts the blame on the individual and her failure to acquire social values because of defective early experience. However, the prevalence of certain crimes among women (shoplifting, prostitution), as well as recent increases in other crimes related to property, is incompatible with the socialization theory. These shifts in the rates of crime indicate that "women have no greater 'morality' or 'decency' than men" (Simon, 1976). Their opportunities have, however, been more limited than those of men. As I shall argue later, sexual status may determine the type of crime and the victim involved, as well as the method used to achieve it.

Sex Roles and Crime

The female criminal is conceived as a "masculine" woman who is rebelling against her sex role (Cowie et al., 1968; Widom, 1978). She is expected to have male physical characteristics (hairy and physically strong) and to be masculine in attitudes and behavior. However, research does not support the view that criminal women are "masculine." In her review of research, Widom (1978) concluded that female offenders are no more "masculine" than females in the general population. Female prisoners' attitudes about sex roles tend to reflect sexual stereotypes in the community. In one study, Widom (1977) found no differences between female offenders and a non-offender group in their attitudes toward women or in their feminine tendencies. Indeed, they were higher on feminine characteristics than university students. Widom concluded that criminal behavior may not be incompatible with femininity; a woman may perceive herself as highly feminine, and yet she may commit criminal acts.

TYPES OF CRIME

Female-related Crimes

Female-related crimes are those committed predominantly by women, such as shoplifting and prostitution in adults and running away, including promiscuity and incorrigibility, in adolescents.

Shoplifting Traditionally, statistics reveal that women are more involved in shoplifting than men. More recent studies in the United States, Ireland, and England, where shoppers were followed until they left the store to see whether or not they stole, indicated that there is no significant differences between the sexes (Mayhew, 1977). Previous studies showing an excess in shoplifting among women are explained by the fact that women are more involved in shopping than men. When the number of female and male shoppers is equal, sex differences in shoplifting tend to diminish.

Yet women and men differ in terms of the items they steal. A British study reveals that women usually steal food, clothes, and other items of little value. Men, on the other hand, steal books and objects other than food and clothes, which are of considerable value (Gibbens & Prince, 1962). In the United States, shoplifting by women also involves items of little value (Hoffman-Bustamante, 1973). That women shop predominantly for household items and groceries is reflected in the items they steal. Smart (1977) noted that stealing of clothes reflects the female role: There is much pressure placed on women to be well dressed and fashionable, on the one hand, and, on the other, the high prices of clothes compared to the low average earnings of women present further incentive to steal.

Since criminal women form a small percentage of criminals, it is thought that there must be something abnormal about women involved in shoplifting and other crimes. It is not unusual that female shoplifters claim that they have no use for the stolen goods and that they cannot understand why they stole, thus conforming to the stereotype of the female kleptomaniac (kleptomania is defined as an obsessive impulse to steal, usually shown by stealing objects for which the individual has no desire or use). It is believed that the high value of goods stolen by men may reflect a goal-directed behavior and a realistic economic need rather than madness. This argument, of course, ignores the fact that a female's position as a housewife may determine her motivation for stealing items, such as groceries and clothes, which are of relatively little value (Smart, 1977; Walker, 1965).

Prostitution   Prostitution is traditionally treated as a female offense. It is legally defined as "the practice of a female offering her body to an indiscriminate intercourse with men, usually for hire" (Hoffman-Bustamante, 1973). This definition indicates that men are immune to the charge of prostitution. Moreover, the law does not punish the male who uses the services of the prostitute.

Female prostitution is justified on the ground that the sex drive of the male is much stronger than that of the female. Men cannot contain their sexual desires and need premarital and extramarital outlets. Brothels may be legalized to satisfy male sexual urges as well as to prevent adultery and illegitimate pregnancies. This argument is used to justify double standards of morality for women and men: Whereas all men can be promiscuous and maintain their respectability, there are two classes of women—the respectable housewife and the prostitute (Smart, 1977).

Clinical psychologists and psychiatrists have traditionally conceived of the prostitute as an abnormal person who is driven to prostitution by her craving for sex rather than because of her economic and social condition. Typically, a prostitute is described as oversexed and alcoholic and as a homosexual who is not sexually responsive to male clients (Walker, 1965). An alternative to the psychiatric interpretation of prostitution is to consider it as an extension of the social position of females in general and housewives in particular (Smart, 1977). *First,* sex as a means to a desired goal is accepted as appropriate to the typical feminine role. The bargaining of sexual favors for marriage is considered as the ultimate goal of girls. In fact, women relinquish their right to their bodies on signing the marriage contract in exchange for financial support by the husband (traditionally husbands can not be accused of raping their wives unless they are legally separated or divorced). However, it is only when sex is used to bargain for an inappropriate goal, such as in prostitution, when a girl fails to bargain at all, or when she bargains while she is too young that her behavior is labeled deviant. *Second,* prostitution should be considered within the framework of the economic limitations put on women in Western society. Women have "relatively limited opportunities . . . to earn a living wage, to win promotion and achieve a secure career, and to be economically independent of men. Complete economic independence remains a possibility for only a small minority of women with the consequence that a majority are not only employed in low-paid, insecure work but are also dependent on husbands, lovers and fathers or, in some cases, a paternalistic Welfare State" (Smart, 1977). Considering this state of affairs, prostitution may constitute an attractive career in which a woman can earn more than in a legitimate job.

Although prostitution may be regarded as a career (Bryan, 1973; Smart, 1977), it should be recognized that it is closely related to the devalued sex role of women. With the women's movement and the demand for equal opportunities for persons, women can fully participate in society without being dependent on transitory and subjective attributes, such as attractiveness.

Runaway Among juvenile girls, running away, which is equivalent to being "in moral danger," is the most frequent offense. Running away is not confined to girls, however. In 1975, a national survey of *noninstitutionalized* juveniles (Justice & Duncan, 1976) has revealed that 10.1 percent of all boys and 8.7 percent of all girls in the 12–17 age range reported running away at least once. A conservative estimate of the children who run away from home each year in the United States tallies over one million. In contrast to the finding that there are more runaways among boys than girls in the general population, there are more girls than boys who are institutionalized for this juvenile offense. Since "runaway" is associated with promiscuity, institutionalization is assumed to protect girls from wandering away and flaunting their sexuality.

In its revision of the *Diagnostic Statistical Manual of Mental Disorders* in 1968, the American Psychiatric Association added the category of *runaway reactions* to its list of mental illness. Running away may, however, be conceived as a simple flight from stress. Contrary to psychiatric thinking, a large number of these runaways report that the reason they ran away was "lifestyle conflicts with parents" on issues such as wearing bras for girls and having long hair for boys (Justice & Duncan, 1976). Running away also tends to be a beneficial rather than a morbid experience for some youngsters. A study by Howell, Emmons, and Frank (1973) revealed that two-thirds of youngsters considered running away as a growing experience.

Male-related Crimes

Although the offenses discussed here, such as homicide, robbery, theft, and larceny, are committed by both sexes, statistics show that they are predominantly male activities.

Homicide   Violent crimes are inconsistent with the traditional concept of the female as loving, caring, and affectionate rather than as aggressive and destructive. Statistics reported by Wolfgang (1958) on homicide in Philadelphia between 1948–1952 reveal a significantly lower rate for females than males. He also found sex differences in the choice of victims and the technique used to carry out the offense. More than half of the victims of female murderers had a family relationship with the offender or were her "paramours." Husbands were often killed by their wives in the kitchen with a butcher knife or other household implement, but nearly half of the wives were beaten to death in the bedroom. Women seem to use less physical strength in committing murder, and, in their violent encounters with men, they have to resort to weapons, such as knives, in order to compensate for their lack of strength relative to the male. Women tend to kill and be killed in self-defense against an aggressive male. A large number of their homicides are not premeditated and seem to be provoked by the victims. For example, more male than female offenders in spouse killings were found guilty and were convicted for more serious degrees of homicide. Consistent with tendencies in the general population, more male than female offenders commit suicide (Wolfgang, 1958). Ward, Jackson, and Ward (1969) found that a large number of females imprisoned for homicide killed their victims while they were unable to defend themselves, at times when they were ill, drunk, asleep, or offguard. Because women are less strong or less adept in the use of weapons or physical strength, they may be less likely to succeed in killing a fully conscious male.

There is now a general belief that there has been a dramatic increase in violence among women. This impression was reinforced by certain events: In 1970, four women made the FBI list for the ten most wanted criminals; also, women became involved in revolutionary movements, such as the Symbionese Liberation Army and Weather Underground. And yet statistics do not support this impression. Figures reported by Norland and Shover (1977) indicate a decline in the proportion of women arrested for homicide from 1966 to 1975. There was, however, a noticeable increase in the percentage of women arrested for armed robbery and other property crimes. Arrests for running away also increased markedly during this period. In general, the increase in female criminality was in nonviolent crime. Even when women are involved in crimes of violence, they normally play supporting roles to men.

Since the rate of violence among women has not increased in recent years, the notion that women's liberation may result in violence has no support. In fact, it is expected that women's "greater freedom and independence will result in a decline in their desire to kill the usual objects of their anger or frustration: their husbands, lovers, and other men upon whom they are dependent, but insecure about" (Simon, 1976). Findings reveal that women who commit violent crimes tend to be the least liberated among female criminals: They are "young, poor, and black, hardly the richest source of feminist militancy" (Price, 1977). These women are more conservative than female nonoffenders (Widom, 1977).

Robbery and property offenses John MacDonald (1975) reported that, in Philadelphia between 1960 and 1966, females consisted of only 5.2 percent of the total number of robbers (most of the females were blacks). FBI statistics reveal that, in 1972, seven of every 100 persons arrested for robbery[1] in the United States were females. Armed robbery is almost exclusively a male crime. According to MacDonald, the female role in armed robbery was confined largely to using sexual charms to entice victims to a suitable spot for robbery, to obtain information from either victims or police, or to distract the attention of police and others from the scene of the crime. Women are also used to hide weapons, to assist in the getaway, or to dispose of the stolen goods. Their passive roles in robbery seem to be compatible with the female stereotype.

The mid-1960s saw an increase in arrests of girls for being gang lookouts and for carrying weapons. By the 1970s, girls had become integrated in male gang activities or had formed independent all-girl gangs. These adolescent girls participate in muggings, burglaries, and extortion rings. They are armed with switchblades, razors, and clubs. One all-girl gang in London is notorious at "granny bashing"—attacking elderly ladies. In large American cities, prostitutes have taken up mugging to supplement their income (Adler, 1975).

Offenses showing the greatest increase in recent years were embezzlement, fraud, forgery, and counterfeiting (white-collar offenses). These trends are shown not only in the United States but also in Western Europe (Price, 1977), suggesting that, in those countries where women are more likely to be employed in white-collar and commercial positions, women are more likely to engage in property offenses and in other economic types of criminal behavior.

Carol Smart (1977) argued that many property offenses committed by women reflect female role expectations and women's opportunities for dishonesty. The handling of stolen goods, for example, is compatible with the female role because it requires a passive role without taking part in the original theft or burglary. Female theft from a machine or an employer requires no great skill, strength, or aggression and consequently is in keeping with the culturally ascribed characteristics of the female role. Jobs in which women are

---

[1]The term robbery or armed robbery is used when stealing is accompanied by violence and force. In theft, there is neither a use or a threat to use violence and force.

frequently employed, such as domestic work and as shop assistants, give women opportunities for stealing without requiring training in violence or the use of weapons and tools. This argument suggests that opportunities for dishonesty and for learning the required skills (for example, safebreaking) may be crucial in sex differences in criminal behavior.

THE FEMALE AND LAW ENFORCEMENT

It is generally believed that society has a protective attitude toward women and that they thus fare better in the process of referral by the police or in the sentences meted out for them by the judiciary system. The evidence, however, shows that, as in other areas of the female spheres of life, sex stereotypes and sex discrimination work against their welfare.

Women and the Police

Women offenders are more likely than men to be let off with a caution instead of being prosecuted (Walker, 1965). In particular, the police tend to deal unofficially with all minor offenses of young girls, in order to save them from the social stigma that follows a court appearance (Pollak, 1950).

Cautioning may, however, be influenced by sex differences in the types of crime (Walker, 1965). Criminal offenses committed by women and girls are considered trivial; for example, males who are caught breaking and entering are rarely let off with a caution when compared with female shoplifters. Also, females are more likely to be first offenders or to play only a secondary role in crime.

Decisions made by the police after arrest—whether to counsel and release or to refer a youth to court—reveal a paternalistic attitude that penalizes women. Girls are charged mainly for juvenile offenses, whereas boys are mostly referred to court for criminal offenses, such as burglary, larceny, and car theft. Parents tend to initiate police action against daughters more than against sons because of double standards of behavior for the two sexes: They expect more obedience from daughters. For example, they rarely complain to the police about a son who does not come home from a date at the expected time, although this complaint is a common reason for the arrest of a daughter. The police seem to comply to the statutes that dictate juveniles' obedience to parents (Chesney-Lind, 1977).

The strict standards parents set for girls are reflected in the number of girls referred to court for juvenile offenses. Whereas girls make up only about one-quarter of the total juvenile court population, they tend to form the majority of those charged with juvenile offenses (Chesney-Lind, 1977). In fact, a female sexual misconduct is treated with greater concern than a criminal act. For example, Andrews and Cohn (1974) found that a parental objection to a daughter's boyfriend was more frequently referred to court by New York intake officers than a charge of larceny. Similarly, a refusal to come home on time, a usual parental complaint about girls, could get a girl before a judge more quickly than arson or illegal entry (crimes usually committed by boys). Pressure from parents on intake officers seems to be responsible for the excess of juvenile offenses among girls. In general, it seems easy to prove that a youth disobeys her parents on some occasions making her susceptible to a court appearance for "ungovernability." It is, howerver, more difficult to prove that a youth has committed a specific criminal act.

Females and the Judiciary System

After arrest, women are not only more likely than men to be charged with violations of their sex roles (for status offenses) and consequently referred to court, but they are also more often held in jails or juvenile detention centers for these offenses (Chesney-Lind, 1977). Since girls are arrested through parental complaints rather than directly by law enforcement officials (as in the case of boys for criminal behavior), the juvenile court is very much concerned with obedience to parents. Parental expectations of what is appropriate behavior for female and male children reflects the attitude of the juvenile court toward girls and boys (Armstrong, 1977). Judges often decide that it is delinquent for a girl, but not for a boy, to return home at an "unreasonable" hour.

Family courts seemingly associate sexual misconduct with female offenses (running away, incorrigibility, curfew violations, truancy). It is assumed that young women who come to the attention of the courts must be in some sort of sexual trouble. Hence all girls brought into family court in New York, including those brought for nonsexual offenses, are given vaginal Wasserman smears to test for venereal disease (Strouse, 1972). This violates the girl's right to privacy, but more importantly, reflects the authorities' assumption that girls who come before the judge are probably promiscuous.

Both female and male juveniles who commit a crime are generally detained for a definite period of time, whereas those detained for status offenses are remanded to a state correctional institution for an indeterminate period of time to be decided upon less by the court than by their parents and the correctional staff. Thus, it seems possible that a girl who is considered promiscuous could be legally detained longer than a boy of a comparable age who had committed a serious crime (Conway & Bogdan, 1977).

Discriminatory Laws Against Women

Most jurisdictions in the United States have statutes in which juvenile delinquency is synonymous with immoral conduct (Armstrong, 1977). These statutes, however, are applied more to females than to males. Sexual delinquency, consisting largely of promiscuity, is the most common offense of female juveniles (Armstrong, 1977). If boys are ever caught for sexual delinquency, it usually involves specific sexual deviations, such as exhibitionism, voyeurism, homosexuality, and public masturbation. Girls, however, face nonspecific charges relating mainly to sexual promiscuity (Weiner, 1970). Although it takes two to make a sexual promiscuous act and although the "crime" of promiscuity is usually shared by both sexes, it is only girls who are charged for this offense. Moreover, the prohibition of promiscuity seems to be selectively enforced on lower-class girls (Conway & Bogdan, 1977). William Thomas (1967) found that the majority of committed girls were from welfare homes. The accusation of immorality or promiscuity may be used to justify the institutionalization of girls who are rejected by their own poor families (Conway & Bogdan, 1977).

Laws related to crimes of sexual jealousy seem to be one-sided (Schofield, 1976). Excuses are usually made for *la crime passionelle* when it is the woman who has been unfaithful: A "crime of honor" usually describes the murder of an unfaithful wife. In Italy, according to Schofield, there was until 1969 a law under which wives but not husbands could be sent to prison for adultery.

There are, however, situations in which the law discriminates against men, in the sense that it treats certain types of male behavior as criminal, but excludes from its scope the female counterpart. In most Western countries, male homosexuality, but not female homosexuality, is unlawful. Women are also never charged with indecent exposure, though this may be because women usually do it in situations where economic gain is the motive, such as in soliciting or striptease performances. Similar sex differences may be seen in attitudes toward voyeurism and exhibitionism: If a man walking past an apartment stops to watch a woman undressing before the window, the man is arrested as a peeper. If a woman walking past an apartment stops to watch a man undressing before a window, the man is arrested as an exhibitionist (MacDonald, 1975).

Females in Prison

Women and particularly girls spend longer terms of confinement than men due to the belief that they are in greater need of rehabilitation (Adler, 1975). In practice, however, women are given no rehabilitation programs. They do laundry, sewing, and other domestic tasks that leave them unprepared for employment and serve only to reinforce their dependency and to affirm the female role (Price, 1977).

Whereas feminine behavior (cooking, sewing) is encouraged, the staff is critical of feminine emotional reactions or of the development of feminine interests, such as hair-styling, fashionable clothes, or cosmetics. This puts many institutionalized girls in a double-bind— that is, being feminine with regard to their domestic role but not being feminine with regard to their sexual role. In other words, "such girls experience all the disadvantages of the traditional female role (i.e., drudgery, boredom, limited horizons) without the 'advantages' (i.e., romance, flirtation and sexual encounters)" (Smart, 1977).

Women tend to have more difficulty in adapting to the prison environment than men. Walker (1965) observed that female prisoners in Britain have more disciplinary problems than men. They tend to have "hysterical outbursts, in which the prisoner smashes everything breakable in the cell." This may not be, as suggested by Walker, because they are more antisocial than men but because the criminal female revolts against institutionalization more than the criminal male. Interestingly, the behavior of hospitalized women described in Chapter 3 is similar to that of imprisoned women, suggesting that their "hysterical outbursts" may be a reaction to institutionalization.

Within the criminal population, female offenders have a higher percentage of mental illness than male offenders (Walker, 1965). In Britain, for example, Holloway, which is a psychiatric hospital for criminals, receives about half of the total number of female prisoners in England and Wales (Smart, 1977). Also, female prisoners are referred more often than males for psychiatric evaluation because of "abnormal" behavior in jail (20 percent of female prisoners vs. 6 percent of male prisoners [Herjanic, Henn, & Vanderpearl, 1977]). Similarly, mental illness is more accepted as a defense in the case of women (Walker, 1965). The diagnosis of mental illness in female and male offenders conforms, to some extent, to that in the general population. Female offenders outnumber male offenders in schizophrenia, depression, and neurosis. Male offenders are higher in alcohol and drug abuse and antisocial personality (Herjanic et al., 1977). A review of research by Widom (1978) reveals that female criminals are described as emotionally unstable, neurotic, anxious, and depressed. However, the number of psychopaths among female offenders is much smaller than that among male offenders.

WOMEN AS CRIME VICTIMS

Rape

"What was the defendent wearing?" That was Mr. Freeman's lawyer.

"I don't know."

"You mean to say this man raped you and you don't know what he was wearing?" He snickered as if I had raped Mr. Freeman.

"Do you know if you were raped?"

A sound pushed in the air of the court (I was sure it was laughter). . . .

Maya Angelou: I KNOW WHY THE CAGED BIRD SINGS

Rape is sexual intercourse committed forcibly and without the person's consent. It is one of the fastest rising violent crimes in the United States. The FBI reported a 68 percent increase in rape between 1968 and 1973. It is estimated that, for every case that comes to their attention, there are ten unreported cases (Offir, 1975). These figures indicate that at least one in ten women living in urban areas will be, at one time or another, confronted by a rapist.

Police records of rape do not represent all segments of the population. The rape experience is so traumatic to women that they are unwilling to describe it to strangers and officials. Middle-class victims tend to go to psychiatrists, gynecologists, and private hospitals, where secrecy is maintained. However, the poor rape victims tend to go to public hospitals, where there is a policy of informing the police of suspected rape cases. Thus, information about rape from the police includes mainly poor victims (Weis & Borges, 1973).

Statistics show that rape victims tend to belong to the same class and race and to be about the same age as their attackers; they can, however, be babies or senile old ladies (Brownmiller, 1975). The single woman between the ages of 17 and 24 appears to be the most frequently reported victim (Notman & Nadelson, 1976). She is vulnerable partly because she is alone and inexperienced. The divorced and separated woman is also vulnerable because her lifestyle and morality are frequently questioned. Her apparent sexual availability makes her seem more approachable sexually.

Rape and the justice system Rape is the least reported crime of violence. Because it is difficult to convict rapists, women are reluctant to report it to the police. This is not surprising, since a relatively small number of rapes known to the police are charged or convicted (Smart, 1977).

Men can get away with rape easily due, in part, to the complexity of the legal system. Corroboration of rape and a proof of the victim's resistance and her good character are needed to convict a rapist. In some states, an eye witness may be required to confirm the occurrence of rape and the rapist's identity (Robin, 1977). Intimate questioning by the police and the prosecution to establish rape can be embarrassing and humiliating:

"How many orgasms did you have? I know why you got raped. How big was he? Was he good-looking? What were you thinking about while he was doing it? Weren't you a little cold in that mini-skirt, Sweetie? Well, why were you out late? Don't you ever wear a bra?" (Robin, 1977).

Victims have to prove to the judge or the jury that they resisted the rapist to the extent that they risked or actually sustained injury. Susan Griffin (1971) noted that it is surprising that women are expected to resist the rapist. Since it is associated with submission, femininity tends to impede rather than encourage self-defense. To be submissive means to defer to masculine strength and to lack muscular development or any interest in defending oneself.

Consent may be determined on the basis of the victim's character and reputation. The jury may decide that the victim is the type of person who would have willingly had intercourse with the defendant on the occasion in question. Thus, the defendant may be acquitted because of the sexual reputation of the victim, and, in some states, this may occur even when the man has previous rape convictions (Griffin, 1971). For example, prostitutes and women with illegitimate children have little chance of securing conviction (Robin, 1977).

The reactions of the police and the court which may reflect firmly held attitudes toward, and stereotypes of, women, make it difficult to convict rapists. It is believed that women cannot be raped: "A hostile vagina will not admit a penis." The victims really desire sex with men, and their physical resistance is seen as part of "the female game of pretending reluctance, or as a desire to be overcome." This is more so when the rapist is not a stranger but somebody she knows. Thus, if a woman is raped by a friend, a date, a lover, an ex-lover, an employer, a teacher, or a doctor, the police as well as other people are unlikely to believe her story (Russell, 1975).

Reaction to rape   The behavior of women during the attack is influenced by their appraisal of the degree of danger involved in the situation. Burgess and Holmstrom (1976) noted that the main coping strategies used by rape victims are *verbal* ("I am a married woman"; "I am a virgin"; "I am sick"). The *physical* action of the victim, which is less frequently used, constitutes either fleeing from the situation or fighting the rapist (trying to push him back out of the apartment). Burgess and Holmstrom reported that one-third of their group could not use any strategy to avoid attack; fear of death tended to paralyze them. Apparently, during first-date rapes, women scream, fight, and threaten to call the police, whereas during rapes by established acquaintances, they can only plead or become paralyzed (Gibbens, 1977).

Rape may cause both physical and psychological damage to the victim. Among the physical symptoms are general soreness and bruising in various parts of the body. Tension headache, insomnia, and early waking are also common symptoms (Burgess & Holmstrom, 1974). Anxiety and depression are major reactions to rape. Victims tend, for example, to develop a fear of being indoors if they have been attacked while sleeping in their beds, whereas they develop a fear of being outdoors if the attack has taken place outside their homes. The Burgess and Holmstrom study has shown that almost all victims reported fears of being alone or a fear of crowds after the rape. Sexual dysfunctions may develop because of the anxiety associated with the traumatic experience. This is more possible when rape is the victim's first experience with sex.

The helpless victim of rape tends to expect support from family and friends after the attack. However, because women are almost always held responsible for the rape, it will often result in a breakdown of close friendship or marriage. Not surprisingly, rape victims themselves begin to feel guilt and to direct the blame toward themselves (Metzger, 1976).

Society and the rapist Rape is a uniquely human experience. Force is not used in the animal kingdom to obtain sexual favors. For example, Williams (1967) stated that "the male monkey cannot in fact mate with the female without her invitation and willingness to cooperate. In monkey society there is not such a thing as rape, prostitution, or even passive consent." Rape is also not found in all human societies. Margaret Mead (1935) reported that rape is hardly practiced by the gentle Arapesh male in New Guinea.

In the West, it is believed that rape is a rare occurrence, carried out by a deviant and insane individual. He is described as a timid and shy male who is unable to obtain normal sexual gratification (Cohen & Seghorn, 1969). Alternatively, he is depicted as a sadist who obtains sexual pleasure through aggression or as an impulsive psychopath who is unable to control his sexual behavior (Calhoun, 1977). Many of these assumptions about the rapist received no empirical support (Amir, 1971; Brownmiller, 1975). Rape is not an impulsive activity but is generally planned by the offender. It is also believed that the rapist is mainly lower class and predominantly black (Amir, 1971). This conclusion is based on police records and must represent a poor sample of rapists in society at large.

In contrast to the view that rape is primarily a deviant sexual act, the behavior of the rapist may represent an extreme state of "masculine" behavior and an expression of aggression, power, strength, and toughness. Deena Metzger (1976) pointed out that "the rapist is educated to his behavior by his society, and rape is the extreme manifestation of approved activities in which one segment of society dominates another. Rape is a ritual of power." If one subscribes to this view, one would expect to find that rape permeates every class of society rather than concentrates among the poor and black. Indeed, Gibbens (1977) found in a randomly selected sample from the general population that 25 percent of the men studied had been involved in sexual aggression with women or girls. Children, because of their powerlessness and almost complete dependency on adults, are the obvious victims of the rapist. Gagnon (1966) found that 24 percent of 4,441 women reported sexual contact as children with an adult. Gagnon estimated that between 20 and 25 percent of children reared in a middle-class environment are victimized by adults. Studies also reveal a high frequency of rape in colleges. Kamin and Kirkpatrick (1953), in a study on the campus of the University of Indiana, found that 20.9 percent of the female students had been offended by "forceful attempts at sexual intercourse in the previous year." The Group for the Advancement of Psychiatry, in a report on *Sex and the College Student* (1965), recorded cases of rape by professors. Since university authorities tend to put the blame on the student, it is understandable that rape victims on university campuses are reluctant to complain (Kamin, 1970). Finally, the acceptance of rape during the Vietnam war is depicted in the confession of Small, a member of the Charlie Company: "That's an everyday affair. You can nail just about everybody on that—at least once. The guys are human, man" (Hersh, 1970).

Conclusion With the exception of a fleeting interest in psychopaths, psychologists have ignored the destructive and aggressive tendencies of the male. However, textbooks of abnormal psychology in the late part of the 1970s started including rape under sexual deviation. This seems to ignore the evidence that rapists are not primarily motivated by a sexual urge but that their main satisfaction is in asserting their power over a woman. Indeed, the majority of the rapists studied do not seem to enjoy sex or even to function adequately in the sexual situation (Russell, 1975). Moreover, rapists are not "insane" individuals, but differ from normal men only in their greater tendency to express aggression and violence (Griffen, 1971).

The psychiatric approach to rape tends to place blame on the victim rather than on the social environment. As Anne Seiden (1976) noted, "Attempts at treatment . . . have often focused, like so much in psychotherapy, on the hope of finding a remediable way in which the victim contributed to her own victimization—inadvertently adding to her victimization—by blaming her."

Rape crisis centers, started recently by the women's liberation movement, are the most effective and promising means of humanizing the treatment of victims (Robin, 1977). These centers provide information, referral services, and temporary shelter, as well as emotional support and counseling before and after the trial. They are operated by women who have been sexually assaulted themselves, by housewives, by practitioners from the helping professions, and by other volunteers. The presence of individuals from the center during the interrogation can increase communication with the authorities and discourage the inhumane treatment of victims.

Briefly, rape is neither a purely sexual nor a purely psychiatric disturbance. It is a problem intimately related to the power structure of society. Unless rape is considered as a social problem and is dealt with as such, it will remain with us for a long time to come.

Battering

. . . 49-year-old Mary McCormick from Ireland testified that she had tried three times to leave her home because of constant beatings, but that she had been unable to support her nine children on her $25 a week salary as a washer-up in a hotel. When she tried to leave, her husband signed her into a mental hospital. The signature of a husband is all that is needed under Irish law. The police forcibly removed her and her family from the train she was fleeing on. They detained her at a police station for a day, refusing to tell her what was happening or why. She was then taken, bound, to a mental hospital where she was given Valium and encouraged to accept shock treatments. Three months and a hunger strike later, her 21-year-old daughter was able to sign her out, but only with the aid of a lawyer.

Diana Russell: Introduction to Del
Martin's BATTERED WIVES

Gayford (1975) defined a battered woman as one "who had received deliberate severe and repeated demonstrable physical injury from her husband." At the very least, this involves punching with closed fist; at the worst, it involves attacks with broken bottles, knives and shootings. In an interview with 100 women from the Chiswick refuge for battered women in England [the first refuge for battered women, opened in 1971 and described by Erin Pizzey (1974) in *Scream Quietly or the Neighbours Will Hear*], Gayford found that all of them were bruised. Some had fractures, dislocations, retinal damage, brain injury, and burns or scrapes. Many of the women reported miscarriages caused by violence. Pizzey (1974) noted that many women coming to the refuge had handicapped children. She raised the possibility that a number of these children were born damaged as a result of their fathers' violence.

It is difficult to estimate accurately the true incidence of physical abuse of women, since many women do not report or acknowledge that they were assaulted by their partners. Also, women from the lower class are more likely to be completely dependent upon their husbands for accommodation and financial help, and thus they are reluctant to seek help (Brandon, 1976). However, estimates of the incidence of physical abuse range from 1 in 500 to 1 in 100 marriages (Gregory, 1976).

Factors in female battering   Female battering represents only one aspect of general violence in the family. It is related to child abuse, drunkenness, and other male antisocial behavior. For example, among parents who abuse their children, one quarter of the mothers also reported that they had been battered by their parents (Smith & Hanson, 1974). Peter Scott (1974) estimated that at least one quarter of men charged with child murder also had a history of wife battering.

Although alcohol cannot entirely explain wife-beating, it may be used as an excuse for violence, or it may trigger an argument that leads to violence. Many men are either drunk at the time of assaulting their wives or have just woken up from an alcohol-induced sleep (Brandon, 1976). That alcohol might contribute to violence in the family is supported by laboratory findings in which large amounts of alcohol tend to increase aggression in men (Taylor & Gammon, (1975).

Second to alcohol, jealousy is mentioned as a factor involved in wife-battering. The husband may become entirely preoccupied with the wife's infidelity. He may start to watch her moves, to ask questions about her activities, and to search her clothing for evidence of sexual activities. Her confessions in response to his continuous pleading with her are very likely to provoke an assault (Brandon, 1976). In Britain, many male suicides are found to follow the murder of a spouse by a jealous husband (Gregory, 1976).

Children who have observed their parents engaging in violence are more likely to be violent with their own spouses. Also, the experience of being hit as a child seems to increase the tendency to use violence in adulthood (Gelles, 1972).

Similar to the common belief that women like to be sexually brutalized and raped is the idea that the battered woman often chooses a violent man: If she doesn't enjoy being beaten, why doesn't she leave? Women, particularly the poor and the uneducated, lack financial resources, housing, and social support, and thus cannot very easily leave to establish a separate home for themselves and their children (Gregory, 1976; Pizzey, 1974). Some women stay either because the husband has promised to reform or because of the children. Others, perhaps those who are brought up in violent homes, believe that "it's part of marriage" (Gregory, 1976). Since many murders are preceded by violence, several women could have been saved by being separated earlier from their husbands (Scott, 1974).

The stereotype of the nagging housewife is often used to put the blame on the woman: The husband hits her to shut her up. The belief that the battered woman is provoking has no support, since 77 percent of the battered women surveyed by Gayford (1975) reported that physical assaults were not preceded by verbal arguments.

Battered women are rarely "mentally ill" (Gregory, 1976). However, they are often on prescribed drugs to relieve their anxiety and depression. It is not surprising that these women are disturbed when their traumatic life situation is taken into consideration. They also tend to be repeatedly admitted to mental hospitals and, often, to be abused by psychiatrists (Pizzey, 1974). They are admitted because they have taken so many overdoses that the local hospital is fed up with them; they are then sent to a psychiatrist, who admits them to a mental hospital for depression. In hospitals, they are tranquilized for a few weeks, told that they are very much improved, and sent home to face another battering.

While in the hospital, many of them undergo brain surgery and ECT. After surgery, their children are taken away and put into care; because of the effects of the operation, these mothers are no longer responsible or capable of looking after them. On the other hand, "the husbands continue to beat them but now they put up with it with cheerful indifference" (Pizzey, 1974). Those who are given ECT "go home and are repeatedly battered until in the end you find a confused, witless forty-year-old sitting in front of you, trying to remember when and where she was last jolted out of her rapidly deteriorated mind" (Pizzey, 1974).

It is clear that battered women are not protected by the law or by the professional. The immediate hope is that the number of refuges administered by women to give accommodation and advice to women in distress will be increased. A long-term prospect is to look into the social and cultural roots of the aggression of men against women.

VIOLENCE AGAINST CHILDREN: CHILD ABUSE

Sinah Jones, of the Parish of St. Mary Woolnoth, was Indicted for Murdering her Bastard Male Child, on the eighteenth December last, being Saturday night, by stopping its Breath with a Cloath put in its Mouth; she being a Servant in the House of Mr. Cousins. The Evidence against her was plain, the Nurse, the Chair-woman, the Mid-wife, the Master and his Servant, all deposing, that she denying the Key, they broke open her Trunk, where they all saw the Child Dead, wrapped up in a Cloath, with a Rag in the Mouth of it, as big as a Handkerchief, and that the Child being something Warm, they tried all they could to recover Life in it, but to no purpose. The Prisoner said little for herself, but that she knew nothing of the Cloath in the Mouth of the Child, and that she had not her Senses, and was Lightheaded. Then the Statute was read to her, wherein, if the Child be found Dead and Concealed, though it were so Born, the Person Concealing it, shall suffer Death as in case of Murder, except she can prove by one Witness at least, that the Child so concealed was born Dead. Upon full evidence, she was brought in guilty of Murder.

Nigel Walker: CRIME AND PUNISHMENT IN BRITAIN

One problem that has been increasingly coming to the attention of the professional and the public is child abuse. This is an important topic in the study of female criminal behavior, since mothers or mother substitutes have more contact with children than fathers and since it is usually assumed that they are more predisposed than fathers to abuse their children.

The most serious areas of child abuse are those related to physical and sexual abuse. In contrast to an adult, the physically abused child is a passive victim who cannot escape from the situation or defend herself or himself. Most societies severely punish aggressive behavior in interactions between adults. However, the use of physical force against children is not equally prohibited. In fact, it is encouraged in specific situations, such as during interactions between parent and child or teacher and child. Most societies give absolute power to parents over their children. Both parents and teachers are usually allowed to use physical force in order to discipline children. There seems to be a tacit acceptance in society of the saying, "Spare the rod and spoil the child."

David Gil (1970) defined physical abuse of children as "the intentional, nonaccidental use of physical force, or intentional nonaccidental acts of omission, on the part of a parent or other caretaker interacting with a child in his care, aimed at hurting, injuring, or destroying that child." Acts of omission or neglect may include withholding food from the child, failing to provide sanitary living conditions, or failing to clothe and to provide medical help for one's child.

Professional interest in the physical abuse of children in the 1960s and 1970s has its origin in a paper by John Caffey, published in 1946. Caffey, a pediatric radiologist, drew attention to unexplainable injuries in young children, such as multiple fractures of the bones and subdural hematomas (a blood clot inside the skull that exerts pressure on the brain). Kempe, Silverman, Steele, Droegemueller, and Silver (1962) were, however, the first to use the label "the battered-child syndrome." They observed that, although child abuse is a major cause of death or maiming of children, physicians are generally unwilling to believe in the possibility of parental abuse of their children.

Parental abuse or neglect may occur at any age, but the majority of cases tend to be found in children under the age of five. Older children suffer from physical abuse because of disciplinary action that often results in battering (Fontana, 1975). The true incidence of child abuse and neglect is uncertain, since many cases are either not taken to physicians and hospitals or may pass unrecognized. Reported cases are estimated to be between two hundred to two hundred and fifty per million (Van Stolk, 1972). Of the 10,920 murders in the United States, one in every 22 involved a child killed by her or his own parent (Fontana, 1975). Girls and boys are equally liable to child abuse (Brandon, 1976).

Who Are the Abusive Parents?

The average age of the mother is 26, and that of the father is approximately 30 (Fontana, 1975; Van Stolk, 1972). They include all educational levels, though they belong predominantly to the lower levels. Gil (1970) found that mental illness plays a minor part in child abuse.

The total number of children who are abused by their mothers is slightly larger than those abused by their fathers. The slight excess of mothers was explained by the finding that 29.5 percent of the children were living in fatherless homes, a factor that increased the mothers' opportunities to abuse their children. Fathers and father substitutes were, in fact, involved in nearly two-thirds of the incidents in homes that did have fathers or father substitutes (Gil, 1970). Thus, the involvement rate of fathers was higher than that of mothers when opportunity to be with children was taken into consideration. The belief that child abuse is a predominantly female crime appears inaccurate.

Abuse by the father is found to be mainly the result of uncontrolled outbursts while disciplining the child (Gil, 1970). The males' attacks tend to be explosive in nature, inflicting serious and multiple injuries (Brandon, 1976). Male violence often results in death. Peter Scott (1974), a British psychiatrist, studied twenty-nine men who were charged with killing a child under the age of five. All these men indicated that the child provoked it: She or he was disobedient, refused to smile, or was dirty. The attacks often occurred when the man was left in charge; in a quarter of the cases, the mother worked, leaving the man to look after the child.

Brandon (1976) described the abusing mothers as being meticulous about standards of care in the home and about the dress and appearance of the child. The first incidence of abuse is often associated with some personal crisis (such as a disagreement with the husband), with a criticism, or with financial or housing difficulties. There is no one common pattern of child abuse, although the majority of the women are under stress (Brandon, 1976).

Maternal infanticide is more likely to occur during the period immediately after childbirth. In Britain, it is found that the mother also tries to kill the rest of her family as well as herself (Walker, 1969). Often, this is caused by the psychological and physiological stress following childbirth. Sometimes, an unmarried woman or girl finds herself pregnant and because of having been prevented from obtaining an abortion, she may dispose of the child, either by abandoning it someplace where it will be found or by killing it.

There are high rates of divorce, alcoholism, drug addiction, mental retardation, mental disturbance, unemployment, and poverty in the background of abusive parents from social agencies and welfare organizations. However, abusive parents undergoing private medical treatment do not have these general characteristics (Fontana, 1975). Abusive parents have often been brutalized as children. This pattern seems to perpetuate itself from one generation to the next (Brandon, 1976; Fontana, 1975; Gil, 1970).

Sexual Abuse of Children

One example of the sexual abuse of children that has been discussed early in this chapter is child rape. Other forms of the sexual exploitation of children are incest and child pornography.

Incest is defined as a sexual relation between members of a family other than the mother's relationship with the father. Brother-sister incest is the most frequent, followed by father-daughter incest; mother-son incest is the least common (Kinsey et al., 1948; Gebhard et al., 1965). The older participant in incestuous relationships is more likely to be a male rather than a female, which may reflect a double-standard for the two sexes; that is, there is a stronger taboo concerning mother-son than father-daughter incest. Brother-sister incest may result from sharing the same bed; this is particularly true of lower-class families living in crammed conditions.

Many cases of incest remain unreported. Weinberg (1955) estimated the annual incidence at 0.73 case per million in Sweden and between 1 to 1.9 cases per million in the United States. However, Kinsey et al. (1948) reported that .5 percent of the males interviewed in their study admitted to acts of incest. Among randomly selected female patients in Britain, Lukianowicz (1972) found paternal incest in the case history of 4 percent of the group.

All the remaining types of incest occurred in another 4 percent of the patients. Patients who experienced paternal incest were classified into four groups, according to the effect that the experience seemed to have had upon them: (1) girls who later became promiscuous, (2) girls who complained of sexual dysfunctions, (3) girls with some neurotic reactions, and (4) girls who showed no ill effects (Lukianowicz, 1972).

Females studied by Maisch (1972) felt positively toward their pregnancies and children from incestuous unions. Research, however, had shown that these children tend to have significantly higher rates of morbidity (deformity, retardation) and mortality (Adams & Neel, 1967; Lindzey, 1967). It has been suggested that sexual stimulation of a girl by her father or by other adults in early adolescence may intensify her sexual drive, leading to promiscuity and prostitution in later years (Teicher, 1975). It is quite possible that seduction of girls in childhood through material inducement may serve as a model for exploitive sexual relationship with men in adulthood.

Pedophilia (literally meaning "love of children") is similar to incest in that it involves a sexual attraction toward children. However, in pedophilia, the increase in the physical maturity of the victim leads to a break in sexual relationship, whereas in incest, physical maturity increases the sexual attraction for the adult partner. The age of the pedophile ranges from adolescence to over seventy. However, the majority of pedophiles are in their thirties and forties. They are often known to their victim—they may be a neighbor, a relative or a friend of the family (Gebhard et al., 1965). Unlike rapists, the pedophiles seldom use violence. In their friendly way, they may masturbate while talking to a girl or stroking her hair. They may also manipulate the child's sex organs, masturbate between her thighs, force the child to masturbate or fellate them, and even have actual intercourse with her.

Associated with pedophilia is child pornography, or so-called "chicken porn," which involves pictures showing the undressing, fondling, and the oral or genital penetration of female children. Customers of this trade are typically middle-class, white, male, middle-aged, and usually married. In recent years, there has been an increase in the number of runaway girls who are exploited sexually in exchange for food and shelter. Yet, law enforcement authorities tend to underestimate the problem; they suggest that children appearing in pornographic films are foreign (Dudor, 1977).

Children represent an extreme state of human powerlessness and dependency; thus, they are unable to defend themselves or to resist violence and exploitation by men. Because children depend entirely on adult assistance and guidance, there is an urgent need for the forming of organizations to protect children's rights.

Women
and
Psychophysiological
Disorders

part five

If a Patient is seiz'd with an Illness during a Passion of his Mind, it uses sometimes to last as long as the Passion; and will rather shift to a Disease of another Form, than quit him altogether. I observed this particularly of late in a Woman of forty Years of Age, that was thrown by the deepest Passions of Mind into a great Flux of Blood from the Womb, of which she was cur'd, after using several Remedies for the space of three Months. But the same Concern, and Passions even of greater Violence, continuing for almost a Year, she was no sooner cur'd of that Flux of Blood, than she was seiz'd with a running from the Womb, that was sometimes white, and sometimes particoloured. After this Running was stopt, she was seiz'd with Anguish at Heart, Anxiety of the Breast, extream Weakness, Leanness, Inappetency, Thirst, a lingring slow Fever, a falling off of the Hair, and the like; which continued, and held out for six Months against all the Power of Remedies. To compleat her Misery, she was taken first with the Swelling of her Legs, then with an Ascites, and at last with an Universal Dropsy all over her Body. After all, being worn out with Care, and miserably tortur'd for five Months with a Legion of Illnesses, she remov'd to the other World.

George Baglivi: THE PRACTICE OF PHYSIC

The Beautiful Female Body: A Key to Mental Health

12

Women are the beautiful sex. Who doubts it? Among birds the male may have the pretty plumage, but among human beings it is the female who wears the peacock feathers.

Una Stannard: "THE MASK OF BEAUTY"

Physical appearance is the first and the most noticeable of our characteristics in interpersonal encounters. There are, however, double standards of beauty for females and males. Most societies seem to give more explicit consideration to the physical beauty of the female than to the handsomeness of the male (Ford & Beach, 1952). Male attractiveness is dependent more on skill and physical strength than on physical appearance. In this chapter, I first discuss standards of physical attractiveness and their implications for the adjustment of women. Included in this discussion are the relationship between physical attractiveness and the hospitalization of women as well as the use of plastic surgery by women to achieve an acceptable level of attractiveness. Second, I discuss obesity and anorexia nervosa, which are considered deviations from prescribed cultural standards of beauty.

PHYSICAL ATTRACTIVENESS

Who Are the Attractive?

Wilson and Nias (1976) suggested that the more exaggerated the sex differences are in an individual's physical appearance, the more sexually attractive the individual will be. They noted: "Basically, the idea of beauty treatment and make-up is to do just this—to emphasize some of the ways in which the female face is different from that of a male (fuller lips, narrower eyebrows, softer complexion, absence of facial hair)." Standards of physical beauty are acquired through learning and experience. If a culture prescribes certain standards of physical beauty, individuals in that culture are more often exposed to such models of pulchritude. The male is frequently exposed to what is considered ideal beauty through the media: This ideal is presented by Miss World or by the "playmate" who appears in magazines, such as *Playboy* and *Penthouse.* These models tend to exaggerate the dimensions of different parts of the female body (breasts, waist, and hips).

Psychologists attempted to find a relationship between attraction to body parts and personality. An amusing instance of this approach is the psychoanalytical suggestion that early breast-feeding experience is associated with later sexual attraction to the breasts. Men who were nursed at the breast in infancy are attracted in adulthood to women with well-developed breasts, whereas men who were bottle-fed tend to like boyish and flat-breasted women (Tridon, 1949). Scodel (1957) hypothesized that men who are attracted to women with large breasts have developed an oral personality and show much concern with the gratification of dependency needs. Hence men who like large breasts are more dependent than those who like small breasts. The results, however, have revealed just the opposite: Subjects who found large breasts attractive were less dependent than subjects who were attracted to small breasts.

Based on the popular stereotype that men can be classified into three groups—breast lovers, buttock lovers, and leg lovers—Wiggins, Wiggins, and Conger (1968) investigated the relationship between these three body parts and personality. They presented 95 male undergraduates with nude female silhouettes where the size of breasts, buttocks, and legs was varied. The preference rating of the subject was then related to various measures of personality charac-

Figure 12.1 The Legs of Your Car. Photo: Veith Pirelli AG.

teristics and behavior. They found that those who like large breasts tended to be readers of *Playboy,* smokers, and sportsmen, whereas those who liked small breasts were nondrinkers, religious, and depressed. Men who liked large buttocks were passive, guilt-prone, and obsessive. In contrast, men who liked small buttocks revealed little interest in sports and were devoted to their work. Large legs were liked by nondrinkers and by submissive and socially inhibited men, whereas small legs were preferred by sociable and exhibitionistic men. The average male, according to the Wiggins study, tended to favor a female with medium-sized legs, medium to small buttocks, and larger than average breasts.

The male physique most popular among women is the one with

thin legs, a medium to thin lower trunk, and a medium to wide upper trunk (the V-look). The pear shape, with either a thin upper trunk or a wide lower trunk, was the least liked by females (Lavrakas, 1975). However, a study carried out in New York appears to indicate that what men imagine women admire is not the same as what women really admire in men. Men thought that women would most admire a muscular chest, shoulders, and arms and a large penis. The women, however, reported that these characteristics disgust them; they cited small buttocks, tallness, and thinness as the most admired characteristic in men (Wilson & Nias, 1976).

All research on the attractiveness of the female body is derived from the male stereotype that women are passive sexual objects to look at. In real-life situations, we normally respond to a total impression of the face and body and other subtle cues, such as smiling, vivaciousness, and health (Holstein, Goldstein, & Ben, 1971; Wilson & Nias, 1976).

"What Is Beautiful Is Good"

Physically attractive persons are more liked, are more popular, and are endowed with many socially desirable characteristics. Both attractive women and men were found to be more popular than unattractive persons (Berscheid, Dion, Walster, & Walster, 1971; Walster, Aronson, Abrahams, & Rottman, 1966). However, physical attractiveness plays a more significant part in the dating popularity of women than in that of men. Moreover, men tend to gain status and to be perceived more favorably when they are associated with an attractive female (Sigall & Landy, 1973).

Attractive persons are not only more liked, they are also assumed to possess socially desirable characteristics. A study by Dion, Berscheid, and Walster (1972) has revealed that physically attractive people are perceived to be more sexually warm and responsive and more sensitive, interesting, sociable, and outgoing than persons of lesser physical attractiveness. Physically attractive persons do not only possess attractive personalities, but they are also perceived as having more prestigious occupations and happier marriages than less attractive persons. Landy and Sigall (1974) found that "beauty is talent": Attractive females are perceived as more capable than unattractive females.

With all these advantages for beautiful women, it is not surprising that they also have financial advantages in that they tend to marry into a higher social class than those who are less attractive (Elder, 1969). As we shall see in the next section, attractive persons are reported to be happier, better adjusted, and have more positive self-concepts than unattractive persons.

Physical Attractiveness and Happiness

In an early study relating physical attraction to adjustment, Clifford Kirkpatrick and John Cotton (1951) argued:

> One could assert that attractive women are relatively free from inferior feelings, they tend to have success in the courtship process, they set the prevailing cultural norms and stereotypes, and finally they may cause their bemused husbands to put up with traits which in less attractive women would cause marital discord. On the other hand, it could be argued that attractive women might be less happily married because of the distinction between the mate-finding process and the mate-satisfying process. Attractive women might capture mates but frustrate them because of narcissism, childishness, superficiality, and general absence of concern for the more solid virtues.

Kirkpatrick and Cotton asked students to nominate some well-adjusted and poorly adjusted couples among their friends and acquaintances. Later, the physical attractiveness of these couples was independently rated by interviewers. Results revealed an excess of attractive persons among the well-adjusted couples. The wife's attractiveness was, however, more important to the adjustment of the couple than that of the husband. Another study by Mathes and Kahn (1975) found that beautiful women tended to be happier, more satisfied with themselves, and more emotionally stable than unattractive women. Again, good looks were not related to the happiness, self-esteem, and emotional adjustment of men.

Lerner and his associates (Lerner & Karabeneck, 1974; Lerner, Orlos, & Knapp, 1976) made a distinction between physical attractiveness and physical effectiveness. Physical attractiveness refers to characteristics that one feels are important to oneself in presenting an attractive physical appearance to members of the opposite sex. Physical effectiveness, on the other hand, refers to how different parts of the body play different roles in helping one to be effective in one's daily functions. It was found that physical attractiveness of body parts, such as the face, chest, profile, ankle, and appearance, is a better predictor of self-concept in the female than in the male. However, physical effectiveness is a better predictor of the self-concept of the male. These findings seem to suggest that the self-concept of the female is based on transitory and subjective characteristics, such as beauty. The male, on the other hand, can obtain prestige through more enduring and objective achievement.

Studies relating attractiveness to happiness and psychological adjustment are usually carried out with persons in their teens or twenties. Since beauty fades with age, women who are attractive when young have more to lose than those who are not, and it may be predicted that they will be more unhappy later in life. Ellen Berscheid and Elaine Walster (1974) reported a study that supports this suggestion: It was found that women who were highly attractive when young, as judged from their college photographs, tended to be less happy and poorly adjusted to life in their forties. No such relationship between physical attractiveness and happiness in later life was observed for men. The problem of the aging attractive female is humorously presented in the so-called "ageing actress syndrome" described by Wilson and Nias (1976) as:

> . . . the stereotype of the woman whose stage success was founded upon her sexual attractiveness, and who in middle-age is reduced to a pathetic, gin-soaked neurotic, waging a losing cosmetic battle against encroaching wrinkles, greyness, and other signs of old age. Perhaps the interest of the men in her life had also been contingent on her beauty, and had subsequently evaporated. Apparently, an inability to grow old gracefully is a danger faced by many attractive women. If happiness is an ultimate criterion, plain women may come into their own in the autumn of their lives.

Physical Attractiveness and Hospitalization

The disadvantages of being "ugly" are undeniable in North American society. This would suggest a relationship between "bad" looks and mental illness. Farina, Fischer, Sherman, Smith, Groh, and Mermin (1977) have indeed found that hospitalized women are rated less attractive than an equivalent group of women living in the community (female shoppers and female students). Attractiveness was also associated with the perception of pathology in patients; for example, the less attractive patients were seen by the ward aides as less adjusted than other patients. Also, the less attractive patients were, the more they regarded themselves as sick and the longer they estimated they would remain in hospital.

Attractiveness also affects the treatment of patients. Unattractive patients tended to remain in hospital for longer periods. In fact, attractiveness was found to be a stronger determinant of the length of institutionalization than assessment of patients' psychological adjustment. Unattractive patients had, in general, a bad deal: They were visited less often, and, inside the hospital, they tended to be less involved with others and were often judged less pleasant (Farina et al., 1977).

Hospitalization could, of course, affect attractiveness; patients may not be allowed to groom themselves adequately or they may simply stop paying attention to their appearance. Hence, hospitalization may cause "bad" looks rather than vice versa. However, Farina and his associates found that patients judged unattractive when ill had poor interpersonal relationships before they were labeled sick. This would suggest that bad looks had caused the patient's life problems even before they were hospitalized. Hospitalization itself may have been only one of many negative life experiences these "unattractive" women had undergone.

The relationship between attractiveness and mental illness raises problems to those who espouse hereditary theories of mental illness. It is quite possible that it is not "madness" that is inherited but that unattractive parents tend to have unattractive children who may, in turn, become liable to being accused of madness.

PLASTIC SURGERY

The importance of physical attractiveness to the female would suggest that beauty aids, such as plastic surgery, can play a major role in improving her social and interpersonal relationships. Although beauty aids are commercially exploited by both business and the surgeon, information about their use and abuse is rather fragmentary and anecdotal (McGregor, 1974; Olley, 1974).

There are two major types of plastic surgery: reconstructive surgery and elective surgery. Reconstructive surgery refers to operations undertaken to correct, as far as possible, the face or other parts of the body that are distorted or maimed as a result of congenital abnormalities, disease, or trauma. Elective surgery, known as esthetic or cosmetic surgery, refers to operations performed in an attempt to improve the appearance of "normal" individuals to conform to acceptable standards of beauty (McGregor, 1974).

About thirty years ago, cosmetic surgery used to be considered a novel procedure and a privilege of the rich. In the 1970s, however, cosmetic surgery has become a booming "industry." Nearly one million Americans had operations in 1971 as compared to 15,000 in 1949 (McGregor, 1974). There seems to be an increase in the number of operations as well as in the types of operations requested. There are now more and more women undergoing breast augmentation to attract and/or hold men whose ideals are featured in magazines such as *Playboy* and *Penthouse*. More middle-aged persons go to doctors who will "lift" their faces or remove wrinkles, double chins, or bags under their eyes. The development of alloplastic materials (silicone) in recent years has extended the capacities of the plastic surgeon and opened many possibilities for persons who wish to improve their looks.

Social Factors in Plastic Surgery

Factors in the increase in the number of clients seeking plastic surgery are almost invariably social and are associated with interpersonal relationships. It has been suggested that, in an urban and mobile society, there is an increase in the number of transitory encounters with people, which tends to lead to an increase in the value attached to physical attractiveness. Brief and superficial meetings do not give persons the opportunity to appreciate other virtues that can be discovered only by prolonged interaction (intelligence, personality traits, social class, etc.). Thus, physical attractiveness has been emphasized in many predominantly "female" jobs that involve brief contact with a large number of people—for example, air hostess, receptionist, and salesperson. The discrimination against "unattractive" women in the job market is illustrated in this citation from *Time* (1972):

What better symbol of exploited womanhood than the pulchritudinous office worker of jest and lore? Lustful male chauvinist bosses chase her around desks, jealous wives plot her undoing, and her alleged lack of brains is a national joke. But at least, says "Washington Post" columnist William Raspberry, she has a job—which is more than can be said for her less well-endowed sisters.

According to Raspberry, discrimination against ugly women ("there's no nice way to say it") is the most persistent and pervasive form of employment discrimination. Men, he argues, face no such bias, except in the movies and in politics. Raspberry's sympathies lie not with the "mere Plain Janes, who can help themselves with a bit of paint and padding," but with the losers, the "real dogs," who supposedly would be working full time if their features were more regular. Such discrimination, he insists, is all the more insidious because no one will admit that it exists. "No personnel officer in his right mind will tell a woman, 'Sorry, lady, but you need a nose job, and your lips don't match.'" And a woman so insulted would not be likely to publicize it.

Other motives for elective surgery may be making friends, attracting a marriage partner, or just submitting to the demands of a husband. McGregor (1974) described the case of a young woman, married less than a year, who requested breast augmentation to please her husband, whose ideal was Raquel Welch. The woman explained, "My poor husband said he never dated anybody under a 36B until he met me, and gee, I'm a 32A and I think I ought to do something about it!"

The plastic surgeon himself can be very sensitive to the slightest deviation or asymmetry in his clients. He may be anxious to make "beautiful people" and be easily tempted to suggest esthetic improvements. Of course, the surgeon's suggestions may also be motivated purely by professional self-interest, such as obtaining experience or recruiting patients.

Apart from the pressure put on women by doctors, they are exposed to a continuous campaign waged by the cosmetic industry. "Every day the billion dollar beauty business tells every woman she is a monster in disguise. Every ad for bras and girdles tells a woman her breasts and hips need reshaping; every ad for high heels that her legs need propping; every ad for cosmetics that her skin, lips, and eyes need masking" (Stannard, 1973). These influences of the media are reflected in the poor self-image of patients who come for plastic surgery (Edgerton, Meyer, & Jacobson, 1961).

Since physical attractiveness is associated with youthfulness, one would expect a high demand for cosmetic surgery among aging females. This is particularly true for women who were considered attractive earlier in life but who are frightened in later life about losing what had been an important source of gratification for them (Goldwyn, 1972). Some of them may be worried about the bags under their eyes or their "awful jowls"; others may demand an overall "mending" and ask the surgeon to lift their faces, augment their breasts, tighten their thighs and abdomens, and remake their noses and chins. They want to regain a youthful identity lost throughout the years.

Effects of Plastic Surgery

Objective research on the effects of plastic surgery is almost nonexistent. Most research in this area appears to be based on the observations of the surgeon or on subjective reports from clients. Reports on the effects of plastic surgery indicate that the majority of clients tend to be pleased with it (Edgerton et al., 1961; Knorr, Hoopes, & Edgerton, 1968; McGregor, 1974; Snyderman & Guthrie, 1971). Thus, it has been suggested by surgeons (Goldwyn, 1972; Knorr et al., 1968) and psychologists (Berscheid & Walster, 1974; Cavior, 1970), that cosmetic surgery might replace psychotherapy to improve the self-image of certain clients:

> Psychotherapists might do well to consider plastic surgery (reconstructive and cosmetic) as an alternative or adjunct to psychotherapy. Anecdotal reports by plastic surgeons and interdisciplinary research by psychologists, sociologists, and plastic surgeons have suggested that plastic surgery can result in marked changes in self-concept, behavior, and the responses of others. For example, if an unattractive girl requests psychotherapy because she feels lonely and rejected and cannot find a husband, it might be more advantageous in terms of time and expense to consider plastic surgery. Rather than have the girl spend months or years in expensive therapy trying to discover her intrapsychic difficulties, it might be better to help her integrate and adjust to the changes which might result from plastic surgery (Cavior, 1970).

Changes in the appearance of the female would undoubtedly affect the reactions of others. However, it is unrealistic to expect immediate improvement after plastic surgery. For example, clients may show disappointment that the operation did not succeed in overcoming restrained relationships with their husbands (Edgerton et al., 1961). Olley (1974) noted that the operation may have adverse effects on those who have been deriving secondary gains, such as sympathy and attention, from their "deformity." In these cases, the "deformity" may be the client's main way of relating to others, and it may serve as an excuse for social or career failures that may be due to factors other than physical attractiveness.

Recently, there has been much interest in the role of plastic surgery after mastectomy. The female breast is a symbol of femininity, beauty, and sexual response (Dietz, 1973). Women may feel mutilated, repulsive, and desexed after the operation. Plastic surgery may restore their former body image and change the reaction of others towards them. Unfortunately, the average surgeon does not recognize the female grief for the missing breast. They only see a patient who should be rescued from cancer rather than "the tender young woman who has had not only the impending fear of mutilation and death but also the knowledge that her feminine personality will be or has been irreparably damaged" (Freeman, 1973).

Emphasis on cosmetic surgery is one of the central issues involved in the controversy over the extent of surgical procedures required to adequately treat breast cancer (Asken, 1975; Garrard, 1975). The possibility of reconstruction of the breast or part of it by the use of various-sized silicone bags under the skin of the chest raises the question of whether the underlying muscles or some parts of the breast can be saved. Traditionally, radical procedures that involve the removal of the breast, the underlying muscles, and the nearby lymph nodes leave no useful skin and muscles on the chest, making reconstruction of the breast very difficult (Hartwell, Anderson, Hall, & Esselstyne, 1976). Early detection of breast cancer before it spreads out makes it possible to save parts of the breast (Garrard, 1975). Millard, Devine, and Warren (1971) observed that 90 percent or more of the cancerous lesions of the breast do not involve the nipple. They offered a procedure for saving the uninvolved nipple and replacing it on the constructed breast. They found this procedure to be a great morale booster for the female.

All in all, both constructive and elective plastic surgery play a major role in the psychological adjustment of the female and in improving her self-image. However, beauty aids in general attempt to exaggerate differences between the sexes and reinforce stereotypes of the female as a sexual object. There is now an increasing number of women who are entering business and other occupations that depend on skills rather than beauty, and it may be predicted that physical attractiveness will not remain the major asset of their lives. Beauty aids may also be rejected by women because they want to be treated as real persons and not as beauty symbols. Fortunately, we are witnessing a unisex trend to break down prejudiced stereotypes in hairstyles, dress, and other aspects of physical appearance.

Standards of female beauty, applied to the body shape, have resulted in a cultural preoccupation with eating, dieting, and weight control. According to Ford and Beach (1952), the majority of societies feel that a plump woman is more attractive than a slim one. That obesity has been admired and even considered a secondary

Figure 12.2a A hottentot woman. From Gustav Theodor Fritsch, *Die Eigenhorenen Sudafrikas,* Breslau: Verlag Ferdinand Hirt, 1872.

Figure 12.2b A nineteenth-century evening dress. Reprinted by permission of the Museum of the City of New York.

sexual characteristic in many cultures was noted by Rudofsky (1972) in *The Unfashionable Human Body*:

> To judge from prehistoric art, fat women either predominated or were chosen by artists for their models, and in the course of time the well-upholstered woman was favored over the scrawny one. A similar taste can frequently be found in modern art; the artist who does not limit his sympathies to the fashionably disembodied female, sides with the primitive, and celebrates massive womanhood. Moreover, a fat body is often thought of as a strong body, and since only women of leisure can afford the luxury of being immobilized, the overfed woman came to represent the well-to-do and beautiful; obesity was promoted to a mark of quality. Hence, among those primitives who gauge female beauty by sheer bulk, brides-to-be go through preparations of excessive fattening. Upon reaching puberty, a girl is placed in a special fattening-house. The time of seclusion varies from several weeks to two years depending on the wealth of the parents.

Apart from cultural obsession with overall bulk, some cultures tend to emphasize specific, strategically placed cushions of fat. One of the most well-known female features is steatopygia, the accumulation of subcutaneous fat to cover a woman's hind parts and upper thighs. In the West, the overweight female is considered grotesque and unattractive; the lean and slender (the unpadded Hollywood version) rather than the chubby and curvy woman is admired. Women tend to succumb to social pressure regarding the shape of their bodies. In the case of both obesity and anorexia nervosa (to be discussed next), the female body may, however, reach abnormal proportions that cannot be entirely explained in terms of conformity to normal standards of beauty.

OBESITY

Obesity is a condition involving an excessive accumulation of fat or adipose (fatty) tissue in the body. Among men, it is prominent during their late twenties and thirties, and among women, it is seen during their forties and fifties. Thus, although obese men outnumber obese women during their early adult years, obese women outnumber obese men during the later stages of adulthood. Longevity of women is only moderately associated with obesity: The percentage

Figure 12.3b *Venus of Willendorf.*   Reprinted   by permission of the Naturhistorisches Museum, Vienna. Alle rechte vorbehalten © by Prahistorische Abteilung Naturhistorisches Museum, Wien.

Figure 12.3a *Venus of Cyrene.* Reprinted by permission of the Museo Nazionale Romano.

of overweight women 75 to 79 years of age is slightly greater than that of women in the 25 to 35 age range. In contrast, longevity in men is significantly associated with weight. Men in the age range of 55 to 64 tend to be less overweight than those in the 25 to 34 year range. Maintaining an average weight appears to be associated with the survival of men in the 65 to 74 age range (Stuart & Davis, 1972).

Factors in Obesity

It is commonly believed that obese persons are emotionally disturbed and that they overeat to reduce their anxiety, depression, and other psychological conflicts (Moore, Stunkard, & Srole, 1962). However, an association between emotional disturbance and overeating has not been supported by research (Rodin, 1977). Schachter, Goldman, and Gordon (1968) found that obese persons did not eat much more when they were anxious and did not show significant anxiety reduction as a result of eating. Holland, Masling, and Copley (1970) found no difference in psychological disturbances between obese and non-obese groups. The finding that one out of every three lower-class persons tended to be significantly overweight indicates that obesity itself may not be considered abnormal among this group. The relationship between obesity and mental health is stronger among middle- and upper-class women because of the great pressure on them to reduce their weight (Rodin, 1977).

Body image disturbance may, however, be related to obesity. Obese persons may perceive their physical appearance negatively. For example, an obese woman says "I call myself a slob and pig. I look in a mirror and say 'You are nothing but a big, fat pig.'" Rodin (1977) noted that this view of one's own body is usually associated with "intense self-consciousness."

It is often observed that overweight tends to run in families. Sixty percent of overweight persons have at least one parent who is overweight (Rodin, 1977). However, it has been demonstrated that although parent-child similarities in body build and diet are higher than expected, there is greater mother-child than father-child similarity—a finding that supports the theory that the mother, and not heredity, influences the eating habits of the child (Stuart & Davis, 1972).

Eating is controlled by external environmental cues as well as by the experience of hunger associated with food deprivation. Obese persons may not be able to control their response to external food cues and may therefore ignore internal signals of hunger. Their eating behavior is initiated and maintained by stimuli outside their body (Rodin, 1977). Thus, obese persons may not know when they are physiologically hungry, since these sensations do not seem to control their eating behavior (Stunkard & Koch, 1964).

Schachter and his associates (1968) suggested that if it is correct that obese persons are unable to label the physiological states associ- ated with food deprivation as hunger, then an empty or full stomach should have no effect on the amount eaten by them. On the other hand, the eating behavior of normal weight subjects should cor- respond to the effects of the bodily states of hunger or satiety. Schachter and his colleagues substantiated this prediction: Whereas obese subjects ate as much or even slightly more crackers when their stomach was full than when they were deprived of food, normal weight subjects ate considerably fewer crackers when they were full than when their stomach was empty.

External cues, such as the presence or prominence of food cues, appear to have a definite influence on the eating behavior of obese persons. Schachter (1971) found that overweight persons ate more almonds when the shells were removed (greater food cue promi- nence) than when the almonds were in their shells and had to be shelled to be eaten. Likewise, Palmer (1973) found that obese per- sons ate significantly more cashews when the lights were bright than when they were dimmed. These influences were not evident in the behavior of normal weight persons.

Effort is another factor that tends to influence obese persons; they tend to expend less effort than normal weight persons to obtain food (Hashim & Van Itallie, 1965). Nisbett (1968) found that obese subjects tended to eat either one or three sandwiches, depending upon the number (one or three) presented on a table in front of them, although they were told that there were many more sand- wiches in a conveniently placed refrigerator.

Obesity is more prevalent in the lower class. Social class differ- ences among men are, however, considerably less than those among women. Social pressure seems to have more influence upon women than upon men (Stunkard, 1975). Stunkard, D'Acquili, Fox, and Filion (1972), in a study of 3,344 school children, found that obesity starts at an early age among lower-class girls. They found that, at age 6, a lower-class group contained 8 percent obese girls, whereas an upper-class group had no obese girls at either age 6 or 7. Obesity was not only more prevalent among poor girls, but its greater prevalence was established earlier and increased at a more rapid rate than among upper-class girls. Stuart and Davis (1972) put forward two explanations of social class differences in obesity:

First, it is possible that poverty may be for obesity what ragweed is for hay fever—a pathogen subtly present but not detected because of the greater prominence of other cues. By this it is suggested that poverty may lead to poor education (including education about health and nutrition), little access to the opportunity for vigorous exercise, and proscription from those aspects of the occupational hierarchy which differentially reward nonobese persons. Second, it is possible that lower socio-economic groups may place a positive value upon obesity either as a means of survival,. . .as an aesthetic trait, or as a countercultural or at least subcultural norm. This would imply that, denied access to the requisites of a sound diet, occupants of lower socio-economic strata might place a positive value upon obesity as a sign of rejection of middle-class values, a possibility which finds some support in the fact that the dominant American reference groups do seem to regard obesity as a form of social deviance.

Methods of Weight Reduction

Dieting seems the obvious method of weight reduction. Strict diet does result in weight reduction, and this is particularly so in a controlled environment, such as in a hospital. Maintenance of weight loss after dieting is, however, extremely difficult in the natural environment. Some studies suggested that weight reduction and the maintenance of weight loss are more effective if the person consumes five to six small meals per day rather than a smaller number of heavy meals. Better controlled studies, however, demonstrated no differences in weight loss on the basis of *meal frequency* (Leon, 1976). *Prolonged fasting or starvation* is effective, but subjects tend to regain the weight they have lost when the fasting is over (Swanson & Dinello, 1970).

Medical treatment consists of drug therapy and intestinal by-pass surgery. In general, the results of *appetite suppressant drugs* are poor, reflecting the failure of medication to deal with obesity. The extensive use of drugs, such as amphetamines, may also result in problems of drug dependency: A woman may become addicted to the drug in addition to her addiction to food.

Intestinal by-pass surgery attempts to reduce the absorptive capability of the small intestine by a surgical procedure that by-passes a major portion of it. Nutritional deficiencies and diarrhea are some of the operation's side effects. Mortality—up to 6 percent—is also reported. It has been suggested that the procedure should be either discontinued (*Drastic Cures for Obesity,* 1970) or used only in cases of intractable massive obesity (Welch, 1973).

Much interest has been shown in the application of learning principles to weight reduction (Leon, 1976; Stuart & Davis, 1972; Stunkard, 1975). Stunkard describes four stages in the behavioral approach to obesity:

1. Description of the behavior to be controlled: Clients are asked to keep careful records of the food they eat. They are asked to put down what they eat, how much, at what time of day, where they are, who they are with, and how they feel. This stage tends to increase the patients' awareness of and the circumstances associated with eating.

2. Control of stimuli that precede eating. The accessibility of food and the amount of high-calorie food kept in the house must be limited.

3. Development of techniques to control the act of eating: This is to enable the individual to develop self-control of eating behavior by interrupting food intake. The person may interrupt the meal for certain periods of time and just sit at the table; she may carry out exercises, such as counting each mouthful of food eaten during a meal.

4. Modification of the consequences of eating: Activities relevant to weight reduction, such as record-keeping, counting chews and swallows, pausing during the meal, and eating in one place are rewarded. Immediate reinforcement is important in the success of the program.

It was found that short-term group psychotherapy that focuses on the problems of adhering to a diet, as well as on the discussion of personal issues, resulted in some degree of weight loss in obese women (Mees & Keutzer, 1967). A number of self-help weight reduction groups have been formed, such as TOPS (Take Off Pounds Sensibly). These groups provide strong pressure by publicly announcing each member's weight at each meeting. Hypnosis may also be used in suggesting new eating habits. The client may be asked during hypnosis to imagine feelings of satiation or aversion to particular foods (Leon, 1976).

In sum, a successful program for the control of obesity should not put the blame of weight gain and the responsibility of weight reduction on the obese person but on the environment. The manipulation of environmental stimuli is important in the reduction and maintenance of weight.

ANOREXIA NERVOSA

Anorexia nervosa is mainly a problem of young females. It is a malnutrition due to a deficient diet in which the caloric restriction is entirely psychological and is not related directly to poverty and to the availability of food (Bliss & Branch, 1960). In describing anorexic women, Bliss and Branch cited Dejerine and Gauckler (1908):

> It sometimes happens that a physician has patients—they are more apt to be women—whose appearance is truly shocking. Their eyes are brilliant. Their cheeks are hollow, and their cheek bones seem to protrude through the skin. Their withered breasts hang from the walls of their chest. Every rib stands out. Their shoulder blades appear to be loosened from their frame. Every vertebra shows through the skin. The abdominal wall sinks in below the floating ribs and forms a hollow like a basin. The thighs and the calves of their legs are reduced to a skeleton. One would say it was the picture of an immured nun, such as the old masters have portrayed. These women appear to be fifty or sixty years old. Sometimes they seem to be sustained by some unknown miracle of energy; their voices are strong and their steps firm. On the other hand, they often seem almost at the point of death, and ready to draw their last breath.
>
> Are they tuberculous or cancerous patients, or muscular atrophies in the last stages, these women whom misery and hunger have reduced to this frightful gauntness? Nothing of the kind. Their lungs are healthy, there is no sign of any organic affection. Although they look so old they are young women, girls, sometimes children. They may belong to good families, and be surrounded by every care. These patients are what are known as mental anorexics, who, without having any physical lesions, but by the association of various troubles, all having a psychic origin, have lost a quarter, a third, and sometimes a half of their weight. The affection which has driven them to this point may have lasted months, sometimes years. Let it go on too long and death will occur, either from inanition or from secondary tuberculosis. However, it is a case of nothing but a purely psychic affection of which the mechanisms are of many kinds.

The term *anorexia* (loss of appetite) is a misnomer. There is usually no loss of appetite in anorexia nervosa; its main feature is, in fact, a conflict between a frantic preoccupation with food and an active restraint from eating. Persons given the label *anorexia nervosa* usually show some of the following characteristics:

1. Age at onset is less than 25 years—cases after the menopause are very rarely reported; see, for example, Kellett, Tremble, and Thorley (1976);

2. The weight loss is at least 25 percent of the original body weight;

3. Eating disturbances are shown in a distorted implacable attitude toward eating (a belief that their weight is normal and that they are only dieting to be attractive);

4. There is no known medical illness that could account for anorexia and weight loss;

5. There is no other known psychiatric disorder, such as depression or schizophrenia;

6. They show certain characteristics, such as amenorrhea (nonoccurrence of menstruation), periods of overactivity, episodes of bulimia (morbid hunger with excessive eating) and vomiting, which may be self-induced (Hogan, Huerta, & Lucas, 1974).

Kendell, Hall, Hailey, and Babigian (1973) reported findings indicating an annual incidence of anorexia nervosa of between 0.37 and 1.6 per 100,000. The male:female ratio ranged from 1:14 to 1:24. However, these data may have underestimated the rates of anorexia nervosa. In the adolescent population of Umea, Sweden, Nylander (1971) estimated that the disorder is present in quite definite and severe form in one of every hundred and fifty 17- to 18-year-old girls. Crisp, Palmer, and Kalucy (1976), in a survey of nine schools for girls in Britain, found one severe case in approximately every 200 girls. In those aged 16 and over, it amounted to one severe case in about every 100 girls.

Crisp and his associates (1976) suggested that anorexia nervosa is associated with an overaffluent and overnourished society and that therefore it appears more often among girls from the upper and upper-middle classes than among those in the lower classes. The sensitivity of adolescent girls about their weight and their concern with dieting may also explain anorexia nervosa. The self-consciousness of these girls about their figures may initiate an extremely restricted diet.

Methods of Weight Increase

Many techniques have been used to increase weight in anorexia nervosa. Tube feeding is, for instance, used to help the female to put on weight. This has, however, serious side effects, such as the risk of infection and death. The use of tranquilizers (chlorpromazine) tends to increase the incidence of bulimia, an excessive appetite. Since one of the symptoms of depression is loss of appetite, it is thought that patients with anorexia nervosa may benefit from electroconvulsive therapy (Moldofsky & Garfinkel, 1974). Two reports also claimed that they cured anorexia nervosa by the use of psychosurgery (Sargent, 1951; Sifneos, 1952). Psychosurgery generally aims at overcoming the resistance of patients to other treatment.

Attempts to hospitalize these patients may pose a problem, since they do not perceive themselves as ill and wonder why they should be treated in hospital and be given drugs, shock therapy, or brain surgery. Hospital investigations are, however, necessary in order to exclude physical illness. In the treatment of anorexia nervosa, it is also thought useful to separate the patient from the family in order to ensure that the therapist can assume full control over the management of the eating problem. Thus, although hospitalization may be indicated to save the life of a patient, the use of drastic organic treatment is unjustified.

Bachrach, Erwin, and Mohr (1965) proposed that eating behavior is largely under the control of its consequences and that it can be maintained and modified by manipulating these consequences. As a first step in dealing with anorexia nervosa, Bachrach and his associates removed a hospitalized woman from an attractive bedroom where flowers, magazines, TV, and a record player were present. The experimenters also started having dinner and breakfast with her, reinforcing her whenever she talked about things that interested her or whenever she lifted the food to her mouth. The amount of food consumed was reinforced by having flowers, magazines, TV, radio, and the like brought into her room. If she did not touch the food, nothing would be done by way of reinforcement. As soon as the reinforcers were effective in increasing the patient's weight (she gained 14 pounds), she was discharged from the hospital.

Other studies also used reinforcement with success. Garfinkel, Kline, and Staucer (1973) established a system of rewards that was tailored for each individual patient. Goals were set for both daily and weekly weight gain. The specific rewards included physical activity, socializing off the wards, overnight and weekend passes, and other privileges on the ward. These were discussed with each patient, and a verbal contract was negotiated (a daily weight gain minimum was set at 0.15 kg and a weekly minimum at 1.0 kg). It was made clear that the patient was responsible for the weight gain. In another study by Azerrad and Stafford (1969), a token system of positive reinforcement (in the form of reward points redeemable for material items and home visits) contingent on the amount of food eaten was found effective in increasing the eating rate in anorexia nervosa. Agras, Barlow, and Chapin (1974) found that giving the client information feedback (concerning weight, caloric intake, and mouthfuls eaten) and serving large meals (the larger the amount of food served, the more food is eaten) are useful for increasing weight.

Anorexia nervosa may involve fear of normal weight and fatness or an anxiety related to eating. Hallsten (1965), for example, reported the treatment of Ann, age 12. Three years earlier, she had been considered obese at 90 pounds and had been called "Fatty." At the time of admission, she was 25 pounds under her age-height-appropriate weight. Desensitizing her fear of storms did not affect her eating habits and weight. Desensitizing her on stimuli dealing with eating, however, brought about positive results. Of particular interest in the present case is that Ann's anxiety related to being fat was reduced. This was necessary in order to counteract the teasing of her peers, since the anxiety evoked by being called "Fatty" had played an important role in causing her anorexia. In another case, desensitization was used to reduce the anxiety associated with normal or fat appearance as well as the anxiety associated with food (Schnurer, Rubin, & Roy, 1973).

Lang (1965) also successfully treated a woman suffering from anxiety, loss of appetite, and nervous vomiting. This twenty-three-year-old registered nurse reported that "not eating and vomiting occurred" whenever there was a new situation or she did "anything opposed to someone's wishes." He desensitized her to three specific situations: traveling to different destinations (the more familiar the destination, the less anxiety arousing it was), disapproval by significant people (e.g., family members), and situations where she was the center of attention.

In conclusion, since some anorexic persons normally die from starvation, overcoming malnutrition should be considered a primary aim. However, weight-gain through tube-feeding and other medical procedures disregard the sensitivities of young females and their life situations, both of which have led to excessive dieting.

Sex Differences in Hypertension, Heart Disease, Ulcer, Asthma, and Headache

13

Emotionality is an intrinsic part of our humanity, but pathological conditions may result from emotional behavior. One aspect of emotions is certain physiological changes, such as heart rate, breathing, and stomach activity. Another aspect of emotions is their overt and external manifestations, such as crying, laughing, smiling, shaking, clenching the teeth, attacking, and running.

The physiological components of emotions are considered predominantly involuntary and are only detectable through instrumentation. The overt components of emotions, on the other hand, are observable and under voluntary control. However, these two aspects of emotion are not unrelated to each other. Physiological responses prepare the individual in an emergency situation for a sudden extensive activity. An increase of the sugar content of the blood prepares the muscles for action. The dilation of the bronchioles of the lung facilitates breathing and provides more oxygen. The decrease of digestive activities parallels increases in heart rate and dilation of the blood vessels. Thus, implicit physiological activities prepare the organism for explicit activities in an emergency situation of danger or stress—the fight or flight reaction. Physiological reactions are adaptive in the face of an emergency situation. However, when neither fight nor flight are possible or appropriate (you can neither hit the boss nor leave the job), the overt manifestations of emotionality can be controlled, but the physiological reaction continues, often resulting in organic damage. The concentration of acidity in the stomach may lead to ulcers. An increase in blood pressure and cardiac activity may rupture blood vessels or may cause a heart attack. These bodily reactions represent some of the main physiological disorders that constitute the main killers in the Western world.

Psychophysiological disorders, such as hypertension (high blood pressure), heart attacks, ulcers, asthma, and headache, which are discussed in this chapter, represent only one facet of people's reaction to stress. We are already familiar with a wide spectrum of other reactions—fears, depression and low activity level, flight into imagination in schizophrenia, adoption of illness behavior in hysteria, indulgence in food or abstinence from food, and the like; these reactions do not involve physical illness and physical damage. In psychophysiological reactions, however, persons are physically ill and in need of medical care to relieve their pain or to save their lives. Psychophysiological disorders may demonstrate how social and psychological factors interact with physiological reactions and result in illness.

ESSENTIAL HYPERTENSION

With aging and the stress of life, our arteries may become hard, thick, or constricted, resisting the flow of blood and in turn raising blood pressure. It is estimated that between 15 to 30 percent of the American population has high blood pressure. Although some of these cases are due to physical factors, the majority have no known etiology and are labeled "essential" (Schwartz & Shapiro, 1973).

The average blood pressure of women is lower than that of men until an age that varies between 30 and 50, depending on the group studied. At older ages, however, men have lower blood pressure than women (Waldron, 1976b). Blood pressure increases with age, but the rate of increase is greater and begins earlier (age 35–40) in women than in men (Weiner, 1977).

Factors in Hypertension

Organic factors. Some studies suggest a relationship between blood pressure and sex hormones (Waldron, 1976b). Experiments with rats indicate that female hormones may increase the constriction of blood vessels, which could cause elevated blood pressure in women. Similarly, oral contraceptives, which contain female hormones, also tend to raise blood pressure, although they may do so only in women with a family history of high blood pressure (Shapiro, 1973). In this case, it is assumed that the pill triggers a genetically determined tendency to high blood pressure (Weiner, 1977). The genetic hypothesis is, however, weakened by the tendency of spouses who are not related to each other except by marriage to have more similar blood pressure levels the longer they remain married to each other (Winkelstein, Ibrahim, & Sackett, 1966). Similarly, other family members besides the spouse tend to share common blood pressure levels.

It has also been suggested that both menopause and ovariectomy may be related to blood pressure. Studies summarized by Waldron (1976b) reveal inconsistent results: They show a slight fall, a slight rise, or no significant change in blood pressure following ovariectomy and early menopause. An elevated blood pressure in women during middle-age or other life stages, may, however, be attributed not only to hormonal changes but also to psychological factors.

A study by Scotch (1963) strongly suggests a relationship between sex roles and elevated blood pressure among women. In a pioneering research, Norman Scotch found that Zulu women between 45 and 64 have higher hypertension rates than men of comparable age, a finding that supports similar observations in the West. He observed, however, that among women, high blood pressure seems to be associated with changes in sex roles. For example, widowed and separated women had higher rates of hypertension than did currently married women of comparable ages. Also, among women living in the city, those with many children (five or more) had a higher rate of hypertension than those with few children. Among women on the reserve, however, it was the menopause rather than the number of children that was related to hypertension: Postmenopausal women were more likely to be hypertensive than premenopausal women of similar age, but again, such a relationship did not hold for women living in the city.

In the traditional Zulu society, a woman's status is related to her ability to bear children, and it is stressful for her not to have children. Thus, for the traditional rural woman, menopause is associated with high blood pressure, whereas the number of children she has is not similarly associated. In the city, however, the opposite situation is found; a large number of children is stressful, whereas the menopause is not. An urban female is not only a wife and a child-bearer, but she is also a wage earner; in this situation, caring for children is of much concern for women. For her, the menopause is not as major an event as it is on the reserve, where it is the end of her major function of childbearing; instead, it frees her for greater productivity as a wage earner (Scotch, 1963). It appears that social rather than organic factors (pregnancy, menopause) are involved in the hypertension of Zulu women. Life events during the middle years may have similar effects on North American women and may elevate blood pressure. The Scotch study, as well as the finding that sex differences in blood pressure vary from one country to the other, strongly suggest the involvement of sociocultural factors in hypertension (Wittkower & Warnes, 1975).

Occupational stress is suggested to explain hypertension in man. Kasl and Cobb (1970) found a relationship between loss or threat of loss of employment and high blood pressure. Available data also reveal that employed women tend to have a slightly lower prevalence of hypertension than housewives of the same race and age. Waldron (1978) cited three studies indicating a consistent trend in this direction. The lower rates of hypertension among employed women would be consistent with the general pattern of better mental health among employed women than among housewives (employed women also have lower rates of coronary heart disease, according to *Vital Health Statistics, U.S., 1965*, cited by Waldron, 1978). Waldron noted that medically treated hypertensive women were more likely to be housewives, supporting their slight disadvantage in the rates of hypertension. However, among women who were *not* taking antihypertension medication, high blood pressure was more common for women who were employed full-time. This finding suggests that employment may actually increase blood pressure but that many women who are hypertensive and on medication may leave their jobs or that they do not seek jobs in the first place. Selective factors may thus have increased the number of employed women with lower blood pressure.

Other studies revealed that women who attend church more frequently have lower blood pressures (Comstock & Partridge, 1972; Kaplan, 1976). Again, selective factors seem to have influenced these findings. A follow-up of females for eight years has revealed that chronically ill persons attended the church less frequently (Comstock & Tonascia, 1977), suggesting that high blood pressure may influence church attendance by keeping sick women at home.

Personality factors Anger and hostility are suggested to explain hypertension. Hypertensive patients, according to this view, are superficially calm, gentle, and affable but are "internally seething with anger" (Lachman, 1972). They are continuously struggling against expressing hostile, aggressive feelings and have difficulty in asserting themselves. As children, these patients had a tendency to attacks of rage and aggression. Gradually, they learned to control their aggression, partly because of the threat of punishment and the fear of losing the affection of the parent (Alexander, French, & Pollock, 1968).

Hokanson and his associates (Hokanson & Burgess, 1962; Hokanson, Willers, & Koropsak, 1968; Hokanson, DeGood, Forrest, & Brittain, 1971; Stone & Hokanson, 1969) have suggested that the relationship between high blood pressure and the inability to express aggression may, however, apply only to men. In their studies, male subjects were angered by a confederate of the experimenter while they were carrying out a task (e.g., counting backward from 99 by twos). This caused the blood pressure of the subjects to rise. Later, half of the subjects were given the opportunity to give a shock to the confederate by pressing a button (or at least they thought they were shocking him, but in fact, no shock was administered). Aggression against the confederate brought the blood pressure back to normal in this group. Blood pressure remained high in the other half of the subjects, who were not given the opportunity to aggress against the confederate. Hokanson also found that aggression directed at a low-status frustrator (a college student) proved helpful in reducing blood pressure but that it was ineffective when directed toward a high-status frustrator (a visiting professor). These findings did not hold for female subjects; that is, aggression in the form of pressing a shock button did not reduce their blood pressure. However, when they made the positive response of pressing a button that rewarded the experimenter, their blood pressure decreased markedly. It appears that aggression by itself is not the key factor in increasing or decreasing blood pressure in male or female subjects. Any social response that helps the individual to terminate or avoid stress in interpersonal relationships seems to be crucial. Females, through socialization, have learned not to respond to frustration by aggression. Other means are more helpful in giving the female control over her environment. Indeed, the sex stereotypes discussed in Chapter 1 show that males are expected to be aggressive and females to be submissive. The Hokanson data suggest that when the male is able to conform behaviorally to sex stereotypes and express aggression, his blood pressure goes down. Breaking away from female sex stereotypes by being aggressive does not reduce the blood pressure of women.

Two studies by Kalis, Harris, Bennett, Sokolow, and Carpenter (1957; 1961) found that hypertensive women adopt male sex-role behavior. These patients were more assertive and expressed more hostility than normal women. The authors noted, however, that assertiveness and overly expressed hostility were maladaptive for these women in most situations where tact and submission were necessary and more effective in dealing with anger stimuli. Hypertensive women were considered inappropriate in their assertiveness and expression of hostility. Women with high blood pressure (prehypertensive group) had significantly more conflicts about sexual identification than women with normal blood pressure. They appeared dissatisfied with themselves and others and were oversensitive to real or imagined criticism. Women with low blood pressure, on the other hand, showed conventionally feminine behavior: They tended to accept social norms appropriate to their age and sex. Harris and Singer (1968) also described the social relationships of hypertensive women as hostile, combative, and abrasive. They were resentful and unable to accept their feminine roles. Of course, the Kalis and associates and the Harris and Singer studies do not demonstrate a *causal* relationship between independence, assertiveness, and aggression on the one hand and high blood pressure in females on the other. They do, however, suggest that a woman who shows these characteristics may be reacted to negatively in our society (for example, she may be rejected and ostracized), which in turn may cause many disturbances, including high blood pressure.

CORONARY HEART DISEASE

The term *coronary* refers mainly to the coronary arteries, which supply blood to the heart. In coronary heart disease, these arteries may be blocked by a blood clot, which may interfere with the blood supply to the heart and cause a heart attack. Angina pectoris is another indicator of coronary heart disease. It is characterized by brief episodes of pain in the chest caused by the inability of the coronary arteries to supply sufficient oxygenated blood to the heart muscle.

Death rates from coronary heart disease are twice as high for men as for women in the United States. The male excess of coronary heart disease is responsible for approximately 40 percent of the total sex differential in mortality (Waldron, 1976a). Murphy (1976a) noted that mortality rates for heart disease under age 70 were almost as high for women as for men in the early 1920s in both Britain and the United States. In 1947, it was noticed in Britain that female mortality rates for heart disease had been decreasing at every age group, whereas male rates at every age group had increased. By 1960, there were at least three male deaths for every female death reported as due to heart disease under age 70.

Factors in Coronary Heart Disease

As in hypertension, the effect of occupational stress seems to be predominant in coronary heart disease. Russek (1959) reported that at the time of their attacks, 91 percent of 100 patients (as compared with only 20 percent of healthy controls) had been holding down two or more jobs; working more than 60 hours per week; or experiencing unusual insecurity, discontent, or frustration in relation to employment. Buell and Breslow (1960) have shown that patients with coronary disease tend to work long hours. Occupational stress is found to differentiate young coronary patients from healthy subjects more readily than heredity, diet, obesity, tobacco consumption, or exercise (Russek & Russek, 1976).

Occupational stress and strain may only reflect Type-A behavior described by Friedman and Rosenman (1974). Type-A behavior is characterized first by a high drive for achievement, recognition, and advancement and a struggle to achieve more and more—what has been called "the quest for numbers." This is coupled with an extraordinary mental and physical alertness. Second, there is a competitive, aggressive, and hostile feeling toward others. Finally, there is an involvement with different responsibilities, coupled with a sense of time urgency and a concern with deadlines for completion— "hurry sickness." Type-B behavior is characterized by the opposite personality traits. In general, Type-A behavior is the lifestyle of the North American male, whereas Type-B behavior is characteristic of the female. However, sex differences in Type-A behavior do not emerge while young persons are still in school (Butensky et al., 1976), a finding that emphasizes the role or learning and experience in the development of such behavior.

Friedman and Rosenman (1974) compared a representative group of San Francisco Junior League members with their husbands. It was found that, as in white American women in general, these women developed coronary heart disease less frequently than their husbands, although they ate as much cholesterol and animal fat as their husbands. The female sex hormones do not seem to protect women from heart disease, since Friedman and Rosenman found that black women were slightly more susceptible than their black husbands to coronary heart disease. The authors concluded that female-male differences in Type-A behavior are the decisive factors. For example, when a group of women were divided into Type-A and Type-B behavior, Type-A women showed a much higher serum cholesterol level than Type-B women. Another finding was that the average blood cholesterol level of Type-A women was higher than that of Type-B men. Similarly, Type-A women not only suffered more coronary heart disease than Type-B women but also had more heart disease than Type-B men. However, on the whole, American white women are protected against coronary heart disease because relatively few of them have Type-A personalities. Furthermore, they are largely excluded from the business and professional sphere normally associated with a Type-A behavior pattern. The housewife's work may be heavy, but it does not involve meeting deadlines, competition, and hostility. In general, females and males have a similar coronary behavior pattern when they are in similar situations, but the female housewife role is associated with a lower level of that behavior.

Waldron, Zyzanski, Shekelle, Jenkins, and Tannenbaum (1977) found that employed women are significantly less Type-A than employed men in the younger age range but that the same distinction does not hold at older ages. The frequency of Type-A behavior for *working* women seems to peak at ages 30–35. One reason that employed women in their twenties are less Type-A is that at this age more than half of the women in the United States have no children and are likely to work, even if they are not Type-A. However, at ages 30–35, over 90 percent of them have at least one child, and fewer women have paid jobs. Among this older group with children, there seems to be a greater tendency for women who are Type-B to stay at home to look after their children, whereas Type-A women tend to hold a job. Waldron and her associates also raised the possibility that, in contrast to those in their early twenties, older women may have greater family responsibilities (a job and children), which tend to increase time pressure and Type-A behavior.

Waldron (1978) found that Type-A behavior is associated with a higher occupational status of women (and men) but not with a greater likelihood of being married or of having a high-status husband. It appears that the coronary behavior pattern contributes more to success in traditional male roles than in traditional female roles (e.g., marrying well).

In general, Type-A behavior is associated with male rather than with female roles in Western societies. Since more women are now seeking jobs and careers, it is not surprising that the gap between men's and women's rates of coronary heart disease is narrowing. This is particularly so among younger women (Waldron & Johnston, 1976).

Smoking and Coronary Heart Disease

Cigarette smoking has been shown to contribute substantially to coronary heart disease. Since smoking is usually considered a male activity, it presents an excellent example of how social stereotyping may influence sex differences in illness. Murphy (1976a) pointed out that when the anginal syndrome was almost exclusively male, smoking was also a male habit. In the nineteenth century, the increase in female angina seems to parallel an increase in the habit of smoking in women. Waldron (1976a) found that the ratio of male to female mortality rates for adults who *never smoked regularly* was much lower than the mortality ratios for the total population, including smokers. Smoking appears to contribute to sex differences in mortality due to heart disease.

Rosenman and Friedman (1961) found that there are differences in the smoking habits of Type-A and Type-B women: More women in Type-A than in Type-B smoked. Among those who smoked, the Type-A group smoked a larger number of cigarettes. No difference between the two groups was found in other habits contributing to heart disease, such as the amount of exercise or diets. Thus, the excess of coronary disease among Type-A persons may be due in part to their tendency to smoke more than Type-B persons.

Murphy (1976a) stated that smoking may affect females and males differently because both the motivation for smoking and the inhalation habits are different. Women in Britain tend to smoke when they are under tension, whereas men smoke when they are bored and understimulated. Because female smokers are under tension, they may play much more with the cigarette and hence may usually inhale less smoke than their bored and understimulated male counterparts. Therefore, heavy smoking may have more deleterious effects on men than on women.

Sex Hormones and Coronary Heart Disease

Evidence relating sex hormones to coronary heart disease is inconsistent. The possibility that male hormones increase the risk of heart disease has no support. For example, castration in men does not reduce death caused by heart disease. Similarly, the androgen levels of coronary patients are not different from those of healthy groups (Waldron, 1976b). Do female hormones, then, affect the risk of heart disease?

Studies of young women with ovariectomy reveal either an increase in coronary heart disease or no relationship at all (Waldron, 1976b). Waldron suggested that hysterectomy may indirectly increase the risk of coronary heart disease through its association with behavioral characteristics, such as cigarette smoking, or with other emotional factors. This may be particularly true in cases of electric hysterectomy (for sterilization). Thus, an increase in coronary heart disease may be due either to the removal of female hormones or to some behavioral characteristics of women who undergo these operations. Hormonal effects can also be investigated in estrogen replacement therapy. However, the evidence is contradictory in this area, revealing a decrease in coronary disease in castrated women after estrogen treatment in one study and no effects on death rates or the prevalence of coronary disease in another (Waldron, 1976b).

High levels of cholesterol in the blood increase the risk of coronary heart disease, and some studies indicated that a decrease in female hormones after ovariectomy of young women is associated with high serum cholesterol levels. In contrast, estrogen therapy generally reduces serum cholesterol. Thus, female sex hormones are assumed to be protective against heart disease. On the negative side, these hormones tend to enhance thrombotic processes: For example, oral contraceptives (see Chapter 4) facilitate blood coagulation, and therefore, women on the pill have an increased risk of death due to vascular troubles (Waldron, 1976b).

One argument against the hormonal interpretation of sex differences in heart disease is that black women have much higher rates of coronary disease than white men and rates about as high as those of black men (Murphy, 1976a). Another argument against the hormonal hypothesis is that, although men tend to have higher rates of coronary disease in Western countries, the sex differential varies from one country to the other. Variations in sex differential would suggest the influence of sociocultural factors rather than hormonal changes (Wittkower & Warnes, 1975).

PEPTIC ULCER

An ulcer is an open wound in the wall of the stomach or the duodenum, the portion of the small intestine lying immediately below the stomach. The term *peptic ulcer* is used for both duodenal and gastric (stomach) ulcers. Duodenal ulcer is more frequent among younger men. Gastric ulcer, on the other hand, occurs in older people and is found with equal frequency in both sexes. It is believed that emotional factors play a more important role in duodenal ulcer than in gastric ulcer (Weiner, 1977).

Women have more acute ulcers, whereas men have more chronic ones. Pflanz (1976), for instance, reported that, in household interviews women more often indicate dyspeptic stomach complaints of the ulcer type than men, in the ratio of 1:0.8. However, when the frequency of ulcers is assessed by other methods, the number of men is greater than that of women (for example, ulcers clinically confirmed by X-ray show the ratio of women to men is 1:4). It is quite possible that the tendency of women to report acute ulcers and other stomach pain enables them to obtain early treatment and thus saves them from chronic conditions and death.

Peptic ulcer as a medical problem has a short history in the Western world. Before around 1830, it was infrequently reported, with no difference in occurrence between the two sexes (Murphy, 1976a). About 1850, there was a shift, with young women becoming much more vulnerable than men. About the turn of the century, the male rate began to rise, eventually overtaking the female rate at every age level. This excess of ulcers in men, like its earlier counterpart in women, started first in the under 30 age group and later spread to older age groups (Murphy, 1976a). In a New York hospital, Mittelmann and Wolff (1942) reported a ratio of 2.5 males to 1 female at the beginning of this century, a ratio that increased to 12 to 1 about thirty years later. After World War II, the incidence of ulcers started to increase in women but remained stable in men (Pflanz, 1976). As the table below indicates, the gap between the sexes has very much narrowed in the 1970s.

CHANGES OF SEX RATIO IN THE INCIDENCE OF ULCERS, FEMALE:MALE
(Adapted from Pflanz, 1976)

	1951	1964	1972
Canada	1:4.3	1:3	1:2.7
U.S.	1:4.3	1:2.6	1:1.9
Finland	1:4.5	–	1:1.3
England and Wales	1:3.4	–	1:1.4

In an attempt to explain the shift in the rates of peptic ulcer, Murphy (1976a) suggested that sex stereotypes may interact in a subtle way with organic factors. He found, for instance, that the most acceptable explanation of the semi-epidemic of peptic ulcer among women in the nineteenth century is the prevalence of "a clothing fashion, the wasp-waisted corset." It had been used throughout the century, becoming more tight and more reinforced by many layers of heavy clothing, until it was gradually replaced by a straight-line fashion just before World War I. These changes in fashion coincided with shifts in the rate of gastric ulcers in young women. The Murphy interpretation is consistent with animal research indicating that immobilization (wrapping rats in a towel) produces gastric lesions (Weiss, 1977).

Murphy (1976a) also noted that, in Australia, the shift in the ratio of ulcers (from 2.3 males to 1 female in 1939 to 1.2 females for each male in the 1960s) can be explained in terms of the readiness of females to take more medication. The switch in the sex ratio was associated with the excessive ingestion of pain killers (tablets containing acid which can produce ulcers).

Mittelmann and Wolff (1942) noted that the increase in the rate of ulcers among men in the first three decades of this century seems to parallel a change in the relationship between the sexes. During this period:

A man was expected to be "master" in his household, yet within this pattern of male dominance men were permitted emotional dependence upon their women. . . . With the gradual change in domestic relationships, however, emotional dependence for a man has become more and more difficult, his freedom limited and his privileges curtailed. . . . Coupled with this change, women now compete with men at work . . . but they do not wish their financial contribution to be "counted upon," since there is social justification for the feeling that in giving themselves in marriage and in "running the household" they have already made an adequate contribution. A woman may become the important financial contributor in the home, in which case she often unwittingly creates in her partner a conviction of inadequacy. If she fails in an occupational venture she is justified by society in retiring and being provided for by her husband, brother or father, while such security for a man has no social approval. If a man fails to "provide" he may be denied the feeling of security which his wife's emotional support could give him. Her humiliation of him under these circumstances is endorsed by cultural sanctions. Thus, while society's requirements of the male are essentially as stringent as before, the emotional support accorded him in return is less (Mittelmann and Wolff, 1942).

More recently, however, Manfred Pflanz (1976) has suggested that the employment of women has increased the rate of female ulcers. He found that the higher the employment level of women in a given country, the higher the percentage of mortality of women from peptic ulcer. This would suggest that the male occupational role is associated with the development of peptic ulcers.

A popular view of the ulcer patient was suggested by Franz Alexander (1934), who described him as efficient, active, and ambitious on the one hand and as having an unconscious need to be dependent and passive on the other. The patient wants to adopt a socially sanctioned male behavior, but this is in conflict with the female behavior pattern.

Since ulcers are prevalent in the male, there are only a few studies of female patients. One study by Cohen, Silverman, and Magnussen (1956) of 200 women with duodenal ulcer found three major groups: a masculine and aggressive group, an immature and inadequate group, and a third group made up of those who accepted their feminine roles in being good mothers, wives, and housekeepers. For the third group, surgery and menopause constituted significant events before the onset of the illness. Other precipitating events in the third group were the birth of a grandchild or the pregnancy of a younger female relative. In contrast, neither surgery nor the menopause played a significant role in the onset of ulcer in the "masculine and aggressive" women or in the "immature and inadequate" group. The loss of someone upon whom they depended seemed to have precipitated ulceration. This study seems to indicate that personality characteristics as well as stressful events associated with ulcers appear to vary in female patients.

In conclusion, there are no definite personality characteristics of female and male ulcer patients; their personalities are seen in other patients as well as in healthy persons. Like patients with other psychophysiological disorders, ulcer patients are not a homogeneous group (Weiner, 1977).

BRONCHIAL ASTHMA

Bronchial asthma is characterized by the obstruction of the bronchial airways because of the tendency of the bronchial tree to respond by bronchoconstriction, edema (excessive tissue fluid), and excessive secretion to a variety of stimuli. The incidence of asthma is between 4.0 percent to 5.7 percent in the general population (Weiner, 1977). It occurs twice as often among boys as among girls, but the sex ratio evens out during the adult years (Purcell & Weiss, 1970). Rates increase with age: Older women (over 45) have it twice to three times more often than younger women (Weiner, 1977).

The Relative Importance of Different
Factors in Asthma

Many stimuli, such as cold air, chemical irritants, odors, exercise, nasal polyps, and psychological factors, can provoke asthma. Life circumstances, combined with a tendency to bronchoconstriction, produce a variable and unstable pattern of asthmatic reaction. Three factors are involved in asthma (Rees, 1956). The allergic factor refers to an increased sensitivity of the cells in the respiratory system to one or more allergens (pollen, dung, dust, etc.). Infections of the respiratory tract may precipitate the first attack of asthma—for example, bronchitis, whooping cough, or pneumonia in childhood. Finally, psychological factors involve emotional, personality, and other experiential factors, any of which may precipitate asthma. These factors seem to change over time, age of onset, and according to the sex of patients.

In children, girls and boys are similar in the incidence of psychological factors. However, females reveal a higher incidence of psychological factors than male patients in all age groups from 16–65. The incidence of infective factors is similar among the two sexes throughout different ages, apart from a low incidence in the 16–25-year-old male group. Allergic factors are similar between girls and boys before 16. After 16, there is a marked increase of allergy as the dominant factor in males in the 16–35-year-old age groups, but this allergic factor starts declining in older asthmatic males. In females, allergic factors are also more dominant in the age groups from 16–35 than in earlier or later age groups. The reasons for the dominance of these factors at a certain life stage are still unknown (Rees, 1956).

Rees (1956) listed many emotions that are assumed to precipitate asthma. These are "anxiety with tension, anticipatory pleasurable excitement, tension due to frustration of any need, anger, resentment, humiliation, depression, laughter, guilt feelings, joy." It appears that any type of emotion may precipitate an asthmatic attack.

The major personality approach to asthma is based on psychoanalytical theory. French and Alexander (1941) described the asthmatic patient as revealing an excessive dependency on the mother that results in hostile impulsive behavior as well as in instability of mood and feeling. Separation from the mother is expected to activate dependency feelings and, presumably, to precipitate asthma. The asthmatic attack (wheezing, gasping for breath) is considered as symbolic of a repressed cry for the lost mother.

The view that there is a specific asthmatic personality is weakened by the finding that female patients may reveal different characteristics from those of male patients. Fine (1963), for example, found that asthmatic girls tend to be less sensitive to maternal rejection, to be depressed, and to strive for independence; asthmatic boys, on the other hand, tend to reveal different traits: They tend to be more sensitive to maternal rejection; to become angry, explosive, and uncontrolled; and they are content to remain dependent. Similarly, Purcell, Turnbull, and Bernstein (1962) found that girls were less outgoing, more anxious, more depressed, and more conscientious than asthmatic boys.

Observations by Groen and Pelser (1964) of patients who were undergoing psychotherapy reveal how asthmatic illness may create similar needs in both sexes—that is, a need to be helped during the asthmatic attack. For example, male patients regarded their partners as protective people from whom they expected love, affection, and understanding. Interviews with the wives of these patients left the impression that the wives were dominant in the relationship and that this situation was induced by the husband. The female patients, like the male patients, wished that their husbands were more kind and loving toward them, and, in particular, they craved a deeper understanding of their sensitivities. They wanted special care and understanding from their husbands during illness, a wish which the male patients had also expressed. Both the women and the men wanted their partners to be at their bedsides during the attack or at least to stay in an adjoining room. A common grievance of both sexes was that their spouses were increasingly indifferent to their illnesses. Thus asthma, like any other organic illness, can create specific relationships, particularly that of dependency, between spouses and their ill partners.

Lachman (1972) argued that asthmatic response may start as the result of an infection, an allergy, or a psychological stress but that it may be perpetuated by the enforcement of others. As the following case reveals, the asthmatic responses of Mrs. Jones became well established because they brought more attention and sympathy from Mr. Jones and reduced his yelling bouts:

. . . Each time Mr. Jones yelled at his wife, her heart rate and pulse pressure sharply increased, she trembled visibly, and there were pronounced constrictions of the bronchioles that led to her gasping for breath, among other responses. The first time this happened, her husband was so concerned about her welfare—particularly about her breathing difficulties—that he immediately stopped his tirade, gave her sympathetic attention, and called a physician. Intermittent tirades of Mr. Jones over the years, with similar subsequent compassion on his part expressed immediately thereafter to his wife's breathing problems, eventually resulted in the gasping pattern being established as a reaction of the wife while changes in heart rate, pulse rate, trembling and other responses tended to diminish and disappear. Further, she then displayed the gasping pattern—which was repeatedly rewarded by the solicitous attention of her husband as well as by other personal gains—very frequently, not only to her husband when he yelled at her, but even when he was present but did not yell at her. And it was also elicited by people who resembled her husband in some way, and to a variety of stimuli associated with her husband—his job, his automobile, his family, his associates, his favorite activities. In short, an asthma-like reaction was developed (Lachman, 1972).

To summarize, bronchial asthma represents a heterogenous disease; therefore, no generalization can be made about the predisposing, initiating, and sustaining factors involved in the illness. At the present state of knowledge, a multiplicity of factors are suggested to explain asthma. As in other psychophysiological reactions, sex differences in the development of asthma are not well understood.

HEADACHE

Migraine and muscle contraction (tension) headaches are the most well-known varieties of headaches. Surveys in the adult population indicate a high rate of migraine: Over a year's time, 23.2 percent of females and 14.9 percent of males reported that they suffered from symptoms of migraine (Waters & O'Connor, 1975). Tension headache is probably more widespread than migraine. There is a general agreement that women tend to report severe headache more than men (Bakal, 1979). Migraine appears to occur with equal frequency in girls and boys until about age 11, after which it predominates in girls (Bille, Ludvigsson, & Sanner, 1977; Oster, 1972). Headache may be preceded by an *aura*—a warning that the headache is coming. Yawning, drowsiness, irritability, and heightened sensitivity to normally ignored everyday sounds are some of the phenomena commonly experienced before an attack. Vomiting and nausea may also occur during the aura state. A sense of well-being may be felt the day before the attack. The person may feel "dangerously well" the day before the attack and may recognize the warning of mood change (Pearce, 1977). Patients may find light unpleasant during the headache attack and prefer to lie down in a darkened room. Some patients have unusual visual experiences (blind or dark spots, unformed flashes of white or colored light).

These visual disturbances may be the result of vasoconstriction (narrowing of the blood vessels) and a decrease in the flow of blood to the retina. Changes in body image may be experienced in migraine. Lance (1973), for example, reported that one patient experienced the following: "My fingers felt as long as telegraphic poles and my mouth with the teeth in it seemed like a case full of tombstones."

Patients experience migraine as an aching, throbbing, unilateral (one-sided) pain, usually coincident with the pulse beat (Bakal, 1975). The pain is more commonly felt in the frontal and temporal regions, but it may extend over the entire head and radiate down to the face, or even to the neck and shoulders. Tension headache is usually bilateral, involving a dull and persistent pain.

Causes of Headache

Both organic and psychological factors have been suggested to explain headache. The genetic hypothesis seems to be supported by the observation of a high incidence of migraine in the families of migraine patients (Goodell, Lewontin, & Wolff, 1954). It is also thought that migraine often occurs in both mother and daughter (Lance, 1973), but this is not supported by the finding that when the mother is the affected parent, both daughter and son are equally afflicted (Deubner, 1977).

Lance (1973) noted that the periodicity of migraine is related to the menstrual cycle in more than half of his female patients—the headache attacks appearing around the time of menstruation. Migraine is also relieved in some pregnant women. Somerville (1972) found both improvement and complete remission of headache during pregnancy. These observations do suggest a relationship between low hormonal levels and migraine. However, the hormonal explanation is inconsistent with the finding that migraine is not influenced when the periods cease (Pearce, 1977).

Some migraine patients report that their attacks are precipitated by eating certain foods, particularly fatty foods, chocolates, and oranges (Lance, 1973). This may, however, result from suggestion. For example, Moffett, Swash, and Scott (1974) studied twenty-five individuals who indicated that their headache was precipitated by the consumption of chocolates. They were told that they would be given two kinds of chocolates, but in fact, one kind was made of noncocoa substance. Results indicated that only a small number reported headache following ingestion of the chocolate and that this percentage was not different from the other condition where noncocoa material was ingested. Exposure to glare (watching TV or being in strong sunlight) and noise is found by some patients to precipitate a migraine attack.

We still do not know any definite organic basis for migraine. Psychological stimuli may, however, precipitate the attack. Life events associated with relaxation are suggested to explain migraine attacks. Migraine occurs during periods when patients are expected to relax and to be tension-free, such as during weekends, the first day of a holiday, Sunday, and planned social engagements (Dalessio, 1972). Pearce (1977) noted sex differences in this respect: For men, weekends and the first days of a holiday are often associated with headache; for the young housewife, who has a husband and children to cope with during the weekends, their departure to work and school may constitute her relaxation, which may bring her a headache on Monday morning (Pearce, 1977).

Attention has also been given to the personality characteristics of migraine patients. They are described as having "an exaggerated sense of personal insecurity . . . perfectionist traits and a tendency to anxiety and to worry unduly. . . . Their emotions were deep, expression of them was frustrated and they had a tendency to revert to self-pity. . . . Amongst the women not one had a successful heterosexual life" (Touraine & Draper, 1934).

Wolff's Headache and Other Head Pain (Dalessio, 1972) a major study on headaches, emphasizes two aspects of the migraine female: She both intensifies her sex role and has sexual problems. Anecdotal evidence from case histories reported by Wolff indicates that the migraine patient is unnecessarily tidy and house-proud and that she is a person who checks and rechecks her actions. Wolff gives the case of a housewife who used to call herself a "Dutch cleaner." Her husband referred to her as a "fanatic with a dust brush." The following remark of the husband tells its own tale: "If you would throw away the mop you would probably feel better." Wolff (Dalessio, 1972) reported that a majority of the migraine women experienced sexual dissatisfaction, with orgasm seldom attained. Generally, they considered sex as an unpleasant marital duty. (It was noted, however, that the sexual functioning of male patients is not similarly affected and appears to be normal.) Unfortunately, most of the characteristics of migraine patients described by Wolff and others are the subjective impressions of clinicians. Rees (1971) found these characteristics to be common in patients with asthma, ulcers, and other disorders. He concluded that "there is no specific personality which is applicable to migraine in general."

Signs of muscular overcontraction are found in most tension headache patients. One simple test of the ability to relax is to lift the patient's arm up in one's hand and to tell the patient to let the arm relax in the examiner's hand as though it were resting on an armchair. The aim is to let the limb go completely loose so that when the examiner's hand is removed, the arm will drop downwards to the patient's side. The majority of tension headache patients are not aware that the arm is not completely relaxed and that it will remain resting on the imaginary armchair when the supporting hand is taken away. Also, normal subjects can let the jaw hang down so that it can be moved rapidly up and down by the examiner. Most tension headache patients hold the jaw so rigidly that the whole head moves with the jaw. These demonstrations should be important before training the patient in muscle relaxation.

Treating Headaches with Biofeedback

Biofeedback is based on operant conditioning in which the response to be learned is followed by a feedback in the form of reward, punishment, or knowledge of results. The technique consists essentially of the use of monitoring instruments to detect and amplify physiological processes in order to make them available to the individual by being fed back in some form. For example, muscle activity is translated into a series of clicks that are spaced in time as a function of the level of tension (rapid clicks indicating greater tension). In a sense, individuals are now able to "hear" their muscle activity. They can also "see" these activities by reading a dial. The level of blood pressure can also be fed to the individual through a series of tones or by reading a dial.

Psychophysiological responses (blood pressure, tension in the muscles) are not ordinarily subject to voluntary control, since they are beyond the awareness of the individual. The aim of biofeedback is to increase the patient's awareness of psychophysiological responses in order to establish control over these responses. It is assumed that continued exposure to and practice (i.e., biofeedback training) of certain physiological responses will eventually enable the patient to bring these responses under voluntary control. It is thought that, during training, the person learns to associate certain thoughts or bodily sensations with changes in feedback (for example, changes in the tones or dial readings). She or he is encouraged to describe these sensations and to use other strategies during the training sessions. For example, patients may use phrases ("I am relaxed," "I am going to sleep") that may be conditioned to the desired physiological response. These so-called autogenic phrases may, in fact, enhance biofeedback. A classic example of the autogenic control of physiological responses is a person reported by Luria (1968) who had exceptionally vivid imagery: He could raise his heart rate 30 beats/minute by imagining that he was running to try to catch a train, and he could produce a 3.5 degree Celsius temperature difference between his two hands by imagining that one hand was on a hot stove, while the other was squeezing a piece of ice.

When biofeedback is used in the treatment of tension headache, the reduction of pain in the head is secondary to dealing with muscle contractions in the scalp, neck, and face. Muscle tension is recorded and measured by an electromyogram (an instrument that indicates levels of muscle tension on a dial). The aim of the biofeedback is the relaxation of specific muscles in the head. The patient is reinforced by auditory feedback in the form of a reduction in the frequency of clicks, which is parallel to the magnitude of the reduction in muscle tension. Through biofeedback, the patient can learn to become aware of the level of tension in the muscles of the head and can learn to reduce it in order to relieve the pain of headache or even to prevent headache (Budzynski, Stoyva, Adler, & Mullaney, 1973).

Since migraine pain is caused by the abnormal dilation of arteries in the head, biofeedback aims at reducing vasodilation and, consequently, reducing pain. Biofeedback of finger temperature has been used in the treatment of migraine. It is assumed that voluntary increase of finger temperature is related to an increase of blood flow to the hands and to a decrease of blood flow to the head. The patient is given instructions in the use of a "temperature trainer" with a dial to indicate the difference between the temperature of the mid-forehead and the right index finger. A positive warmth response, as indicated by the trainer, is accomplished by increasing the temperature of the hands in comparison to that of the forehead. Autogenic training is relevant to the treatment of migraine since it aims at bringing somatic functions (heaviness of the limbs as an indicator of relaxation and warmth in the extremities) under voluntary control (Schultz & Luthe, 1969). By repeating certain phrases ("My mind is calm and quiet"), patients can relax and focus on the achievement of warmth in the hands (Sargent, Walters, & Green, 1973).

Certainly, if successful, biofeedback can be used to prevent headache attacks; patients who developed voluntary control of headache could also detect preheadache symptoms and manage to relax in order to avoid migraine attacks. Unfortunately, biofeedback techniques are only in the preliminary stages of development. Recent studies reveal that migraine patients treated by finger warming do not show better improvement than other patients with no biofeedback training (Miller, 1978).

In the treatment of hypertension, results vary from one patient to the other or from one study to the other (Miller, 1978). Patients can control and decrease their blood pressure (Kristt & Engel, 1975; Patel & North, 1975), but this is far from curing hypertension. Since irreversible anatomical changes occur within the walls of blood vessels when the illness is well advanced, biofeedback should be considered as a preventive measure in both hypertension and cardiac troubles.

In addition to biofeedback, muscle relaxation may be used in the treatment of headache and other disorders. Jacobsen's (1938) progressive relaxation is the most widely used method. The client is taught to tense each muscle group in her body separately, to start feeling this tension, and then, gradually, to "untense" these muscles. One may start by asking the client to grip the arm of the chair and observe the sensations in the hand and the arm. She may also be asked to push and pull against the therapist while he grips her left wrist so that she becomes more aware of muscle tension feelings in the arm. She is also asked to give the feeling of tension her fullest attention and then, gradually, to reduce it while the therapist decreases his counteraction. These preliminary exercises enable her to distinguish between the sensation of a contracting muscle and that of a relaxed muscle. The tense housewife may continue to exercise with other muscles. She may lie down for 5 to 10 minutes and first lift the legs one at a time, hold them up for 30 seconds, and then relax the muscles so that the leg slumps heavily onto the bed. The arms could be similarly exercised. The arm is raised and the muscles are relaxed to allow it to drop down. Similar exercises with the muscles of the eyes, forehead, and jaws are also practiced. These exercises enable muscle tension patients to become aware of the pressure sensations in the forehead, temple, or neck and to reverse the process by relaxing the muscles involved. Patients also learn to avoid becoming tense in emotional situations.

SUMMARY

Psychophysiological illnesses, which are often associated with sex roles, are the major killers of Western people. Men, for example, generally tend to have higher blood pressure than women until middle-age when the level of blood pressure in women surpasses that of men. It is suggested that when the male conforms behaviorally to sex stereotypes and expresses hostility and anger, his blood pressure goes down. But because women are punished for being assertive and aggressive, exhibiting the same behavior does not reduce their blood pressure. Also, stress associated with middle-age may explain high blood pressure among women during this period; evidence linking the menopause and low hormonal levels with high blood pressure is inconsistent. Occupational stress, such as loss or threat of loss of employment, is linked to high blood pressure in men.

Death from heart disease is twice as high for men as for women. Type-A personality (meeting deadlines, competition, and hostility), which is associated with professional and business success, is suggested as a major cause of heart disease. Type-A personality is more characteristic of a working man than a housewife. Male occupational stresses tend to differentiate heart disease patients from healthy subjects more readily than heredity, diet, obesity, tobacco consumption, or exercise. Smoking which is usually considered a male activity presents an excellent example of how sex stereotypes may influence sex differences in illness. It is observed that an increase in the female habit of smoking has been accompanied by an increase in heart disease among women. A high rate of heart disease among black women contradicts the hypothesis that female hormones protect women from heart trouble.

The rate of ulcers is also associated with activities peculiar to women and men. For example, the high rate of ingestion of acid drugs (pain killers) by women may cause ulcers. (The semiepidemic of ulcers among young women during the nineteenth century may have been caused by the tight corsets which used to be fashionable during that period.) Although it is believed that ulcers are associated with the efficient, active, and ambitious executive, there are no definite personality characteristics of female and male ulcer patients. However, employment tends to increase ulcers among women.

Asthma occurs twice as often among boys as among girls; but the sex-ratio evens out during adulthood. It may be precipitated by infection of the respiratory system, by an allergy to such material as dust and pollen, or by psychological factors. The relative effect of these factors on females and males is very little understood.

The rates of headache are higher among women than men. Some believe that headache is transmitted through the mother to her daughter, but this belief has no support. The suggestion that headache is associated with menstruation is inconsistent with the finding that headache does not disappear after the menopause. The clinical description of female patients as sexually inadequate housewives and obsessively house-proud homemakers may represent only a selected group of patients.

The medical treatment of headache as well as other psychophysiological reactions primarily aims at alleviating symptoms rather than curing the illness. A promising new method of treatment is biofeedback, which attempts to make patients aware of their physiological reactions and to control such reactions. Treatment by biofeedback is still in the experimental stage.

Afterword

It is now quite evident that both the diagnosis and the treatment of mental illness are related to sex roles. Rates of mental illness reveal that there are more females than males with the diagnosis of depression, phobia, anxiety, hysteria, and chronic schizophrenia, and more males than females with the diagnosis of personality disorders (psychopathy, alcoholism, and addiction) and psychophysiological disorders (ulcers, heart, and respiratory disorders). Since the overall number of females as patients in psychiatric facilities is greater than that of males, it is not surprising that women are prescribed more drugs, and are given more psychotherapy, shock therapy, and psychosurgery.

Sex-related patterns of mental illness are consistent with feminine role orientation, which emphasizes expressive behavior and relation between persons, and with masculine role orientation which is concerned with instrumental behavior and the achievement of goals. In our society, persons who react to stress by intensifying their sex role or by breaking away from it are considered mad. Thus, a woman is labeled phobic or depressive when she is hyper-feminine (helpless, hopeless, passive, and dependent) and a man may be diagnosed as a psychopath when he becomes hyper-masculine (aggressive and antisocial). Sex-role reversal (aggression and overt sexuality in the female or apathy and social withdrawal in the male) is also regarded as an important aspect of schizophrenia.

And yet, the intensification of sex roles is more tolerated by society than the reversal of it. For example, crying as a symptom of depression is more tolerated in women than in men. Clinicians also attribute more serious pathology to men who express dependency (a female pattern) than to women who reveal the same level of such behavior. In contrast, women who become aggressive (a male pattern) are considered more disturbed than men who show similar behavior. Thus, in order to avoid rejection, persons tend to be reluctant to express behavior indicating sex-role reversal. Men, in particular, tend to avoid feminine behavior because femininity is more associated with psychopathology and undesirable characteristics than masculinity.

Sex roles may determine the nature of stressful life situations which precipitate psychological disturbance. It seems that female disturbance originates within the family, whereas male disturbance is closely linked to occupational problems. The mental health of women is defined in terms of their function as mothers and housewives or as attractive sexual objects. Because of the limitations of family roles, psychiatric symptoms of females are often due to difficulties beyond their control. Among family stresses conducive to psychiatric disturbance in females is having three or more young children and the lack of an intimate relationship with a mate. Women are also sensitive to bereavement and to loss of the mother in childhood. Further, the housewife role itself appears to be compatible with a phobic or depressive lifestyle. Many women who had been active, independent, and self-sufficient before marriage develop agoraphobia and depression (fears of going out, fears of being alone, lack of initiative, and so on) immediately after marriage. Even of those women who acquire phobias and depression before marriage, the marital situation and the housewife role seem to reinforce and aggravate their disturbance. The marital conflicts of educated females are sometimes related to the diagnosis of schizophrenia.

Female sexuality and her reproductive organs are considered paramount to her psychological adjustment. The belief that sexual frustration is the cause of female psychological problems is partly responsible for the use and abuse of sexual intercourse in psychotherapy. Further, unattractive women are more vulnerable to hospitalization and are more perceived as sick and hopeless than attractive women. Since female psychological adjustment is defined in terms of transitory physical characteristics such as beauty, the excess of middle-aged females among chronic schizophrenics and other residents of mental hospitals is understandable. Also, the popularity of hysterectomy (and hormone treatment) among physicians may be traced to the old Greek belief that the *hystera*—the womb—can explain virtually all female troubles.

Although marriage and family life protect men against many physical and mental hazards, it is not entirely safe to be a man. Certain sex-linked behavior may expose men, more than women, to physical injury and death. For example, men are exposed more to accidents on the road and at work. A relatively high rate of male suicide is associated with occupational problems and old-age retirement. Male mortality from respiratory diseases (lung cancer, emphysema) as well as from cirrhosis of the liver are primarily caused by excessive smoking and drinking. Occupational stress (so-called Type-A behavior, such as being pressured by deadlines, competing, and feeling hostile) is also implicated in the high rate of mortality due to heart disease, and other psychophysiological disorders. Men are also more involved than women in homicide and other violent crimes (female crimes are usually victimless, and therefore, women do not kill or get killed as often as men).

The study of sex differences in mental illness, within the framework of the female family role and the male occupational role, represents a shift of emphasis from biological factors and the psyche to the social environment. The investigation of stresses and strains in the family has been more useful in understanding female psychiatric disturbance than the study of psychic conflicts and hormonal cycles. One example I gave in this book is the change in the study of female sexual dysfunction during the last two decades. Traditionally, psychoanalysts conceived female sexual dysfunction as a sickness, using the awful label "frigid" to emphasize the insensitivity and inadequacy of women. Since the sixties, however, it has been found that many environmental factors affect the female sexual response. Because female sexuality is more repressed by society than male sexuality, a woman may develop fear, anxiety, and guilt that might inhibit her sexual response. Also, in many cases of sexual dysfunction, it has been found that the husbands rather than the wives are inadequate: These husbands are clumsy, crude, inept, and ignorant of the female sexual response. Such findings have revolutionized sex therapy, which now aims at teaching couples adequate sexual techniques and at changing their negative attitudes toward sex. Similar advances have been made in the study of homosexuality. Old beliefs about homosexuality as illness have been discredited by research emphasizing bisexuality and the human potential for both homosexuality and heterosexuality.

Research findings on the relationship between psychopathology, femininity, and the role of the housewife challenge current theory and practice in psychiatry and psychology. Adaptation to sex roles (being passive, submissive, dependent, or obedient) as the ultimate criterion for female mental health is inconsistent with these research findings. Similarly, therapists who reinforce the female for carrying out domestic chores and homemaking may be intensifying rather than relieving her troubles. Indeed, having less family involvement or having a job outside the home seem to protect the female from psychological disturbance, even in the presence of other risk factors, such as stressful life events.

Overall, research presented in this book reflects a period of social change and turmoil: We are now witnessing a noticeable breakdown of rigid sex roles and sex stereotypes, as well as the emergence of an androgynous person who can combine the best of both worlds of femininity and masculinity and who will be able to adapt to situations calling for desirable feminine-typed behavior (warmth and expressiveness) or desirable masculine-typed behavior (initiative and independence) without being ostracised or labeled "mad." Future development of the research outlined in this volume may reveal more about the negative nature of sex roles, and yet it may also lead to an adaptive lifestyle that transcends both "femininity" and "masculinity."

Finally, professionals who subscribe to a medical view of abnormal behavior may raise two objections to the idea that mental illness is largely a deviation from sex roles. First, they may note that persons who are labeled mentally ill engage in unusual and bizarre behavior that is seemingly unrelated to sex-role norms: for example, hallucinations (hearing voices from outer space) or delusions (believing that one is the Virgin Mary). Second, it may be observed that there are many people who deviate from traditional sex roles but are not labeled mentally ill. These two objections are based on the false psychiatric belief that abnormal symptoms are *sufficient* for referral to a psychiatrist. Community studies, however, reveal that at least 10 percent of the "normal" population report hallucinations (almost 80 percent report at least one psychiatric symptom), and yet they are not labeled "mad." Deviation from social norms, including sex-role norms may not necessarily lead to psychatric diagnosis and treatment. It appears—as I have repeatedly pointed out in this volume—that it is the power inherent in social roles in general and in sex roles in particular that makes a great difference: In a role conflict in which one partner does not fulfill role expectations, it is more likely that the less powerful could be degraded to the status of "madness." That is, perhaps, why housewives and children are more often accused of madness than husbands. That is also why there are more working-class psychiatric patients of both sexes than there are middle- or upper-class, and why there are more blacks under treatment than whites. It is a fact that in our society a woman playing the traditional role of housewife and mother has less legitimate power than her husband; she is, therefore, more vulnerable to the accusation of madness. The weakness of the female in comparison with her husband and the professional is well depicted in a James Thurber story (1945). Once upon a time, there was a man who announced to his wife that there was a unicorn in the garden. She replied, "You are a booby, and I am going to have you put in the booby-hatch." The husband, who had never liked the words "booby" and "booby-hatch" said, "We'll see about that." The wife sent for the police and the psychiatrist. When they arrived, she told them her story. "Did you tell your wife you saw a unicorn?" the police asked the husband. "Of course not. The unicorn is a mythical creature," said the husband. "That's all I wanted to know," said the psychiatrist. So they took her away, cursing and screaming, and shut her up in an institution. The husband lived happily ever after.

References

Abbott, S., & Love, B. Is women's liberation a lesbian plot? In V. Gornick & B.K. Moran (Eds.), *Woman in sexist society.* New York: Basic Books, 1971.

——. *Sappho was a right-on woman: A liberated view of lesbianism.* New York: Stein & Day, 1972.

Abelson, H., Cohen, R., Schrayer, D., & Rapperport, M. Drug experience, attitudes and related behavior among adolescents and adults. In National Commission on Marijuana and Drug Abuse, *Drug use in America: Problems in perspective* (Appendix, Vol. I). Washington, D.C.: U.S. Government Printing Office, 1973.

Aberle, D.F. "Arctic hysteria" and latah in Mongolia. *Transactions of the New York Academy of Sciences,* 1952, *14,* 291-297.

Abramowitz, S.I., Abramowitz, C.V., Jackson, C., & Gomes, B. The politics of clinical judgement: What nonliberal examiners infer about women who do not stifle themselves. *Journal of Consulting and Clinical Psychology,* 1973, *41,* 385-391.

Abse, D.W. Sexual disorder and marriage. In D.W. Abse, E.M. Nash, & L.M.R. Louden (Eds.) *Marital and sexual counseling in medical practice* (2nd ed.). New York: Harper & Row, Pub., 1974.

Adams, M.S., & Neel, J.V. Children of incest. *Paediatrics,* 1967, *40,* 55-62.

Adler, F. *Sisters in crime.* New York: McGraw-Hill, 1975.

Agras, W.S., Barlow, D.H., & Chapin, H.N. Modification of anorexia nervosa. *Archives of General Psychiatry*, 1974, *32*, 279–286.

Alexander, F. The influence of psychologic factors upon gastrointestinal disturbances: A symposium. *Psychoanalytic Quarterly*, 1934, *3*, 501–539.

Alexander, F., French, T.M., & Pollock, G.H. *Psychosomatic specificity*. Chicago: University of Chicago Press, 1968.

Alexander, F.G., & Selesnick, S.T. *The history of psychiatry: An evaluation of psychiatric thought and practice from prehistoric times to the present.* New York: Harper & Row, Pub., 1966.

Al-Issa, I. Social and cultural aspects of hallucinations. *Psychological Bulletin*, 1977, *84*, 570–587.

——. Sociocultural factors in hallucinations. *International Journal of Social Psychiatry*, 1978, *24*, 167–176.

Al-Issa, I., & Al-Issa, B. Psychiatric problems in a developing country: Iraq. *International Journal of Social Psychiatry*, 1970, *16*, 15–22.

American Psychological Association. Report of the task force on sex bias and sex role stereotyping in psychotherapeutic practice. *American Psychologist*, 1975, *30*, 1169–1175.

Amir, M. *Patterns of forcible rape.* Chicago: University of Chicago Press, 1971.

Ananth, J. Psychopathology in Indian females. Paper presented at the Sex, Culture and Illness Symposium, 25–27 March, 1976, Montreal, Canada.

Anastasi, A. Four hypotheses with a dearth of data: Response to Lehrke's "A theory of X-Linkage of major intellectual traits." *American Journal of Mental Deficiency*, 1972, *76*, 620–622.

Andrews, J.D. Psychotherapy of phobias. *Psychological Bulletin*, 1966, *66*, 455–480.

Andrews, R., & Cohn, A. Governability: The unjustifiable jurisdiction. *Yale Law Journal*, 1974, *83*, 1383–1409.

Angelou, Maja. *I know why the caged bird sings.* New York: Bantam, 1971.

Angrist, S., Dinitz, S., Lefton, M., & Pasamanick, B. Rehospitalization of female mental patients. *Archives of General Psychiatry*, 1961, *4*, 363–370.

Angrist, S., Lefton, M., Dinitz, S., & Pasamanick, B. *Women after treatment: A study of former mental patients and their normal neighbors.* Englewood Cliffs, N.J.: Prentice-Hall, 1968.

Anonymous. Psychiatric recommendations. *Bulletin of the British Psychological Society*, 1973, *31*, 20–21.

Antunes, C.M.F., Stolley, P.D., Rosenshein, N.B., Davies, J.L., Tonascia, J.A., Brown, C., Burnett, L., Rutledge, A., Pokempner, M., & Gracia, R. Endometrial cancer and estrogen use. *The New England Journal of Medicine*, 1979, *300*, 9–13.

Argeriou, M., & Paulino, D. Women arrested for drunken driving in Boston. *Journal of Studies on Alcohol,* 1976, *37,* 648–658.

Armstrong, G. Females under the law—"protected" but unequal. *Crime and Delinquency,* 1977, *23,* 109–120.

Asken, M.S. Psychoemotional aspects of mastectomy: A review of recent literature. *American Journal of Psychiatry,* 1975, *132,* 56–59.

Azerrad, J., & Stafford, R.L. Restoration of eating behavior in anorexia nervosa through operant conditioning and environmental manipulation. *Behavior Research and Therapy,* 1969, *7,* 165–171.

Bachrach, A.J., Erwin, W.J., & Mohr, J.P. The control of eating behavior in an anorexic by operant conditioning techniques. In L.P. Ullman & L. Krasner (Eds.), *Case studies in behavior modification.* New York: Holt, Rinehart and Winston, 1965.

Baglivi, G. *The Practice of Physic, reduc'd to the ancient Way of Observations, containing a just Parallel between the Wisdom of the Ancients and the Hypothesis's of Modern Physicians.* 2nd ed. London: Midwinter, Linton, Strahan, etc., 1723.

Bahr, S.J. Effects on power and division of labor in the family. In L.W. Hoffman and F.I. Nye (Eds.), *Working Mothers.* San Francisco: Jossey-Bass, 1974.

Bailey, D.S. *Homosexuality and the Western Christian tradition.* London: Longmans, Green & Co., 1955.

Bailey, M.B., Haberman, P., & Alksne, H. Outcomes of alcoholic marriages: Endurance, termination or recovery. *Quarterly Journal of the Study of Alcohol,* 1962, *23,* 610–623.

Baird, D. Sterilization and therapeutic abortion in Aberdeen. *British Journal of Psychiatry,* 1967, *113,* 701–709.

Bakal, D.A. Headache: A biopsychological perspective. *Psychological Bulletin,* 1975, *82,* 369–382.

——. Headache. In R.H. Woody (Ed.), *Encyclopedia of clinical assessment.* San Francisco: Jossey-Bass, 1979 (in press).

Baker, A.A., Morison, M., Game, J.A., & Thorpe, J.G. Admitting schizophrenic mothers with their babies. *Lancet,* 1961, *2,* 237–239.

Ball, J.C., & Chambers, C.D. *The epidemiology of opiate addiction in the U.S.* Springfield, Ill.: Chas. C Thomas, 1970.

Bardwick, J.M. *The psychology of women.* New York: Harper & Row, Pub., 1971.

Barry, H., III. Cross-cultural evidence that dependency conflict motivates drunkenness. In M.W. Everett, J.O. Waddell, & D.B. Heath (Eds.), *Cross-cultural approaches to the study of alcohol.* The Hague: Mouton Publishers, 1976.

Barry, H., III, Bacon, M.K., & Child, I.L. A cross-cultural survey of some sex differences in socialization. In I. Al-Issa & W. Dennis (Eds.), *Cross-cultural studies of behavior.* New York: Holt, Rinehart and Winston, 1970.

Bart, P.B. Social structure and vocabularies of discomfort: What happened to female hysteria. *Journal of Health and Social Behavior,* 1968, *9,* 188–193.

——. Depression in middle-aged women. In V. Gornick & K. Moran (Eds.), *Woman in sexist society.* New York: Basic Books, 1971.

Barton, R., & Whitehead, J.A. The gas-light phenomenon. *Lancet,* 1969, *1,* 1258–1260.

Bateson, G., Jackson, D.D., Haley, J., & Weakland, J. Toward a theory of schizophrenia. *Behavioral Science,* 1956, *1,* 251–264.

Bazzoui, W., & Al-Issa, I. Psychiatry in Iraq. *British Journal of Psychiatry,* 1966, *112,* 827–832.

Beach, F. Cross-species comparisons and the human heritage. In F. Beach (Ed.), *Human sexuality in four perspectives.* Baltimore: Johns Hopkins University Press, 1977.

Beck, A.T. *Depression: Clinical, experimental and theoretical aspects.* New York: Harper & Row, Pub., 1967.

——. *Cognitive therapy and the emotional disorders.* New York: International Universities Press, Inc., 1976.

Beck, A.T., & Greenberg, R.L. Cognitive therapy with depressed women. In V. Franks & Y. Burtle (Eds.), *Women in Therapy.* New York: Brunner/Mazel, 1974.

Becker, J., & Siefkes, H. Parental dominance, conflict and disciplinary coerciveness in families of female schizophrenics. *Journal of Abnormal Psychology,* 1969, *74,* 193–198.

Beckman, L.J. Women alcoholics. A review of social and psychological studies. *Journal of Studies on Alcohol,* 1975, *36,* 797–825.

——. Alcoholism problems and women: An overview. In M. Greenblatt & M.A. Schuckitt (Eds.), *Alcoholism problems in women and children.* New York: Grune & Stratton, 1976.

——. Sex-role conflict in alcoholic women: Myth or reality. *Journal of Abnormal psychology,* 1978, *87,* 408–417.

Beech, H.R. Approaches to understanding obsessional states. In H.R. Beech (Ed.), *Obsessional states.* London: Methuen & Co., Ltd., 1974.

Belfer, M.L., Shader, R.I., Carroll, M., & Hormatz, J.S. Alcoholism in women. *Archives of General Psychiatry,* 1971, *25,* 540–544.

Bell, A.P. The homosexual as patient. In R. Green (Ed.), *Human sexuality.* Baltimore: Williams & Wilkins, 1975.

Bem, S.L. Sex role adaptability: One consequence of psychological androgyny. *Journal of Personality and Social Psychology.* 1975, *31,* 634–643.

Benedek, T.F., & Rubenstein, B. *The sexual cycle in women: The relation between ovarian function and psychodynamic processes.* Washington, D.C.: National Research Council, 1942. (Cited in Bardwick, 1971.)

Bernard, J. The fourth revolution. *Journal of Social Issues,* 1966, *22,* 76-87.

Berne, E. *Games people play.* New York: Grove Press, 1967.

Berscheid, E., Dion, K., Walster, E., & Walster, G.W. Physical attractiveness and dating choice: A test of the matching hypothesis. *Journal of Experimental Social Psychology,* 1971, *7,* 173-181.

Berscheid, E., & Walster, E.H. *Interpersonal attraction.* Reading, Mass.: Addison-Wesley, 1969.

——. Physical attractiveness. In L. Berkowitz (Ed.), *Advances in experimental social psychology* (Vol. 7). New York: Academic Press, 1974.

Bieber, I., Dain, H.J., Dince, P.R., Drellich, M.G., Grand, H.G., Gundlach, R.G., Kremer, M.W., Rifkin, A.H., Wilbur, C.B., & Bieber, T.B. *Homosexuality: A psychoanalytic study of male homosexuals.* New York: Basic Books, 1962.

Bille, B., Ludvigsson, J., & Sanner, G. Prophylaxis of migraine in children. *Headache,* 1977, *17,* 61-63.

Bittner, E. Police discretion in emergency apprehension of mentally ill persons. *Social Problems,* 1967, *14,* 278-292.

Blane, H.T. *The personality of the alcoholic: Guises of dependency.* New York: Harper & Row, 1968.

Bleuler, M. The offspring of schizophrenics. *Schizophrenia Bulletin,* 1974, *8,* 93-107.

Bliss, E.L., & Branch, C.H.H. *Anorexia nervosa.* New York: Harper & Row, 1960.

Blitch, J.W., & Haynes, S.N. Multiple behavioral techniques in a case of female homosexuality. *Journal of Behavior Therapy and Experimental Psychiatry,* 1972, *3,* 319-322.

Block, J.H. Issues, problems and pitfalls in assessing sex differences: A critical review of the psychology of sex differences. *Merrill-Palmer Quarterly,* 1976, *22,* 283-308.

Blood, R.O., Jr. The husband-wife relationship. In F.I. Nye & L.W. Hoffman (Eds.), *The employed mother in America.* Chicago: Rand McNally, 1963.

Bloom, B.L., Asher, S.J., & White, S.W. Marital disruption as a stressor: A review and analysis. *Psychological Bulletin,* 1978, *85,* 867-894.

Blurton-Jones, N.G., & Leach, G.M. Behavior of children and their mothers at separation and greeting. In N.G. Blurton-Jones (Ed.), *Ethological studies of child behavior.* Cambridge, England: Cambridge University Press, 1972.

Boggs, M.H. The role of social work in the treatment of inebriates. *Quarterly Journal of the Study of Alcohol,* 1944, *4,* 557-567.

Bowker, L.M. College student drug use: An examination and application of the epidemiological literature. *Journal of College and Student Personnel,* 1975, *16,* 137–144.

Brady, J.P., & Lind, D.L. Experimental analysis of hysterical blindness. *Archives of General Psychiatry,* 1961, *4,* 331–339.

Braginsky, B.M., & Braginsky, D.D. *Mainstream psychology: A critique.* New York: Holt, Rinehart & Winston, 1974.

Brandon, S. Physical violence in the family: An overview. In Marie Borland (Ed.), *Violence in the family.* Manchester: Manchester University Press, 1976.

Brecher, R., & Brecher, E. The Work of Masters and Johnson. In R. Brecher & E. Brecher (Eds.), *An analysis of human sexual response.* New York: New American Library, 1966.

Breuer, J., & Freud, S. Studies on hysteria (1893–1895). In *The standard edition of the complete psychological works of Sigmund Freud* (Vol. II). London: Hogarth Press, 1955.

Briscoe, C.W., & Smith, M.D., Depression and marital turmoil. *Archives of General Psychiatry,* 1973, *29,* 812–817.

Brockway, B.S. Assertive training with professional women. Paper presented at the Ninth Annual Convention of the Association for the Advancement of Behavior Therapy, December 11–14, 1975, San Francisco, California.

Brodman, K., Erdman, A., Lorge, I., & Wolff, H. The Cornell medical-index health questionnaire. VI. The relation of patients' complaints to age, sex, race and education. *Journal of Gerontology,* 1953, *8,* 339–342.

Brody, E.B., & Sata, L.S. *Comprehensive textbook of psychiatry.* Baltimore: Williams & Wilkins, 1967.

Brody, H., Meikle, S.T., & Gerritse, R. Therapeutic abortion: A prospective study. *American Journal of Obstetrics and Gynecology,* 1971, *109,* 347–353.

Bromet, E., & Moos, R. Sex and marital status in relation to the characteristics of alcoholics. *Journal of Studies on Alcohol,* 1976, *37,* 1302–1312.

Brooks, J., Ruble, D., & Clark, A. College women's attitudes and expectations concerning menstrual-related changes. *Psychosomatic Medicine,* 1977, *39,* 288–298.

Broverman, I.K., Broverman, D.M., Clarkson, F.E., Rosenkrantz, P., & Vogel, S.R. Sex-role stereotypes and clinical judgments of mental health. *Journal of Consulting and Clinical Psychology,* 1970, *34,* 1–7.

——. Sex-role stereotypes: A current appraisal. *Journal of Social Issues,* No. 2, 1972, *28,* 59–78.

Brown, B.S., Gauvey, S.K., Meyers, M.B., & Stark, S.D. In their own words: Addicts reasons for initiating and withdrawing from heroin. *International Journal of Addiction,* 1971, *6,* 635–645.

Brown, D.G. Female orgasm and sexual inadequacy. In R. Brecher & E. Brecher (Eds.), *An analysis of human sexual response.* New York: New American Library, 1966.

Brown, G.W., Bhrolchain, M.N., & Harris, T. Social class and psychiatric disturbance among women in an urban population. *Sociology,* 1975, *9,* 225–254.

Brown, G.W., & Harris, T. *Social origins of depression. A study of psychiatric disorders in women.* London: Tavistock Publications, 1978.

Brown, G.W., Harris, T., & Copeland, J.R. Depression and loss. *British Journal of Psychiatry,* 1977, *130,* 1–18.

Brownmiller, S. *Against our will: Men, women and rape.* New York: Simon & Schuster, 1975.

Bryan, J. "Apprenticeship in prostitution" and "Occupational ideologies and individual attitudes of call girls." In E. Rubington & M. Weinberg (Eds.), *Deviance: The interactionist perspective* (2nd ed.). London: McMillan, 1973.

Budzynski, T.H., Stoyva, J.M., Adler, C.S., & Mullaney, D.J. EMG biofeedback and tension headache: A controlled outcome study. In L. Birk (Ed.), *Biofeedback: Behavioral medicine.* New York: Grune & Stratton, 1973.

Buell, P., & Breslow, L. Mortality from coronary heart disease in California men who work long hours. *Journal of Chronic Disease,* 1960, *11,* 615–626.

Burgess, A.W., & Holmstrom, L. Rape trauma syndrome. *American Journal of Psychiatry,* 1974, *131,* 981–986.

———. Coping behavior of the rape victim. *American Journal of Psychiatry,* 1976, *133,* 413–418.

Burton, A., & Sjoberg, B., Jr., The diagnostic validity of human figure drawings in schizophrenia. *Journal of Psychology,* 1964, *57,* 3–18.

Buss, A.H. *Psychopathology.* New York: John Wiley, 1966.

Busse, E.W. *Theory and therapeutics of aging.* New York: Modern Press, 1973.

Butensky, A., Farralli, V., Heebner, D., & Waldron, I. Elements of the coronary prone behavior pattern in children and teen-agers. *Journal of Psychosomatic Research,* 1976, *20,* 436–444.

Butler, C., & Wagner, N. Sexuality during pregnancy and post-partum. In R. Green (Ed.), *Human sexuality: A health practitioner's text.* Baltimore: Williams & Wilkins, 1975.

Caffey, J. Multiple fractures in the long bones of infants suffering from chronic subdural hematoma. *American Journal of Roentgenology,* 1946, *56,* 163–173.

Cahalan, D., Cislan, I.H., & Crossley, H.M. *American drinking practices: A national study of drinking behavior and attitudes.* New Haven: College & University Press, 1969.

Calhoun, J.F. *Abnormal psychology: Current perspectives* (2nd ed.). New York: Random House, 1977.

Cameron, D.E. Sexuality and the sexual disorders. In J.R. Rees (Ed.), *Modern practice in psychological medicine.* New York: Harper & Row, Pub., 1949.

Caprio, F.S. *Female homosexuality.* New York: Citadel Press, 1954.

Carstairs, G.M., & Kapur, R.L. *The great universe of Kota stress, change and mental disorder in an Indian village.* London: The Hogarth Press, 1976.

Cash, F. Methodological problems and progress in schizophrenia research: A survey. *Journal of Consulting and Clinical Psychology,* 1973, *40,* 278–286.

Cashdan, S. *Interactional psychotherapy: Stages and strategies in behavioral change.* New York: Gruen & Stratton, 1973.

Cavior, N. *Physical attractiveness, perceived attitude, similarity, and interpersonal attraction among fifth and eleventh grade boys and girls.* Unpublished doctoral dissertation, University of Houston, 1970.

Chafetz, M.E., Blane, H.T., Abram, H.S., Golner, J., Lacy, E., McCourt, W.F., Clark, E., & Meyers, W. Establishing treatment relations with alcoholics. *Journal of Nervous and Mental Disease,* 1962, *134,* 395–409.

Chalfant, H.P. The alcoholic in magazines for women. *Sociological Focus,* 1973, *6,* 14–26.

Chambers, C., Hinesley, R.K., & Moldestad, M. Narcotic addiction in females: A race comparison. *International Journal of the Addictions,* 1970, *5,* 257–278.

Cheek, F.E. A serendipitous finding: Sex roles and schizophrenia. *Journal of Abnormal and Social Psychology,* 1964a, *69,* 392–400.

——. The "schizophrenogenic mother" in word and deed. *Family Forces,* 1964b, *3,* 155–177.

Cherry, S.H. *The Menopause Myth.* New York: Ballantine Books, 1976.

Chesler, P. Patient and patriarch: Women in the therapeutic relationship. In V. Gornick & B. Moran (Eds.), *Woman in sexist society.* New York: Basic Books, 1971.

——. *Women and madness.* Garden City, New York: Doubleday, 1972.

Chesney-Lind, M. Judicial paternalism and the female status offender: Training women to know their place. *Crime and Delinquency,* 1977, *23,* 121–130.

Chesser, E. *Strange loves, the human aspects of sexual deviation.* New York: Random House, 1971.

Child, I.L., Barry, H., III, & Bacon, M.K. Sex differences: A cross-cultural study of drinking. *Quarterly Journal of Studies of Alcohol,* Supplement, 1965, *3,* 49–61.

Chodoff, P., & Lyons, H. Hysteria: The hysterical personality and hysterical conversion. *American Journal of Psychiatry*, 1958, *114*, 734–740.

Chorover, S.L. The pacification of the brain. *Psychology Today*, 1974, *7*, 59–70.

Clark, A.L., & Wallin, P. Women's sexual responsiveness and the duration and quality of their marriages. *American Journal of Sociology*, 1965, *71*, 187–196.

Clausen, J.A. The impact of mental illness: A twenty-year follow-up. In R.D. Wirt, G. Winokur, & M. Roff (Eds.), *Life History Research in Psychopathology* (Vol. 4). Minneapolis: The University of Minnesota Press, 1975.

Clausen, J.A., & Yarrow, M.R. Paths to the mental hospital. *Journal of Social Issues*, 1955, *11*, 25–32.

Clendenin, W.W., & Murphy, G.E. Wristcutting: New epidemiological findings. *Archives of General Psychiatry*, 1971, *25*, 465–469.

Clinical Psychiatry Committee. Clinical trial of treatments of depressive illness. *British Medical Journal*, 1965, *1*, 881–886.

Cohen, M., & Seghorn, T. Sociometric study of the sex offender. *Journal of Abnormal Psychology*, 1969, *74*, 249–255.

Cohen, S.I., Silverman, A.J., & Magnussen, F. New psychophysiologic correlates in women with peptic ulcer. *American Journal of Psychiatry*, 1956, *112*, 1025–1026.

Coleman, J.C. *Abnormal psychology and modern life*. Glenview, Illinois: Scott, Foresman, 1964.

——. *Abnormal psychology and modern life*. (2nd ed.) Glenview, Illinois: Scott, Foresman, 1976.

Comfort, A. *The joy of sex: A gourmet guide to love making*. New York: Crown, 1972.

Comstock, G.W., & Partridge, K.B. Church attendance and health. *Journal of Chronic Disease*, 1972, *25*, 665–672.

Comstock, G.W., & Tonascia, J.A. Education and mortality in Washington County, Maryland. *Journal of Health and Social Behavior*, 1977, *18*, 54–61.

Conger, J.J. *Adolescence and youth: Psychological development in a changing world* (2nd ed.). New York: Harper & Row, Pub., 1977.

Conway, A., & Bogdan, C. Sexual delinquency: The persistence of a double standard. *Crime and Delinquency*, 1977, *23*, 131–135.

Cooper, D. *The death of the family*. New York: Pantheon Books, 1970.

Cooperstock, R. Sex differences in psychotropic drug use. Paper prepared for Symposium on Sex, Culture and Illness. 25–27 March, 1976a, Montreal, Canada.

——. Women and psychotropic drugs. In A. MacLennan (Ed.), *Women: Their use of alcohol and other legal drugs.* Toronto: Addiction Research Foundation of Ontario, 1976b.

Coppen, A., & Kessel, N. Menstruation and personality. *British Journal of Psychiatry,* 1963, *109,* 711–721.

Cosentino, F., & Heilbrun, A.B. Anxiety correlates of sex-role identity in college students. *Psychological Reports,* 1964, *14,* 729–730.

Costello, C.G., Electroconvulsive therapy: Is further investigation necessary? *Canadian Psychiatric Association Journal,* 1976, *21,* 61–67.

Costello, C.G., & Belton, G.P. Depression: Treatment. In C.G. Costello (Ed.), *Symptoms of psychopathology.* New York: John Wiley, 1970.

Costello, C.G., Christensen, S.J., Bobey, M., & Hall, M.K. The relationship of illness and non-illlness variables to the administration of ECT. *Canadian Psychiatric Association Journal,* 1972, *17,* 325–326.

Costrich, N., Feinstein, J., Kidder, L., Marecek, J., & Pascale, L. When stereotypes hurt: Three studies of penalties for sex-role reversals, *Journal of Experimental Social Psychology,* 1975, *11,* 520–530.

Cowie, J., Cowie, V., & Slater, E. *Delinquency in Girls.* London: Heinemann, 1968.

Crisp, A.H., Palmer, R.L., & Kalucy, R.S. How common is anorexia nervosa? A prevalence study. *British Journal of Psychiatry,* 1976, *128,* 549–554.

Curlee, J. A comparison of male and female patients at an alcoholic treatment center. *The Journal of Psychology,* 1970, *74,* 239–247.

Dahlberg, C.C. Sexual contact between patient and therapist. *Contemporary Psychoanalysis,* 1970, *6,* 107–124.

Dalessio, D.J. *Wolff's headache and other head pain.* New York: Oxford University Press, 1972.

Dalton, K. Menstruation and crime. *British Medical Journal,* 1961, *2* (part 2), 1752–1753.

Damon, G. The least of these: The minority whose screams haven't yet been heard. In R. Morgan (Ed.), *Sisterhood is Powerful.* New York: Random House, 1970.

Davenport, W.H. Sex in cross-cultural perspectives. In F. Beach (Ed.), *Human sexuality in four perspectives.* Baltimore: John Hopkins University Press, 1977.

Davis, D., Lambert, J., & Ajans, Z. Crying in depression. *British Journal of Psychiatry,* 1969, *115,* 597–598.

Davis, M. *The sexual responsibility of woman.* New York: Dial Press, 1956.

Davison, G., & Neal, J.M. *Abnormal psychology: An experiental clinical approach.* New York: John Wiley, 1974.

Davison, G.C. Homosexuality: The ethical challenge. Paper presented at the

Annual Convention of the Association for Advancement of Behavior Therapy, November 2, 1974, Chicago, Illinois.

Dawkins, S., & Taylor, R. Non-consummation of marriage. A survey of seventy cases. *Lancet,* 1961, *11,* 1029–1030.

Deubner, D.C. An epidemiologic study of migraine and headache in 10–20 year olds. *Headache,* 1977, *17,* 173–180.

Deutsch, H. *The psychology of women.* New York: Grune & Stratton, 1945.

Deykin, E.Y., Jacobson, S., Klerman, G., & Solomon, M. The empty nest: Psychosocial aspects of conflict between depressed women and their grown children. *American Journal of Psychiatry,* 1966, *122,* 1422–1426.

Diamant, L. An investigation of a relationship between liberalism and lesbianism. Paper presented at the Annual Meeting of the American Psychological Association, August-September, 1977, San Francisco, California.

Diamond, M. Human sexual development: Biological foundations for social development. In F. Beach (Ed.), *Human sexuality in four perspectives.* Baltimore: Johns Hopkins University Press, 1977.

Dickinson, R.L., & Beam, L. *A thousand marriages.* Baltimore: Williams & Wilkins, 1932.

Dietz, H. Commentary on "psychologic adjustment to mastectomy." *Medical Aspects of Human Sexuality,* 1973, *7,* 65.

Dion, K.K., Berscheid, E., & Walster, E. What is beautiful is good. *Journal of Personality and Social Psychology,* 1972, *24,* 285–290.

Distler, L.S., May, P.R., & Tuma, A.H. Anxiety and ego-strength as predictors of response to treatment in schizophrenic patients. *Journal of Consulting Psychology,* 1964, *28,* 170–177.

Dodson, B. *Liberating masturbation: A meditation on self-love.* New York: Body Sex Designs, 1974.

Dohrenwend, B. Social status and stressful life events. *Journal of Personality and Social Psychology,* 1973, *28,* 225–235.

Dohrenwend, B., & Dohrenwend, B. *Social status and psychological disorders.* New York: John Wiley, 1969.

———. Sex differences in psychiatric disorders. *American Journal of Sociology,* 1976, *81,* 1447–1471.

Douglas, M. *Purity and Danger: An analysis of concepts of pollution and taboo.* Baltimore: Penguin, 1970.

Draguns, J.G. Psychological disorders of clinical severity. In H.C. Triandis & J.G. Draguns (Eds.), *Handbook of cross-cultural psychology. Volume five: psychopathology.* Boston: Allyn & Bacon, 1979 (in press).

Drastic cures for obesity. *Lancet,* 1970, *2,* 1094.

Drellich, M.G., & Bieber, I. The psychological importance of the uterus. *Journal of Nervous and Mental Disease,* 1958, *126,* 322–336.

Driscoll, G.Z., & Barr, H.L. *Comparative study of drug dependent and alcoholic women.* Selected papers from the 23rd Annual Meeting of Alcohol and Drug Problems Association of North America, 1972, 9–20 (cited in Beckman, 1975).

Drug use in America: Problems in perspective. Second Report of the National Commission on Marijuana and Drug Abuse. Washington, D.C.: U.S. Government Printing Office, March 1973.

Dudor, H. America discovers child pornography. *Ms.,* August, 1977, *6*, pp. 45–47, 80.

Dunnell, K., & Cartwright, A. *Medicine takers, prescribers and hoarders.* London: Routledge & Kegan Paul, 1972.

Eastwood, M.R., & Stiasny, S. The use of electroconvulsive therapy. *Canadian Psychiatric Association Journal,* 1978, *23,* 29–33.

Edgerton, M.T., Meyer, E., & Jacobson, W.F. Augmentation mannaplasty II. Further surgical and psychiatric evaluation. *Plastic Reconstructive Surgery,* 1961, *27,* 279–301.

Edwards, P., Harvey, C., & Whitehead, P.C. Wives of alcoholics: A critical review and analysis. *Quarterly Journal of Studies on Alcohol,* 1973, *34,* 112–132.

Eisler, R.M., Miller, P.M., & Hersen, M. Components of assertive behavior. *Journal of Clinical Psychology,* 1973, *29,* 295–299.

Ekblad, M. Induced abortion on psychiatric grounds. *Acta Psychiatrica et Neurologica Scandinavica,* 1955, Supplement 99.

Elder, G. Appearance and education in marriage mobility. *American Sociological Review,* 1969, *34,* 519–533.

Elgosin, R.B. Premarital counseling and sexual adjustment in marriage. *Connecticut State Medical Journal,* 1951, *15,* 999–1002.

Ellinwood, E.H., Jr., Smith, W.G., & Vaillant, G.E. Narcotic addiction in males and females: A comparison. *International Journal of the Addictions,* 1966, *1,* 33–45.

Engs, R.C. Drinking related behaviors among college students. *Journal of Studies of Alcohol,* 1978 (in press).

Eysenck, H.J. *Crime and personality.* Boston: Houghton Mifflin, 1964.

Eysenck, S.B.G., & Eysenck, H.J. The personality of female prisoners. *British Journal of Psychiatry,* 1973, *123,* 693–698.

Fabian, A.A., & Donahue, J.F. Maternal depression: A challenging child guidance problem. *American Journal of Orthopsychiatry,* 1956, *26,* 400–405.

Fairnbairn, A.S., & Acheson, E.D. The extent of organ removal in the Oxford area. *Journal of Chronic Diseases,* 1969, *22,* 111–122.

Farina, A., Felner, R., & Boudreau, L. Reactions of workers to male and female patient job applicants. *Journal of Consulting and Clinical Psychology,* 1973, *41,* 363–372.

Farina, A., Fischer, E.H., Sherman, S., Smith, W.T., Groh, T., & Mermin, P. Physical attractiveness and mental illness. *Journal of Abnormal Psychology*, 1977, *8*, 510–517.

Farley, F.H., & Farley, S.V. Stimulus-seeking motivation and delinquent behavior among institutionalized delinquent girls. *Journal of Consulting and Clinical Psychology*, 1972, *39*, 94–97.

Farley, F.H., & Mealiea, W.L. Dissimulation and social desirability in the assessment of fears. *Behavior Therapy*, 1971, *2*, 101–102.

Feinblatt, J.A., & Gold, A.R. Sex roles and the psychiatric referral process. *Sex Roles*, 1976, *2*, 109–122.

Fejer, D., & Smart, R. The use of psychoactive drugs by adults. *Canadian Psychiatric Association Journal*, 1973, *18*, 313–319.

Feld, S. Feelings of adjustment. In F.I. Nye & L.W. Hoffman (Eds.). *The employed mother*. Chicago: Rand McNally, 1963.

Feldman, M.P., & MacCulloch, M.J. The application of anticipatory avoidance learning to the treatment of homosexuality. I. Theory, technique and preliminary results. *Behavior Research and Therapy*, 1965, *2*, 165–183.

——. *Homosexual behavior: Theory and assessment*. Oxford: Pergamon Press, 1971.

Fidell, L.S. Psychotropic drug use by women: Health, attitudinal personality and demographic correlates. Paper presented at the American Psychological Association, August 28, 1977, San Francisco, California.

Field, M.J. *Search for security: An ethnopsychiatric study of rural Ghana*. Evanston, Ill.: Northwestern University Press, 1960.

File, K.N. Sex roles and street roles. *The International Journal of the Addictions*, 1976, *11*, 263–268.

Fine, R. The personality of the asthmatic child. In H.I. Schneer (Ed.), *The asthmatic child*. New York: Harper & Row, Pub., 1963.

Fodor, I.G. The phobic syndrome in women: Implications for treatment. In V. Franks & M. Burtle (Ed.), *Women in Therapy*. New York: Brunner/Mazel, 1974.

Fontana, A.F. Familial etiology of schizophrenia. *Psychological Bulletin*, 1966, *66*, 214–227.

Fontana, V.J. Childhood maltreatment and battered child syndromes. In A.M. Freeman, H.I. Kaplan, & B.J. Sadock (Eds.), *Comprehensive textbook of psychiatry* (Vol. 2). Baltimore: Williams & Wilkins, 1975.

Ford, C.S., & Beach, F.A. *Patterns of sexual behavior*. New York: Ace Books, 1952.

Forslund, M.A., & Gustafson, T.J. Influence of peers and parents and sex differences in drinking by high-school students. *Quarterly Journal of Studies on Alcohol*, 1970, *31*, 868–875.

Frank, R.T. The hormonal cause of premenstrual tension. *Archives of Neurology and Psychiatry,* 1931, *26,* 1053–1057.

Freeland, J.B., & Campbell, R.S. The social context of first marijuana use. *International Journal of Addictions,* 1973, *8,* 317–324.

Freeman, B. Commentary on "psychologic adjustment to mastectomy." *Medical aspects of human sexuality,* 1973, *7,* 65.

French, T.M. & Alexander, F. Psychogenic factors in bronchial asthma. Part I, *Psychosomatic Medicine Monographs,* 1941, *1,* No. 4. Pp. 92.

Freud, S. Further recommendations in the technique of psychoanalysis, observations of transference of love. In E. Jones (Ed.), *Collected papers* (Vol. 2). London: Hogarth Press, 1956. (Originally published, 1915.)

——. The aetiology of hysteria. In J. Strachey (Ed.), *The standard edition of the complete psychological works of Sigmund Freud.* London: Hogarth Press, 1962. (Originally published, 1896.)

Friday, N. *My secret garden: Women's sexual fantasies.* New York: Simon & Schuster, 1973.

——. *Forbidden flowers: More women's sexual fantasies.* New York: Simon & Schuster, 1975.

Friedman, M., & Rosenman, R. *Type A behavior and your heart.* New York: Knopf, 1974.

Fromm-Reichmann, F. Notes on the development of treatment of schizophrenia by psychoanalytic psychotherapy. *Psychiatry,* 1948, *11,* 263–273.

——. *Principles of intensive psychotherapy.* Chicago: University of Chicago Press, 1950.

Gadpaille, W.J. Research into the physiology of maleness and femaleness. *Archives of General Psychiatry,* 1972, *26,* 193–206.

Gagnon, J. Female child victims of sex offenses. *Social Problems,* 1966, *13,* 176–192.

Gall, M.D. The relationship between masculinity–femininity and manifest anxiety. *Journal of Clinical Psychology,* 1969, *25,* 294–295.

Ganer, E., Gallant, D., & Grunebaum, H. Children of psychotic mothers. *Archives of General Psychiatry,* 1976, *33,* 311–317.

Gardner, G.G. The relationship between childhood neurotic symptomatology and later schizophrenia in males and females. *Journal of Nervous and Mental Disease,* 1967, *144,* 97–100.

Garfinkel, P.E., Kline, S.A., & Stancer, H.C. Treatment of anorexia nervosa using operant conditioning techniques. *Journal of Nervous and Mental Disease,* 1973, *157,* 428–433.

Garmezy, N., with the collaboration of S. Streitman. Children at risk: The search for the antecedents of schizophrenia. Part I. Conceptual models and research methods. *Schizophrenia Bulletin,* 1974, *8,* 14–90.

Garrard, A. News about breast cancer—for you and your doctor. *Ms.*, 1975, *3*, 28-29.

Gayford, J.J. Wife battering: A preliminary survey of 100 cases. *British Medical Journal*, 1975, *1*, 194-197.

Gebhard, P.H., Gagnon, J.H., Pomeroy, W.B., & Christenson. C.V. Sex offenders: New York: Harper & Row, Pub., 1965.

Geer, J.H. The development of a scale to measure fear. *Behavior Research and Therapy*, 1965, *3*, 45-53.

Geis, G. Hypes, hippies and hypocrites. *Youth and Society*, 1970, *1*, 368-379.

Gelles, R. *The violent home.* Beverly Hills, Calif.: Sage Publications, Inc., 1972.

Gerty, U.M. The adaptive behavior of adolescent children whose mothers were hospitalized at St. Elizabeth's Hospital with a diagnosis of schizophrenia. *Catholic University of America Studies in Social Work*, 1955, No. 22.

Gibbens, T.C.N. More facts about rape. *New Society*, 1977, *39*, 275-276.

Gibbens, T.C.N., & Ahrenfeldt, R.H. Cultural factors in delinquency. London: Tavistock Publications Limited, 1966.

Gibbens, T.C.N., & Prince, J. *Shoplifting.* London: ISTD Publications, 1962.

Gil, D.G. *Violence against children: Physical child abuse in the United States.* Cambridge, Mass.: Harvard University Press, 1970.

Gillespie, D.L. Who has the power? The marital struggle. In J. Freeman (Ed.), *Women: A feminist perspective*, Palo Alto, Calif.: Mayfield, 1975.

Gillie, O. Is it time to stop taking the tablets? *Sunday Times*, December 7, 1975, p. 42.

Ginsberg, G.L., Frosch, W.A., & Shapiro, T. The new impotence. *Archives of General Psychiatry*, 1972, *26*, 218-220.

Goffman, E. *Asylums.* Garden City, New York: Doubleday (Anchor Books) 1961.

Goldfarb, W. Childhood psychosis. In Paul H. Mussen (Ed.), *Carmichael's manual of child psychology* (3rd ed.). New York: John Wiley, 1970.

Goldstein, A.J. A case conference: Some aspects of agoraphobia. *Journal of Behavior Therapy and Experimental Psychiatry*, 1970, *1*, 305-313.

Goldwyn, R.M. Operating for the aging face. *Psychiatry in Medicine*, 1972, *3*, 187-195.

Gomberg, E.S. Women and alcoholism. In V. Franks & V. Burtle (Eds.), *Women in Therapy.* New York: Brunner/Mazel, 1974.

Goode, E. *The marijuana smokers.* New York: Basic Books, 1970.

Goodell, H., Lewontin, R., & Wolff, H.G. Familial occurrence of migraine headache. *Archives of Neurology and Psychiatry*, 1954, *72*, 325-334.

Goodman, R.M., & Gorlin, R.J. *The face in genetic disorders.* St. Louis: Mosby, 1970.

Gove, W.R. The relationship between sex roles, marital status, and mental illness. *Social Forces,* 1972a, *51,* 34–44.

———. Sex roles, marital status and suicide. *Journal of Health and Social Behavior,* 1972b, *13,* 204–213.

———. Sex, marital status and mortality. *American Journal of Sociology,* 1973, *79,* 45–67.

———. Sex differences in mental illness: Evidence and explanations. Paper prepared for Symposium on Sex, Culture, and Illness, 25–27 March, 1976, Montreal, Canada.

Gove, W.R., & Tudor, J.F. Adult sex roles and mental illness. *American Journal of Sociology,* 1973, *78,* 812–835.

Grafenberg, E. The role of urethra in female orgasm. *International Journal of Sexology,* 1950, *3,* 145–148.

Gray, J. *The psychology of fear and stress.* New York: McGraw-Hill, 1971a.

———. Sex differences in emotional behavior in mammals including man: Endocrine bases. *Acta Psychologica,* 1971b, *35,* 29–46.

Gray, S.W. Masculinity-femininity in relation to anxiety and social acceptance. *Child Development,* 1957, *28,* 203–214.

Greer, G. *The female eunuch.* New York: McGraw-Hill, 1971.

Greer, S., & Morris, T. Psychological attributes of women who develop breast cancer: A controlled study. *Journal of Psychosomatic Research,* 1975, *19,* 147–153.

Gregory, M. Battered wives. In M. Borland (Ed.), *Violence in the family.* Manchester: Manchester University Press, 1976.

Griffin, S. Rape: The all-American crime. *Ramparts,* 1971, *10,* 26–35.

Groen, J.J., & Pelser, H.E. Experiences with and results of group psychotherapy in patients with bronchial asthma. In J.J. Groen (Ed.), *Psychosomatic Research.* New York: Macmillan, 1964.

Gross, H.S., Herbert, M.R., Knatterud, G.L. and Donner, L. The effect of race and sex on the variation of diagnosis and disposition in a psychiatric emergency room. *Journal of Nervous and Mental Disease,* 1969, *148,* 638–642.

Grossberg, J.M., & Wilson, H.K. A correlational comparison of the Wolpe-Lang fear survey schedule and the Taylor Manifest Anxiety Scale. *Behavior Research and Therapy,* 1965, *3,* 125–128.

Group for the Advancement of Psychiatry. *Sex and the college student. Report No. 60.* New York: Mental Health Materials Center, Inc., 1965.

Grunebaum, H.U., & Weiss, J.L. Psychotic mothers and their children: Joint admission to adult psychiatric hospital. *American Journal of Psychiatry,* 1963, *119,* 927–933.

Gundlach, R.H., & Riess, B.F. Self and sexual identity in the female: A study of female homosexuals. In B.F. Riess (Ed.), *New Directions in Mental Health*. New York: Grune & Stratton, 1968.

Guttentag, M., Salasin, S., Legge, W.W., & Bray, H. *Sex differences in the utilization of publicly supported mental health facilities: The puzzle of depression.* Unpublished report for the National Institute of Mental Health – MH 26523–02, 1977.

Haberman, P.W. Some characteristics of alcoholic marriages differentiated by level of deviance. *Journal of Marriage and Family*, 1965, *27*, 34–36.

Hafner, R.J. The husbands of agoraphobic women and their influence on treatment outcome. *British Journal of Psychiatry*, 1977, *131*, 289–294.

Haggard, H.W., & Jellinek, E.M. *Alcohol explored.* New York: Doubleday, 1942.

Hall, S. Vaginismus as cause of dyspareunia. Report of cases and method of treatment. *Western Journal of Surgery, Obstetrics and Gynecology*, 1952, *60*, 117–120.

Hallsten, E.A., Jr. Adolescent anorexia nervosa treated by desensitization. *Behavior Research and Therapy.* 1965, *3*, 87–91.

Hallstrom, T. *Mental disorder and sexuality in the climacteric.* Gateberg, Sweden: Orstadius Biktryckeri AB, 1973.

Hamilton, G.V. *A research in marriage.* New York: Albert & Charles Boni, 1929.

Hamilton, P. *Angel street, a victorian thriller in three acts* (Copyright 1939 under the title "Gas Light"). New York: French, 1942.

Hammen, C.L., & Padesky, C.A. *Sex differences in the expression of depression.* Paper presented at the meetings of the American Psychological Association, August, 1977, San Francisco, California.

Hammen, C.L., & Peters, S.D. Differential responses to male and female depressive reactions. *Journal of Consulting and Clinical Psychology*, 1977a, *45*, 994–1001.

———. Consequences of interactions with depressed men and women, 1977b. Unpublished paper.

Hammer, E.F. Symptoms of sexual deviation: Dynamics and etiology. *Psychoanalytical Review*, 1968, *55*, 5–27.

Harder, T. The psychopathology of infanticide. *Acta Psychiatrica Scandinavica*, 1967, *43*, 196–245.

Harris, R.E., & Singer, M.T. Interaction of personality and stress in the pathogenesis of essential hypertension. In *Hypertension: Neural control of arterial pressure* (Vol. 16). Proceedings of the Council for High Blood Pressure Research. New York: American Health Association, 1968.

Hartwell, W., Jr., Anderson, R., Hall, M.B., & Esselstyne, C., Jr. Reconstruction of the breast after mastectomy for cancer. *Plastic and Reconstructive Surgery,* 1976, *57,* 152–157.

Hashim, S.A., & Van Itallie, T.B. Studies in normal and obese subjects with a monitored food dispensing device. *Annals of the New York Academy of Sciences,* 1965, *131,* 654–661.

Haslam, M.T. The treatment of psychogenic dyspareunia by reciprocal inhibition. *The British Journal of Psychiatry,* 1965, *111,* 280–282.

Hastings, D.W. Can specific training procedures overcome sexual inadequacy? In R. Brecher & E. Brecher (Eds.), *An analysis of human sexual response.* New York: New American Library, 1966.

Heilbrun, A.B., Jr. Sex-role, instrumental-expressive behavior, and psychopathology in females. *Journal of Abnormal Psychology,* 1968, *73,* 131–136.

Heiman, J.R. The physiology of erotica: Women's sexual arousal. *Psychology Today,* 1975, *8,* 90–94.

———. A psychophysiological exploration of sexual arousal patterns in females and males. *Psychophysiology,* 1977, *14,* 266–274.

Hemminki, E. Diseases leading to psychotropic drug therapy. *Scandinavian Journal of Social Medicine,* 1974, *2,* 129–134.

Herjanic, M., Henn, F.A., & Vanderpearl, R.H. Forensic psychiatry: Female offenders. *American Journal of Psychiatry,* 1977, *134,* 556–558.

Hersen, M. Self-assessment of fear. *Behavior Therapy,* 1973, *4,* 241–257.

Hersh, S.M. *My Lai 4: A report of the massacre and its aftermath.* New York: Random House (Vintage Books), 1970.

Higgins, J. Effects of child rearing by schizophrenic mothers. *Journal of Psychiatric Research,* 1966, *4,* 153–167.

Hill, C. Sex of the client and sex and experience level of counselor. *Journal of Counseling Psychology,* 1975, *22,* 6–11.

Hirschfeld, M. *Sexual anomalies and perversions.* London: Francis Adler, 1948.

Hite, S. *The Hite Report: A nationwide study of female sexuality.* New York: Dell, 1976.

Hoffman, M.L. Moral development. In P.H. Mussen (Ed.), *Carmichael's Manual of Child Psychology* (Vol. 2). New York: Wiley, 1970.

———. Sex differences in moral internalization and values. *Journal of Personality and Social Psychology,* 1975, *32,* 720–729.

———. Sex differences in diabetes mellitus. Paper presented at the Symposium on Sex, Culture, and Illness. March 25–27, 1976, Montreal, Canada.

———. Personality and social development. *Annual Review of Psychology,* 1977, *28,* 295–321.

Hoffman, M.L., & Saltzstein, H.D. Parent discipline and the child's moral development. *Journal of Personality and Social Psychology,* 1967, *5,* 45–57.

Hoffman-Bustamante, D. The nature of female criminality. *Issues in Criminology*, 1973, *8*, 117–136.

Hogan, W.M., Huerta, E., & Lucas, A.R. Diagnosing anorexia nervosa in males. *Psychosomatics*, 1974, *15*, 122–126.

Hokanson, J.E., & Burgess, M. The effects of three types of aggression on vascular processes. *Journal of Abnormal and Social Psychology*, 1962, *65*, 446–449.

Hokanson, J.E., DeGood, D.E., Forrest, M.S., & Brittain, T.M. *Availability of* avoidance behaviors for modulating vascular-stress responses. *Journal of Personality and Social Psychology*, 1971, *19*, 60–68.

Hokanson, J.R., Willers, K.R., & Koropsak, E. Modification of autonomic responses during aggressive interchange. *Journal of Personality*, 1968, *36*, 386–404.

Holden, C. Psychosurgery: Legitimate therapy of laundered lobotomy? *Science*, 1973, *179*, 1109–1112.

Holiday, B., with Dufty, W.F. *The lady sings the blues*. New York: Doubleday, 1956.

Holland, J., Masling, J., & Copley, D. Mental illness in lower class normal, obese and hyperobese women. *Psychosomatic Medicine*, 1970, *32*, 351–357.

Hollingshead, A.F., & Redlich, F.C. *Social class and mental illness*. New York: Wiley, 1958.

Holstein, C.M., Goldstein, J.W., & Ben, D.J. The importance of expressive behavior, involvement, sex, and need-approval in inducing liking. *Journal of Experimental Social Psychology*, 1971, 7, 534–544.

Holzberg, J.D. Sex differences in schizophrenia. In H. Beigel (Ed.), *Advances in Sex Research*. New York: Harper & Row, Pub., 1963.

Hooker, E. The adjustment of the male overt homosexual. *Journal of Projective Techniques*, 1957, *21*, 18–31.

Hoover, R., Guay, L.A., Cole, P., & MacMahon, B. Menopausal estrogen and breast cancer. *New England Journal of Medicine*, 1976, *295*, 401–405.

Hopkins, J.H. The lesbian personality. *British Journal of Psychiatry*, 1969, *115*, 1433–1436.

Horner, M.S. Toward an understanding of achievement-related conflicts in women. *Journal of Social Issues*, 1972, *28*, 157–75.

Horton, D. The functions of alcohol in primitive societies: A cross-cultural study. *Quarterly Journal of Studies on Alcohol*, 1943, *4*, 299–320.

Hotchner, A.E. *Papa Hemingway: a personal memoir*. New York: Random House, 1966.

Houck, J.H. The intractable female patient. *American Journal of Psychiatry*, 1972, *129*, 27–31.

Howard, E.M., & Howard, J.L. Women in institutions: Treatment in prisons and mental hospitals. In V. Franks & V. Burtle (Eds.), *Women in therapy.* New York: Brunner/Mazel, 1974.

Howard, J., & Borges, P. Needle sharing in the Haight: Some social and psychological functions. *Journal of Health and Social Behavior,* 1970, *11,* 220–230.

Howell, M.C., Emmons, E.B., & Frank, D.A. Reminiscences of runaway adolescents. *American Journal of Orthopsychiatry,* 1973, *43,* 840–853.

Huffman, J.W. The effect of gynecological surgery on sexual reactions. *American Journal of Obstetrics and Gynecology,* 1950, *59,* 915–917.

Hunt, M. *Sexual Behavior in the 1970's.* Chicago: Playboy Press, 1974.

Jackson, B. Treatment of depression by self-reinforcement. *Behavior Therapy,* 1972, *3,* 298–307.

Jacobsen, E. *Progressive relaxation.* Chicago: University of Chicago Press, 1938.

Jacoby, S. Feminism in the $12,000-a-year family: "What do I do for the next 20 years?" *New York Times Magazine,* June 17, 1973, 10. © 1973 by The New York Times Company. Reprinted by permission.

Jakubowski-Spector, P. Facilitating the growth of women through assertive training. *The Counseling Psychologist,* 1973, *4,* 75–86.

James, J.E., & Goldman, M. Behavior trends of wives of alcoholics. *Quarterly Journal of the Study of Alcohol,* 1971, *32,* 373–381.

Jellinek, E.M. *The disease concept of alcoholism.* New Haven, Connecticut: Hill House Press, 1960.

Jick, H., Watkins, R.N., Hunter, J.R., Dinan, B.J., Madsen, S., Rothman, K.J., & Walker, A.M. Replacement endrogens and endometrial cancer. *The New England Journal of Medicine,* 1979, *300,* 218–222.

Johnson, A. Recent trends in sex mortality differentials in the United States. *Journal of Human Stress,* 1977, *3,* 22–23.

Johnson, J.W. The effect of group assertiveness training on assertiveness, self-concept, and sex-role stereotypy in married women. Paper presented at 9th Annual Conference of the Association for the Advancement of Behavior Therapy, December 11–14, 1975, San Francisco, California.

Johnson, K.G., Donnely, J.H., Scheble, R., Wine, R.L., & Weitman, M. Survey of adolescent drug use: Sex and grade distribution. *American Journal of Public Health,* 1971, *61,* 2418–2431.

Johnson, M.W. Physicians' views on alcoholism: With special reference to alcoholism in women. *Nebraska State Medical Journal,* 1965, *50,* 378–384.

Johnston, R., & Planansky, K. Schizophrenia in men: The impact on their wives. *The Psychiatric Quarterly,* 1968, *42,* 146–155.

Jones, B.M., & Jones, M.K. Women and alcohol: Intoxication, metabolism and the menstrual cycle. In M. Greenblatt & M.A. Schuckit (Eds.), *Alco-*

holism problems in women and children. New York: Grune & Stratton, 1976.

Jones, J. Non-ECT. *World Medicine*, 1974, *9*, 24.

Jones, K.L., Smith, D.W., Ulleland, C.N., & Streissguth, A.P. Patterns of malformation in offspring of chronic alcoholic mothers. *Lancet*, 1973, *1*, 1267–1271.

Jones, W.H., Chernovetz, M.E. O'C., and Hansson, R.O. The enigma of androgyny: Differential implications for males and females? *Journal of Consulting and Clinical Psychology*, 1978, *46*, 298–313.

Justice, B., & Duncan, D. Running away: An epidemic problem of adolescence. *Adolescence*, 1976, *11*, 367–371.

Kaats, G.R., & Davis, K.E. The dynamics of sexual behavior of college students. *Journal of Marriage and the Family*, 1970, *32*, 390–399.

——. The social psychology of sexual behavior. In L.S. Wrightsman (Ed.), *Social psychology in the seventies*. Monterey, California: Brooks/Cole Publishing Co., 1972.

Kagan, J. Acquisition and significance of sex typing and sex role identity. In M. Hoffman & L. Hoffman (Eds.), *Review of child development research* (Vol. 1). New York: Russell Sage, 1964.

——. *Change and continuity in infancy*. New York: John Wiley, 1971.

——. Psychology of sex differences. In F.A. Beach (Ed.), *Human Sexuality in Four Perspectives*. Johns Hopkins University Press, 1977.

Kahne, J. Suicide among patients in mental hospitals. A study of psychiatrists who conducted their therapy. *Psychiatry*, 1968, *31*, 32–43.

Kalashian, M.M. Working with the wives of alcoholics in an outpatient clinic setting. *Marriage and Family*, 1959, *21*, 131–133.

Kalinowsky, L.B. Effects of somatic treatments on the sexual behavior of schizophrenics. In H.C. Beigels (Ed.), *Advances in sex research*. New York: Harper & Row, Pub., 1963.

Kalis, B.L., Harris, R.E., Bennett, L.F., & Sokolow, M. Personality and life history factors in persons who are potentially hypertensive. *Journal of Nervous and Mental Disease*, 1961. *132*, 457–468.

Kalis, B.L., Harris, R.E., Sokolow, M., & Carpenter, L.G. Response to psychological stress in patients with essential hypertension. *American Heart Journal*, 1957, *53*, 572–578.

Kamin, E.J. Sex aggression by college men. *Medical Aspects of Human Sexuality*, 1970, *4*, 25–40.

Kamin, E.J., & Kirkpatrick, C. Male sex aggression on university campuses. *American Sociological Review*, 1953, *22*, 52–58.

Kandel, D. Inter- and intragenerational influences on adolescent marijuana use. *Journal of Social Issues*, 1974, *30*, 107–135.

Kane, F.J. Postpartum disorders. In A.M. Freedman, H.I. Kaplan, & B.J. Sadock (Eds.), *Comprehensive textbook of psychiatry* (Vol. 1). Baltimore: Williams & Wilkins, 1975.

Kaplan, B. A note on religious beliefs and coronary heart disease. *Journal of South Carolina Medical Association*, 1976, 72, Suppl., 60–64.

Kaplan, H. *The new sex therapy: Active treatment of sexual dysfunctions.* New York: Brunner/Mazel, 1974.

Kardener, S.M., Fuller, M., & Mensh, I.N. A survey of physicians' attitudes and practices regarding erotic and nonerotic contact with patients. *American Journal of Psychiatry*, 1973, *130*, 1077–1081.

Kasl, S.V., & Cobb, S. Blood pressure changes in men undergoing job loss: A preliminary report. *Psychosomatic Medicine*, 1970, *6*, 95–106.

Kaya, H.E., Berl, S., Clare, J., Eleston, M.R., Gershwin, B.S., Gershwin, P., Kogan, L.S., Torda, C., & Wilbin, C.B. Homosexuality in women. *Archives of General Psychiatry*, 1967, *17*, 626–634.

Kayton, R., & Biller, H.B. Sex-role development and psychopathology in adult males. *Journal of Consulting and Clinical Psychology*, 1972, *38*, 208–210.

Kegel, A. Sexual functions of the pubococcygeus muscle. *Journal of Obstetrics and Gynecology*, 1952, *60*, 521–524.

Keil, T.J. Sex role variations and women's drinking. Results from a household survey in Pennsylvania. *Journal of Studies on Alcohol*, 1978, *39*, 859–868.

Kellett, J., Tremble, M., & Thorley, A. Anorexia nervosa after the menopause. *British Journal of Psychiatry*, 1976, *128*, 555–558.

Kempe, C.H., Silverman, F.N., Steele, B.V., Droegemueller, W., & Silver, H.K. The battered child syndrome. *Journal of the American Medical Association*, 1962, *181*, 17.

Kendell, R.E., Hall, D.J., Hailey, A., & Babigian, H.M. The epidemiology of anorexia nervosa. *Psychological Medicine*, 1973, *3*, 200–203.

Kesey, K. *One Flew Over the Cuckoo's Nest.* New York: Viking Press, 1964. Copyright © 1962, by Ken Kesey.

Kessel, N., & Shepherd, M. Neurosis in hospital and general practice. *Journal of Mental Science*, 1962, *108*, 159–166.

Kessler, J.W. *Psychopathology of childhood.* Englewood Cliffs, N.J.: Prentice-Hall, 1966.

Kinsey, A.C., Pomeroy, W.B., & Martin, C.E. *Sexual behavior in the human male.* Philadelphia: Saunders, 1948.

Kinsey, A.C., Pomeroy, W.B., Martin, C.E., & Gebhard, P. H. *Sexual behavior in the human female.* Philadelphia: Saunders, 1953.

Kinsey, B.A. *The female alcoholic.* Springfield, Ill.: Chas. C Thomas, 1966.

——. Psychological factors in alcoholic women from a state hospital sample. *American Journal of Psychiatry*, 1968, *124*, 1463–1466.

Kirkegaard-Sorensen, L., & Mednick, S.A. Registered criminality in families with children at high risk for schizophrenia. *Journal of Abnormal Psychology*, 1975, *84*, 197–204.

Kirkpatrick, C., and Cotton, J. Physical attractiveness, age, and marital adjustment. *American Sociological Review*, 1951, *16*, 81–86.

Kirsh, B. Consciousness-raising groups as therapy for women. In V. Franks & V. Burtle (Eds.), *Women in therapy*. New York: Brunner/Mazel, 1974.

Klein, R. A crisis to grow on. *Cancer*, 1971, *28*, 1660–1665.

Kleiner, R.J., & Parker, S. Goal striving, social status and mental disorder: A research review. *American Sociological Review*, 1963, *28*, 189–203.

Knorr, N.J., Hoopes, J.E., & Edgerton, M.R. Psychiatric-surgical approach to adolescent disturbance in self-image. *Plastic and Reconstructive Surgery*, 1968, *41*, 248–253.

Koedt, A. The myth of the vaginal orgasm. In *Notes from the second year*. Boston: New England Free Press, 1970.

Kohlberg, L. The cognitive developmental approach to moral education. *Phi Delta Kappan*, 1975, *56*, 670–677.

Kokonis, N.D. Choice of gender on the DAP and measures of sex-role identification. *Perceptual and Motor Skills*, 1972, *35*, 727–730.

Kolstad, P. Therapeutic abortion. *Acta Obstetrica et Gynecologica Scandinavica*, 1957, *36*: Suppl., 6.

Komarovsky, M. *Dilemmas of masculinity: A study of college youth*. New York: W.W. Norton & Co., Inc., 1976.

Kraepelin, E. *Lectures on Clinical Psychiatry* (Authorized trans. from German, rev. and ed. by Thomas Johnstone). New York: Macmillan (Hafner Press), 1968. (Originally published, 1904.) Courtesy of the Library of the New York Academy of Medicine.

Kraft, T., and Al-Issa, I. Behavior therapy and the recall of traumatic experience. *Behavior Research and Therapy*, 1965a, *3*, 55–58.

——. Treatment of traffic phobia. *British Journal of Psychiatry*, 1965b, *111*, 1013.

——. Brief behavior therapy for the general practitioner. *Journal of the College of General Practitioners*, 1966, *12*, 270–276.

——. Behavior therapy and the treatment of frigidity. *American Journal of Psychotherapy*, 1967, *21*, 116–120.

Kreitman, N., Sainsbury, P., Pearce, K., & Costain, W.R. Hypochondriasis and depression in outpatients at general hospital. *British Journal of Psychiatry*, 1965, *3*, 607–615.

Kristt, D.A., & Engel, B.T. Learned control of blood pressure in patients with high blood pressure. *Circulation*, 1975, *51*, 370–378.

Kuriansky, J.B., Deming, W.E., & Gurland, B.J. On trends in the diagnosis of schizophrenia. *American Journal of Psychiatry*, 1974, *131*, 402–408.

Lachman, S.J. *Psychosomatic disorders: A behavioristic interpretation.* New York: John Wiley, 1972.

Laing, R.D. *The divided self: An existential study of sanity and madness.* New York: Pantheon Books, a Division of Random House, Inc., 1965.

Laing, R.D., & Esterson, A. *Sanity, madness and the family. Families of schizophrenics* (2nd Ed.). London: Tavistock Publications, 1970.

Lance, J.W. *The mechanism and management of headache.* London: Butterworths, 1973.

Landy, D., & Sigall, H. Beauty is talent: Task evaluation as a function of the performer's physical attractiveness. *Journal of Personality and Social Psychology*, 1974, *29*, 299–304.

Lang, P.J. Behavior therapy with a case of nervous anorexia. In L.P. Ullman & L. Krasner (Eds.), *Case studies in behavior modification.* New York: Holt, Rinehart and Winston, 1965.

LaTorre, R.A. The psychological assessment of gender identity and gender role in schizophrenia. *Schizophrenia Bulletin*, 1976, *2*, 266–285.

Lavrakas, P.T. Female preferences for male physiques. *Journal of Research in Personality*, 1975, *9*, 324–334.

Lazarus, A.A. The treatment of chronic frigidity by systematic desensitization. *Journal of Nervous and Mental Disease*, 1963, *136*, 272–278.

——. Behavior therapy with identical twins. *Behaviour Research and Therapy*, 1964, *1*, 313–320.

——. On assertive behavior: A brief note. *Behavior Therapy*, 1973, *4*, 697–699.

——. Women in behavior therapy. In V. Franks & V. Burtle (Eds.), *Women in Therapy.* New York: Brunner/Mazel, 1974.

Lazarus, R.S. *Psychological stress and the coping process.* New York: McGraw-Hill, 1966.

Lehrke, R. A theory of X-linkage of major intellectual traits. *American Journal of Mental Deficiency*, 1972, *76*, 611–619.

Lennane, K.J., & Lennane, R.J. Alleged psychogenic disorders in women—a possible manifestation of sexual prejudice. *New England Journal of Medicine*, 1973, *288*, 288–292.

Leon, G.R. Current directions in the treatment of obesity. *Psychological Bulletin*, 1976, *83*, 557–578.

Lerner, R.M., & Karabeneck, S.A. Physical attractiveness, body attitudes, and self-concept in late adolescents. *Journal of Youth and Adolescence*, 1974, *3*, 307–316.

Lerner, R.M., Orlos, J.B., & Knapp, J.R. Physical attractiveness, physical effectiveness and self-concept in late adolescence. *Adolescence*, 1976, *11*, 313–326.

Lester, D., & Lester, G. *Suicide: The gamble with death.* Englewood Cliffs, N.J.: Prentice-Hall, 1971.

Levine, J. The sexual adjustment of alcoholics: A clinical study of a selected sample. *Quarterly Journal of Studies on Alcohol*, 1955, *16*, 675–680.

Levinson, L.J. Hysterectomy complications. *Clinical and Obstetrical Gynecology*, 1972, *15*, 802–826.

Levy, S.J., & Doyle, K. Attitudes towards women in a drug abuse treatment program. *Journal of Drug Issues*, 1974, *4*, 428–435.

Lewinson, P.M. A behavioral approach to depression. In R.J. Friedman & M.M. Katz (Eds.), *The psychology of depression: Contemporary theory and research.* New York: John Wiley, 1974.

Lewis, C., & Berman, M. Studies of conversion hysteria. *Archives of General Psychiatry*, 1965, *13*, 275–282.

Lewis, H.B. *Psychic war in men and women.* New York: New York University Press, 1976.

Lewis, M., and Brooks, J. Self, other, and fear: Infants' reactions to people. In M. Lewis and L.A. Rosenblum (Eds.) The origins of fear. New York: John Wiley, 1974.

Lewis, M.F. Alcoholism and family casework. *Family*, 1937, *18*, 39–44.

Lidz, T., Cornelison, A.R., Fleck, S., & Terry, D. The intrafamilial environment of schizophrenic patients II. Marital schism and marital skew. *American Journal of Psychiatry*, 1957, *114*, 241–248.

Lindbeck, V.L. The woman alcoholic. A review of the literature. *International Journal of the Addictions*, 1972, *3*, 567–580.

Lindemann, E. Observations on psychiatric sequelae to surgical operations in women. *American Journal of Psychiatry*, 1941, *98*, 132–137.

Lindzey, G. Some remarks concerning incest, incest taboo and psychoanalytic theory. *American Psychologist*, 1967, *22*, 1057–1059.

Linn, E.L. Agents, timing and events leading to mental hospitalization. *Human Organization*, 1961, *20*, 90–98.

Linsky, A.S. Community structure and depressive disorders. *Social Problems*, 1969, *17*, 120–131.

Lisansky, E.S. Alcoholism in women: Social and psychological concomitants. I. Social history data. *Quarterly Journal of Studies on Alcohol*, 1957, *18*, 588–623.

Lobitz, W.C., & Lo Piccolo, J. New methods in the behavioral treatment of sexual dysfunction. *Journal of Behavior Therapy and Experimental Psychiatry*, 1972, *3*, 265–271.

Logan, W.P.D., & Cushion, A.A. *Morbidity statistics from general practice.* London: H.M. Stationery Office, 1958.

Lombroso C., and Ferrero, W. *The female offender.* London: Fisher Unwin, 1895.

London, P. *The modes and morals of psychotherapy.* New York: Holt, Rinehart and Winston, 1964.

Lo Piccolo, J., & Lobitz, W. The role of masturbation in the treatment of orgasmic dysfunction. *Archives of Sexual Behavior,* 1972, *2,* 163-171.

Lowenthal, M.F., Thurnher, M., Chiriboga, D., and associates. *Four stages of Life: A comparative study of women and men facing transitions.* San Francisco: Jossey-Bass, 1975.

Lucas, C.J., Sainsbury, P., & Collins, J.C. A social and clinical study of delusions in schizophrenia. *Journal of Mental Science,* 1962, *108,* 747-758.

Ludwig, M.L., Marx, A.J., Hill, P.A., & Browning, R.M. The control of violent behavior through faradic shock: A case study. *Journal of Nervous and Mental Disease,* 1969, *148,* 624-637.

Lukianowicz, N.Z. Incest I: Paternal incest. *British Journal of Psychiatry,* 1972, *120,* 301-313.

Luria, A.R. *The mind of a mnemonist* (trans., L. Solotaroff). New York: Basic Books, 1968.

Maccoby, E.E., & Jacklin, C.N. *Psychology of sex differences.* Stanford, California: Stanford University Press, 1974.

MacDonald, D.E. Mental disorders in wives of alcoholics. *Quarterly Journal of the Study of Alcohol,* 1956, *17,* 282-287.

MacDonald, J.M. *Armed robbery: Offenders and their victims.* Springfield, Ill.: Chas. C Thomas, 1975.

Mace, D. *Success in marriage.* New York: Abingdon Press, 1958.

MacFarlane, J., Allen, L., & Honzik, M. *A developmental study of the behavior problems of normal children.* Berkeley: University of California Press, 1954.

Madden, J.S., & Jones, D. Bout and continuous drinking in alcoholism. *British Journal of Addiction,* 1972, *67,* 245-250.

Maher, B.A. *Principles of psychopathology.* New York: McGraw-Hill, 1966.

Maisch, H. *Incest* (trans., Colin Bearne). New York: Stein & Day, 1972.

Malmfors, K. The problem of women seeking abortions. In M. Calderone (Ed.), *Abortion in the United States.* New York: Harper & Row, Pub., 1958.

Manheimer, D.I., & Mellinger, G.D. Personality characteristics of the child accident repeater. *Child Development,* 1967, *38,* 491-513.

Manheimer, D.I., Mellinger, G.D., & Balter, M.B. Psychotherapeutic drugs. *California Medicine,* 1968, *109,* 445-451.

Mann, J. Experimental induction of human sexual arousal. In W.C. Wilson

(Executive Director), *Technical report of the commission on obscenity and pornography, Vol. I. Preliminary studies.* Washington, D.C.: U.S. Government Printing Office, 1971.

Mannes, M. The roots of anxiety in modern woman. *Journal of Neuropsychiatry,* 1964, *5,* 412.

Marecek, J. Psychological disorders in women: Indices of role strain. In I.H. Frieze, J.E. Parsons, P.B. Johnson, D.N. Ruble, & G.L. Zellman, *Women and Sex Roles. A social psycholgical perspective.* New York: W.W. Norton & Co., Inc., 1978.

Marecek, J., & Kravetz, D. Women and mental health: A review of feminist change efforts. *Psychiatry,* 1977, *40,* 323–329.

Marks, I. *Fears and phobias.* New York: Academic Press, 1969.

———. Phobias and obsessions: Clinical phenomena in search of laboratory models. In J.D. Maser & M.E.P. Seligman (Eds.). *Psychopathology: Experimental models.* San Francisco: W.H. Freeman & Company, Publishers, 1977.

Mark, V.H. A psychosurgeon's case *for* psychosurgery. *Psychology Today,* 1974, *8,* pp. 28, 30, 33, 84–86.

Mark, V.H., & Ervin, F.R. *Violence and the brain.* New York: Harper & Row, Publishers, 1970.

Martin, D., & Lyon, P. *Lesbian/Woman.* San Francisco: Glide Publications, 1972.

Masserman, J.H. *Principles of dynamic psychiatry.* Philadelphia: Saunders, 1961.

Masters, W., & Johnson, V. *Human sexual response.* Boston: Little, Brown, 1966.

———. *Human sexual inadequacy.* Boston: Little, Brown, 1970.

Mathes, E.W., & Kahn, A. Physical attractiveness, happiness, neuroticism and self-esteem. *Journal of Psychology,* 1975, *90,* 27–30.

Mayer, J., Myerson, D.J., Needham, M.A., & Fox, M. The treatment of the female alcoholic: The former prisoner. *American Journal of Orthopsychiatry,* 1966, *36,* 248–249.

Mayer-Gross, W., Slater, E., & Roth, M. *Clinical psychiatry.* London: Cassell, 1960.

Mayhew, P. Crime in a man's world. *New Society,* 1977, *40,* 560.

Mayou, R. The social setting of hysteria. *British Journal of Psychiatry,* 1975, *127,* 466–469.

McCartney, J.L. Overt transference. *Journal of Sex Research,* 1966, *2,* 227–237.

McCary, J.L. *Human sexuality.* New York: Van Nostrand, 1967.

McClelland, D.C., Davis, W.N., Kalin, R., & Wanner, E. *The drinking man.* New York: Free Press, 1972.

McClelland, D.C., & Watt, N.F. Sex role alienation in schizophrenia. *Journal of Abnormal Psychology*, 1968, *74*, 226–238.

McGregor, F.M.C. *Transformation and identity; the face and plastic surgery.* New York: Quadrangle/The New York Times, 1974.

McGrew, W.C. *An ethological study of children's behavior.* New York: Academic Press, 1972.

McKeever, W.F., May, P.R.A., & Tuma, A.H. Prognosis in schizophrenia: Prediction of length of hospitalization for psychological test variables. *Journal of Clinical Psychology*, 1965, *21*, 214–221.

McKinley, S.M., & Jeffreys, M. The menopausal syndrome. *British Journal of Preventive Social Medicine*, 1974, *28*, 108–115.

McLean, P. Therapeutic decision-making in the behavioral treatment of depression. In P.O. Davidson (Ed.), *The behavioral management of anxiety, depression and pain.* New York: Brunner/Mazel, 1976.

Mead, M. *Sex and temperament in three primitive societies.* New York: Morrow, 1935.

———. *Male and female.* New York: Morrow, 1949.

Mechanic, D. The influence of mothers on their children's health attitudes and behavior. *Pediatrics*, 1964, *33*, 444–453.

———. "Sex, illness behavior and the use of health service." Paper prepared for Symposium on Sex, Culture and Illness, March 25–27, 1976, Montreal, Canada.

Mednick, M.T.S., & Weissman, H.J. The psychology of women—selected topics. *Annual Review of Psychology*, 1975, *26*, 1–18.

Mednick, S.A. Breakdown in individuals at high risk for schizophrenia: Possible predispositional perinatal factors. *Mental Hygiene*, 1970, *54*, 50–63.

Mednick, S.A., & Schulsinger, F. Some premorbid characteristics related to breakdown in children with schizophrenic mothers. In D. Rosenthal & S.S. Kety (Eds.), *The transmission of schizophrenia.* Oxford: Pergamon Press, 1968.

Mees, H.L., & Keutzer, C.S. Short-term group psychotherapy with obese women. *Northwest Medicine*, 1967, *66*, 548–550.

Meikle, S. The psychological effects of hysterectomy. *Canadian Psychological Review*, 1977, *18*, 128–141.

Meikle, S., Brody, H., & Pysh, F. An investigation into the psychological effects of hysterectomy. *The Journal of Nervous and Mental Disease*, 1977, *164*, 36–41.

Melges, F.T., & Hamburg, D.A. Psychological effects of hormonal changes in women. In F.A. Beach (Ed.), *Human sexuality in four perspectives.* Baltimore, Maryland: Johns Hopkins University Press, 1977.

Mellet, P.G. The clinical problem. In H.R. Beech (Ed.), *Obsessional States*. London: Methuen and Co. Ltd., 1974.

Mensh, I.N. The aging population and mental health. In S.C. Plog & R.B. Edgerton (Eds.), *Changing perspectives in mental illness*. New York: Holt, Rinehart & Winston, 1969.

Metzger, D. It is always the woman who is raped. *American Journal of Psychiatry*, 1976, *133*, 405–408.

Meyer, V. Modification of expectancies in cases with obsessional rituals. *Behavior, Research and Therapy*, 1966, *4*, 273–280.

Millard, D.R., Devine, J. Jr., & Warren, W.D. Breast reconstruction: A plea for saving the uninvolved nipple. *American Journal of Surgery*, 1971, *122*, 763–764.

Miller, J.S., Sensenig, J., Stocker, R.B., & Campbell, R. Value patterns of drug addicts as a function of race and sex. *International Journal of the Addictions*, 1973, *8*, 589–598.

Miller, L.C., Hampe, R., Barrett, C.L., & Noble, H. Children's deviant behavior within the general population. *Journal of Consulting and Clinical Psychology*, 1971, *37*, 16–22.

Miller, N.E. Biofeedback and visceral learning. *Annual Review of Psychology*, 1978, *29*, 373–404.

Mirsky, A.F., & Orzack, M.H. *Final report on psychosurgery pilot study. Appendix: Psychosurgery*. National Commission for the Protection of Human Subjects, U.S. Department of Health, Education and Welfare. Washington, D.C.: U.S. Government Printing Office, 1977.

Mischel, W. Sex-typing and socialization. In P.H. Mussen (Ed.), *Carmichael's Manual of Child Psychology*. New York: John Wiley, 1970.

Mittelmann, B., & Wolff, H.G. Emotions and gastroduodenal function. *Psychosomatic Medicine*, 1942, *4*, 5–61.

Modlin, H.C. Psychodynamics in the management of paranoid states of women. *Archives of General Psychiatry*, 1963, *8*, 263–268.

Moffett, A.W., Swash, M., & Scott, D.F. Effect of chocolate on migraine: A double-blind study. *Journal of Neurology, Neurosurgery and Psychiatry*, 1974, *37*, 445–448.

Moldofsky, H., & Garfinkel, P.E. Problems of treatment of anorexia nervosa. *Canadian Psychiatric Association Journal*, 1974, *19*, 169–175.

Mondanaro, J. Pregnancy, children and addiction. *Journal of Psychedelic Drugs*, 1977, *9*, 59–68.

Moore, M.E., Stunkard, A.J., & Srole, L. Obesity, social class and mental illness. *Journal of the American Medical Association*, 1962, *181*, 962–966.

Moos, R.H. Psychological aspects of oral contraceptives. *Archives of General Psychiatry*, 1968, *19*, 87–94.

———. A typology of menstrual cycle symptoms. *American Obstetrics and Gynecology*, 1969, *103*, 390–402.

Mostow, E., & Newberry, P. Work role and depression in women: A comparison of workers and housewives in treatment. *American Journal of Orthopsychiatry*, 1975, *45*, 538–548.

Moulton, R. Some effects of the new feminism. *The American Journal of Psychiatry*, 1977, *134*, 1–6.

Mulford, H.A. Women and men problem drinkers sex differences in patients served by Iowa's communities alcoholism centers. *Journal of Studies of Alcohol*, 1977, *38*, 1624–1639.

Murdock, G.P. *Social structure*. New York: Macmillan, 1949.

Murphy, H.B.M. Cultural aspects of the delusion. *Studium Generale*, 1967, *20*, 684–692.

———. The schizophrenia evoking role of complex social demands. In A.R. Kaplan (Ed.), *Genetic factors in schizophrenia*. Springfield, Ill.: Chas. C Thomas, 1972.

———. Changing sex ratios. Paper prepared for the Symposium on Sex, Culture and Illness. March 25–27, 1976a, Montreal, Canada.

———. Notes for a theory of latah. In W. Lebra (Ed.), *Culture-Bound syndromes, ethnopsychiatry and alternate therapies*. Honolulu: An East-West Center book, The University Press of Hawaii, 1976b.

———. Male/female differences in psychiatric morbidity; their use in transcultural studies. Paper read at IX congreso Latinamericano di psiquiatria (APAL). February, 1977, La Habana, Cuba.

Murstein, B.I. Physical attractiveness and marital choice. *Journal of Personality and Social Psychology*, 1967, *22*, 8–12.

Myerson, D.J. Clinical observations on a group of alcoholic prisoners with special reference to women. *Quarterly Journal of Studies on Alcohol*, 1959, *20*, 555–572.

Nadelson, C.C., Notman, M.T., & Bennett, M.B. Success or failure: Psychotherapeutic considerations for women in conflict. *American Journal of Psychiatry*, 1978, *135*, 1092–1096.

Nance, W.E., & Engel, E. One X and four hypotheses: Response to Lehrke's "A theory of X-linkage of major intellectual traits." *American Journal of Mental Deficiency*, 1972, *76*, 623–625.

Nathanson, C.A. Illness and the feminine role: A theoretical review. *Social Science and Medicine*, 1975, *9*, 57–62.

———. Sex, illness and medical care: A review of data, theory, and method. Paper prepared for the Symposium on Sex, Culture and Illness, March 25–27, 1976, Montreal, Canada.

Nell, R. Sex in a mental institution. *Journal of Sex Research*, 1968, *4*, 303–312.

Nisbett, R.E. Determinants of food intake in obesity. *Science*, 1968, *159*, 1254–1255.

Norland, S., & Shover, N. Gender roles and female criminality: Some critical comments. *Criminology*, 1977, *15*, 87–104.

Notman, M., & Nadelson, C.C. The rape victim: Psychodynamic considerations. *American Journal of Psychiatry*, 1976, *133*, 408–412.

Noyes, A.P., & Kolb, L.C. *Modern clinical psychiatry* (6th ed.). Philadelphia: Saunders, 1963.

Nylander, I. The feeling of being fat and dieting in a school population. *Acta Sociomedica Scandinavica*, 1971, *3*, 17–26.

O'Donnell, J.A. *Narcotic addicts in Kentucky*. Washington, D.C.: U.S. Government Printing Office, 1969.

Offir, C.W. Rape: Don't take it lying down. *Psychology Today*, 1975, *8*, 73.

Ohlson, E.L., & Wilson, M. Differentiating female homosexuals from female heterosexuals by use of the MMPI. *The Journal of Sex Research*, 1974, *10*, 308–315.

Olley, P.C. Aspects of plastic surgery: Social and psychological sequelae. *British Medical Journal*, 1974, *3*, 322–324.

Orford, J. Alcohol and marriage. The argument against specialism. *Journal of Studies on Alcohol*, 1975, *36*, 1537–1561.

Oster, J. Recurrent abdominal pain, headache and limb pains in children and adolescents. *Pediatrics*, 1972, *50*, 429–436.

Padfield, M. The comparative effects of two counseling approaches on the intensity of depression among rural women of low socioeconomic status. *Jouranl of Counseling Psychology*, 1976, *23*, 209–214.

Paffenberger, R.S., & McCabe, L.J. The effect of obstetric and perinatal events on risk of mental illness of women of childbearing age. *American Journal of Public Health*, 1966, *56*, 400–407.

Paige, K. *The effects of oral contraception of affective fluctuations associated with the menstrual cycle*. Unpublished doctoral dissertation, University of Michigan, 1969. (Cited in Bardwick, 1971.)

Palmer, R.J. The effects of food cue prominence and concern about weight on the eating behavior of obese and normally weighted humans. Doctoral Dissertation, Indiana University, 1972. *Dissertation Abstracts International*, 1973, *33*, 3921B. (University Microfilms No. 73-2743, 67.)

Parker, S. Eskimo psychopathology in the context of Eskimo personality and culture. *American Anthropologist*, 1962, *64*, 76–96.

Parlee, M.B. The premenstrual syndrome. *Psychological Bulletin*, 1973, *80*, 454–465.

Parrinder, G. *Witchcraft*. Harmondsworth, Middlesex, England: Penguin, 1958.

Patel, C., & North, W.R.S. Randomized controlled trial of yoga and biofeedback in the management of hypertension. *Lancet*, 1975, *2*, 93.

Patterson, R.M., & Craig, J.B. Misconceptions concerning the psychological effects of hysterectomy. *American Journal of Obstetrics and Gynecology*, 1963, *85*, 104–111.

Pattison, E.M. *Personality profiles of 50 alcoholic women*. Abstract of paper in preparation. University of California, Irvine, 1975. (Cited in Wilsnack, 1976.)

Paykel, E.S. Life stress, depression and attempted suicide. *Journal of Human Stress*, 1976, *1*, 3–12.

Paykel, E.S., & Dienelt, M.N. Suicide attempts following acute depression. *Journal of Nervous and Mental Disease*, 1971, *153*, 234–243.

Paykel, E.S., Prusoff, B., & Uhlenhuth, E. Scaling of life events. *Archives of General Psychiatry*, 1971, *25*, 340–347.

Paykel, E.S., & Weissman, M.M. Social adjustment and depression: A longitudinal study. *Archives of General Psychiatry*, 1973, *28*, 659–663.

Pearce, J. Migraine: A psychosomatic disorder. *Headache*, 1977, *17*, 125–128.

Peck, A., & Marcus, H. Psychiatric sequelae of therapeutic interruption of pregnancy. *The Journal of Nervous and Mental Disease*, 1966, *143*, 417–425.

Perrot, R. The man who says we're all mad. *The Observer*, 20 September 1970, p. 17.

Persons, R., Persons, M., & Newmark, I. Perceived helpful therapists' characteristics, client improvement and sex of therapist and client. *Psychotherapy: Theory Research and Practice*, 1974, *11*, 63–65.

Pflanz, M. Sex differences in abdominal illness. *Social Science and Medicine*, 1978, *12B*: 171–176.

Phillips, D.L. Rejection of the mentally ill: The influence of behavior and sex. *American Sociological Review*, 1964, *29*, 679–687.

Phillips, D.L., & Segal, B.E. Sexual status and psychiatric symptoms. *American Sociological Review*, 1969, *34*, 58–72.

Pitt, B. Atypical depression following childbirth. *British Journal of Psychiatry*, 1968, *114*, 1325–1335.

Pizzey, E. *Scream quietly or the neighbours will hear*. Harmondsworth, Middlesex, England: Penguin, 1974.

Podolsky, E. The woman alcoholic and premenstrual tension. *Journal of American Medical Women's Association*, 1963, *18*, 816–818.

Polatin, P., & Douglas, D.E. Spontaneous orgasm in a case of schizophrenia. *Psychoanalytic Review*, 1953, *40*, 17–26.

Pollak, O. *The Criminality of Women*. Philadelphia: University of Pennsylvania Press, 1950.

Pomeroy, W.B. The Masters-Johnson report and the Kinsey tradition. In R. Brecher & E. Brecher (Eds.), *An analysis of human sexual response.* New York: New American Library, 1966.

Post, F. The social orbit of psychiatric patients. *Journal of Mental Science,* 1962, *108*, 759–771.

Prather, J.E., & Fidell, L.S. Drug use and abuse among women: An overview. *The International Journal of the Addiction,* 1978, *13*, 863–885.

Price, R.R. The forgotten female offender. *Crime and Delinquency,* 1977, *23*, 101–108.

Pugh, T.F., Jerath, B.K., Schmidt, W.M., & Reed, R.B. Rates of mental disease related to childbearing. *New England Journal of Medicine,* 1963, *268*, 1224–1228.

Purcell, K., Turnbull, J.W., & Bernstein L. Distinctions between subgroups of asthmatic children: Psychological tests and behavioral rating comparisons. *Journal of Psychosomatic Research,* 1962, *6*, 283–291.

Purcell, K., & Weiss, J.H. Asthma. In C.G. Costello (Ed.), *Symptoms of psychopathology.* New York: John Wiley, 1970.

Radloff, L. Sex differences in depression. *Sex Roles,* 1975, *1*, 249–265.

Ramey, E. Men's cycles (They have them too, you know). *Ms,* 1972, *1*, pp. 8, 11,12, 14, 15.

Rao, S. Birth order and schizophrenia. *Journal of Nervous and Mental Disease,* 1964, *38*, 87–89.

Raskin, M., & Dyson, W.L. Treatment problems leading to readmission of schizophrenic patients. *Archives of General Psychiatry,* 1968, *19*, 356–360.

Rathod, N.H., & Thomson, I.G. Women Alcoholics: A clinical study. *Quarterly Journal of the Study of Alcohol,* 1971, *32*, 45–52.

Rawlings, E.I., & Carter, D.K. Feminist and nonsexist psychotherapy. In E.I. Rawlings & D.I. Carter (Eds.), *Psychotherapy for women.* Springfield, Ill.: Chas. C Thomas, 1977.

Reed, E.W., & Reed, S.C. *Mental retardation: A family study.* Philadelphia: Saunders, 1965.

Reed, M.R. Masculinity-femininity dimension in normal and psychotic subjects. *Journal of Abnormal and Social Psychology,* 1957, *55*, 289–294.

Rees, L. Physical and emotional factors in bronchial asthma. *Journal of Psychosomatic Research,* 1956, *1*, 98–114.

——. Background to migraine. In J.N. Cummings (Ed.), *4th migraine symposium.* London: Heinemann, 1971.

Reich, W. *The function of the orgasm.* New York: Orgone Institute Press, 1942.

Reiss, I.L. *The social context of premarital sexual permissiveness.* New York: Holt, Rinehart & Winston, 1967.

——. Heterosexual relationships of patients: Premarital, marital and extramarital. In R. Green (Ed.), *Human sexuality. A health practitioners text.* Baltimore: Williams and Wilkins, 1975.

Report of the Commisson on Obscenity and Pornography. New York: Bantam, 1970.

Resnich, P.J. Child murder by parents: A psychiatric review of filicide. *American Journal of Psychiatry,* 1969, *126,* 325-334.

Rich, A.R., & Schroeder, H.E. Research issues in assertiveness training. *Psychological Bulletin,* 1976, *83,* 1081-1096.

Richards, D.H. A post-hysterectomy syndrome. *Lancet,* 1974, *2,* 983-985.

Rickles, N.K. The angry woman syndrome. *Archives of General Psychiatry,* 1971, *24,* 91-94.

Riess, B.F. New viewpoints on the female homosexual. In V. Franks & V. Burtle (Eds.), *Women in Therapy.* New York: Brunner/Mazel, 1974.

Rimm, D.C., & Somervill, J.W. *Abnormal psychology.* New York: Academic Press, 1977.

Rimmer, J., Pitto, F.N., Jr., Reich, T., & Winokur, G. Alcoholism II. Sex, socioeconomic status and race in two hospitalized samples. *Quarterly Journal of Studies on Alcohol,* 1971, *32,* 942-952.

Rimmer, J., Reich, T., & Winokur, G. Alcoholism V. Diagnosis and clinical variation among alcoholics. *Quarterly Journal of Studies on Alcohol,* 1972, *33,* 658-666.

Rinehart, J.W. Mobility, aspiration-achievement discrepancies and mental illness. *Social Problems,* 1968, *15,* 478-488.

Roberts, B. Psychosurgery: The final solution to the woman problem. *Rough Times: Journal of Radical Therapy,* 1972, *3,* 16-17.

Robin, G.D. Forcible rape: Institutionalized sexism in the criminal justice system. *Crimes and Delinquency,* 1977, *23,* 136-153.

Robinson, M.N. *The power of sexual surrender.* Garden City: Doubleday, 1959.

Robson, K.S., Pederson, F.A., and Moss, H.A. Developmental observations of dyadic gazing in relation to the fear of strangers and social approach behavior. *Child Development,* 1969, *40,* 619-627.

Rodin, J. Bidirectional influences of emotionality, stimulus responsivity, and metabolic events in obesity. In J.D. Maser & M.E.P. Seligman (Eds.), *Psychopathology: Experimental models.* San Francisco: Freeman, 1977.

Roeske, N.A. Women in psychiatry: A review. *American Journal of Psychiatry,* 1976, *133,* 365-372.

Rogers, D. *The psychology of adolescence* (3rd Ed.). Englewood Cliffs, N.J.: Prentice-Hall, 1977.

Rosen, B. *Witchcraft.* London: Edward Arnold, 1969.

Rosenbaum, B. Married women alcoholics at the Washington hospital. *Quarterly Journal of Studies on Alcohol,* 1958, *19,* 79–89.

Rosenman, R.H., & Friedman, M. Association of specific behavior pattern in women with blood and cardiovascular findings. *Circulation,* 1961, *24,* 1173–1184.

Rosenthal, D. *Genetic theory and abnormal behavior.* New York: McGraw-Hill, 1970.

——. Searches for the mode of genetic transmission in schizophrenia: Reflections and loose ends. *Schizophrenia Bulletin,* 1977, *3,* 268–276.

Ross, A.O. *Psychological disorders of children. A behavioral approach to theory, research and therapy.* New York: McGraw-Hill, 1974.

Rotkin, K. The phalacy of our sexual norm. *Rough times: A journal of radical therapy,* 1972, *3,* 20–22.

Roueche, B. Annals of medicine: As empty as Eve. *New Yorker,* 1974, *50,* 84–100.

Rubin, I. Sex after forty and after seventy. In R. Brecher & E. Brecher (Eds.), *An analysis of human sexual response.* New York: New American Library, 1966.

Rubinstein, L.M. The role of identifications in homosexuality and transvestism in men and women. In I. Rosen (Ed.), *The pathology and treatment of sexual deviation: A methodological approach.* London: Oxford University Press, 1964.

Rudofsky, B. *The unfashionable human body.* New York: Doubleday, 1972.

Rule, J. *Lesbian images.* New York: Doubleday, 1975.

Russek, H.I. Role of heredity, diet, and emotional stress in coronary heart disease. *Journal of the American Medical Association,* 1959, *171,* 503–508.

Russek, H.I., & Russek, L.G. Is emotional stress an etiologic factor in coronary heart disease? *Psychosomatics,* 1976, *17,* 63–67.

Russell, D.E.H. *The politics of rape.* New York: Stein & Day, 1975.

——. Introduction. In D. Martin, *Battered wives.* San Francisco: Glide Publications, 1976.

Rutter, M. Children of sick parents. An environmental and psychiatric study. Institute of Psychiatry, *Maudsley Monographs* (No. 16). London: Oxford University Press, 1966.

Rutter, M., & Graham P. Epidemiology of psychiatric disorders. In M. Rutter, J. Tizard, & K. Whitmore (Eds.), *Education, health and behaviour.* London: Longman, 1970.

Safilios-Rothschild, C. *Love, sex, and sex roles.* Englewood Cliffs, N.J.: Prentice-Hall, 1977.

Saghir, M.T., & Robins, E. Homosexuality: I. Sexual behavior of the female homosexual. *Archives of General Psychiatry*, 1969, *20*, 192–201.

——. *Male and female homosexuality: A comprehensive investigation.* Baltimore: Williams and Wilkins, 1973.

Saghir, M.T., Robins, E., & Walbran, B. Homosexuality: II. Sexual behavior of the male homosexual. *Archives of General Psychiatry*, 1969, *21*, 219–229.

Sales, E. Women's adult development. In I.H. Frieze, J.E. Parsons, P.B. Johnson, D.N. Ruble, & G.L. Zellman. *Women and sex roles. A social psychological perspective.* New York: Norton, 1978.

Sameroff, A.J., & Zax, M. Perinatal characteristics of the offspring of schizophrenic women. Paper presented at the Annual Meeting of the American Psychological Association, September, 1972, Honolulu, Hawaii.

——. In search of schizophrenia: Young offspring of schizophrenic women. In Lyman L. Wynne, Rue L. Cromwell, & Steven Mattysse (Eds.), *The nature of schizophrenia.* New York: John Wiley, 1978.

Sanua, V.D. Sociocultural factors in families of schizophrenics. *Psychiatry*, 1961, *24*, 246–265.

Sarbin, T.R. The concept of hallucination. *Journal of Personality*, 1967, *35*, 359–380.

——. The scientific status of the mental illness metaphor. In S.C. Plog & R.B. Edgerton (Eds.), *Changing perspectives of mental illness.* New York: Holt, Rinehart & Winston, 1969.

Sarbin, T.R., & Juhasz, J.B. The social context of hallucinations. In R.K. Siegel & L.J. West (Eds.), *Hallucination.* New York: John Wiley, 1975.

——. The social psychology of hallucinations. *Journal of Mental Imagery*, 1978, *2*, 117–144.

Sargent, J.D., Walters, E., & Green, E.E. Psychosomatic self-regulation of migraine headache. In L. Kirk (Ed.), *Biofeedback: Behavioral medicine.* New York: Grune & Stratton, 1973.

Sargent, W. Leucotomy in psychosomatic disorders. *Lancet*, 1951, *2*, 87–91.

Schachter, J., Elmer, E., Ragins, N., Winkerly, F., & Lachin, J.M. Assessment of mother-infant interaction: Schizophrenic and nonschizophrenic mothers. *Merrill-Palmer Quarterly*, 1977, *23*, 193–206.

Schachter, S. Some extraordinary facts about obese humans and rats. *American Psychologist*, 1971, *26*, 129–144.

Schachter, S., Goldman, R., & Gordon, A. Effects of fear, food deprivation, and obesity on eating. *Journal of Personality and Social Psychology*, 1968, *10*, 91–97.

Schachter, S., & Singer, J.E. Cognitive, social and physiological determinants of emotional state. *Psychological Review*, 1962, *69*, 379–399.

Scheff, T.J. *Being mentally ill. A sociological theory.* Chicago: Aldine, 1966.

Schmidt, G., Sigusch, V., & Schafer, S. Responses to reading erotic stories: Male-female differences. *Archives of Sexual Behavior,* 1973, *2,* 181–199.

Schnurer, A.T., Rubin, R.R., & Roy, A. Systematic desensitization of anorexia nervosa seen as a weight phobia. *Journal of Behavior Therapy and Experimental Psychiatry,* 1973, *4,* 149–153.

Schofield, M. *Promiscuity.* London: Victor Gollancz Ltd., 1976.

Schofield, W. *Psychotherapy: The purchase of friendship.* Englewood Cliffs, N.J.: Prentice-Hall, 1963.

Schuckit, M.A. Sexual disturbance in the woman alcoholic. *Medical aspects of human sexuality,* 1972a, *6,* 44–65.

———. The alcoholic woman: A literature review. *Psychiatry in Medicine,* 1972b, *3,* 37–42.

Schuckit, M.A., & Morrissey, E.T. Alcoholism in women: Some clinical and social perspectives with an emphasis on possible subtypes. In M. Greenblatt & M.A. Schuckit (Eds.), *Alcoholism problems in women and children.* New York: Grune & Stratton, 1976.

Schuckit, M.A., Pitts, F.N., Jr., Reich, T., King, L.J., & Winokur, G. Alcoholism I. Two types of alcoholism in women. *Archives of General Psychiatry,* 1969, *20,* 301–306.

Schuckit, M.A., Rimmer, J., Reich, T., & Winokur, G. The bender alcoholic. *British Journal of Psychiatry,* 1971, *119,* 183–184.

Schultz, J.H., & Luthe, W. *Autogenic Therapy* (Vol. 1). New York: Grune & Stratton, 1969.

Schulz, C.G., & Kilgalen, R.K. *Case studies in schizophrenia.* New York: Basic Books, 1969.

Schwab, M.E. A study of reported hallucinations in a Southeastern county. *Mental Health and Society,* 1977, *4,* 344–354.

Schwartz, G.E., & Shapiro, D. Biofeedback and essential hypertension: Current findings and theoretical concerns. In L. Birk (Ed.), *Biofeedback: Behavioral medicine.* New York: Grune & Stratton, 1973.

Schwarz, O. *The psychology of love.* Baltimore: Penguin, 1949.

Scodel, A. Heterosexual somatic preference and fantasy dependency. *Journal of Consulting Psychology,* 1957, *21,* 371–374.

Scotch, N.W. Sociocultural factors in the epidemiology of Zulu hypertension. *American Journal of Public Health,* 1963, *53,* 1205–1213.

Scott, P.D. Battered wives. *British Journal of Psychiatry,* 1974, *125,* 433–441.

Seaman, B. The new pill scare. *Ms.,* 1975, *3,* pp. 61–64, 98–102.

Seiden, A.M. Overview: Research on the psychology of women I. Gender differences and sexual reproductive life. *American Journal of Psychiatry,* 1976, *133,* 995–1007.

Seidenberg, R. Drug advertising and perception of mental illness. *Mental Hygiene*, 1971, *55*, 21–32.

——. The trauma of eventlessness. *The Psychoanalytic Review*, 1972, *59*, 95–109.

Selby, H., Jr. *Last exit to Brooklyn.* New York: Grove Press, 1957.

Seligman, M.E.P. Depression and learned helplessness. In R.J. Friedman & M.M. Katz (Eds.), *The psychology of depression: Contemporary theory and research.* New York: John Wiley, 1974.

——. *Helplessness: On depression, development, and death.* San Francisco: Freeman, 1975.

Shapiro, A.P. Essential hypertension—Why idiopathic? *American Journal of Medicine*, 1973, *54*, 1–5.

Sharp L.J., & Nye, F.I. Maternal mental health. In F.I. Nye and L.W. Hoffman (Eds.), *The employed mother in America.* Chicago: Rand McNally, 1963.

Sherfey, M.J. A theory on female sexuality. In Robin Morgan (Ed.), *Sisterhood in power.* New York: Random House, 1970.

——. *The nature and evolution of female sexuality.* New York, Random House, 1972.

Siegelman, M. Adjustment of homosexual and heterosexual women. *British Journal of Psychiatry*, 1972, *120*, 477–481.

——. Parental background of homosexual and heterosexual women. *British Journal of Psychiatry*, 1974, *124*, 14–21.

Sifneos, P.S. Case of anorexia nervosa treated successfully by leucotomy. *American Journal of Psychiatry*, 1952, *109*, 356–360.

Sigall, H., & Landy, D. Radiating beauty: Effects of having a physically attractive partner on person perception. *Journal of Personality and Social Psychology*, 1973, *28*, 218–224.

Simon, R.J. American women and crime. *Annals of the Academy of Political and Social Science*, 1976, *423*, 31–46.

Simpson, R. *From the closet to the courts: The lesbian transition.* New York: Viking Press, 1976.

Singer, J.E., Westphal, M., & Niswander, K.R. Sex differences in the incidence of neonatal abnormalities and abnormal performance in early childhood. *Child Development*, 1968, *39*, 103–122.

Sirois, F. Epidemic hysteria. *Acta Psychiatrica Scandinavica*, 1974, Supplementum *252*.

Slater, A.D. A study of the use of alcoholic beverages among high-school students in Utah. *Quarterly Journal of Studies on Alcohol*, 1952, *13*, 78–86.

Slater, E., & Roth, M. *Clinical psychiatry* (3rd ed.). London: Bailliere, Tindall & Cassell, 1969.

Smart, C. *Women, crime and criminology: A feminist critique.* London: Routledge & Kegan Paul, 1977.

Smart, R., & Fejer, D. Drug use among adolescents and their parents: Closing the generation gap in mood modification. *Journal of Abnormal Psychology,* 1972, *79,* 153–160.

Smibert, J. Pitfalls of sterilization. *Medical Journal of Australia,* 1972, *2,* 901–903.

Smith, C.G., & Sinanan, K. "The gas-light phenomenon" reappears. A modification of the ganser syndrome. *British Journal of Psychiatry,* 1972, *120,* 685–686.

Smith, D.C., Prentice, R., Tompson, D.J., & Herrman, W.L. Association of exogenous estrogen and endometrical carcinoma. *New England Journal of Medicine,* 1975, *293,* 1164–1167.

Smith, K.P. Social and situational determinants of fear in the play group. In M. Lewis & L.A. Rosenblum (Eds.), *The origins of fear.* New York: John Wiley, 1974.

Smith, S.M., & Hanson, R. 134 battered children: A medical and psychological study. *British Medical Journal,* 1974, *3,* 606–670.

Snyderman, R.K., & Guthrie, R.H. Reconstruction of the female breast following radical mastectomy. *Plastic Reconstruction Surgery,* 1971, *47,* 565–567.

Sobel, D.E. Children of schizophrenic patients: Preliminary observations on early development. *American Journal of Psychiatry,* 1961, *118,* 512–517.

Solberg, D.A., Butler, J., & Wagner, N.N. Sexual behavior in pregnancy. *New England Journal of Medicine,* 1973, *288,* 1098–1103.

Somerville, B.W. A study of migraine in pregnancy. *Neurology,* 1972, *22,* 324–328.

Soranus of Epherus. *Gynecology* (Trans. and with an introduction by Owsei Temkin). Baltimore: Johns Hopkins University Press, 1956. (Originally published, circa 130 A.D.)

Sorensen, R.C. *Adolescent sexuality in contemporary America: Personal values and sexual behavior ages 13–19.* New York: Abrams, 1973.

Sotile, W.M., & Kilmann, P.R. Treatments of psychogenic female sexual dysfunctions. *Psychological Bulletin,* 1977, *84,* 619–633.

Spanos, N.P. Witchcraft in histories of psychiatry: A critical analysis and an alternative conceptualization. *Psychological Bulletin,* 1978, *85,* 417–439.

Spiro, M.E. *Kibbutz: Venture in Utopia.* Cambridge: Harvard University Press, 1956.

Squire, L.R. A stable impairment in remote memory following electroconvulsive therapy. *Neuropsychologia,* 1975, *13,* 51–58.

Squire, L.R., Slater, P.C., & Chace, P.M. Retrograde amnesia: Temporal gradient in very long term memory following electroconvulsive therapy. *Science*, 1975, *87*, 77–79.

Stannard, U. The mask of beauty. In V. Gornic & B. Moran (Eds.), *Woman in sexist society*. New York: Basic Books, 1971.

——. Commentary on psychosexual adjustment of the unattractive women. *Medical Aspects of Human Sexuality*, 1973, *7*, 77.

Stekel, W. *Sexual aberrations*. Santa Ana, California: Vision Press, 1963.

Stengel, E. *Suicide and attempted suicide*. London: Penguin, 1964.

Stevens, B.C. *Marriage and fertility of women suffering from schizophrenia and affective disorders*. London: Oxford University Press, 1969.

——. Illegitimate fertility of psychotic women. *Journal of Biosocial Science*, 1970, *2*, 17–30.

Stimson, G. Women in a doctored world. *New Society*, 1975, *32*, 265–267.

Stockburger, D.W., & Davis, J.O. Selling the female image as mental patient. *Sex Roles*, 1978, *4*, 131–134.

Stoller, R.J. Sexual deviations. In F. Beach (Ed.), *Human sexuality in four perspectives*. Baltimore: Johns Hopkins University Press, 1977.

Stone, L.J., & Hokanson, J.E. Arousal reduction via self-punitive behavior. *Journal of Personality and Social Psychology*, 1969, *12*, 72–79.

Stoppard, J.M., & Kalin, R. Can gender stereotypes and sex-role conceptions be distinguished? *British Journal of Social and Clinical Psychology*, 1978, *17*, 211–217.

Straus, R. Drinking in college. In S.L. Maddox (Ed.), *The domesticated drug: Drinking among collegians*. New Haven: College & University Press, 1970.

Straus, R., & Bacon, S.D. *Drinking in college*. New Haven: Yale University Press, 1953.

Streissguth, A.P. Maternal alcoholism and the outcome of pregnancy: A review of the fetal alcohol syndrome. In M. Greenblatt & M.A. Schuckit (Eds.), *Alcoholic problems in women and children*. New York: Grune & Stratton, 1976.

Stricker, G. Implications of research for psychotherapeutic treatment of women. *American Psychologist*, 1977, *32*, 14–22.

Strouse, J. To be minor and female: The legal rights of women under 21. *Ms.*, 1972, *1*, p. 74.

Stuart, R.B., & Davis, B. *Slim chance in a fat world*. Champaign, Ill.: Research Press, 1972.

Stunkard, A.J. From explanation to action in psychosomatic medicine: The case of obesity. *Psychosomatic Medicine*, 1975, *37*, 195–236.

Stunkard, A.J., D'Acquili, E., Fox, S., & Filion, R.D.L. The influence of social class on obesity and thinness in children. *Journal of the American Medical Association*, 1972, *221*, 579–584.

Stunkard, A.J., & Koch, C. The interpretation of gastric motility: 1. Apparent bias in the reports of hunger by obese persons. *Archives of General Psychiatry*, 1964, *11*, 74–82.

Suchman, E.A. The "hang loose" ethic and the spirit of drug use. *Journal of Health and Social Behavior*, 1968, *9*, 146–155.

Suffet, F., & Brotman, R. Female drug use: Some observations. *The International Journal of the Addictions*, 1976, *11*, 19–33.

Suicide mortality 1950–1968. Health and Welfare Division, Catalogue 84–528. Ottawa: *Statistics Canada*, Nov. 1972.

Sussex, J.N., Gassman, F., & Raffel, S.C. Adjustment of children with psychotic mothers in the home. *American Journal of Orthopsychiatry*, 1963, *33*, 849–854.

Swanson, D.W., Bohmert, P.J., & Smith, J.A. *The paranoid*. Boston: Little, Brown, 1970.

Swanson, D.W., & Dinello, F.A. Follow-up of patients starved for obesity. *Psychosomatic Medicine*, 1970, *32*, 209–214.

Symonds, A. Phobias after marriage: Women's declaration of dependence. *The American Journal of Psychoanalysis*, 1971, *31*, 144–152.

Szasz, T.S. *The manufacture of madness*. New York: Harper & Row, Pub., 1970.

———. *The second sin*. Garden City, N.Y.: Doubleday Books, 1973.

———. *The myth of mental illness: Foundations of a theory of personal conduct* (Revised edition). New York: Harper & Row, Pub., 1974.

Taylor, K.F. *Psychopathology: Its causes and symptoms*. London: Buttersworth, 1966.

Taylor, S.P., & Gammon, C.B. Effects of type and dose of alcohol on human physical aggression. *Journal of Personality and Social Psychology*, 1975, *32*, 169–175.

Taylor, S.P., Vardaris, R.M., Rawitch, A.B., Gammon, C.B., Cranston, J.W., & Lubetkin, A.I. The effects of alcohol and delta-9-tetrahydrocannabinol on human physical aggression. *Aggressive Behavior*, 1976, *2*, 153–162.

Teicher, J.D. Sexual deviations. In A.M. Freeman, H.I. Kaplan, & B.J. Sadock (Eds.), *Comprehensive textbook of psychiatry* (vol. 2). Baltimore: Williams and Wilkins, 1975.

Telfer, M.A., Richardson, C.E., & Chock, E.S. X chromosome errors in female criminals. *Journal of the American Medical Association*, 1968, *206*, 1087.

Tennes, K.H., & Lampl, E.E. Stranger and separation anxiety in infancy. *Journal of Nervous and Mental Diseases*, 1964, *139*, 247–254.

Tennov, D. *Psychotherapy: The hazardous cure.* New York: Abelard-Schuman, 1975.

Teoh, J.I., & Tan, E.S. An outbreak of epidemic hysteria in West Malaysia. In W. Lebra (Ed.), *Culture-bound syndromes, ethnopsychiatry, and alternate therapies.* Honolulu: An East-West Center book, The University Press of Hawaii, 1976.

Terhune, W. The phobic syndrome. A study of 86 patients with phobic reactions. *Archives of Neurology and Psychiatry,* 1949, *62,* 162–172.

Terman, L.M., Buttenwieser, P., Ferguson, L.W., Johnson, W.B., & Wilson, D.P. *Psychological factors in marital happiness.* New York: McGraw-Hill, 1938.

Thacore, V.R., Gupta, S.C., & Suraiya, M. Psychiatric morbidity in a North Indian Community. *British Journal of Psychiatry,* 1975, *126,* 364–369.

Thigpen, C.H., & Cleckley, H.M. *Three faces of Eve.* New York: McGraw-Hill, 1975.

Thomas, W. *The unadjusted girl.* New York: Harper & Row, Pub., 1967.

Thompson, A.W.S. Prescribing of hypnotics and tranquilizers in New Zealand. *Pharmaceutical Journal of New Zealand,* 1973, *35,* 15–18.

Thurber, J. *The Thurber Carnival* (2nd ed.). New York: Harper and Brothers, 1945.

Tietze, T. A study of mothers of schizophrenic patients. *Psychiatry,* 1949, *12,* 55–65.

Time. Equalities for uglies, February 21, 1972, *99,* 12.

——. Gays on the march, September 8, 1975, *106,* 440–450.

——. Culture and the curse, February 23, 1976, *107,* 50–51.

Todd, J., & Dewhurst, K. The Othello syndrome. *Journal of Nervous and Mental Disease,* 1955, *122,* 367–374.

Touraine, G.A., & Draper, G. Migrainous patient—A constitutional study. *Journal of Nervous and Mental Disease,* 1934, *8,* 1–23.

Tridon, A. *Psychoanalysis and Love.* New York: Permabooks, 1949.

Udry, J.R., & Morris, N.M. Distribution of coitus in the menstrual cycle. *Nature,* 1968, *220,* 593–596.

Ulleland, C.N. The offspring of alcoholic mothers. *Annals of the New York Academy of Science,* 1972, *197,* 167–169.

Ulleland, C.N., Wennberg, R.P., Igo, R.P., & Smith, N.J. The offspring of alcoholic mothers. *Pediatric Research,* 1970, *4,* 474 (Abstract).

Ullman, A.D. First drinking experience as related to age and sex. In D.J. Pittman & C.R. Snyder (Eds.), *Society, culture and drinking patterns.* New York: John Wiley, 1970.

Ullmann, L.P., & Krasner, L. *A psychological approach to abnormal behavior.* Englewood Cliffs, N.J.: Prentice-Hall, 1969.

——. *A psychological approach to abnormal behavior* (2nd ed.). Englewood Cliffs, N.J.: Prentice-Hall, 1975.

Valenstein, E.S. *Brain control.* New York: John Wiley, 1973.

——. The practice of psychosurgery: A survey of the literature (1971–1976). In *Appendix: Psychosurgery.* The National Commission for the Protection of Human Subjects of Biomedical and Behavioral Research, U.S. Department of Health, Education and Welfare. Washington, D.C.: U.S. Government Printing Office, 1977.

Vance, E.B., & Wagner, N. Written descriptions of orgasm: A study of sex differences. *Archives of Sexual Behavior,* 1976, *5,* 87–98.

Van Emde Boas, C. The doctor-patient relationship. *Journal of Sex Research,* 1966, *2,* 215–218.

Van Stolk, M. *The battered child in Canada.* Toronto: McClelland & Stewart, 1972.

Veith, I. *Hysteria: The history of a disease.* Chicago: University of Chicago Press, 1965.

Wadsworth, M.E.J., Butterfield, W.J.H., & Blaney, R. *Health and sickness: The choice of treatment.* London: Tavistock, 1971.

Wahl, O.F. Sex bias in schizophrenia research: A short report. *Journal of Abnormal Psychology,* 1977, *86,* 195–198.

Waldron, I. Type A behavior and heart disease in men and women. Paper given at the Symposium on Sex, Culture and Illness, March 25–27, 1976a, Montreal, Canada.

——. Why do women live longer than men? *Social Science and Medicine,* 1976b, *10,* 349–362.

——. The coronary-prone behavior pattern, blood pressure, employment and socioeconomic status in women. *Journal of Psychosomatic Research,* 1978, *22,* 79–87.

Waldron, I., & Johnston, S. Why do women live longer than men? Part II. *Journal of Human Stress,* 1976, *2,* 19–30.

Waldron, I., Zyzanski, S., Shekelle, R.B., Jenkins, D., & Tannenbaum, S. The coronary-prone behavior pattern in employed men and women. *Journal of Human Stress,* 1977, *3,* 2–18.

Walker, N. *Crime and punishment in Britain: The penal system in theory, law and practice.* Edinburgh: Edinburgh University Press, 1965.

——. *Crime and insanity in England.* Edinburgh, Scotland: Edinburgh University Press, 1969.

Walster, E., Aronson, E., Abrahams, D., & Rottman, L. Importance of physical attractiveness in dating behavior. *Journal of Personality and Social Psychology,* 1966, *4,* 508–516.

Wanberg, K.W., & Horn, J.L. Alcoholism syndromes related to sociological classifications. *International Journal of Addictions*, 1973, *8*, 99–120.

Wanberg, K.W., & Knapp, J. Differences in drinking symptoms and behavior of men and women alcoholics. *British Journal of Addiction*, 1970, *64*, 347–355.

Ward, D.A., Jackson, M., & Ward, R.E. Crime and violence by women. In D.J. Mulvihill & M.M. Tumin (Eds.), *Crimes of violence. A staff report submitted to the National Commission on the causes and prevention of violence.* Washington, D.C.: U.S. Government Printing Office, 1969.

Warheit, G.J., Holzer, C.E., III, & Arey, S.A. Race and mental illness: An epidemiological update. *Journal of Health and Social Behavior*, 1975, *16*, 243–256.

Warheit, G.J., Holzer, C., III, & Schwab, J. An analysis of social class and racial differences in depressive symptomatology: A community study. *Journal of Health and Social Behavior*, 1973, *14*, 291–299.

Waters, W.E., & O'Connor, P.J. Prevalence of migraine. *Journal of Neurology, Neurosurgery and Psychiatry*, 1975, *38*, 613–616.

Watson, J.B., & Rayner, R. Conditioned emotional reactions. *Journal of Experimental Psychology*, 1920, *3*, 1–14.

Webb, A.P. Sex-role preferences and adjustment in early adolescents. *Child Development*, 1963, *34*, 609–618.

Wechsler, H., & McFadden, M. Sex differences in adolescent alcohol and drug use. A disappearing phenomenon. *Journal of Studies on Alcohol*, 1976, *37*, 1291–1301.

Weeke, A., Bille, M., Videbach, Th., Dupont, A., & Juel-Nielsen, N. The incidence of depressive syndromes in a Danish county, *Acta Psychiatrica Scandinavica*, 1975, *51*, 28–41.

Weich, M.J. Behavioral differences between groups of acutely psychotic (schizophrenic) males and females. *The Psychiatric Quarterly*, 1968, *42*, 107–122.

Weideger, P. *Menstruation and menopause.* New York: Knopf, 1975.

Weinberg, S.K. *Incest behavior.* New York: Citadel Press, 1955.

Weiner, H. *Psychobiology and human disease.* New York: Elsevier North-Holland, 1977.

Weiner, I.B. *Psychological disturbance in adolescence.* New York: John Wiley, 1970.

Weinstein, E.A. *Social aspects of delusions. A psychiatric study of the Virgin Islands.* New York: Free Press, 1962.

Weis, K., & Borges, S. Victimology and rape: The case of the legitimate victim. *Issues in Criminology*, 1973, *8*, 71–115.

Weiss, J.L., Grunebaum, H.U., & Schell, R.E. Psychotic mothers and their children. *Archives of General Psychiatry*, 1964, *11*, 90–98.

Weiss, J.M. Psychological and Behavioral Influences on gastrointestinal lesions in animal models. In J.D. Maser & M.E.P. Seligman (Eds.), *Psychopathology: Experimental models.* San Francisco: W.H. Freeman, and Co., Publishers, 1977.

Weissman, M.M. The epidemiology of suicide attempts, 1960 to 1971. *Archives of General Psychiatry,* 1974, *30,* 737-746.

Weissman, M.M., Fox, K., & Klerman, G.L. Hostility and depression associated with suicide attempts. *American Journal of Psychiatry,* 1973, *130,* 450-455.

———. Sex differences and the epidemiology of depression. *Archives of General Psychiatry,* 1977, *34,* 98-111.

Weissman, M.M., Klerman, G.L., Paykel, E.S., Prusoff, B., & Hanson, B. Treatment effects on the social adjustment of depressed patients. *Archives of General Psychiatry,* 1974, *30,* 771-778.

Weissman, M.M., & Paykel, E.S. *The depressed woman.* Chicago: University of Chicago Press, 1974.

Weissman, M.M., Paykel, E.S., Siegel, R., & Klerman, G.L. The social role performance of depressed women: Comparison within a normal group. *American Journal of Orthopsychiatry,* 1971, *41,* 390-405.

Weissman, M.M., & Slaby, A.E. Oral contraceptives and psychiatric disturbance: Evidence from research. *British Journal of Psychiatry,* 1973, *123,* 513-518.

Weitz, S. *Sex roles: Biological, psychological and social foundations.* New York: Oxford University Press, 1977.

Welch, C.E. Abdominal surgery. *New England Journal of Medicine,* 1973, *288,* 609-616.

Werry, J.S. Childhood psychosis. In H.C. Quay & J.S. Werry (Eds.), *Psychopathological disorders of childhood.* New York: John Wiley, 1972.

Werry, J.S., & Quay, H.C. The prevalence of behavior symptoms in younger elementary school children. *American Journal of Orthopsychiatry,* 1971, *41,* 136-143.

West, D.J. *Murder followed by suicide.* Cambridge, Mass.: Harvard University Press, 1966.

Whalen, T. Wives of alcoholics: Four types observed in a family service agency. *Quarterly Journal of the Study of Alcohol,* 1953, *14,* 632-641.

Whitehead, P.C., & Ferrence, R.G. Women and children last: Implications of trends in consumption for women and young people. In M. Greenblatt & M.A. Schuckit (Eds.), *Alcoholism problems in women and children.* New York: Grune & Stratton, 1976.

Widom, C.S. Self-esteem, sex role identity, and feminism in female offenders. Paper presented at the American Psychological Association Annual Meetings, 25-30, August 1977, San Francisco, California.

———. Toward an understanding of female criminality. In B.A. Maher (Ed.),

Progress in experimental personality research (Vol. 8). New York: Academic Press, 1978.

Wiggins, J.S., Wiggins, N., & Conger, J.C. Correlates of heterosexual somatic preference. *Journal of Personality and Social Psychology,* 1968, *10,* 82–89.

Wilkinson, G.S. Patient-audience social status and the social construction of psychiatric disorders: Toward a differential frame of reference hypothesis. *Journal of Health and Social Behavior,* 1975, *16,* 28–38.

Williams, J.H. *The psychology of women. Behavior in a biosocial context.* New York: W.W. Norton & Co., Inc., 1974.

Williams, L. *Man and monkey.* London: Duetsch, 1967.

Wilsnack, S.C. Sex-role identity in female alcoholism. *Journal of Abnormal Psychology,* 1973, *82,* 253–261.

Wilsnack, S.N. The impact of sex roles on women's alcohol use and abuse. In M. Greenblatt & M.A. Schuckit (Eds.), *Alcoholism problems in women and children.* New York: Grune & Stratton, 1976.

Wilson, G.D., & Nias, D.K.B. *Love's mysteries: The psychology of sexual attraction.* London: Open Books, 1976.

Winkelstein, W., Jr., Ibrahim, M., & Sackett, D.L. Familial aggregation of blood pressure, Preliminary report. *Journal of the American Medical Association,* 1966, *195,* 848–850.

Winokur, G., & Clayton, P.J. Family history study. A comparison of male and female alcoholics. *Quarterly Journal of Studies of Alcohol,* 1968, *29,* 885–891.

Winokur, G., & Pitts, F.N., Jr. Affective disorder: 1. Is reactive depression an entity? *Journal of Nervous and Mental Disease,* 1964, *138,* 541–547.

Winokur, G., Rimmer, J., & Reich, J. Alcoholism IV. Is there more than one type of alcoholism? *British Journal of Psychiatry,* 1971, *118,* 525–531.

Wittkower, E.D., & Robertson, B.M. Sex differences in psychoanalytic treatment. Paper prepared for Symposium on Sex, Culture and Illness, 25–27 March, 1976, Montreal, Canada.

Wittkower, E.D., & Warnes, H. Transcultural psychosomatics. *Canadian Psychiatric Association Journal,* 1975, *20,* 143–149.

Wolf, S.R. Emotional reactions to hysterectomy. *Post-Graduate Medicine,* 1970, *47,* 165–169.

Wolfgang, M.E. *Patterns in criminal homicide.* Philadelphia: University of Pennsylvania Press, 1958.

Wolpe, J. Reciprocal inhibition as the main basis of psychotherapeutic effects. In H.J. Eysenk (Ed.), *Behavior therapy and the neuroses.* Oxford: Pergamon Press, 1960.

Wood, H.P., & Duffy, E.L. Psychological factors in alcoholic women. *American Journal of Psychiatry,* 1966, *123,* 341–345.

Wright, H. *More about the sex factor in marriage* (2nd ed.). London: Williams & Norgate, 1959.

Zigler, E., & Phillips, L. Social effectiveness and symptomatic behaviors. *Journal of Abnormal and Social Psychology,* 1960, *2,* 231–238.

Zilboorg, G. *The medical man and the witch during the renaissance.* New York: Cooper Square, 1935.

Zilboorg, G., & Henry, G.W. *A history of medical psychology.* New York: W.W. Norton & Co., Inc., 1941.

Zuckerman, M. Physiological measures of sexual arousal in humans. In W.C. Wilson (executive director), *Technical report of the commission on obscenity and pornography. Vol. 1: Preliminary studies.* Washington, D.C.: U.S. Government Printing Office, 1971.

Index